The Internal Foe

The Internal Foe:
Judaism and Anti-Judaism
in the Shaping of Christian Theology

By

Jeremy F. Worthen

CAMBRIDGE
SCHOLARS

P U B L I S H I N G

The Internal Foe: Judaism and Anti-Judaism in the Shaping of Christian Theology,
by Jeremy F. Worthen

This book first published 2009

Cambridge Scholars Publishing

12 Back Chapman Street, Newcastle upon Tyne, NE6 2XX, UK

British Library Cataloguing in Publication Data
A catalogue record for this book is available from the British Library

ISBN (10): 1-4438-0207-7, ISBN (13): 978-1-4438-0207-9

For Peter Worthen (1938-2002)

TABLE OF CONTENTS

FOREWORD

The Old City of Jerusalem is perhaps among the most resonant places on earth for attending to the presence of the past. Certainly that was my experience when I visited it for the first time during the final stages of writing this book. The remarkable excavations in the grounds of the Crusader church of St Anne enable one to gaze down precipitously at buildings from the Middle Ages and late antiquity and rest one's eyes on pavement and pools far beneath even them, which date from more than two thousand years ago. This is but one confirmation of the reality continually encountered in and around the City: that the ground on which we stand, apparently enduring and stable, is only the latest stratum in a series of layers going back over many centuries.

Nor is the sedimentation of these multiple levels simply the result of the cumulative process of intensive human habitation across the millennia. What was built at one level may have been deliberately destroyed by new powers, whose representatives either raised or left others to raise on the remains new monuments to new orders. Or then again it may have been appropriated, its use redefined. The Romans flattened the temple in 70 CE as a mark of the permanent defeat of the Jewish nation. When a Christian emperor became interested in the places most directly related to his new faith's history in the fourth century, the blank ruin where the temple had once stood was carefully preserved as a theological symbol of the end of the former covenant and the replacement of Jewish Israel by the "Catholic" Church. That Church's worship was focused instead on Constantine's immense Basilica of the Resurrection, from which the empty site of the former temple could be properly contemplated. By contrast, the Islamic rulers of Jerusalem in the seventh century eventually turned the Temple Mount into a new holy place, a centre for devout pilgrimage and learning whose twin foci are the still breathtaking Dome of the Rock and Al-Aqsa mosque. When Christian Crusaders then occupied Jerusalem in the twelfth century, rather than destroying or ignoring what the Islamic empire had created on the site they brought an altar into the Dome of the Rock and rendered it a church for several decades, before, conquered again, it reverted to its original use.

The buildings of Jerusalem's Old City, hidden, excavated and fully standing, testify to the complex processes of negation, adaptation and assimilation by which the power of the present engages with the given, the resistance of the physical past. Yet that by itself is too bloodless, because for each successive wave of occupation the stones that had been established represented also the lives of those opponents who may have killed and been killed in the battle for supremacy. The ground on which one stands today therefore is not only a complex archaeological record; it has been stained with blood shed in violence many times over, and not just in the distant past. The cost of the beauty that is radiantly present in so many places here is not comfortable to consider. The stones of centuries are traces of human lives and the deaths that ended them.

Yet just as physical remains were not simply erased in their totality but contributed in various ways to the creation of the next new order, so too there was, at different levels in different periods, a cohabitation of peoples and a rich exchange of cultures in this place. In another Crusader church, some distance from Jerusalem itself at Abu Ghosh, Islamic elements show through the stonework and Eastern and Western styles of Christian art come together in the still largely visible frescoes; the conquerors preserve as well as destroy what they sought to overcome, may even indeed arrive at a certain appreciation of it through the very proximity of occupation. Jerusalem itself can be considered a symbol of meeting as well as of conflict, not least between the religious traditions that have contested it and for which it remains a place of intense significance: Judaism, Christianity and Islam.

How these—and other—traditions can relate to one another today without violence and the replication of historic hostility, yet also without dissolving their distinctive identities and claims about truth into the corrosive relativism that too easily accommodates a pluralist human world, is a question of great importance, and not only in Jerusalem.[1] For the past fifty years it has steadily progressed into the mainstream of institutional and scholarly attention, as an area of concern not just for adherents of those traditions but for national and even international politics. This study both reflects and hopes to contribute in a small way to that wider discussion.

It does so as a historical study that focuses on Christianity and its relation to Judaism, a relation which remains arguably decisive for the way that Christianity situates itself with regard to all subsequent religious "others", including Islam. In his correspondence during World War I with his friend Eugene Rosenstock-Huessy, Franz Rosenzweig wrote of the Judaism with which he had re-identified in relation to the Christianity to which Rosenstock-Huessy had converted:

> We are the internal foe; don't mix us up with the external one! Our enmity
> may have to be bitterer than any enmity for the external foe—but all the
> same—we and you are within the same frontier, in the same Kingdom.[2]

Of course, there would be differing evaluations of the theological position
indicated here. And which foe, which other, is ever wholly external? Yet
Rosenzweig was convinced that the relationship between Christianity and
Judaism differs from the relationship between Christianity and its many
subsequent opponents and partners because it is somehow interior to
Christianity's identity and development. As an "internal foe," Judaism is
both uniquely provocative and uniquely generative for Christianity. Anti-
Judaism keeps the Church facing Judaism even as it seeks to push it away:
"we are the louse in your fur," as Rosenzweig says in the same passage.
The book that follows is perhaps best understood as an attempt to test the
value of Rosenzweig's insight with regard to the history of Christian
theology.

The findings of such historical inquiry matter not only to scholars but
also to all those who speak about and on behalf of Christianity in the
contemporary context, because they need to attend with great care to the
ground beneath their feet when they do so. Christian theology—the
discourse invoked consciously or less consciously by those speaking about
or on behalf of Christianity—is itself shaped by a complex series of
engagements, often though not always characterized by hostility and
violence, with what has been rendered as "other", beginning with Judaism
itself. Although those engagements may not be easily visible or accessible
to us now, those who would seek to address issues today of religious
identity and difference from the perspective of Christian theology need to
be aware of how that perspective is itself generated by the shifting and
conflicted construction of identity and difference in relation to the other
over two thousand years. The more conservative may be fearful of
influence through interaction with other religions while the more liberal
eagerly anticipate enlightenment from it, but neither may fully appreciate
the extent to which the very position from which they approach such
interaction in the present has been shaped beneath the surface by a dense
maze of intersecting exchanges from the past.

Notes

[1] See e.g. Richard Harries, Norman Solomon and Tim Winter, eds., *Abraham's Children: Jews, Christians and Muslims in Conversation* (London: T & T Clark, 2005); David F. Ford and C. C. Pecknold, eds., *The Promise of Scriptural Reasoning* (Oxford: Blackwell, 2006); David Burrell, *Faith and Freedom: An Interfaith Perspective* (Oxford: Blackwell, 2004).

[2] In Eugen Rosenstock-Huessy, ed., *Judaism despite Christianity: The "Letters on Christianity and Judaism" between Eugen Rosenstock-Huessy and Franz Rosenzweig* (Alabama: University of Alabama Press, 1969), 130.

ACKNOWLEDGMENTS

This book is primarily the result of two brief periods of immersion in the work of researching and writing separated by five years when attention to it had to be fitted around my role as Vice Principal and then Principal of the South East Institute for Theological Education. I am grateful to the Council of the Institute for granting me the two sabbaticals without which a project of this scope would have been utterly impossible, and to my colleagues who have encouraged and supported me in innumerable ways. Without the continuing expressions of interest from them and from many of my students over that time, I would probably have despaired of ever bringing it to completion.

An invitation from John Court to teach a course on Jewish-Christian theological dialogue at the University of Kent gave me a focus for some important background work, and I have appreciated John's calm and professional guidance on many occasions since then. I also valued the enthusiasm about the project expressed by Gareth Jones, from Christ Church Canterbury University, when I shared some early drafts with him. I have given short papers on various occasions relating to aspects of the material covered here, and I am especially grateful to Randi Rashkover and Robin Gill for insightful criticism of previous attempts at a concluding synthesis. Matt Ham encouraged me to explore the unfamiliar waters of art history as an additional dimension of the project.

Thanks are due to all who read draft versions of different parts. Ross Hutchison applied his sharpness of mind to the chapter on early modernity and made many helpful suggestions. The rich diversity of gifts among my colleagues at SEITE, Justine Allain Chapman, Andrew Angel, Lincoln Harvey, Nick Townsend and Mark Wakelin, was reflected in the range of stimulating comments I received on the chapters they graciously agreed to read. The two readers for CSP also provided valuable advice from which I hope I have learnt. Johanna Guerney's attention to detail has helped to limit my numerous errors. Finally, I owe particular debts to Marc Saperstein and Susannah Ticciati for grappling with my unruly text and giving me vital feedback on both specific points and the work as a whole.

The opportunity to participate in a course on "Abraham, Yesterday and Today" in 2007 at St George's College in Jerusalem opened up new perspectives from which I was able to find a clarity of overarching purpose that had previously eluded me. It also allowed me the privilege of meeting Tony Muir, whose continuing encouragement has been a spur for perseverance on the home straight. Michael Last was my guide and companion for some extended extracurricular excursions into the Old City, including the visit to the church of St Anne and its grounds which inspired the Foreword. Michael kindly allowed me to use one of his photographs of that location for the cover. I am deeply grateful to the Saint George's College Jerusalem Trust and to the St Boniface Trust for helping to make all this possible through their financial support.

I have exchanged intellectual interests, research ideas and academic writing at different stages of completion with Jennifer Harris since the time when we were both at the University of Toronto nearly two decades ago. Looking back over that time, I struggle even to begin to quantify the benefits I have received from such sharing, and that is how it should be between friends. In Canterbury, Jeremy Carrette has encouraged, attended to and challenged me in my thinking for some years now and has also provided invaluable practical advice on shaping my material for publication. Those who most inspired me earlier on by their teaching, their guidance and their very different vocations to scholarship, including Peter Barnett, Myles Burnyeat, Rowan Williams and Brian Stock, might be surprised to see where their influence has eventually led me; I hope they would not be too disappointed. My wife, Lizzie, and my daughters, Hannah and Sarah, have given incalculable support without which nothing at all could have been achieved.

I started work on the early stages of this book while sitting with my sleeping father in the autumn of 2002, not knowing that the reason for his constant drowsiness was a terminal illness that would soon kill him. Not having had the opportunity to share it with him in any other way, yet knowing that without the wonderful things he gave me it could not exist, I dedicate the book to him.

INTRODUCTION

The book that follows this Introduction is a study of the past for the sake of the present. It offers a partial and inevitably highly selective engagement with the vast topic of Christianity's interaction over two thousand years with Judaism as, in Rosenzweig's phrase, its "internal foe"—Judaism defined by the end of the second century CE as an enemy but one somehow uniquely positioned inside and across the borders of Christian self-understanding. It focuses on theological writings that would only have been accessible to a small number of people at the time yet have remained in many cases profoundly influential. Through reflecting on the history of Christian thinking in relation to Judaism, it hopes to clarify some of the urgent questions facing Christian theology today in our particular context of religious pluralism.

The idea that a richer appreciation of historical realities, however painful the truths with which it confronts us, can enable a more constructive approach to present challenges in inter-religious dialogue, and specifically dialogue between Christians and Jews, is hardly a novel one. Since the 1960s, Christian scholars and formal Church statements have sought to identify what material from the accumulation of theological traditions might need to be rejected or reinterpreted in the light of the imperative to overcome antisemitism and anti-Jewish prejudice within Christianity. The first section of the Introduction presents a brief review and analysis of this literature.

On the other hand, Christian animosity towards Jews and Judaism is only one dimension of the history of Jewish-Christian relations. The significance of the complex processes of interchange between Judaism and Christianity for both religious traditions, not least when attitudes were apparently characterized by violent hostility or resolute indifference, is a theme that has come strongly to the fore in a number of recent historical studies spanning the entirety of Christian history and is perhaps likely to grow more prominent with further exploration.[1] Yet it is not clear that the consequences of that theme for the self-understanding of Christianity in the present and for its deployment of theological resources in dialogue with others have really begun to be grasped.

This book seeks to sketch out new ground in relating these two areas of inquiry not only to one another but to important developments within

Christian theology itself. It attempts to show that the actuality of exposure to Judaism (always mediated through the prior assumptions and expectations of Christians) and the deep commitment to maintaining as (theologically) rational a stance of anti-Judaism together contributed to significant shifts in the articulation of Christian doctrine, not least as dominant forms of rationality themselves changed and brought various degrees of disorientation. Christian thinking is committed to making claims about newness and to situating these claims in relation to Israel—and thereby to engaging with the enduring Judaism that identifies itself as Israel and yet resists them. The second section of the Introduction sets out this approach in more detail while the third provides an overview of the chapters that follow. Their clear implication is that we need to attribute a much more active role to both Judaism and anti-Judaism in the shaping of Christian theology over two thousand years than has previously been recognized.

Christian-Jewish Dialogue and the Interpretation of Christian History

"The Christian-Jewish debate that started nineteen hundred years ago," writes Israel Yuval, "in our day came to a conciliatory close." He gives as the primary factors here the Nazis' Final Solution and the founding of the State of Israel: because of the first, "the anti-Jewish position of Christianity became reprehensible and illegitimate" while the second "made the Christian exegesis of exile and destruction irrelevant."[2] Although forcefully expressed, the general accuracy of this statement needs to be acknowledged. Since the Second World War, a series of important church statements have not only emphatically rejected racist antisemitism but also renounced anti-Judaism in the sense of condemnation of the continuing existence of Judaism as a form of religion, thereby repudiating much that would have passed for normal Christian teaching about Judaism for close to two millennia.[3] These documents are concerned to make it clear that God has not abandoned Israel as his people for the sake of the Church since the coming of Christ, that Jews through history and today are not to be held collectively accountable for the death of Christ, and that therefore in no sense can their sufferings be claimed to reflect God's desire to punish their rejection of him, as if anyone adding to those sufferings might be deemed to be doing something meritorious.[4] There is an evident determination here to cut the connection between Christian theology and the legitimation of any kind of antisemitic attitude or behaviour. This determination and the theological commitments underpinning it are today shared by influential theologians from across the whole range of major Christian denominations.[5] Sweeping assertions about the legalistic decadence of Judaism by the first century CE, for instance, or Jewish culpability for Jesus' crucifixion, commonplaces of academic Christian theology well into the 1960s, have disappeared from mainstream scholarship, if not necessarily from popular preaching and teaching.[6]

Yet while Christian theologians and church leaders can agree on the rejection of the most prominent aspects of the anti-Judaism that has been a feature of virtually all Christian culture in the past, they find it harder to reach consensus on just what such a rejection might actually entail. Does the negation of those theses about Judaism associated with the "teaching of contempt" have any deeper implications for Christian doctrine, or can they simply be sloughed off and left behind while the enterprise of Christian teaching continues essentially unaffected?[7] It is at this point that historical analysis becomes clearly relevant, because the extent to which other features of Christian doctrine are bound up with a discredited anti-Judaism is at least at one level an invitation to careful historical investigation.

In one of the seminal contributions to the debate within the churches from over thirty years ago, Rosemary Radford Ruether traced the failings of Christianity in its relationship to Judaism right back to the incipient high Christology of the New Testament documents themselves, famously describing anti-Judaism as the "left hand" of (what became) the orthodox doctrine of Christ: if he is the divine Son of God allegedly foretold in the Hebrew scriptures, then those who continue to read those scriptures after his coming and yet still reject him can only thereby render themselves wilfully blind, culpably disobedient and therefore rightly rejected by their God.[8] In line with this analysis, many contemporary advocates of the need for a "post-Holocaust theology" would make the adoption of a "modest" Christology and the abandoning of claims about scriptural fulfilment necessary points of departure for such an endeavour.[9] Ruether's approach might be compared with that of others who, while focusing on different cardinal points of Christian doctrine, such as the resurrection of Christ or salvation through him alone, concur in diagnosing the cause of anti-Judaism in the "absolute" claims of historic Christianity, and therefore recommending a cure that amounts to their relativization.[10] In its assumption that less doctrine means less anti-Judaism, her approach might also be said to find a parallel in the curious argument of Stephen Haynes that the problem with all Christian theological understandings of Judaism is that they understand Judaism in terms of Christian theology. For

Haynes, such theology can only be read as fluctuating expressions of an abiding "witness people myth" whose existence is inherently threatening for Jews.[11]

This kind of response has not however met with universal endorsement in contemporary writing about Christian doctrine, let alone official church statements, even if it retains much currency in liberal circles. Relativism may indeed effectively blunt traditional condemnations, but the same acid equally erodes the value of any theological affirmations Christianity might seek to make. As John Howard Yoder noted,

> Christian shame about Auschwitz is clear, but seldom is it clear what the needed correction is, or why the adjustments that some propose (abandoning Christology? abandoning theology? abandoning God language?) would be good news.[12]

Yoder himself was not entirely unsympathetic to the suggestion that part of the necessary "correction" might involve re-examining some of the inherited Christological language of the Christian churches. Yet this was not because of any willingness on his part to dilute the decisive significance of Jesus as Lord and Christ in the manner that Ruether advocated. It was rather because, according to Yoder, the separation of Christianity from the Judaism within which it originally grew and the consequent development of supersessionism (the notion of the "supersession" or replacement of Israel by the Church as the people of God) as what might be termed an ideology of self-legitimation involved a decisive and regrettable turn toward the Hellenistic, Gentile world in the latter half of the second Christian century, and the attempt to find there the primary resources for Christian theology.[13]

Yoder's identification of the root of supersessionism and therefore anti-Judaism not in the Bible or the claims of historic orthodoxy as such but in the post-biblical development of doctrine in a Hellenizing key can be paralleled in some other influential recent works. For R. Kendall Soulen, for instance, the bracketing out of Israel's history and scripture in the "standard canonical narrative" of creation, fall, redemption and consummation that took hold in the course of the second century left Christian doctrine marked despite its best efforts by the Gnostic tendencies it was struggling to overcome; the Enlightenment then pushed still further the process of removing God from actual history with its contingency and physicality.[14] Dawson, following Hans Frei, tries to identify an understanding of scriptural fulfilment in early Christian sources (from Paul to Origen) that is quite different from Hellenistic allegorizing and its intellectual successors, in order to argue that the fulfilment hermeneutics encountered here are not in fact generative of supersessionism.[15] If supersessionism, understood as the core of theological anti-Judaism, can be linked to the distortion of Christian teaching by Gnosticism and Hellenism, subsequently compounded by the Enlightenment, then its overcoming can be fruitfully tied to the wider project of re-appropriating biblical and traditional teaching by identifying the misleading effects of those various alien lenses. This is, broadly speaking, the approach of recent contributions by Robert Jenson and Scott Bader Saye as well as Yoder and Soulen.[16] For these theologians, the price of abandoning supersessionism is not the relinquishing of historic Christian orthodoxy but the careful restatement of that orthodoxy from its original texts and sources.

We might note at this point some potential limitations of the perspective represented by these writers, despite the undoubted value of their contributions. To begin with, the terminology of supersessionism itself is open to question, despite its pivotal role in much of the writing on this topic. Rowan Williams' comment about the need for "a better typology of anti-Judaism" is relevant here.[17] One might begin by noting that it is not an inconsequential difference as to whether one speaks of people or of covenant as being superseded. As will be shown in the course of this book, a case can be made that the normative position of pre-modern Christianity at least and of much that follows it is that the Jewish people after Christ remain within God's covenant with Abraham. If they do not accept Jesus as Lord and Messiah, then they remain in it as disobedient children, liable to God's wrath and judgment, but children of the covenant nonetheless. On the other hand, that normative position also takes it absolutely for granted that the covenant made at Sinai with Moses *has* come to an end with the coming of Christ. In other words, the Jewish people as such has not been superseded by the Church, because the covenant with Abraham remains and now includes *both*, but the covenant to which "unconverted" Jews (if religious) think they adhere has indeed been superseded by Christ. Hence their religious way of life is superseded and therefore theologically redundant, but their status as children of Abraham is definitely not.

Such observations are congruent with the argument of George Lindbeck that supersessionism does not stand still but takes significantly different forms over time, particularly before and after the advent of modernity in the seventeenth century.[18] This may be relevant for unravelling the disagreement among contemporary writers wishing to articulate a Christian position "beyond supersessionism" as to whether Christian theology should now be affirming two distinct (if related and complementary) covenants, for Israel and the Church, Jews and Gentiles, or rather a single covenant within which the currently divergent paths of Israel and Church are nonetheless somehow included. A lack of conceptual clarity about the initial terms of discussion and their historical development perhaps hampers constructive discussion, and the chapters that follow may have something to contribute in this regard.[19]

Another arguable limitation of the perspective offered by Yoder and others is that the historical narratives deployed by these writers could all be described as variations on a version of theological historiography oriented towards establishing a point of "fall", of disintegration or distortion away from some kind of wholeness and balance that can be located in the original witnesses of the tradition. It also tends to be assumed that after this point the same anti-Jewish themes are repeated with only minor variations until the events referred to by Yuval begin to shake theology out of its fateful complacency. As this point of "fall" is judged to lie somewhere between the earliest New Testament texts and the reign of Constantine (earlier for Ruether, later for e.g. Yoder), historical attention tends to be focused on the first three centuries in particular. Beyond what is presumed to be the definitive separation of Christianity and Judaism and the former's adoption of supersessionism as essential teaching, there may be—as Soulen's approach in particular suggests—interest in how that teaching is affected by wider developments within subsequent Christian theology, such as the rise of the Enlightenment in the eighteenth century and liberal Protestantism in the nineteenth, but these are seen as essentially secondary matters. Moreover, anti-Judaism is taken to be the result of the successive infection of the purity of original sources by various kinds of malign "outside" influence (Gnosticism, Hellenism, the Enlightenment). This seems to close down a number of important questions before they can be properly explored, on the one hand about Christian origins and the extent to which anti-Judaism arises directly from their inherent dynamics rather than from some subsequent process of cultural importation, and on the other about Christian history beyond the supposed site of "fall" and the intertwining of Judaism and anti-Judaism with its subsequent unfolding in ways that remain significantly creative as well as deadening or merely repetitive. One of the ways in which this study seeks to offer a fresh account of theological history is in opening up precisely these areas for careful inquiry.

Jewish-Christian Exchange and the Shaping
of Christian Theology

The chapters that follow assume that drawing on some of the more recent historical research about Jewish-Christian interaction, as well as a close reading of specific Christian texts, can enhance the interpretation of the past development of Christian theology in relation to Judaism in important ways. Not least, such research has significantly undermined one of the assumptions that pervaded earlier historical analysis and tends to be reflected also in the work just discussed of Christian theologians when they turn to history: that Jews and Judaism themselves were not significant participants in relevant developments within Christian thought, functioning primarily as the unwilling objects of Christian speculation. That assumption can yield at best a "two-dimensional" view of theological history, in which there is a relationship between Christian theology *about* Jews and internal shifts *within* Christian theology as such.

This book advocates instead the investigation of a "three-dimensional" historical process in which major changes *within* Christian theology, the theological exchange *between* Judaism and Christianity and the (more or less hostile) Christian understanding *of* Judaism are inseparable from one another in their dynamic development. The insertion of theological exchange as a "middle term" here is critical, for it will be argued in the individual chapters that follow that significant shifts in Christian theology cannot in fact be adequately comprehended without some attention to this. As this process of exchange has continued—with peaks and troughs of activity—throughout the history of Christianity in the West, acknowledging its potential importance means attending to periods where it has been particularly intense and creative, periods that have not necessarily received extensive treatment in previous work on Christian theology and anti-Judaism. It is not therefore simply a question of plotting changing Christian understandings of Judaism, or even correlating them with shifting patterns in Christian theology itself. Rather, the internalized anti-Judaism of Christian thinking paradoxically left it open to continual challenge and disturbance from the persisting Jewish "other", encountered both as a cultural force (manifested in texts, learned exchanges and formal debates) and as a presence actual, reconstructed and amplified in the Christian imagination.

This perspective makes it apparent that contemporary dialogue between the two religions, for all the changing terms of reference rightly highlighted by Yuval, nonetheless remains the continuation of a long-standing conversation. The fact that the discourse by which it was conducted was, from a modern point of view, for the most part disfigured by polemic, misunderstanding and prejudice until very recently cannot render it of no interest to the historian of Christian thought, or allow this interaction to be regarded as therefore inherently valueless and unproductive.[20] The classic writings from the fourth and fifth century doctrinal controversies of Christianity are by and large no better in the handling of their opponents. Polemic was the ordinary mode of self-conscious theological exchange on major issues in the pre-modern period and, to a considerable extent, beyond it. The setting aside of such exchanges and the presentation of Judaism and Christianity instead as parallel but essentially discrete and quite separate religious realities blinkers our reading of this rich history of interaction between the two.[21] However much regret we may have for the ways in which the conversation between Jews and Christians has been conducted in the past, there is nothing to be gained from the illusion that we are doing something wholly original in engaging in dialogue today, not least because the language of our present conversation will have been profoundly shaped by earlier layers of interaction, whether or not we attend to them and no matter how stridently we may repudiate them. To return to the image of the Foreword, we need to understand the shifting levels that constitute the ground on which we stand—and the encounters, conflicts and exchanges that are expressed in that bewildering stratification.

In order to trace this dynamic three-dimensional process and relate it to broader issues in cultural history, the book, after the opening chapter on Christian origins from the New Testament to the second century, deals at some length with three critical periods in the development of Western Christianity: from the later eleventh to the thirteenth century; from the late sixteenth to the early eighteenth century; and the first half of the twentieth century. These periods are recognizable as times of major transition both for Western Christian theology and for the wider culture in which it was embedded—and as times where the process of Jewish-Christian exchange just referred to acquired particular momentum, which prompts the question of how adapting to new forms of theological reason and responding to new realities of experienced Judaism might be correlated in the development of Christian theology. The "three-dimensional" historical approach, then, will seek to relate transitions in Christian thinking both to the encounter with Jews and Judaism and the exchanges that it generated, and to attempts to make sense of Israel's place in the divine purpose in the past, present and future. One implication of this analysis is that it is misleading to narrate the history of Christian theology—at any point—as the progressive working-out of a set of internally generated questions, rather than as a story which always involves contingent interaction between a diversity of Christian and non-Christian characters, including, at crucial points, Jewish critics and commentators. The approach taken is, to repeat a point made earlier, necessarily selective; to revert again to the image of the Foreword, the book is better understood as a series of attempts to dig down and thereby shed light on a few of the major layers in the shaping of Christian theology that disclose the importance of Judaism and anti-Judaism in that process, rather than as any kind of comprehensive excavation.

Overview of Chapters

An attempt to interpret the shaping of Christian theology in terms of its interplay with Judaism and anti-Judaism could be seen as a minor scholarly variation on Tom Stoppard's rereading of Hamlet in *Rosencrantz and Guildenstern are Dead*: by taking the perspective of some minor characters and viewing the story through their eyes, one might show ingenuity and gain peripheral insights, but little else. The approach that is taken in the chapters that follow, however, reflects my concern to test a specific hypothesis as to why the three-dimensional process of exchange just described might be of much more than marginal significance for the development of Christian theology. The first part of the hypothesis is that since Christian faith begins with the proclamation of good news about Jesus as the Christ, Christian thinking has to produce and explore assertions about what is made new in this Christ. The second part is that because Christian thinking cannot forget that "Christ" means the one though whom God's promises to Israel would come to pass, it also has to consider what account to give of those who identify as Israel after Jesus and yet do not accept him as Christ. The third is that these two subjects are interrelated in Christian thinking: newness in Christ, as the primary subject of Christian theology, cannot easily be severed from the secondary subject of (apparently) enduring, "old" Israel without Christ. Finally, thinking about this secondary subject, in turn, happens in tension with Christians' actual experience (including interpretive prejudgments) of Jews.

If this hypothesis is right, then changing perceptions of Jews might lead to changing theological evaluations of Judaism and hence to shifts in the understanding of the primary subject for Christian theology, newness in Christ. Equally, the direction of influence might run the other way: how newness is understood theologically might shift with implications both for Christian discourse about Judaism and for Christian interaction with, and treatment of, contemporary Jews. In either case, the shaping of Christian theology via exchanges with Judaism and rationalization of anti-Judaism would be of considerable significance. In fact, I will argue, the influence works in both directions.

The first chapter, "Origins: Towards the Classic Framework," begins by tracing various ways in which the texts of the New Testament negotiate resistance to the central claims about newness made by their writers and communities. Through a reading of Justin Martyr's *Dialogue with Trypho* it then shows how in the second century claims about newness and judgments about resistance begin to crystallize in relation to three major issues: scripture, covenant and people. In relation to scripture, the claim is that Jesus Christ is the definitive fulfilment of the scriptures (fulfilment in Christ), with the emerging judgment that Judaism without faith in Christ cannot understand its own Bible (interpretive blindness). In relation to covenant, the claim is that the covenant with Israel has been renewed by God for Jews and Gentiles through Jesus' death and resurrection (renewal in Christ), with the judgment that the Torah has now been removed from its temporarily central place as the matrix for the divine-human covenant (displacement of Law). In relation to people, the claim is that God's purpose of blessing is being restored in present history through the Christian assemblies / churches (restoration in Christ), with the judgment that history is now marked by a separation between the Church as the faithful people of God and recipient of divine blessing, and the Judaism that holds onto the Law and rejects Jesus Christ as a disobedient people henceforth subject to divine punishment (division of history). This set of claims and corresponding arguments becomes the "classic" framework in Christianity for understanding the newness of Christ in relation to an enduring Judaism that is now conceived as external and hostile to the Catholic Church. It is at this point that facing the other of Judaism and perpetuating a legitimating anti-Judaism both become embedded in the practice of Christian theology.

The second chapter, "Before Modernity: Questions and Continuity," focuses on the Western Middle Ages, in particular the critical period 1050-1300. It argues that the "three-dimensional" interaction between the development of Christian theology, its encounter with Judaism and its perpetuation of anti-Judaism can be traced in the shifts that occurred in explication of the covenant claim and judgment (renewal in Christ / displacement of Torah) and in the process of questioning generated by the people claim and judgment (restoration in Christ / division of history). The emerging preoccupation with reason at this point in Christian theology can be seen as in part provoked by increased awareness of the religious "other" (Islam as well as Judaism) and as fostering modes of theological thinking that tended to be either more rigorously abstract (Anselm on salvation) or more rigorously historical (Aquinas on the Mosaic Law) than in the first millennium. Ultimately, however, confidence in the scripture claim and judgment (fulfilment in Christ / interpretive blindness), with the practice of allegorical interpretation linking them together, guided Christian theologians in their negotiation of the emerging tensions in this area. It ensured that history in its totality remained the subject of a sustained theological hermeneutics and hence underpinned the adjustments to the classic framework that contributed to its endurance.

The third chapter, "Modernity: Against Fulfilment," considers the very different situation that began to obtain from the seventeenth century onwards. The growing prominence of historical approaches to the Bible decisively affected the normative framework of pre-modernity by undermining confidence in the scripture claim, its attendant judgment and the related principle of scripture's pervasive figural meaning. Instead, what had been a subordinate strategy for articulating Christ's newness, the claim that he represented the culmination of progressive revelation, became the primary way to restate what was "new" about the good news. As in the previous chapter, a dynamic process of interaction is described, centred on the relationship between polemical Jewish-Christian theological exchange, the revolution in the interpretation of scripture within Christian theology and the changing evaluations of Judaism in "modern" theology. The effective replacement of prophetic fulfilment by narratives of historical development (immediately contested) in modernizing Christianity had profound implications, as writers sought to resist the relativization of particular religions by Enlightenment thinkers such as Lessing with the Enlightenment tools of supposedly objective historical scholarship.

"At the End of Modernity: What Is New?" is the title of the fourth chapter. It considers the first five decades of the twentieth century, a period when Judaism and anti-Judaism became conscious subjects for Christian theological consideration in an unprecedented way. It begins with Harnack's *Essence of Christianity* as a revealing summation of the project of "modern" Christian theology outlined in the previous chapter, a project that radically revised claims about newness in Christ while replicating and even intensifying the three judgments about enduring Judaism from the classic framework. Ultimately, Harnack advocated a Christian canon without the Old Testament and Christian history as an era with no use for a Jewish presence. Although they both rejected the liberal world view of nineteenth-century modernity represented by Harnack and both came from Jewish backgrounds, Eugen Rosenstock-Huessy and Franz Rosenzweig reached sharply divergent conclusions in their 1916 correspondence regarding the enduring significance of Judaism for Christianity, eventually leading Rosenzweig to propose a remarkable analysis of the relationship between Christian theology, Jewish reality and anti-Jewish attitudes. Karl Barth's radical re-description of the newness proclaimed by the Christian gospel enabled him to engage in a sustained re-examination of critical elements from the classic framework, a task for which the rise of state sponsored antisemitism in Germany provided the catalyst. Yet the dynamics of that framework in correlating the claim of the gospel with judgment on Judaism continued in his thought. Finally, writings of three Roman Catholic thinkers from these decades, Jacques Maritain, Henri de Lubac and Edith Stein, are shown both to parallel some of the theological moves already identified in the chapter and to suggest points of tension emerging between new theological insights forged in the confrontation with Nazism and the pre-modern framework which none of these writers explicitly repudiated.

"The Misshaping of Christian Theology?" takes a step back from Christian theology to review writings on Christianity by Leo Baeck and Martin Buber, two contrasting Jewish writers from the same period just considered, the first half of the last century. It argues that in their presentation of Christian theology's rejection of elements of Judaism as historically decisive and enduringly problematic, they provide a significant precedent for the current work in its attempt to show the importance of anti-Judaism in the shaping of Christian theology. Yet they also mirror the assumptions of many Christian writers about the essential externality of Judaism to Christianity. Ultimately, their "critical histories" of Christianity in relation to Judaism cannot accommodate the important insights of the preceding chapters.

The final chapter, "Conclusion: The Internal Foe," therefore returns to the model initially proposed by Franz Rosenzweig in his correspondence with Rosenstock-Huessy. It compares this model with two alternative and influential models for understanding the relation of Judaism to Christianity, the "exterior other" and the "estranged sibling". Reflection on the book as a whole, particularly with regard to the important themes of the hermeneutics of history and of reason, ethics and Law, underlines the interpretive power of Rosenzweig's approach. The deep intertwining of Christian self-understanding with Christian understanding of Judaism, and hence experience of Judaism, confirms the initial hypothesis sketched out above as a productive way of developing Rosenzweig's insight through the study of theological history. Yet that approach also leaves us with the uncomfortable question of whether anti-Judaism is indeed intrinsic to Christianity: is Christian theology always bound to regard Judaism as its "foe", however much it struggles for reconciliation? Two responses are briefly outlined, deriving from contrasting views as to whether Christian claims about the gospel must always generate judgment about the Judaism that does not appear to heed them.

Notes

---

[1] Judith Lieu, *Image and Reality: The Jews in the World of the Christians in the Second Century* (Edinburgh: T & T Clark, 1996); Daniel Boyarin, *Border Lines: The Partition of Judaeo-Christianity* (Philadelphia: University of Pennsylvania Press, 2004); Israel Jacob Yuval, *Two Nations in Your Womb: Perceptions of Jews and Christians in Late Antiquity and the Middle Ages*, trans. Barbara Harshav and Jonathan Chipman (Berkeley: University of California Press, 2006); Jeremy Cohen, *Living Letters of the Law: Ideas of the Jew in Medieval Christianity* (Berkeley: University of California Press, 1999); Frank E. Manuel, *The Broken Staff: Judaism through Christian Eyes* (Cambridge: Harvard University Press, 1992); David N. Myers, *Resisting History: Historicism and Its Discontents in German-Jewish Thought* (Princeton: Princeton University Press, 2003).

[2] Yuval, *Two Nations*, 20-21.

[3] See Helga Croner, ed., *Stepping Stones to Further Jewish-Christian Relations: An Unabridged Collection of Christian Documents* (New York: Paulist Press, 1977). For a collection of Roman Catholic texts including more recent pronouncements, see *Catholic Jewish Relations: Documents from the Holy See*, introduction by Eugene J. Fisher (London: Catholic Truth Society, 1999). The process leading to the statement of the 1988 Lambeth Conference of Anglican Bishops on "Jews, Christians and Muslims: The Way of Dialogue" is reviewed by Richard Harries, in *After the Evil: Christianity and Judaism in the Shadow of the Holocaust* (Oxford: Oxford University Press, 2003), 119-124. There are no obvious parallels to be drawn in relation to the Orthodox Churches; cf. the comments of Yves Dubois, "An Orthodox Perspective," in *Christian-Jewish Dialogue: A Reader*, ed. Helen P. Fry (Exeter: University of Exeter Press, 1996), 32-35.

[4] E.g. WCC Resolution on Anti-Semitism 1961 and the report of Faith and Order recommended for study in 1968, in Croner, ed., *Stepping Stones*, 72-85; "Notes on the Correct Way to Present the Jews and Judaism in Preaching and Catechesis in the Roman Catholic Church (June 24, 1985)," in *Catholic Jewish Relations*, introduction by Fisher, 34-49.

[5] See e.g. Carl E. Braaten and Robert W. Jenson, eds., *Jews and Christians: People of God* (Grand Rapids: Eerdmans, 2003); Judith H. Banki and John T. Pawlikowski, eds., *Ethics in the Shadow of the Holocaust: Christian and Jewish Perspectives* (Franklin: Sheed & Ward, 2001).

[6] Charlotte Klein, *Anti-Judaism in Christian Theology*, trans. Edward Quinn (London: SPCK, 1978).

[7] For an excellent survey of the different positions taken in response to this basic question, see Stephen R. Haynes, "Beware Good News: Faith and Fallacy in Post-Holocaust Christianity," in *Good News after Auschwitz? Christian Faith within a Post-Holocaust World*, ed. Carol Rittner and John K. Roth (Macon: Mercer University Press, 2001), 3-20.

[8] Rosemary Radford Ruether, *Faith and Fratricide: The Theological Roots of Anti-semitism* (New York: Seabury Press, 1974).

[9] Mary C. Boys, *Has God Only One Blessing? Judaism as a Source of Christian Self-Understanding* (New York: Paulist Press, 2000); cf. Stephen R. Haynes, *The Bonhoeffer Legacy: Post-Holocaust Perspectives* (Minneapolis: Fortress, 2006), xi, 89 and 97-98.

[10] On the resurrection, see the work of A. Roy Eckhardt, for instance "Salient Christian-Jewish Issues of Today: A Christian Exploration," in *Jews and Christians: Exploring the Past, Present and Future*, ed. James H. Charlesworth (New York: Crossroad, 1990), 151-184. On soteriology rather than Christology as the critical issue, see Helen Fry, "Towards a Christian Theology of Judaism," in *Christian-Jewish Dialogue*, ed. Fry, 27-30. On the wider question of whether a dose of relativism is the cure to supersessionism, see the remarks of Harries, *After the Evil*, 95-105, commenting on comparable issues in van Buren and Pawlikowski.

[11] Stephen Haynes, *Reluctant Witnesses: Jews and the Christian Imagination* (Louisville: Westminster John Knox Press, 1995).

[12] John Howard Yoder, *The Jewish-Christian Schism Revisited*, ed. Michael G. Cartwright and Peter Ochs (London: SCM, 2003), 111.

[13] See especially chapter 1, "It Did Not Have To Be," in Yoder, *Jewish-Christian Schism*, 43-66.

[14] R. Kendall Soulen, *The God of Israel and Christian Theology* (Minneapolis: Fortress, 1996).

[15] John David Dawson, *Christian Figural Reading and the Fashioning of Identity* (Berkeley: University of California Press, 2002). At one point, Dawson appears to trace supersessionism to "the failure of trinitarianism" stemming from the philosophy of Hegel (134).

[16] See for instance Robert W. Jenson, "Towards a Christian Theology of Judaism," in *Jews and Christians*, ed. Braaten and Jenson, 1-13; Scott Bader-Saye, *Church and Israel after Christendom: The Politics of Election* (Boulder: Westview, 1999), e.g. 53-55.

[17] Rowan Williams, "Bulgakov and Anti-semitism," appendix to *Towards a Russian Political Theology*, by Sergii Bulgakov, ed. Rowan Williams (Edinburgh: T & T Clark, 1999), 300.

[18] See for instance George Lindbeck, "The Church as Israel: Ecclesiology and Ecumenism," in *Jews and Christians*, ed. Braaten and Jenson, 78-94. Cf. Michael G. Cartwright, "'If Abraham is Our Father. . .' The Problem of Christian Supersessionism *after* Yoder," Afterword to *Jewish-Christian Schism*, by Yoder, 207-214, on attempts to differentiate various types of supersessionism.

[19] For contrasting Roman Catholic views, compare e.g. Claudia J. Setzer, "The Jewish-Christian Schism: Reflections on the Vatican Document *We Remember*," in *Ethics in the Shadow*, ed. Banki and Pawlikowski, 35-50, with Richard John Neuhaus, "Salvation Is from the Jews," in *Jews and Christians*, ed. Braaten and Jenson, 65-77. Bader-Saye, in *Church and Israel*, emphatically rejects the "two-covenant" approach favoured by many scholars, including Setzer, and pioneered by the Anglican writer between the wars, James Parkes (see e.g. 1-3, 95-102, and compare Harries, *After the Evil*, 100-01); on Parkes himself, see the recent biography by Colin Richmond, *Campaigner against Antisemitism: The Reverend James Parkes, 1896-1981* (London: Vallentine Mitchell, 2005).

[20] For a careful and sophisticated treatment of New Testament texts as polemical documents, see Craig A. Evans and Donald A. Hagner, eds., *Anti-semitism and Early Christianity: Issues of Polemic and Faith* (Minneapolis: Fortress, 1993). We need to learn to read polemic as a genre or dimension of different genres of theological literature, rather than simply a term of contempt.

[21] For a sustained attempt to do this, see Jacob Neusner, *Jews and Christians: The Myth of a Common Tradition* (London: SCM, 1991) and the series of books co-written by Neusner with Bruce Chilton, which includes *Jewish and Christian Doctrines: The Classics Compared* (London: Routledge, 2000), with an introduction setting out their joint approach (vii-xi).

CHAPTER ONE

ORIGINS:
TOWARDS THE CLASSIC FRAMEWORK

A primary purpose of this study is to analyse the significance of processes of theological exchange between Christianity and Judaism in periods other than those that have received the most intense scholarly attention—the first 150 years of Christianity on the one hand and the past six decades on the other. Yet in order to engage with that task in the following chapters, some discussion of Christian origins is necessary. Those chapters will repeatedly refer to something that I call the "classic framework" for relating the newness of Christ to the endurance of Israel, a framework that is largely settled by the third century in Catholic Christianity and against which subsequent shifts within Christian understanding can be helpfully mapped, as the rest of the book seeks to show. The concept of the classic framework that binds Christian self-understanding to engagement with Judaism is pivotal for the book as a whole, and therefore it is necessary to give some attention to tracing the processes whereby it achieved initial articulation. That is the aim of this first chapter.

To order to achieve this, the first section explores within some texts of the New Testament the emergence of a number of interrelated claims. These claims, arising from a shared concern to communicate the message of good news through Jesus Christ, can be described in relation to scripture, covenant and people: fulfilment of scripture in Christ, renewal of the covenant in Christ, restoration of God's people in Christ. From the time of the earliest Christian documents, however, it is also evident that these claims about newness were strongly contested within the Jewish contexts where they first originated, prior to the destruction of the temple in 70 CE. Judaism at this time was characterized by a pluriformity of interpretation about what faithfulness to Israel's God might mean, with vigorous debate and sometimes overt hostility between adherents of different points of view.[1] Some scholars are therefore happier to talk about "Judaisms" than Judaism in the singular. The New Testament evidence indicates the formation of distinctively Christian claims about newness in the context of encounter with various levels of opposition, both from within the plurality of Jewish voices that shared some kind of allegiance to Jesus of Nazareth and from the many and varied Jewish voices that did not.

Within this early period, it would be misleading to think of Christianity and Judaism as distinct religions or social groupings. The dynamics of claim and resistance described in the first section of the chapter are likely to have unfolded within what Boyarin calls "Judaeo-Christianity", with resistance to particular articulations of gospel claims coming from other Jesus-believing Jews as well as from Jews who rejected any idea that Jesus of Nazareth should be accorded particular status.[2] The destruction of the temple in 70 CE undoubtedly had incalculable effects on Jewish life generally and specifically on the relationship between the early Christian movement and the Jewish context in which it originated, some of which may be reflected in the New Testament, depending on how individual texts are dated. After the catastrophic failure of the Jewish revolt in the 130s, a fundamental transition from the New Testament period becomes apparent, whereby the ultimately dominant form of Christianity comes to define itself over against a contemporary Judaism which is struggling to re-establish its own identity. That transition is briefly surveyed in the second section of the chapter.

Justin Martyr's *Dialogue with Trypho* has been seen as both an index of and a contribution to the changing situation of Jewish-Christian relations in the second half of the second century.[3] In the third section of the chapter, an analysis of Justin's text shows perceived resistance to the claims arising from the formative articulation of the Christian message becoming the focus of judgment, judgment now directed against the "other" of Judaism construed as both mirroring and opposing the Christianity from which it is (at least in Justin's rhetoric) now distinct and separate. It is at this point that the "classic framework" for correlating Christian self-understanding with the interpretation of enduring Judaism begins to come into view. Positive claims about newness in Christ as prophetic fulfilment are translated into a set of parallel verdicts about oldness, as the fulfilment of a different strand in the prophetic tradition, the strand of judgment on God's people. "Old" Israel's resistance to the fulfilment of scripture in Christ is linked to Judaism's interpretive blindness. Resistance to the renewal of the covenant is linked to the displacement of Torah from God's dealings with his people after Christ. Resistance to the restoration of God's people through the new assemblies of Jews and Gentiles meeting in Christ's name is linked with the division of history, between the church which God blesses and faithless Israel which he chastises, with every misfortune befalling those Jews who refuse to be gathered in for salvation interpreted as a sure sign of divine punishment. The fourth and final section of the chapter reviews these developments and sums up the classic framework that arises from them. It also opens the question of the extent to which this framework implicates Christian theology that flows from it in both the sustaining of anti-Judaism and the perpetuation of exchanges with the Judaism of Christian experience and imagination. That is the question that lies at the heart of the remaining chapters of the book.

Newness and Resistance in the New Testament

In this first section of the chapter, it is argued that proclamation of a "new thing" in Christ led early Christian writers to articulate claims about newness in relation to scripture, covenant and people. Across the diversity of New Testament writings, we can recognize shared themes around fulfilment of scripture in Christ, renewal of covenant in Christ and restoration of God's people in Christ. These claims are shaped in relation to resistance both from within the plurality of the early Christian movement and from the plurality of the much larger Judaism within which it originated as itself one strand among many.

Perhaps it is worth adding a point of clarification about what this section will *not* do. For the sake of the chapters that follow, it is necessary to establish in very broad outline how these claims about newness might be passed on to attentive readers of the New Testament in later centuries with certain tensions and questions already bound up with them. I will not however attempt to provide a rigorous historical analysis of how these claims might have developed within the New Testament period, for instance by careful comparison of the different histories and perspectives of all the relevant individual texts. In particular, from the standpoints of both Christian history and Christian theology, the extent to which these claims in fact originated in the ministry of Jesus of Nazareth and the way he represented himself is clearly a matter of the utmost importance, and one that is of direct relevance to much of the so-called "Third Quest" for the historical Jesus.[4] I do not, however, intend to engage with it here. That does not mean, of course, that my treatment will not tend to reflect certain prejudgments about it, however hard I try to avoid that. It is not clear to me, however, that I could have begun to do justice to the immensely significant and much debated issues at stake here and still found space to open up the largely neglected questions about the shaping of Christian theology over two millennia which are the focus for this study.

The Scripture Claim: Fulfilment in Christ

The writers of the New Testament were convinced that God had done something new in Christ that left nothing as it had been before. They also regarded that deed as belonging within the one story of God's dealings with Israel which included themselves as the successors of the patriarchs and prophets. The new thing of God that had broken in and transformed everything also affirmed and was indeed affirmed by the former things of God, as they were held in the people's memory through the still somewhat fluid canon of first-century Judaism.[5] Indeed, their reading of this scripture taught the early Christians to have faith in a God whose truly new things were deeds to keep faith with the oldest promises. Already in the prophetic literature of the Hebrew scriptures there is a clear connection between newness and prophetic foretelling; "See, the former things have come to pass, and new things I now declare; before they spring forth, I tell you of them" (Isa. 42:9).[6] This power to proclaim the new, the unexpected, before it unfolds, is a demonstration of the power of Yhwh that humiliates the idols of the nations (Isa. 48:3-7). The foretelling divine word, however, also releases the power of events to function as signs, as communication between Yhwh and his people. Hence "newness" within history becomes theologically significant within the prophetic tradition precisely when it corresponds to some already recorded word of God, to something God *has* done. The verse which serves as the most majestic proclamation of God's *novum*, "Do not remember the former things, or consider the things of old," is followed by an anticipatory description of the "new thing" Yhwh is doing which explicitly reprises the original journey through the wilderness after the exodus from Egypt (Isa. 43:18-22).[7]

The new thing reveals the purposes of God by at once matching and, so to speak, exceeding both the things God has done in the distant past (creation, exodus, giving the law, entering the land) and the words God has spoken in the recent past of prophecy. The documents of the New Testament originated among communities that lived in continuity with this prophetic thinking. If it were truly the case that the present generation was witnessing a new communicative act of God, then this act had to be one that both matched and exceeded the authoritative testimony of the past as represented in Torah narrative and prophetic promise. Only in this way could God's people recognize the historically unprecedented as God's doing, God's word to them.

It is important to emphasize that this mode of interpreting present and (anticipated) future events in the light of scriptural texts and thereby reinterpreting those texts themselves in the light of perceptions of unfolding history is something already well-established *within* the Hebrew scriptures.[8] Moreover, the New Testament describes a Jewish world in which it is accepted that devout people, like Zechariah and Elizabeth, Simeon and Anna in the opening chapters, recognize a "prophetic surplus" in the scriptures they read and hope for the closing of the gap between present reality and the horizon of hope arising from that surplus; they are "looking for the redemption of Jerusalem" (Luke 2:38). Nor is this representation without historical plausibility; as Wright concludes, "The great story of the Hebrew scriptures was therefore inevitably read in the second-temple period as a story in search of a conclusion."[9] The discoveries at Qumran have made it abundantly clear that expectation of divine action to fulfil past prophecy and a willingness to discern such action taking shape amidst present events were features of at least one group in first-century Palestinian Judaism.[10] Moreover, it is likely that for most Jews living under Roman occupation in the land of God's promise, such expectations could be awakened if circumstances were suitable.[11]

Yet it is also clear that early Christian practices of interpretation had some highly distinctive features as well. The passage in Luke's Gospel about the appearance of the risen Christ to two disciples on the way to Emmaus (Luke 24:13-35) might be used as a point of departure for reflection on this, if we read it as (at one level) a dramatization of the relationship between believing in the good news of the resurrection and re-conceiving the relationship between scriptural texts and present experience.[12] The passage assumes, to begin with, that the reason Jesus had followers at all in his lifetime was because some people saw in him a prophetic figure: Jesus of Nazareth had been recognized as "a prophet mighty in deed and word before God and all the people" (Luke 24:19b). This has been a theme from the outset of Jesus' ministry in Luke's Gospel, when in the synagogue at Nazareth he describes himself as a prophet—a self-identification which the people of his home town then dramatically reject (Luke 4:16-30).[13] What makes the followers of Jesus different from other Jews who are hoping for the fulfilment of God's promises is the way that they relate the realization of prophetic hope to one particular prophet, Jesus of Nazareth.

Luke's two disciples are on the Emmaus road heading away from Jerusalem, convinced that the crucifixion has rendered that relationship between hope in God's action and faith in Jesus of Nazareth impossible. He was handed over to death; "But we had hoped that he was the one to redeem Israel" (Luke 24:21a). Yet the impasse is not final. The grieving followers suddenly hear another voice: "Was it not necessary that the Messiah should suffer these things and then enter into his glory?" (Luke

24:26). The voice, not recognized at this stage, raises the question: was it possible that the Lord's death was, despite everything, "according to the scriptures"—that indeed this is what the scriptures were all about? In order to accept this, these Jews who shared the not uncommon idea that decisive scriptural fulfilment could be touching their lifetimes would have to discover a new kind of interpretation, a new way of figuring fulfilment. And this comes to them, while they continue to walk away from Jerusalem, the site of hope's destruction, as the gift of the risen but as yet unknown Lord, who "interpreted to them the things about himself in all the scriptures" (Luke 24:27b); but equally, only through that gift can they be brought to the point of seeing him for who he is—the risen one, the Lord, the Messiah and Son of God. "Were not our hearts burning within us while he was talking to us on the road, while he was opening the scriptures to us?" (Luke 24:32). Yet burning as their hearts already were, "he had been made known to them in the breaking of the bread" (Luke 24:35b)—their eyes were finally and decisively opened in the recalling through present encounter of the symbolic and prophetic action he had undertaken on the night before he died, giving them bread and calling it his body, giving them wine and calling it his blood.

The passage, then, suggests that belief in the gospel of the resurrection of the crucified involves a rereading of Israel's scripture. Faith in the resurrection requires an acceptance that the cross which initially appeared to Jesus' followers as a terrible impasse in the fulfilment of God's purposes communicated through the scriptures is actually at their heart, and therefore those scriptures can now be reread, re-described, re-appropriated in its light. Paul's summary of the original core of belief in Christ, perhaps the earliest summary we have of the Christian proclamation, might be understood as expressing these same dynamics:

> Now I should remind you, brothers and sisters, of the good news that I proclaimed to you, which you in turn received, in which also you stand, through which also you are being saved. . . . For I handed on to you as of first importance what I in turn had received: that Christ died for our sins in accordance with the scriptures, that he was buried, that he was raised on the third day in accordance with the scriptures. (1 Cor. 15:1-2a, 3-4)

As in the Emmaus road narrative, here too the articulation and reception of the Christian proclamation is inseparable from a hermeneutics of fulfilment. The bare assertion of Jesus' death and resurrection only becomes meaningful as gospel insofar as it is understood as taking place "in accordance with the scriptures"—as God's new thing that is also in

profound continuity with the "old" things that God is known to have said
and done.

From the beginning of this chapter, we have been using the terminology
of fulfilment to express the claim that Christian faith has wanted to make
from its origins about the correlation between the scriptures and the events
around Jesus of Nazareth. Yet occurrences of fulfilment language in the
context of prophetic interpretation of scripture in the New Testament
(where in English they translate passive forms of the Greek verb *pleroo*)
are in fact absent from Paul's letters and restricted to the Gospels and
Acts—with James 2:23 as perhaps the exception that proves this rule, given
it relates to correspondences within the Abraham narrative of Genesis. In
the light of this concentration and the presence of only one direct
antecedent in the Hebrew scriptures (2 Chron. 36:21), it would be advisable
not to assume too readily that the term with its connotations of
completeness and finality should have a determinative role in explicating
New Testament approaches to interpreting sacred scripture.

Moreover, the distribution of fulfilment language in Mark and John is
directly linked to the narrative of the passion. Assuming the priority of
Mark, for instance, the earliest example of the term in a Christian
hermeneutical context is the hanging subordinate clause at Mark 14:49b,
which constitutes the very last words Jesus says in the presence of his
disciples in Mark's Gospel before his death: "but so that the scriptures
might be fulfilled . . ." (to follow the syntax of the original Greek). This is
the only place that the verb occurs in Mark's gospel, and its occurrence at
this critical juncture in the text is hardly incidental.[14] The language of
fulfilment, which carries within it the concept of completion, appears only
in this grammatically incomplete sentence. Nor does the author of Mark
give us a great deal of direct guidance about how one might understand
Jesus' suffering and death as fulfilling scripture, although the composition
of the Gospel as a whole seems to reflect the belief that what is most
important for faith in Christ—including the resurrection itself—cannot be
directly stated.[15] Some commentators have argued that it is through the
deeper pattern of scriptural allusions within the Gospel, rather than in the
explicit citations of scriptural texts, that the author wants to help his readers
towards an understanding of how it could be that through the death of the
Son of God "the scriptures might be fulfilled," with Isaiah 53, Zechariah 9-
14 and Psalms about righteous suffering all having some claim to being
invoked as interpretive background via careful patterns of allusion.[16]

Only once, and that at the outset, is explicit scriptural citation deployed
by the narrative / editorial voice in Mark's Gospel, at Mark 1:2-3 to
introduce John the Baptist. Matthew and John make much greater use of

this possibility, both of them sometimes introducing quotations with formulas using fulfilment language rather than the more neutral "it is written". It has been suggested that the original focus—historically and theologically—for Christian discourse about fulfilment was Jesus' rejection, suffering and death. John's Gospel reflects this in its restriction of fulfilment language by the narrative voice to passages from chapters 12-19, which concern Jesus' final days in Jerusalem. On the other hand, Matthew's contrasting concentration of the fulfilment formulas that are characteristic of his Gospel in the early chapters indicates a concern to highlight "point for point" correspondences between texts from the Hebrew scriptures and specific details in the life of Jesus from its very beginning, indeed from his conception itself. From the other side of the resurrection, Matthew presents the whole of Jesus' life as an appropriate subject for interpretation as prophetic fulfilment.

In Acts, Luke extends forward that same confidence in prophetic reading that treats the death and resurrection of the Christ as its centre of theological gravity, to the post-resurrection experiences of the disciples in Jerusalem and beyond. In this respect Luke could be seen as adapting and continuing the "ecclesiocentric" hermeneutics that Hays identified in Paul's letters: since "These things happened to them to serve as an example, and they were written down to instruct us, on whom the ends of the ages have come" (1 Cor. 10:11), texts relating to Adam, Abraham and Moses, passages from the Law, the Prophets and the Writings, can all be drawn on by Paul for teaching about what is happening within the church of Jews and Gentiles.[17] As already noted, this is also a process in which the "original" texts are thereby themselves reinterpreted in the light of the present experiences of those claiming to be the people of God.

What is also clear from the New Testament documents, however, is that the interpretive claims about scripture bound up with faith in the resurrection of the crucified from the beginning met resistance and hostility from the unconvinced. Paul, for instance, is acutely aware that the shared ground of scripture within the Diaspora Jewish communities that provide the context for his work is also sharply contested ground. Some of his most sustained exegesis, e.g. in Galatians 4, is prompted by the need to wrest particularly strategic textual "sites" away from his opponents and assimilate them instead to his own understanding of the Christian gospel.

At no point does Paul in his letters set out a formal demonstration that Jesus' death and resurrection happened "according to the scriptures"; rather, he writes from and for the confidence that this is indeed the case. There is therefore a certain distance between the presentation of the scripture claim of fulfilment in Christ in Paul's own letters and the presentation of the same claim ascribed to him by Luke in Acts. Almost as soon as he has come to believe in Jesus, Paul is described by Luke as engaging in adversarial exchanges with other Jews who do not share this faith; indeed, he "confounded the Jews who lived in Damascus by proving that Jesus was the Messiah" (Acts 9:22). This claim that Jesus' Messiahship could be proved by attentive interpretation of the scriptures to the satisfaction of an open-minded Jewish hearer is one that is neither explicit nor implicit in Paul's own writing and interpretive practice. Yet it seems to be of some importance to later Pauline Christian such as we might presume the author of Luke-Acts to be. In Thessalonica, Paul again starts his ministry by "explaining and proving that it was necessary for the Messiah to suffer and rise from the dead" (Acts 17:3a); moreover, Apollos is judged to have been highly effective in the same task (Acts 18:28; cf. 6:8-10 on Stephen), so this is not a special ability conferred on Paul alone. The question of how to interpret the resistance to belief in Christ of Jews who have been presented with such overwhelming proof is something to which we will return later in this section of the chapter.

The Covenant Claim: Renewal in Christ

In Luke's account of the last supper, one of the crucial interpretive sentences uttered by Jesus is, "This cup that is poured out for you is the new covenant in my blood" (Luke 22:20b).[18] Although each of the four New Testament accounts of the last supper attributes somewhat different words to Jesus, all represent him as referring to covenant in relation to the cup. "New covenant" appears in this context in Paul's version at 1 Cor. 11:25 and also in some manuscripts of Matthew. Given the pivotal importance of this scene for framing our understanding as Gospel readers of the passion narrative that follows, the significance of the deployment of (new) covenant language at this point would be hard to overestimate. One cardinal theme for understanding Jesus' death as "according to the scriptures," then, at least among some of those early Christian groups whose texts have come down to us in the New Testament, was that of the renewal of the covenant with Israel.

Perhaps the most important scriptural text for informing this theme was Jeremiah 31:31-34. Although he does not cite it directly, it seems clear that these verses on new covenant, together with the references to new spirit in Ezek. 36:26-27 (and cf. Ezek. 11:19-20), were in Paul's mind in writing the remarkable passage about the newness of Christ that we find in 2 Corinthians 3.[19] At the beginning of the chapter, Paul describes the Corinthians as a letter of recommendation for him, "written not with ink but with the Spirit of the living God, not on tablets of stone but on tablets of human hearts" (2 Cor. 3:3b). The final phrase, *kardiais sarkinais*, precisely corresponds to *kardian sarkinen* in the Septuagint translation of Ezek. 36:26 likely to have been familiar to Greek-speaking Jewish communities at this time. With it an allusion is already being made to Ezekiel's promise of the giving of (the) spirit so that obedience to the divine command may be interiorized and thereby rendered complete. Yet where the passages from the Hebrew prophets speak of the resistance of God's people to God's Torah being decisively overcome in the renewal of the covenant, for Paul it seems the issue is rather the inexorable resistance of writing itself to the work of the Spirit. The contrast is made still more starkly shortly afterwards, as Paul introduces the "new covenant" language of Jeremiah 31: God has made us "ministers of a new covenant, not of writing [*gramma*] but of Spirit; for the writing kills, but the Spirit gives life" (2 Cor. 3:6), to translate with as little paraphrase as possible. The association between writing, Mosaic covenant and death is continued in what follows: "Now if the ministry of death, chiselled in letters on stone tablets, came in glory so that the people could not gaze at Moses' face . . ." (2 Cor. 3:7a).

In the remainder of 2 Corinthians 3, further contrasts are added to those already introduced between old covenant / new covenant, writing / Spirit, life / death: ministry of death / ministry of Spirit; ministry of condemnation / ministry of justification; what was set aside / what is permanent; veil over face and minds / veil removed (2 Cor. 3:7-16). Death and condemnation are cardinal dimensions of what has now been rendered "past" by the newness of Christ; but so too, it would seem, are writing, the tablets of stone, Moses himself and the Mosaic books, which can now be re-described as "the old covenant" (2 Cor. 3:14). The verb *katargeo*, meaning "to set aside, abolish", occurs repeatedly in this passage (verses 7, 11, 13, 14)—the same verb that is used in 1 Cor. 15:26 to refer to the eschatological abolition of death, the final enemy. Whereas in Ezekiel and Jeremiah, new covenant and new spirit promised complete adherence to Torah as the covenant bond, in Paul the institution of the Mosaic Torah seems to stand somehow over against the "new thing" that God is doing and, furthermore, becomes implicated in a whole bundle of "former things," including condemnation and death, that have now been abolished.

Commentators have struggled to make coherent sense of the lacunae and sudden jumps in Paul's train of thought in 2 Corinthians 3, as they have in other important passages of his work and perhaps in particular in contexts where questions of Torah / Law are paramount. "Law" was already recognized as a bewilderingly multivalent term in Paul by Origen

in the third century, and it would be foolhardy to extrapolate with
confidence from one strand within a complex and arguably ultimately
fragmentary whole.[20] Nonetheless, there is clearly a significant connection
for Paul between claims about new covenant through Christ and concerns
about making sense of Torah / Law as text and practice, a connection that
is also visible in his more extended treatment of Torah / Law in Galatians
and then again in Romans, where questions about justification come to the
fore. Scholarship associated with the so-called "new perspective" on Paul
has taught us to read his language of justification as being concerned
primarily with the issue of entering into the covenant of God with God's
people.[21] Paul's insistence, on almost any reading of his letters, that the
renewal of the covenant in Christ means that Gentiles who believe in Jesus
can enter the covenant without becoming fully Torah observant as that was
customarily accepted within the Judaism(s) of the time was evidently
deeply controversial. Again, it was a focus for dissension both within the
still predominantly Jewish Christian movement and with other Jewish
groups with whom the Jesus movement continued to have various levels of
relationship.

Questions of practice, it would seem, were the catalyst here. If Gentiles
who believed in the gospel of Jesus Christ were not required to take on
certain practices set down in the Torah / Law, such as circumcision, dietary
restrictions and Sabbath observance, what sense was to be made of both the
past institution of such practices by divine revelation (via writing on stone
and, later, in ink) and the present continuation of them by Jews (both some
of those professing allegiance to Christ and those rejecting such
allegiance)? One way of reading Paul's complex thinking on these issues in
Galatians and Romans is to see him as starting from utter conviction on the
"policy" question of the admission of Gentiles into full status membership
of God's covenant people without the observance of some characteristically
Jewish practices based on Torah / Law. Faced with considerable opposition
on this point, he seeks to deploy a number of interweaving theological
arguments for his position. As he does so, he moves in a non-systematic
way towards articulating an understanding of the place of Moses' Torah /
Law within the purposes of God that represents a radical departure from
previous Jewish thinking (in all its diversity).[22] Yet this new understanding
remains very much a "work in progress" in Paul's writings and contains
persistent tensions that Paul is not able to resolve satisfactorily (if indeed
he was fully aware of them). This approach certainly gains some
plausibility from the trajectory of Paul's thinking in Galatians 3-4, where
he begins by forcibly defending the reality of Gentiles belonging to God's
people, as true children of Abraham, through believing in the message

about Jesus Christ rather than by "works of the law" (Gal. 3:3). Yet Paul is quickly drawn from Gal. 3:10 onwards into a series of points about the status and purpose of the Law itself. Initially and then again in chapter 4 he locates exegetical and speculative grounds for a negative evaluation of Torah / Law, while between these points we see him striving for positive formulations about the Law's God-given purpose.

The same issues can be seen in the more extended treatment of Christ's transforming work in Romans, in particular in chapters 5-7. In chapter 5, Paul develops the contrasting parallel between Adam and Christ, again as one in a series of contrasts: trespass / free gift, condemnation / justification, dominion of death / dominion of life, many made sinners / many made righteous. In the course of the discussion, "law" is linked to the regime of Adam as one of trespass, condemnation and death, in contrast with the newness of Christ.[23] At Rom. 5:13 Paul inserts the observation: "sin was indeed in the world before the law, but sin is not reckoned when there is no law." This rather opaque statement seems to prepare the ground for a further "intervention" in the Adam / Christ exposition at Rom. 5:20: "But law came in, with the result that the trespass multiplied; but where sin increased, grace abounded all the more." That triggers the immediate question of Rom. 6:1: "Should we continue in sin in order that grace may abound?" Paul responds by explaining union with the crucified and risen Christ as crucifixion of the "old [Adamic] self" (Rom. 6:6) and therefore death to sin for the believer (Rom. 6:11). Yet the question of law keeps springing back for Paul. He ends this section with the conclusion: "For sin will have no dominion over you, since you are not under law but under grace" (Rom. 6:14)—immediately prompting the further question, "Should we sin because we are not under law but under grace?" (Rom. 6:15).

Paul has to clarify why it is that the newness Christ has brought means an end *both* to endless *anomia*, "lawlessness" (Rom. 6:19), *and* to being "under law." Paul returns to the image of being crucified with Christ, interpreted not now in terms of death of the old man and new creation, but of how "you have died to the law through the body of Christ, so that you may belong to another, to him who has been raised from the dead" (Rom. 7:4). Reprising the passage from 2 Corinthians 3 analysed earlier, Paul offers another vivid conclusion:

> But now we are discharged from the law, dead to that which held us captive, so that we are slaves not under the old written code [*en palaioteti grammatos*, literally "in oldness of writing"] but in the new life of the Spirit [*en kainoteti pneumatos*, "in newness of Spirit"]. (Rom. 7:6)

Here we find perhaps the most vivid instance of apparent association in Paul between Torah practice and the whole Adamic "dominion of death" to which God in Christ has put a decisive end: dying to the old, Adamic man of sin means being released from "the oldness of writing."

Such association clearly prompted, in Paul's mind and in the minds of his first readers, exactly the question it may prompt for us: "What then should we say? That the law is sin?" (Rom. 7:7). The exegesis of what follows in Romans 7 is complex and much debated, but the important point to be noted with regard to this study is that Paul will not allow a simple *equivalence* of law and sin, but neither will he allow a complete *disconnection* of law and sin. He will insist that far from being capable of being identified with sin, "the law is holy, and the commandment is holy and just and good" (Rom. 7:12); moreover, "the law is spiritual" (Rom. 7:14). Yet it nonetheless serves as a kind of germ or point of departure, an *aphorme* (Rom. 7:8, 11) for sin. Now Paul returns to the thesis he began to develop in Rom. 5:20-21 before he had to break off in order to defend himself against the charge of encouraging sin. Within the narrative of God's purposes, Law given through Moses (Rom. 5:13-14) serves the purpose of intensifying the dynamic of sin that has its source in Adam, bringing it to a head, keeping it constantly working and active within humanity, at the same time reminding humanity that it finds itself in impossible contradiction between commandment and desire, good and evil, spirit and flesh (Rom. 7:7-20). In this way, Paul can (at least to his own satisfaction) maintain that the giving of the law was a work of God, that it prepared for the new and final work of God in Christ, *and* that it has no authority over those who are now in Christ, that indeed they are free from it and deny their identity "in Christ" if they place themselves under it.

Accepting the newness of Christ is incompatible, for Paul, with being "under law", however precisely that might have been interpreted in terms of forms of Torah practice Paul might have considered appropriate within the Christian communities that he knew, particularly in the case of other Jewish believers.[24] This did not mean *anomia*, lawlessness, according to Paul's way of thinking: rather, the *novum* that had come in Christ still included the fulfilment of those prophetic texts in Ezekiel and Jeremiah that spoke of a direct "inscription" of God's teaching on the heart, of an interior transformation that included a complete internalization of the divine command, effected through union with Christ crucified and raised. Paul, however, unlike those prophetic writers, inferred that such internalization must cause a radical re-evaluation of the status of the exterior, "scripted" Torah. Such re-evaluation of Torah in relation to belief and practice in all likelihood presented significant problems for the relationship between Pauline Christian communities and the wider "umbrella" of first-century Jewish life within which the Christian movement had originated.[25]

Paul's approach to the claim of the making new of God's covenant in Christ can be compared with the appearance of the same theme in the letter to the Hebrews. The letter, unlike any of Paul's, quotes Jer. 31:31-34 directly and in full, at Heb. 8:8-12; indeed, this is the longest direct quotation anywhere in the New Testament. Paul is focused in Galatians and Romans at least on how the renewal of the covenant affects the admission of Gentiles and therefore how the renewed covenant is to relate to the Law once given to Moses and the specific practices arising from it that have come to be constitutive for Jewish identity. Hebrews, on the other hand, is concerned with contrasting the covenant given through Moses and the covenant through the blood of Christ as two parallel frameworks for divine worship, with purification of the worshippers and the appropriate means of atonement to ensure this as primary issues.[26]

A rather different set of practices than in Paul, also based on the reading of Torah, is therefore presented in Hebrews as in tension with faith in Jesus Christ and thereby re-described as "old". The old covenant is explicated here quite specifically in terms of the instructions in Exodus for worship in the tent in the wilderness, with its attendant rituals of priestly cleansing and animal sacrifice. The new covenant comes with Jesus as both high priest and "once for all" cleansing sacrifice through self-offering. The writer seems motivated by concern that his readers might miss (and perhaps be attracted to) the rituals associated with the temple, not by debates about those aspects of Torah practice that appear to have been the flashpoints for Paul's writing in Galatians and Romans, such as circumcision and dietary observance. Conversely, nowhere in his letters does Paul express any judgment at all about how the "new thing" God has done in Christ might change the relationship of Jewish believers in particular to the *worship* of Torah-based Judaism, and above all to the temple, although Luke attributes to Paul at the synagogue in Thessalonica the argument that Christ offers the hitherto lacking possibility of complete forgiveness of sin (Acts 13:38-39), which certainly has parallels with Hebrews.

While Hebrews focuses on biblical texts relating to the tabernacle (and thereby highlights the themes of priesthood and sacrifice on the one side, and the wilderness journey on the other), the book of Revelation engages with issues of right worship in a rather different way. In it, the symbolic centrality of Jerusalem within the prophetic texts is recognized and celebrated. In trito-Isaiah, for instance, the restoration of the city of Zion is a crucial theme, with the creation of new heaven and new earth directly

linked to the (new, renewed) creation of Jerusalem (Isa. 65:17-18). Yet in
Revelation's concluding vision of Jerusalem restored, there is no temple.
Readers familiar enough with prophetic writings to be aware of the partial
"mapping" of the book's structure on the book of Ezekiel would have been
particularly aware of the striking lacuna at this point.[27]

For Revelation as for Hebrews, then, the practices of temple worship—
based on sacrifice—cannot be imagined as having any place in the life of
God's people after the renewal of the covenant in the blood of Jesus, priest
and sacrifice, either in the midst of present struggles or following the final
triumph of the holy warrior / slaughtered lamb. The same might be said of
Luke on the basis of the speech he attributes to Stephen in Acts 7, where
scripture is invoked against the institution of the temple (Acts 7:44-50), and
indeed of the Gospel writers generally given their narration of prophecies
of the temple's destruction (e.g. Mark 13:1-2 and parallels). All this, it
would seem, has come to an end with the new thing God has done in
Christ; as Luke's Jesus says at the last supper, "This cup that is poured out
for you is the new covenant in my blood" (Luke 22:20b). What further use,
then, the blood of the sacrifices laid down in the covenant of Sinai? At the
end of the citation of Jer. 31:31-34, the writer of Hebrews comments: "In
speaking of 'a new covenant', he has made the first one obsolete. And what
is obsolete and growing old will soon disappear" (Heb. 8:13).

The People Claim: Restoration in Christ

It is difficult to be certain about the precise context, and therefore
meaning, of Hebrews' prediction that the old covenant "will soon
disappear," but it might reasonably be taken as evidence for the way that
early Christians, perhaps particularly from the second generation onwards,
found it difficult to understand the persistence of what they experienced as
resistant to the claims that followed from their belief in Jesus crucified as
Messiah and Lord in accordance with the scriptures. In Christ, those
scriptures had been fulfilled, the covenant renewed and wonderful things
experienced in the churches where those who received him assembled for
proclamation, teaching and celebration. And yet most Jews were
unconvinced or indifferent. Of course, most Gentiles who came across the
Jesus movement were unconvinced or indifferent as well, but it was other
Jews who, by continued adherence to traditional practices without regard
for the implications of the renewal of the covenant in Jesus Christ, kept
alternative ways of reading the scriptures in relation to those practices both
current and prevalent.

There were various ways for early Christians to make sense of the resistance of most of those who claimed to be God's people to their claims about restoration in Jesus Christ. It is likely that from the outset one aspect of articulating the claim that Christ's death was indeed "according to the scriptures" was the identification of the rejection of Jesus' message by those he encountered in his ministry, especially the Jerusalem leadership, as itself the fulfilment of prophecy. The very first time that Jesus himself quotes from scripture in Mark's Gospel, for instance, is his citation of Isa. 6:9-10 at Mark 4:12, when commenting on the parable of the sower to his disciples. Mark's Jesus interprets the mixed reception of the word of God in his teaching from the start as "according to the scriptures", scriptures which show God's people as incapable of turning and responding in unity to the call of God at pivotal points in their history. The parable as subsequently expounded deals with indifference and transient responses, yet Mark's Jesus has already faced outright opposition by this point from "scribes" (Mark 2:6), "Pharisees" (Mark 2:24), unnamed people in a synagogue (Mark 3:2) and "scribes who had come from Jerusalem" (Mark 3:22). Reference to scriptural fulfilment is also implicit in the *dei* ("must") of Mark 8:31, the first time Jesus foretells his rejection, suffering and death in Jerusalem:

> Then he began to teach them that the Son of Man must undergo great suffering, and be rejected by the elders, the chief priests, and the scribes, and be killed, and after three days rise again.

The same word, *dei*, is used by Luke's Jesus in the Emmaus road narrative and is immediately explicated there in terms of Jesus giving an explanation of what has happened from "all the scriptures" (Luke 24:26-27).

One text that seems to have been particularly appealed to by early Christian writers as finding fulfilment in the rejection of the Messiah by the people's leaders and his subsequent exaltation by God's own hand is Psalm 118:22-23, cited by Mark's Jesus at the conclusion of the parable with which he ends a debate within the temple courts with "the chief priests, the scribes, and the elders" (Mark 11:27): "The stone that the builders rejected has become the chief cornerstone; this was the Lord's doing, and it is amazing in our eyes" (Mark 12:10-11). As well as appearing in the parallel versions of the parable in Matthew and Luke, it also occurs independently in Acts 4:11 and 1 Pet. 2:7. Clearly such texts functioned at an early stage on two levels: their original purpose was to explain how the rejection of the Messiah by his own people could be a fulfilment of the scriptures, but they are also implicitly assisting the Christian community to make sense of the fact that even after Jesus' resurrection, his vindication by God as Lord and

Messiah, so many Jews, and most importantly the Jewish leadership in Judea, the Galilee and the Diaspora, continue to resist the gospel message. Particular texts aside, Levenson has drawn attention to the likelihood of the New Testament's first readers hearing clearly in the Gospels the motif from the Patriarchal narratives in Genesis of the suffering of the beloved son at the hands of those brothers jealous of his unique chosenness—and interpreting their own marginal position in the same light. In recapitulating the plight of Isaac, Jacob / Israel and in particular Joseph, Jesus' hostile reception from "his own" reveals him as the chosen and anointed one in whom the scriptures find fulfilment.[28]

We noted earlier how re-interpretation of scripture in the light of the gospel of resurrection has as one horizon in the New Testament the reality of resistance to this practice. Paul regards such resistance as provisional, as Romans 9-11 makes clear with its central affirmation that after the time of hardening and judgment has been completed "all Israel will be saved" (Rom. 11:26). As we would expect, Paul seeks to understand what is happening in the story of God's relationship with God's people as one of prophetic fulfilment and therefore as one within which a certain dialectical tension of old and new is maintained. He moves rapidly across a kaleidoscope of passages from the Law and the Prophets to maintain both that Israel was, is and will always be God's elect people *and* that rejection by Jews of faith in Jesus Christ constitutes a hardening of heart comparable to that of Pharaoh, the archetypal enemy of God's people, and will incur the judgment of God. He finds prophetic texts relating both to a division within the body of Israel between the faithful remnant, the true Israel, and the unfaithful, and to the inclusion of the Gentiles within the promises of God. Thus the disorienting pattern of development in the early Christian movement, with non-acceptance by most of Israel both in the Land and in the Diaspora, yet growing interest and adherence from Gentiles not all of whom were Torah observant, is deemed to be, after all, the work of God, because it corresponds to significant patterns of prophecy discernible within Israel's past as set out in its scripture. These new things too can be understood as God's communicative activity, because they match and exceed and therefore fulfil what is read from the past.

Here again, however, the distance between Paul's own writings and the "Paul" who appears in Luke-Acts is significant. We have already noted that Luke's Paul is committed to a notion of theological necessity that is not evident in Paul's letters: the notion that things *had* to happen this way, and that the way they had to happen was clearly signalled in advance in the scriptures.[29] This is important not just because it suggests a more "linear" and less dialectical relation between the oldness of the writing and the newness of the Spirit than we find in Paul, but also because in itself it becomes a critical step in the interpretation of Jewish resistance and rejection with regard to the newness of the gospel. If Paul, along with Apollos and others, proved unequivocally from the scriptures that Jesus was the Messiah, as, according to Acts, they did, and if Jews in Israel and the Diaspora still refused to believe the good news—then this was clearly because of a profound moral and spiritual failing on the part of those Jews. And God's response to the fact of such moral and spiritual failing is clear: in the words of Jesus speaking in the temple to the Jewish leaders in Matthew's Gospel, "Therefore, I tell you, the kingdom of God will be taken away from you and given to a people that produces the fruits of the kingdom" (Matt. 21:43). So, in Acts, Paul may begin by giving the Jews the opportunity to come to faith in Christ by "proving" his Messiahship from the scriptures, but he keeps moving away from the synagogue as focus to speak directly to the (more receptive) Gentiles.

Paul's discussion in Rom. 9-11 includes the assertions that Israel must remain the elect people of God and that the eschatological fulfilment of God's purposes cannot take place without their inclusion. Other New Testament writers—such as the writer of Matthew's Gospel—seem at some points to take the blunter view that if those who reject faith in Christ are disobedient to God, then those who persist in such disobedience must simply cease to be the people of God, which is now to be found instead among the new and spreading Christian "assemblies" (*ekklesiai*). It is possible that Matthew, like Luke-Acts, reflects a changed mentality following the destruction of the temple in 70 CE, now identified in Christian understanding as marking the definitive end of the "old" covenant based on the Mosaic Torah. Up to a point, they are also here pursuing the logic of Paul's own writings about the displacement of practices hitherto emblematic of faithfulness to the Law in the light of the newness of Christ: if Law no longer "frames" the covenant relationship between God and God's people, but rather Christ, then those who continue to hold to the Law while rejecting Christ risk drifting outside that covenant relationship and ceasing to be God's people.

The final element in the emerging interpretation of widespread Jewish resistance to Christian claims in Luke-Acts, and one that corresponds to other New Testament documents including Paul's letters as noted above, is that this rejection by much of Israel and the counterbalancing phenomenon of the inclusion of Gentiles within the covenant people of God are themselves understood as something prophesied clearly in the scriptures. For instance, in the "sample speech" to a Diaspora synagogue that Luke provides (Acts 13:16-43), Paul ends with a quotation from Habakkuk warning those in attendance of the dangers of failing to attend to the new thing God is doing. When the Jews of the city turn against him, we are to understand that the "negative" prophetic word about Israel's failure has been confirmed, as Paul and Barnabas turn instead to the Gentiles and cite a prophecy from deutero-Isaiah as being fulfilled in what they are doing (Acts 13:46-47). One might compare the final incident recounted in Acts, Paul's meeting with the Jewish leaders in Rome; their mixed reaction is interpreted by Paul as fulfilment of the same prophetic text from Isa. 6:9-10 about Israel's blindness and deafness that had been cited by Jesus in commenting on the failure of the word of God to take root and grow, in the context of his own lack of acceptance (Acts 28:23-28; cf. Luke 8:10b). Indeed, while Mark and Matthew quote the verses in full within their Gospels, Luke saves the complete version until this point, at the very end of his two-volume work, for Paul's last speech, whose valedictory words are a brief commentary on it: "Let it be known among you then that this salvation of God has been sent to the Gentiles; they will listen" (Acts 28:28).

By the end of Luke-Acts, the correspondence between the indifference of his contemporaries to Jesus and the indifference of most Jews known to Luke's readers to the Jesus movement is made very clear, as is the outcome of such hardness of heart. The last piece of exegesis in Acts has an uncomfortable echo of the first, where Peter applies the idea of the "necessity" of the fulfilment of scripture to the case of Judas, ending with the text "Let another take his position as overseer" (Acts 1:15-20). As faithless Judas (*Ioudas* in Greek) is replaced by faithful Matthias at the beginning, so by the end of Acts unbelieving Jews (in Greek *Ioudaioi*) are being replaced by believing Gentiles as the people of God. For Luke, the "old" scriptures prophesy unambiguously not only the saving death and resurrection of the Messiah, but the rejection of him by the majority of the Jewish people and the inauguration of a new form of the people of God that includes Gentiles without requiring Torah observance from them. Although Luke does not dwell on the point explicitly, it would seem an evident inference from his narrative in the Gospels that the sack of Jerusalem and destruction of the temple by the Romans in 70 CE should be understood as a result of the rejection of Jesus by the Jewish leadership and people at large (Luke 19:41-44; cf. 21:20-24, 23:28-31).

The translation of Paul's dialectical and eschatological theology into more linear and historical thinking that is partially reflected in Hebrews reaches a kind of terminus in Acts. Paul as a character in the narrative mediates the shift of the Christian movement from Jerusalem to Rome, from the heart of ancient Judaism to the centre of the contemporary Gentile empire, from the fringes of the synagogue to its own still embryonic independent presence in the bustling religious marketplace of the Greco-Roman city. Luke wants to reassure Theophilus and all his readers that continuing history is the scene for the unfolding fulfilment of Christian claims about newness in the life of God's people, through their restoration in Christ, regardless of the indifference and opposition to those claims from most Jews.

Between Paul the Apostle and Justin the Apologist

Christianity began as a movement within Judaism, at a time when Judaism was characterized by a high degree of internal diversity and disagreement. At this early stage, to talk about the Church in relation to Judaism and anti-Judaism makes little or no historical sense. Christian assemblies were one competing subgroup within the spectrum of first-century Judaism(s). By the second half of the second century, however, such talk does begin to make sense, insofar as it directly reflects the discourse of influential Christian writers, although of course it nonetheless needs to be treated with due scholarly caution. Before we consider in the next section one of the most important texts for marking this transition, we need to review briefly some of the issues that might be relevant for understanding it.

Scholarship of Christian origins has increasingly recognized that the eventual emergence of Christianity as a religion over against Judaism was a complex process that unfolded at different speeds in different contexts and was driven by a variety of factors.[30] The documents assembled to form the Christian New Testament belong, at least for the most part, to the period when adherence to faith in Christ, sometimes coupled with a radically open policy on admission of Gentiles, characterized some groups within the broad spectrum of Jewish existence. Their place within that spectrum may well have been a contentious one, not least because of the way that non-acceptance of their distinctive claims by others was interpreted by them as faithless disobedience and continuing practices taken for granted by some or most others were dismissed as belonging to a previous phase of God's dealings with God's people. Despite the realities of polemic and hostility that are evident from the New Testament documents, then, it remains anachronistic to speak about anti-Judaism in this context. The debates reflected in the New Testament can be understood as unfolding within the conflicted field of Boyarin's Judaeo-Christianity, where the winning over of Israel as a whole to faith in Jesus remained a vital project for the Jewish leaders of the early Christian movement.

   The crucial point for our purposes here is that Judaism is not conceived
as some kind of homogenous "other" external to Christianity at this stage,
even by those voices within the New Testament which are most sharply
critical of the behaviour and attitudes of some other Jews.[31] How it could
and did come to be so conceived, it has become clear in recent studies, is
not a straightforward question to answer. Judaism itself changed
profoundly during this same period and became less internally diverse;
after 70 CE, for instance, there were no longer Sadducees, a group with
whom some New Testament writings give explicit evidence for conflict,
nor Essenes, with whom the evidence for conflict is arguably implicit in
Hebrews. It is likely that general hostility to Christian claims from other
Jewish groups, for which there is evidence in the New Testament, was
increasingly accompanied by specific measures to exclude Jesus believing
Jews from synagogues and associated Jewish life.[32] While we need to be
wary of oversimplifying the issues here, by the second half of the second
century some Christian writers were representing Judaism as a single,
coherent entity opposed to the Church, whether or not the boundaries
between Christians and Jews were quite so precise in terms of actual
religious life. At this point, with the re-description of the now
predominantly Gentile Church as the "new" Israel in contrast to the old,
what had been polemical exchanges about how to be Israel in the case of
Paul and other Jewish New Testament writers began to be read instead as
polemic against an externalized and objectified Judaism and against the
Jews who identified with it—and moreover read, by the second half of the
second century, as canonical scripture.[33]
   The Judaism that was thereby rendered the enemy of the Christian
Church, and thus the object of what we can begin to call anti-Judaism,
cannot be identified in a straightforward way with any actual form of
Jewish life. Jewish existence was itself during this period in the early
stages of an extended process of contested transition towards Rabbinic
Judaism, a transition arguably not finally complete until the redaction of
the Babylonian Talmud in the sixth century. Moreover, as Gentile Christian
groups became more estranged from Jewish contexts, knowledge of
Judaism based on actual encounters with Jews and Jewish leaders
inevitably tended to diminish. It has been suggested, for instance, that
attempting to reconstruct some kind of historical picture for the "Judaism"
written about by Ignatius of Antioch in the early second century is likely to
be futile: Ignatius simply deploys it as a negative term within his own
theological rhetoric.[34] The question of just how much contact persisted
between Jews and Christians after 135 CE is a complex one.[35] What is
clear, however, is that the need to respond to and make theological sense of

continuing Judaism was inherent in the self-construction of "Catholic" Christianity as a body seeking to define itself by definite boundaries, rejecting the claims of perceived heretics to belong to the Church just as it rejected the claims of non-Jesus Jews to belong to Israel.

Aside from continuing contacts between Jews and Christians, not least among the many on both sides who did not accept their leaders' attempts to inhibit overlap and exchange, the non-Jews who probably constituted the majority in most churches by the third century and to whom Christianity sought primarily to appeal in the cities of the Roman empire would have been in most cases very aware of Judaism as a significant presence. It has been estimated that at the start of the second century, there were perhaps around 100,000 Christians, but approximately 6-7 million Jews, perhaps between a seventh and a tenth of the population of the Roman empire as a whole.[36] Non-Jews would also be likely to be aware that Christians characteristically related their claims of "newness" regarding Christ to Judaism's holy books in a way that almost all these Jews discounted. Therefore even as the Church became predominantly Gentile in its outlook, the *apologetic* need to relate the newness of Christ to the enduring "oldness" of the Jews and their scriptures became more pressing. What did it mean to say that what God had done in Christ was confirmed by its fulfilment of ancient prophecies entrusted to a people that were almost entirely indifferent to this supposedly decisive event? The endurance of the Jews outside the Church, their failure to "fade away" as the writer of Hebrews perhaps had hoped, posed a major obstacle to the credibility of mainstream Christianity as this had developed by the mid-second century. Thus it should not necessarily be surprising that Luke-Acts, perhaps the New Testament text most self-consciously directed towards a non-Jewish, Hellenistically educated readership, also makes the strongest and most specific claims about the fulfilment of prophecy in post-resurrection history. Indeed, it comes closest to anticipating the development of the claims identified in the previous section into the later, "classic" framework that is first clearly discernible in Justin Martyr.

It should not then be surprising either that this framework can best be seen emerging in the writings of a second-century Christian known primarily as an "Apologist", i.e. as a Christian writer of texts purporting to explain to (influential, educated) pagans that Christianity is not only undeserving of persecution but indeed deserving of adherence from them.[37] The central part of Justin Martyr's *First Apology* comprises an extended account of how the birth, life, death and resurrection of Christ, and the subsequent history of the Church, fulfil ancient Hebrew prophecies. This is evidently the strongest positive argument for Christianity that Justin

believes he can offer his almost certainly hypothetical addressees, the
Emperor Antoninus Pius along with his sons and the Roman senate.[38] His
most important work from our point of view, however, is his *Dialogue with
Trypho*, which is presented as the record of a conversation with a Jew who
has fled to Greece following the war in Palestine precipitated by Bar
Kochba's revolt.[39] While the parallels with his *First Apology* indicate the
numerous intersections between Jewish-Christian debates and the questions
asked of Christianity by Gentiles steeped in Greco-Roman culture, the
Dialogue with Trypho also offers potential evidence of just what those
Jewish-Christian debates may have been like in the second century and
how far they had an impact upon the formation of the mainstream Christian
tradition.

While Trypho, Justin's Jewish interlocutor in the dialogue, is evidently
a stylized figure designed to fit Justin's literary and theological purposes,
as is only to be expected in a work presented within the classical genre of
the philosophical dialogue, we can still posit some (mediated) relationship
between the particular objections made by him and the objections of which
Justin would have been likely to be aware as actually circulating within
Hellenistic Jewish communities.[40] This would apply most obviously to
Trypho's arguments against Christian exegesis which involve questioning
the Septuagint translation that quickly became standard in early
Christianity.[41] It would also apply to his opening line of questioning with
Justin, summarized in the words: "resting your hopes on a man that was
crucified, you yet expect to obtain some good thing from God, while you
do not obey His commandments."[42] How could Christians appeal to the
scriptures as prophecy while setting them aside as law and teaching? How
could they assert their faithfulness to the revelation of the God of Israel
when they ignore the instructions given to God's servant Moses to stand for
all time? In such questions we can see the shadow—not necessarily the
direct reproduction—of Christian-Jewish exchange at the formative period
when the two were beginning to establish their distinct though still
intertwined identities.

Against "Judaism": Justin's *Dialogue with Trypho*

The classic framework within subsequent Christianity for understanding
the newness of Christ in relation to "old" Israel first comes clearly into
focus in the writings of Justin Martyr, the subject of this third section of the
chapter. Here we can also observe the intersection of distinctively Christian
anti-Judaism with the formulation of distinctively Christian theology at a
common point of origin. Justin's work develops further the three positive

theological claims about the newness of Christ identified in the first section of the chapter from New Testament writings. It also sets out corresponding negative judgments on a Torah observing Judaism now conceived, by contrast with the New Testament writings, as separate from the Christian Church: interpretive blindness with regard to scripture, displacement of Torah with regard to covenant and division of history with regard to people. In this process, the extension of biblical thinking about fulfilment of prophecy to subsequent events generates a theological hermeneutic of continuing history that has a crucial role in making these judgments and the anti-Judaism they convey "reasonable" within the terms of Christian thought.

The Scripture Judgment: Interpretive Blindness

In the first section of this chapter, it was argued that for New Testament writers, coming to faith in Christ was bound up with a recognition that in his life, death and resurrection the scriptures of Israel found their fulfilment. Such a process of course presupposed prior familiarity with the texts and traditions of Israel, including an acceptance that they conveyed a "prophetic surplus" and an expectation that this surplus might find actualization within the present time. Justin recounts his own conversion in the first pages of the *Dialogue* as also hinging on the reading of biblical texts. An adherent of Hellenistic philosophy, he has worked his way through its major schools and first encounters the scriptures via an enigmatic Christian teacher who is himself highly adept at philosophical argument. It is not philosophical argument alone that convinces Justin to become a Christian, however, but an invitation to read the prophetic writings of Israel—as prophecy of "those events which have happened and those which are happening." Justin's response at this point recalls the travellers on the Emmaus road:

> But straightway a flame of love was kindled in my soul; and a love of the prophets, and of those men who are friends of Christ, possessed me; and whilst revolving his words in my mind, I found this philosophy alone to be safe and profitable.[43]

Here too, therefore, coming to faith in Christ and participating in a particular form of interpretive activity in relation to the scriptures are inextricably linked. The tensions involved in sustaining that faith within the religious marketplace of the Hellenistic city are also evident in what follows in the *Dialogue*.

In the opening exchanges of the *Dialogue* referred to at the end of the preceding section, Trypho presents the Jewish half of the dilemma that must have seemed to confront many second-century Christians such as Justin in this context: either the Christian gospel depends on the Jewish scriptures, in which case convert fully to Judaism as a way of acknowledging the authority of those writings in their entirety; or it does not, in which case the Jewish Bible as a whole, like the Jewish Law contained within it, needs to be "displaced" and, at best, relegated to the past.[44] There was no shortage of influential teachers in the mid-second century churches arguing that Israel with its Torah was in fact from the outset a failed expression of God's will, and therefore its scriptures could not be expected to convey anything reliable or ultimately illuminating about the new thing God had done in Christ—that newness now being understood not via the fulfilment of prophecy within a dialectic of old and new but as an absolute, cosmic newness. Marcion resolved at a stroke the complexities around Paul's "bundling" of holy Torah with the old order of sin and death: according to him and to other figures associated with the Gnostic tendency in early Christian thought, the god of the Jews and of their Bible is simply not the same as the God of Jesus and of Christianity. For such "Christian" teachers, the newness of Christ is not the fulfilment of Israel's prophecies at all but an utterly radical newness without precedent or parallel. In his *Antitheses*, Marcion set out contrasting pairs of texts from the Jewish Bible and his own version of the Christian canon in order to make the case that Christ could not be seen as in any way fulfilling the testimony about God provided by the Jewish people. In the name of Paul, he undercut the fundamental claim that we identified in the New Testament writers, including Paul himself: that the newness of Christ is to be understood as the fulfilment of the already given word of God.

It is hardly surprising, therefore, that we can find hints of an odd sort of alliance between Marcion and Christianity's Jewish critics, in that both agreed that the Jewish Bible had nothing to do with the Christian Church, and a corresponding overlap between responses to Judaism and responses to Marcionism from within Christianity.[45] "Catholic" Christianity was having to compete to attract and retain converts against the impressiveness of Judaism as a major religious presence in the empire with a very ancient pedigree, and against the radical appeal of Marcionism and related Gnostic groupings preaching a gospel of the new in absolute opposition to everything old. Both competitors agreed on one thing alone, that Christian claims to "own" the Jewish Bible were absurd. It can be seen as a condition of the survival of what became orthodox Christianity that it should find a way to retain the claim of fulfilment in Christ that was written through the

New Testament documents and bound the Christian gospel to the Hebrew scriptures and the history of Israel, and thereby to keep the dialectic of old and new within its theological apprehension of that gospel. This claim needed to be carefully but determinedly defended not only against Jewish critics, who might be presumed to have only limited knowledge of Christianity itself, but also against Marcionite and Gnostic Christians who knew Christian traditions and scriptures from the inside. It is noteworthy, then, that Justin Martyr also wrote a now lost work against the Marcionites, which reprised some of the material contained both in the *Apology* and the *Dialogue with Trypho*. Whether Justin is attending to Gentile non-Christians, Jewish non-Christians or what he regards as false teaching within the Church, the need to defend at length and in detail the claim that Jesus Christ is the fulfilment of the prophetic scriptures is paramount.

At one point in the exchange with Trypho, Justin, appealing, as usual, to a variety of texts from the scriptures to make his point, asks him:

> Are you acquainted with them, Trypho? They are contained in your Scriptures, or rather not yours but ours. For we believe them; but you, though you read them, do not catch the spirit that is in them.[46]

This sweeping claim of Church ownership of the contested scriptures, with its clear implication of Jewish dispossession, requires, Justin is aware, some careful defence. That defence appears in a non-systematic way throughout the dialogue, and we might distinguish three particular aspects of his approach. To begin with, by way of contrast with much of the New Testament (though here again Acts and Hebrews point the way), Justin cites and comments on extended passages of scripture, more on the scale of whole chapters and individual psalms, rather than just isolated verses or short extracts.[47] He thus seeks to extend the scope of a prophetic reading of scripture beyond the relatively narrow range of texts cited in the New Testament. Secondly, Justin is also aware of the dimension of waiting in Christian experience, and the clear implication carried with it that in fact all prophecy is not yet fulfilled. He therefore explicitly develops the doctrine of the two advents of Christ—one in suffering, which has already taken place, and one in glory, which is yet to come—as a hermeneutical principle, such that where potentially messianic passages of scripture do not appear to relate to the first, to the events recorded in the New Testament, they are made to refer instead to the second, to the completion of Christ's work that lies in the future.[48] This distinction and the assumption that the Hebrew prophets were quite capable of "mixing" references to the two within a single passage help Justin to formulate sustained Christian interpretations of the lengthy portions of scripture he tends to cite.

The third important feature of Justin's defence of the Catholic Church's ownership of the scriptures is his extension of the idea of correspondences between events, persons and places that enable us to interpret unfolding history in the light of prior scriptural text and thereby also reinterpret that text in the light of our own perceived experience of God's action. Not only does he apply it far more widely than any New Testament writer to scriptural narratives, he also takes the particularly important step of applying it specifically to the commandments of the Mosaic Torah.[49] The task of articulating this approach systematically in verse-by-verse commentary would be taken up in the third century by Origen, again with an awareness of the relevance of his work to defending Christianity from charges of incoherence made by Jews and Gentiles with some knowledge of Judaism.[50] To provide a Christological reading of the Torah, via the hermeneutics of allegory, was especially important in defending Christian claims to possess the whole of Israel's scripture—that it is indeed "not yours, but ours"—by generating a "counter-reading" of the Law that explains why Christians appear to ignore its actual prescriptions while continuing to appeal to its theological authority.

Appropriating all of scripture via allegorical interpretation was also a vital strategy against less extreme versions of the Gnostic tendency, where some parts of it were graded as more inspired than others, some as divine revelation and others as human—or demiurgic—corruption. It is not hard to see how these internal Christian debates tended to push the Church towards a "maximalist" version of the original claim as expressed in 1 Cor. 15:3b-4: everything in the Law and the prophets corresponds to something in the story of Jesus Christ, and everything in the story of Jesus Christ corresponds to something in the Law and the prophets. We might consider such New Testament texts as John 5:39 as already anticipating this approach, with Matthew's Gospel an attempt to vindicate it through an extended treatment of Jesus' origins. Indeed, at one level the entire edifice of biblical interpretation in pre-modern Christianity is no more than an elaborate and systematic extension of the process generated by the attempted vindication of the "maximalist" version of the claim of prophetic fulfilment in Christ that has its roots in the New Testament itself.

For Justin, it is clear that the Christian Church has found in Christ the hermeneutical key that unlocks the meaning of Israel's scriptures. Jews, like Trypho, who do not "see" the truth of Christological interpretation can only be accounted somehow blind in their understanding. One critical question for later Christian anti-Judaism will be what kind of account to give of this interpretive blindness, specifically the extent to which it might indicate either deliberate disobedience or sub-rational ignorance.

The Covenant Judgment: Displacement of Torah

While the application of allegory enables Justin to suggest an alternative, Christological interpretation of Torah, he still has to answer Trypho's opening line of questioning: why do Christians not keep the Torah in its fullness? Justin's dialogue indicates a number of overlapping responses here rather than a single, coherent answer. At times he uses what we might call a philosophical approach, arguing that divinely sanctioned moral commands must be eternal, and therefore cannot come into being at a particular point in time.[51] In other passages he resorts to a "moralizing" form of allegorical reading already developed in Hellenistic Judaism, relating particular ritual prescriptions of the Torah to particular aspects of the moral life, but asserting, against Hellenistic Judaism, that identifying the moral meaning must lead one to discard the actual practice.[52] Yet none of this really touches on the question of why God gave Israel the Torah in the first place, why its observance ever possessed any value at all. To answer that question, Justin finds an overarching theme in one particular remark of Jesus in the Gospels, in his exchange with the Pharisees about divorce: "For your hardness of heart he [Moses] wrote this commandment" (Mark 10:5; cf. Matt. 19:8). The first exposition of this line of understanding comes in chapters XVIII-XXIII, following Justin's statement to Trypho:

> For we too would observe the fleshly circumcision, and the Sabbaths, and in short all the feasts, if we did not know for what reason they were enjoined you—namely, your transgressions and the hardness of your hearts.[53]

According to Justin, it was because Israel was so prone to sin and idolatry, so ready to forget God, that much—though not all—of the Torah was given, not because there was anything inherently good about its regime and certainly not because observance of its ritual commands was in any way pleasing to God. At one point, Justin suggests a categorization of the divine commands which brings his somewhat diffuse treatment of the Law together. Some commands are given "in reference to the worship of God and practice of righteousness," presumably those that could be taken as part of the eternal law kept by righteous people in every generation. Some refer to "the mystery of Christ," i.e. can be interpreted allegorically as prophecies of the New Testament. Those that remain are there "on account of the hardness of your people's hearts."[54] Such categorizations would become a commonplace strategy for Christian hermeneutics up until the present day.[55] Many of the ritual prescriptions of the Law, then, are explained by Justin as designed to minimize occasions for sin and supply constant reminders of God's demands. He is also able to invoke a number of passages from the prophets in apparent support of both the assertion that Israel is uniquely faithless and disobedient and the assertion that Israel's attempts at superficial Torah observance are rejected by God because of this.[56] Israel is elect of God, it would appear, in the rather paradoxical sense that this people was peculiarly hard-hearted and therefore required the particular and otherwise somewhat arbitrary constraints of the Law in order to be kept in some kind of relationship to God, which constraints it in fact consistently ignored.[57] The Law marks out Israel as uniquely prone to sin— in the past and still today. This is a weakness not, it is implicitly asserted, in any way shared by the Church, the new Israel as it becomes in Justin's account.[58]

This line of thought about the Law in Justin touches on several strands from the New Testament material noted earlier. For instance, the thematic association between sin and the Law found in Paul is preserved, but in a way that still upholds the essential goodness of the giver of the Law even as it limits it to a purely negative, restraining purpose, and thus acts as a counter to Marcionite appropriations of the Pauline writings. Justin accommodates Pauline motifs within a framework that is shaped rather by the "historical" theology of Acts and Hebrews, within which Israel as defined by observance of Torah serves as a stage in the story of God's marvellous works that has now come to a definitive end. This end is itself, moreover, already foretold by the scriptures: the fulfilment of God's promises was always going to include the ending of the Mosaic regime. Justin does not only rely on the already traditional Christian exegesis of prophetic texts such as Jeremiah 31 to make the point here; he demonstrates from a detailed allegorical exegesis of the injunctions about the Passover that they can no longer obtain once the fulfilment of the Passover lamb's "type", i.e. Christ, has come.[59]

Justin's conclusion is that the Law has served its purpose in preserving the people of Israel, entrusted with the prophecies about Christ, from altogether falling away before Christ's coming. Just as the old covenant with its law has passed away now the prophesied Christ has come, so now a new covenant and a new law, the covenant and law of Christ, have arrived—and here Justin picks up and develops further the theme of Hebrews 8 in a way that blunts the edge of the sharp Pauline dialectic of gospel and law, letter and spirit that so appealed to Gnosticizing Christians:

for I have read that there shall be a final law, and a covenant, the chiefest of all, which it is now incumbent on all men to observe, as many as are seeking after the inheritance of God. For the law promulgated at Horeb is now old, and belongs to yourselves alone; but *this* is for all universally.[60]

The contrast for Justin is not between law and something else—gospel, spirit, freedom—but between old, passing law and new, eternal law. Moreover, the new law that is allied with the new covenant must be a law for all and therefore have the qualities of universality; and only Christianity, according to Justin, can claim those. Old Israel, the Israel of the Mosaic Law, continues merely as an act of indifference to, indeed defiance of, the God who has acted in complete consistency with his revelation to Israel by putting to one side the covenant with Moses and establishing the new covenant of Christ to which the former covenant was always only intended to lead.

The People Judgment: Division of History

At this point, we are approaching the people judgment of the emerging classic framework, namely the division of post-resurrection history, with prophesied condemnation and prophesied grace mapped against the contrasting developments of Judaism and Christianity. If for Justin the Law originated as a way of setting old Israel aside from the ways of the nations, because of Israel's proneness to sin and hardness of heart against the demands of God, it survives after the culmination of that sin in the rejection and crucifixion of the Christ as a kind of inverted image of its original purpose: it ensures that those who committed the ultimate sin and refuse to repent by acknowledging Jesus as the Christ can continue to be punished for their wickedness.[61] Torah observance means that the Jews, banished from the land of Israel in the aftermath of 135 CE and increasingly distrusted and disliked in the cities of the Roman empire, are isolated from wider society and easily identified.

Attribution of responsibility for Jesus' death to hostile Jews has some precedent in the New Testament itself, both in the passion accounts of the Gospels and in 1 Thess. 2:14-16. Yet something changes with the second-century sources, including the *Epistle of Barnabas* and the *Peri Pascha* of Melito of Sardis as well as Justin's writings. The guilt of the Jews for the crucifixion of the Son of God is wholly detached from the Roman context of Jesus' death and rendered a perpetual condition of Judaism insofar as it continues to refuse to acknowledge Jesus as Christ. For Justin, the events of 70 and 135 CE are clearly decisive in the articulation of this charge of collective Jewish guilt.[62] They constitute proof of divine rejection of old Israel following Israel's rejection of God's Christ. The end of the temple, the end of life in the land of promise and therefore the end of the possibility of observance of the Torah linked to temple and land demonstrate beyond all refutation that the old covenant and the old law belong to the past, and that the old Israel that continues to cling to them can only provoke the continuing effects of divine wrath and judgment. This Israel remains a people elect and set apart—for suffering and humiliation.

For Justin, therefore, the fulfilment of prophecy does not finish even with the events recounted in the Acts of the Apostles. For him, the failure of the two Jewish revolts and the consequent and continuing suffering of the Jewish people fulfil the prophecies of judgment on Israel's faithlessness and disobedience in a way that is decisive for Christianity's understanding of enduring Israel: suffering God's punishment for rejecting Christ and clinging to Law is now the meaning of Jewish existence. This extension of the concept of prophetic fulfilment found in the apostolic writings into history occurring after those writings themselves, and in particular after the "partings of the ways" between Judaism and Christianity, is critical both to the normative understanding of Judaism in Christian theology, and to the political question of how "Christian" regimes would treat Jewish communities existing under them. If the Christian gospel is vindicated by the historical reality of Jewish humiliation and suffering, would it be threatened by apparent Jewish achievement and success? And is the gospel then properly assisted by the authorities of church and government taking measures to ensure that this humiliation and suffering continue in a reassuringly demonstrable way? There is a dark shadow to Justin's extension of prophetic fulfilment to account for 70 and 135 CE that we will need to keep returning to in the course of this study.

History since the resurrection is not only for Justin a drama of judgment fulfilled, but a drama of promise fulfilled as well. The rise of the Church, its spread across all nations, is the other dimension of prophetic fulfilment that needs to be set against the defeat and suffering of Israel. At the time of Justin, of course, the triumph of the Church could not be described in political terms; for all the hardships that befell Jewish communities in the second century, Christians probably remained in general more vulnerable to social marginalization and arbitrary violence. Rather, the Church's incipient victory and its part in the fulfilment of scriptural prophecies of redemption is judged by Justin to consist in such things as: its gathering of the nations into the people of God;[63] its turning them from idolatry;[64] its manifestations of spiritual gifts;[65] its overcoming of demons;[66] and its putting an end among its adherents to sin, paradigmatically sexual sin.[67] In all of this the Church acts for Justin as a living demonstration of the newness that God has brought about in Christ.

The importance of this line of argument for him is evident from the much more concise and focused account of the claim of prophetic fulfilment in the *First Apology*, where he concludes a review of the detailed correspondence between Jesus' life, death and resurrection with texts from the scriptures by appealing again to recent history to clinch his case:

> For with what reason should we believe of a crucified man that He is the first-born of the unbegotten God, and Himself will pass judgment on the whole human race, unless we had found testimonies concerning Him published before He came and was born as man, and unless we saw that things have happened accordingly—the devastation of the land of the Jews, and men of every race persuaded by His teaching through the apostles, and rejecting their old habits . . . ?[68]

It is worth underlining two points about this passage. First, Justin appears to assert that without the argument from prophetic fulfilment, the claim that Jesus of Nazareth was God's Son would be groundless. The weight of the Christian answer to the question of why this man rather than any other should be acknowledged as the Son of God is placed firmly, even exclusively, on the claim that his life exhibits a unique and compelling correlation with the prophecies contained in Israel's scripture. Secondly, it is the correlation of post-resurrection history and its division between Christianity and Judaism with the twofold prophetic message of blessing and judgment that seals the validity of the Christian "reading" of divine revelation in history as centred in Christ as the incarnate Son of God. Justin almost seems to indicate that it is the power of this secondary prophetic correlation in present history that establishes the truth of the primary prophetic correlation for Christian theology, that of the birth, life, death and resurrection of Jesus with Israel's scripture.

This point then returns us to Justin's account of his own conversion in the opening chapters of the *Dialogue*, and the assertion of the Christian teacher he mysteriously encounters that the prophets "spoke by the Divine Spirit, and foretold events which would take place, and are even now taking place."[69] It is surely not accidental that the one major recent event referred to so far in the book, in the very first chapter, is the failure of the Bar Kochba revolt; Justin only meets Trypho at all because "having escaped from the war lately carried on there, I am spending my days in Greece, and chiefly at Corinth."[70] Yet even in the face of such evident—for Justin—demonstration of scriptural fulfilment underlining the truth of Christian claims, Trypho, and most Jews with him, continued to resist the

Gospel, a resistance which placed them on the other side of the division of history after Christ as the object of God's promised judgment.

The Emergence of the Classic Framework

In Justin's writings, the classic framework that will form a vital point of reference for the rest of this study comes into relatively clear focus. First, the claim in relation to scripture of fulfilment in Christ is corroborated by the development of a scriptural hermeneutic in which the identification of specific prophecies of Christ is accompanied by strategies which are ready to find reference to him and to life in his body, the Church, on every page and even in every verse. "Old" Israel is thereby dispossessed of its Bible and its own continuing practice of interpretation is ruled out in advance as reflecting only its interpretive blindness. Secondly, the claim in relation to covenant of renewal in Christ is judged to entail a displacement of Law as religious practice that hardens into the specific view that observance of the Torah is no longer of any value, at best neutral and at worst (as eventually became the orthodox view) to be considered as disobedience and sin for Jewish and Gentile Christians alike. Thirdly, the claim in relation to people of restoration in Christ is accompanied by an interpretation of continuing prophetic fulfilment in the division of history between judgment for unbelieving Israel and blessing for the believing Church that is gathering in the Gentiles. Such a reading of present history gained sharper focus with the failure of the Bar Kochba revolt and consequent end to Israel as a political and indeed territorial entity in 135 CE. The social and political humiliation of non-Jesus believing Israel and its perpetual exile from the once-promised land are now deemed by Christian writers to be definitive "proof" of its punishment by God and rejection as God's people. On the other hand, the spread of Gentile Christianity is judged a sign that the Church is completing the fulfilment of the messianic promises that converge on Jesus Christ.

Justin is thereby able to interpret his "Judaism" as an unwilling but still decisive witness to the truth of the Church's gospel. Far from the endurance of forms of Jewish life wholly resistant to Christian influence constituting some kind of problem or obstacle for Christian belief, their undeniable decline is read as evidence of the former Israel's punishment for continuing to reject the Messiah and, when set against the rise and spiritual vitality of the Church, as evidence that Jesus' teaching in the temple as reported by Matthew has come true: "the kingdom of God will be taken away from you and given to a nation producing the fruits of it" (Matt. 21:43). Justin's teaching showed how the emerging Catholic Church could avoid the dilemma with which the "fact" of old Israel's endurance appeared to present it: either old Israel was truly elect, in which case one should convert to Judaism, or old Israel was not, in which case there was no need to preserve its scriptures or hallow its memory. Instead, Justin offered a powerful response to both Judaizing and Gnosticizing objections. Old Israel was and must remain an ineradicable part of the Christian past, but it has no positive place in the Christian present. The newness of Christ can allow no positive meaning for the endurance of Torah observing Israel beyond it. Because Israel was the carrier of the Christological prophecy by which alone the truth of the gospel of the new covenant could be made known and established, the Marcionite version of Christian newness as the absolutely unprecedented has to be rejected. Yet because that prophecy is now being fulfilled between the first and second comings of Christ by the blessing of new Israel and the punishment of disobedient, old Israel, there is nothing to be learnt from those non-Jesus Jews whom Justin names as Judaism. By refusing to acknowledge the newness of the Christian gospel the old Israel of the old covenant can paradoxically only confirm it, as it staggers on isolated from the times and diminishing in strength, the object of unyielding divine chastisement.

In order to retain the New Testament's understanding of the newness of Christ as the unparalleled work of the one God of Israel in faithfulness to his word, Justin extended its treatment of prophetic fulfilment both backward and forward: backward to cover the entirety of the scriptures, through the development of a distinctive Christological hermeneutic at the service of the Church; and forward to "read" recent history as a continuation of the one prophetic story of judgment and grace, with judgment exemplified in the condition of old Israel and grace in the burgeoning life of the new Church. He recognized that the status of the Torah both in the past and the present remained a critical issue for the theology he was participating in shaping, and he outlined a multi-faceted approach in response, reflecting something of the Pauline "bundling" of sin and Law but ultimately assigning it a clear providential role in the past and providing Christian interpreters with a categorization of commands that could provide the basis for detailed exegesis within a Christian theological framework.

As to why Torah is no longer binding, Justin makes this hinge on the interpretation of covenantal history, and although his treatment of this theme remains somewhat undeveloped, he at least pointed the way ahead to the later second century when the theology of the two covenants emerges as a fundamental structuring device not only for the immensely influential thought of Irenaeus of Lyons but indeed for the Christian canon itself.[71] For

Justin, although he knew much of what we would call the New Testament, scripture remained a common and contested set of texts for Jews and Christians. By the time of Irenaeus, writing perhaps a few decades later, Christians had a distinctive scriptural canon of their own, divided into two: the Old "Covenant" (or "Testament") and the New. The most basic feature of their Bible now taught Christians that history—and God's work in history—has two periods, each looking towards the one Christ, the one "new thing" of God; one period, that of the old covenant, leading up to his coming, and the other, that of the new covenant, flowing from it and towards his second advent. That people remain who still adhere to the old covenant regardless of the coming of the one to whom it was always pointing is a reflection of human sin, pride and stubbornness—and an invitation to recognize the judgment of God upon such things.

If the scripture judgment and the covenant judgment embed the oldness of Israel in Christian theology as a theme for the interpretation of what is now appropriated as part of Christian scripture, the people judgment embeds the same theme also in the theological interpretation of continuing history. Within this emerging framework, the newness of the gospel can only be expressed by also recounting the pastness of Torah-observant Judaism as "old Israel". At the very moment, therefore, when the separation of "Christianity" from "Judaism" is asserted in the construction of these two concepts in Justin's discourse, the permanent insertion of Judaism as a difficult presence within Christian theologizing is also ensured. From now on, shifts in the understanding of scripture and history alike will precipitate repeated returns to the problematic site of old Israel, its finished Law and its continuing existence, particularly when consciousness stirs of the persisting reality of independent Jewish life that "ought" to be have come to an end after Christ.

At this point, what we are calling the classic framework for Christian understanding of the newness of Christ in relation to the oldness of Israel is, in all essentials, in place. The three judgments that form the core of Christian anti-Judaism are enmeshed in the emerging theological tradition along with the three positive claims that arise from the original articulation of the gospel in relation to scripture, covenant and people, ensuring a continuing and complex linkage between Christian interpretation of Jewish existence, Christian-Jewish exchange and internal Christian self-understanding. The following chapters will explore that linkage in relation to three particularly crucial periods for the formation of Western Christian theology: from the mid-eleventh century to Thomas Aquinas; from the Reformation to the early Enlightenment; and from the dawn of the twentieth century to the end of the Second World War. While the classic framework will be shown to undergo significant shifts along the way, the resilience of its components, and in particular its judgments, will also be demonstrated, along with their power to replicate the dynamic of anti-Judaism across epochal changes in the culture and outlook of Christian theology.

Notes

[1] See e.g. the classic work of Gerd Theissen, *The Shadow of the Galilean: The Quest of the Historical Jesus in Narrative Form*, trans. John Bowden (London: SCM, 1987); also N. T. Wright, *The New Testament and the People of God* (London: SPCK, 1992), 167-214.

[2] Boyarin, *Border Lines*.

[3] Boyarin, *Border Lines*, 67.

[4] For a survey of related scholarship, see N. T. Wright, *Jesus and the Victory of God* (London: SPCK, 1996), 83-124.

[5] For introductory overviews, see John M. Court, ed., *New Testament Writers and the Old Testament: An Introduction* (London: SPCK, 2002), and Steve Moyise, *The Old Testament in the New* (London: T & T Clark, 2001).

[6] Biblical citations are from *The Holy Bible Containing the Old and New Testaments: New Revised Standard Version Anglicized Edition* (Oxford: Oxford University Press, 1995), unless otherwise indicated.

[7] See the discussion in Michael Fishbane, *Biblical Interpretation in Ancient Israel* (Oxford: Clarendon, 1985), 363-64.

[8] Fishbane, *Biblical Interpretation*, 350-379.

[9] Wright, *New Testament*, 217.

[10] See e.g. James C. VanderKam, *The Dead Sea Scrolls Today* (Grand Rapids: Eerdmans, 1994), especially 180-82, and Moyise, *Old Testament*, 9-16.

[11] Wright, *New Testament*, 280-338.

[12] Cf. the discussion of this passage in Louis-Marie Chauvet, *The Sacraments: The Word of God at the Mercy of the Body*, trans. Madeleine Beaumont (Collegeville: Liturgical Press, 2001), 23-28.

[13] The importance of the theme of Jesus as prophet in Luke-Acts, and indeed of prophecy as such for the composition of the work as a whole, is emphasized in Luke Timothy Johnson's commentary, *The Gospel of Luke* (Collegeville: Liturgical Press, 1991).

[14] I am following the consensus of modern textual scholars that Mark 15:28 is a later interpolation.

[15] Frank Kermode, *The Genesis of Secrecy: On the Interpretation of Narrative* (Cambridge: Harvard University Press, 1979).

[16] Moyise, *Old Testament*, 29-31.

[17] Richard B. Hays, *Echoes of Scripture in the Letters of Paul* (New Haven: Yale University Press, 1989).

[18] This verse is absent from the shorter version of the last supper which appears in some early manuscripts of Luke's Gospel; on this and the parallel sayings in other New Testament sources, see the discussion in Paul F. Bradshaw, *Eucharistic Origins* (London: SPCK, 2004), 1-23.

[19] Hays, *Echoes of Scripture*, 128-29.

[20] See the extended discussion of this passage, and defence of its coherence, in Hays, *Echoes of Scripture*, 122-53.

[21] The question of "Paul and the Law" has been a sharply contested one in recent New Testament studies, particularly with the emergence of the so-called new perspective on Paul associated e.g. with E. P. Sanders, *Paul and Palestinian Judaism: A Comparison of Patterns of Religion* (London: SCM, 1977).

[22] The idea advocated by some scholars, that Paul has no view about Jews and the Law, being only concerned about its imposition on Gentiles, is briefly but effectively criticized in Brendan Byrne, "Interpreting Romans Theologically in a Post-'New Perspective' Perspective," *Harvard Theological Review* 94:3 (2001): 227-41, in particular at 228n10. The article also usefully reviews some wider issues in this controversial area.

[23] I have tried to capitalise "Law" when referring specifically to the Torah / Law of Moses, in contrast to "law" as a general term, whilst recognizing that the line between the two is sometimes blurred, particularly in Paul.

[24] For a recent attempt to change conventional perspectives on these issues, see the work of Mark D. Nanos, e.g. *The Mystery of Romans: The Jewish Context of Paul's Letter* (Minneapolis: Fortress, 1996) and *The Irony of Galatians: Paul's Letter in First-Century Context* (Minneapolis: Fortress, 2002).

[25] On Paul's part in the estrangement of some and eventually all Christian communities from the Jewish context of their origins, see e.g. James D. G. Dunn, *The Partings of the Ways between Christianity and Judaism and Their Significance for the Character of Christianity* (London: SCM, 1991), especially 117-39; Alan Le Grys, *Preaching to the Nations: The Origins of Mission in the Early Church* (London: SPCK, 1998), in particular 71-87.

[26] On the possible contexts for the composition of Hebrews, see the Introduction of William L. Lane, *Hebrews 1-8* (Dallas: Word, 1991), xlvii-lxvi.

[27] Moyise, *Old Testament*, 117-21.

[28] Jon D. Levenson, *The Death and Resurrection of the Beloved Son: The Transformation of Child Sacrifice in Judaism and Christianity* (New Haven: Yale University Press, 1993), in particular 200-32.

[29] Compare the reference in the prayer at Acts 4:24ff. to "whatever your hand and your plan had predestined to take place" (Acts 4:28).

[30] The literature on this subject is vast. Contributions in English would include: Dunn, *Partings of the Ways*; Wayne A. Meeks, "Breaking Away: Three New Testament Pictures of Christianity's Separation from the Jewish Communities," in *Essential Papers on Judaism and Christianity in Conflict: From Late Antiquity to the Reformation*, ed. Jeremy Cohen (New York: New York University Press, 1991), 89-113; Lieu, *Image and Reality*; Boyarin, *Border Lines*; Yoder, *Jewish-Christian Schism*.

[31] See the final chapter of Bruce Chilton and Jacob Neusner, *Judaism in the New Testament: Practices and Beliefs* (London: Routledge, 1995), 175-88, for an argument that Hebrews should perhaps be seen as the exception here.

[32] William Horbury, *Jews and Christians in Contact and Controversy* (Edinburgh: T & T Clark, 1998), 67-110 and 155-61.

[33] On this subject, see Evans and Hagner, eds., *Anti-semitism*. The arguments presented by a variety of authors in this collection suggest the need for significant re-evaluation of the influential approach to anti-Judaism in early Christian tradition in Ruether, *Faith and Fratricide*.

[34] Lieu, *Image and Reality*, 51.

[35] The classic study here is Marcel Simon, *Verus Israel: A Study of the Relations between Christians and Jews in the Roman Empire (AD 135-425)*, trans. H. McKeating (London: Littman Library of Jewish Civilization, 1996).

[36] Lee Martin McDonald, "Anti-Judaism in the Early Church Fathers," in *Anti-semitism*, ed. Evans and Hagner, 241-42. Lieu argues for "a continuing pattern of competing legitimation" between Jews and Christians in the cities of second-century Asia Minor (*Image and Reality*, 94).

[37] Robert M. Grant, *Greek Apologists of the Second Century* (London: SCM, 1988).

[38] Justin Martyr, *The First Apology of Justin*, Ante-Nicene Fathers, vol. 1 (Grand Rapids: Eerdmans, 1985), 163-186; see chapters XXXI-LIII.

[39] Justin Martyr, *Dialogue with Trypho, a Jew*, Ante-Nicene Fathers, vol. 1 (Grand Rapids: Eerdmans, 1985), 194-270.

[40] On the extent to which Justin's Trypho tells us anything about second-century Judaism and its approach to Christianity, contrast the wholly negative verdict of Ruether, *Faith and Fratricide*, 119-120, with the more nuanced position of e.g. McDonald, "Anti-Judaism," especially 225-229, and Lieu, *Image and Reality*, ix and 12-13.

[41] See the summary discussion of Trypho's exegetical objections to Justin's case in Simon, *Verus Israel*, 157-60.

[42] Justin, *Dialogue* X (199). One might compare the objection to Christianity of Celsus' Jew, as recorded by Origen (*Contra Celsum* I.49-50), and Augustine's (much later) imaginary Jewish interlocutor as discussed by Simon, *Verus Israel*, 93-94.

[43] Justin, *Dialogue* VII-VIII (198-99).

[44] Terminology in this area is a difficult and sensitive issue, but I have tried to use Jewish Bible when I mean specifically the canon of continuing Judaism, Old Testament when referring to the first part of the Christian Bible and Hebrew scriptures when a more neutral term seems appropriate.

[45] Lieu, *Image and Reality*, 264-65; cf. Simon, *Verus Israel*, 69-70.

[46] Justin, *Dialogue* XXIX (209).

[47] Justin, *Dialogue*, e.g. chapters XIII (citing Is. 53.10-54.6), XXII (texts from Ezekiel, Amos, Jeremiah and Isaiah, as well as the whole of Psalm 50). Five further psalms are cited in full between chapters XXXII and XXXVIII.

[48] Justin, *Dialogue* XIV (201-202), XXX-XXXII (209-210). Justin finds a particularly clear exegetical basis for his approach in Jacob's prophecy to Judah in Gen. 49; see LII (221).

[49] Justin, *Dialogue*, e.g. XL-XLII (214-216).

[50] See for example Origen, *Homilies on Leviticus 1-16*, trans. Gary Wayne Barkley, Fathers of the Church vol. 83 (Washington, DC: Catholic University of America Press, 1990).

[51] Justin, *Dialogue* e.g. XXIII, XXIX, XLVIII, XCIII. On later versions of this line of thought, see Simon, *Verus Israel*, 82-83 (cf. 163-164).

[52] Justin, *Dialogue* e.g. XIV-XV.

[53] Justin, *Dialogue* XVIII (203).

[54] Justin, *Dialogue* XLIV (217).

[55] See the defence of Justin on this point and the tradition that followed him in Oliver O'Donovan, *Resurrection and Moral Order: An Outline for Evangelical Ethics*, 2nd ed. (Leicester: Apollos, 1994), 159-60.

[56] Justin, *Dialogue* XXI-XXII.

[57] Cf. Justin, *Dialogue* XLVI (217-218).

[58] Cf. Lieu, *Image and Reality*, 136-137.

[59] Justin, *Dialogue* XL (214-215).

[60] Justin, *Dialogue* XI (199-200); cf. also XXIV, XLIII, CXVIII.

[61] On the Law as identifying Jews for punishment, see Justin, *Dialogue* XVI-XVII, XIX, XCII; on Jews as the killers of Christ, XCV, CXXXIII, CXXXVI.

[62] On subsequent uses of this basic position, see Simon, *Verus Israel*, 67-68.

[63] Justin, *Dialogue* XCI, CXI, CXXI-CXXII, CXXX-CXXXI. Justin explicitly rejects suggestions that prophecies about the in-gathering of the nations might be fulfilled by Gentile converts to Judaism.

[64] Justin, *Dialogue* XI, LXXXIII.

[65] Justin, *Dialogue* XXXIX, LXXXII, LXXXVII-LXXXVIII.

[66] Justin, *Dialogue* XXX, XLVI, XLIX, LXXXIII, LXXXV, CXXI.

[67] Justin, *Dialogue* CXVI; cf. Wayne A. Meeks, *The Origins of Early Christian Morality: The First Two Centuries* (New Haven: Yale University Press, 1993), e.g. 31-32, and Peter Brown, *The Body and Society: Men, Women and Sexual Renunciation in Early Christianity* (London: Faber, 1989).

[68] Justin, *First Apology* LIII (180).

[69] Justin, *Dialogue* VII (198).

[70] Justin, *Dialogue* I (194).

[71] On Justin and Irenaeus, see Soulen, *God of Israel*, 34-48.

CHAPTER TWO

BEFORE MODERNITY:
QUESTIONS AND CONTINUITY

In the previous chapter, we traced the emergence by the latter half of the second century of what I am calling the classic Christian framework for understanding the newness of Christ in relation to the endurance of Israel. The framework can be expressed in terms of a threefold pattern of claim and judgment in relation to scripture, covenant and people, where the judgments carry the intellectual force of Christian anti-Judaism. Thus the scripture claim of fulfilment in Christ is linked to the judgment of interpretive blindness on the part of continuing Judaism; the covenant claim of renewal in Christ is linked to the judgment that Torah observance belongs to an earlier, now finished covenant which has therefore been displaced; and the people claim of a restoration in Christ is linked to the judgment of a consequent division of history between the Church which embodies that restoration and the Torah observing Judaism that rejects it and thereby renders itself forever "old" and subject to divine wrath. Calling this pattern of understanding classic is intended to indicate its historical significance both as the framework for all mainstream Christian theology at least before the period of early modernity (considered in the next chapter) and as exercising a persistent gravitational pull thereafter.

Some of the most influential accounts of Christian theology in relation to Judaism have tended to leapfrog over the Western Middle Ages altogether, as if nothing of very much consequence happened after the conversion of Constantine until at least the Protestant Reformation and the Enlightenment.[1] Yet while it is true that certain features of inter-religious polemic achieved a stereotypical form by the end of antiquity that was repeated with little variation for the next thousand years, this is hardly the whole story.[2] The twelfth century in particular has long been acknowledged as a crucial period for the development of Western culture generally, and for Western Christian theology in particular.[3] Over the past two decades, a number of influential studies have explored the extent to which it also represented a decisive stage in the relationship between

Christianity and Judaism in Europe.[4] It is now widely recognized by historians, then, that the period 1050-1300 represents, on the one hand, a time of considerable creativity for Western theology and, on the other, a decisive point in the development of Jewish-Christian relations in Western Europe. It therefore seems well worth exploring the possible relationship between these two phenomena and their combined effects on the articulation of the classic framework outlined in the previous chapter.

The present chapter seeks to make a contribution to that task by tracing within this period the three-dimensional process described in the Introduction: how significant changes *within* Christian theology, the fluctuating theological exchange *between* Judaism and Christianity and the Christian understanding *of* Judaism interacted with one another. Its four sections highlight different aspects of that process. The first section argues for a shift in the people judgment (division of history) in that Christian thought became less confident about identifying the blessing of the Church with specific aspects of its public history, while nonetheless retaining as axiomatic an identification of the curse on old Israel with visible Jewish suffering and political powerlessness. In order to understand how this shift is reflected in Western Christianity in the period with which we are principally concerned in this chapter, 1050-1300, it will be necessary first to consider some important developments in late antiquity, above all the theology of history proposed by Augustine of Hippo.

The next section sets out a corresponding shift in the people claim (restoration in Christ), as theologians in the eleventh and twelfth centuries developed new ways of articulating what Christ had done for God's people that could be presented in relative detachment from any kind of transformation in the present, and indeed from traditional anchorage in scriptural sources. The focus then shifts to the covenant judgment (displacement of Torah), which generated intensified questioning in the scholastic theology of the twelfth and thirteenth centuries about the past and present purpose of the Mosaic Law, with Aquinas eventually producing a more radically historicizing account than had previously been current in Christian theology. Finally, speculation as to whether the new stage in history signalled by the covenant claim (renewal in Christ) might itself be succeeded by a further stage of newness to come provoked contrasting responses in the thirteenth century. Yet the resulting debate highlights the significance of a shared if also in some respects contested horizon of eschatological expectation in the modulations of the classic framework over time. Across the four sections that deal with these points, there is also a recurring motif: unquestioning adherence to the scripture claim and judgment (fulfilment in Christ / interpretive blindness), and the tradition of allegorical interpretation that bound them together, ensured that shifts and questions alike did not ultimately destabilize the unifying power of the classic framework in the medieval period.

Shift in the People Judgment: Asymmetry in History

Justin's confidence in the evident fulfilment of God's promises of blessing and restoration in the life of the second-century Church is, in retrospect, rather remarkable. Christians were still at this stage a very small minority of the population even where they had a significant presence, and were far fewer in total numbers than contemporary Jews. They were also socially marginalized and subject to harassment and sometimes violence, both popular and legally sanctioned. Over the following millennium, we can trace points where the Church's historically visible "success" fostered strong reassertion of the claim that God's purpose was being fulfilled in its achievements. Yet questions about this also become apparent, posed with increasing directness by Christianity's Jewish interlocutors. While we can tentatively posit a growing degree of ambivalence about the people claim as the Middle Ages unfold on the one hand, on the other it is clear that the corresponding judgment, about the division of history and the political humiliation of Israel as testimony to divine punishment, becomes if anything more starkly and stridently asserted, particularly in the fourteenth and fifteenth centuries.

The Loss of Jerusalem

The intimate relationship that we identified in Justin Martyr's work between apologetics, the place of Israel and the fundamental contours of Christian doctrine can still be clearly discerned a century later in the *Three Books of Testimonies* of Cyprian of Carthage.[5] Cyprian presents this work, which comprises for the most part collections of biblical texts to support theological assertions, as a kind of introduction to biblical theology for someone who is a recent convert to Christian faith.[6] While the second book sets out the Church's teaching about Christ, and the third its expectations about the Christian life, the first, which we might reasonably assume to have some sort of foundational purpose, is solely concerned with the transfer of election from "the Jews" to "us". The first seven propositions of the first book, all explicated by scriptural passages, relate to the punishment of the Jews for their faithlessness in general and refusal to follow Christ in particular as fulfilment of Old Testament prophecy. The continuing importance for early Christian discourse of the events of 135

CE is underlined in the sixth proposition, "That the Jews should lose Jerusalem, and should leave the land which they had received."[7] Cyprian could well have expected an educated pagan to be impressed by the argument that Jewish political failure invalidated the Jewish claim to be the elect people of God; it had been used in the first century by the Egyptian writer Apion, and refuted by Josephus.[8] The next eleven propositions then set out the oldness of everything pertaining to Judaism (circumcision, Mosaic Law, Jerusalem temple with its sacrifices and priesthood) as evidence that God has now replaced it with the newness of the Church and its corresponding features, as he had always intended and indeed foretold through Israel's prophets.

The final six propositions of the first Book of the *Testimonies* then contrast the old people of the Jews with the new people of the Gentile Church. The twentieth sets out how it had been predicted "That the church which before had been barren should have more children from among the Gentiles than what the synagogue had had before."[9] While at one level this is a simple reiteration of the claim that the Church by its "gathering in" of the Gentiles fulfils a vital dimension of Old Testament prophecy, the explicit appeal to numbers suggests a new confidence by the mid-third century that the Church now had many more Gentile members than Judaism had Gentile converts or adherents. It is also a plea that such numerical growth should itself be read as prophetic fulfilment validating the assertion that the Church is the place to look for God's work of restoration and blessing in history, by contrast with exiled and humiliated Israel which is the object of his wrath—despite the fact that Cyprian lived through and eventually died in one of the first waves of empire-wide persecution of Christians.

Not surprisingly, the conviction found in Justin and Cyprian that God's purpose is made plain through the divided post-resurrection histories of Judaism and Christianity reaches something of a high-water mark in the fourth century. Following the "conversion" of Constantine, there were Theodosius' attempts to make Nicene orthodoxy the universal religion of the empire. Christian writers had suggested much earlier that the flourishing of the Roman empire was the work of divine providence in preparing the way for the spread of Christianity. Even when Christianity was still subject to persecution under the empire, its apologists, as we have seen with Justin and Cyprian, regarded contemporary history as the scene of prophetic fulfilment in the attainments of the divinely blest Church. With the victory of Constantine, it was a relatively small step for a writer such as Eusebius of Caesarea, who had written in that same apologetic vein even in the latter part of the third century, to discern the fulfilment of

Old Testament prophecies of God's rule on earth in the new kingdom of the Christian emperor, indeed to present "the reign of Constantine as the culmination of human history."[10] The commitment of the Theodosian regime in the latter part of the fourth century to eradicating paganism completely helped to facilitate a second outbreak of such theological enthusiasm in interpreting the political success of the Christian emperors as the sign of the work of God.[11]

The confidence that growth in the political and social power of the Church affirmed it to be the recipient of God's blessing would have been likely, by itself, to reinforce the view that the relative political weakness of Judaism showed it to be the object of God's wrath. That view could only be intensified by reports of the attempt to rebuild the Jerusalem temple under the brief reign of the pagan emperor Julian.[12] The ruins of the temple in Jerusalem had long been considered by Christians to be both vivid symbol and concrete proof of the end of the "old" temple of Judaism and its replacement by the new temple of the body of Christ. In the third century, Origen's exegetical focus on the spiritual Jerusalem had stressed the irrelevance to Christians of the present state of the land of Israel beyond this lesson from the rubble. Constantine's establishment of new church buildings in Jerusalem on reclaimed "holy" sites, however, and the deliberate neglect of the ruined remains of the temple area provided the opportunity for Eusebius to find a more positive demonstration of the division of contemporary history between the triumphant Church and humiliated Israel, in fulfilment of biblical prophecy.[13] Such rhetoric is likely to have been very familiar to Julian and its conscious subversion one of his motivations for initiating the project of rebuilding the temple for renewed Jewish use.

The project had not proceeded very far before Julian's death, but for a preacher such as John Chrysostom the failure of this unholy coalition of Christ's enemies to undo what Christ had accomplished underlined the finality of history's division.[14] That the history of Judaism after and apart from Christ should be one of failure and humiliation is for him a matter of divine judgment; it is itself the work of Christ, demonstrating that the one who was crucified is now risen and reigns. As Chrysostom expresses it,

> You Jews did crucify him. But after he died on the cross, he then destroyed your city; it was then that he dispersed your people; it was then that he scattered your nation over the face of the earth. In doing this, he teaches us that he is risen, alive, and in heaven.[15]

God's desire that his revelation should be manifest through such political events as the destruction of the Jewish temple and the exile of the Jewish

people is shown once again for Chrysostom by the account of miraculous
intervention to prevent the progress of the attempted rebuilding under
Julian.[16] Julian himself clearly understood the logic of Christian discourse
that the truth about God's election of the Church is etched into public
history and sought to refute it on its own terms. His subsequent public
failure could only reinforce the claims of that logic to unassailable
plausibility. "Believing—unhappy man—that he could destroy the Lord's
word, he only demonstrated its truth all the more through what he did," as
Cassiodorus would comment later.[17]

Augustine of Hippo: The Witness of the Jews

Despite the triumphant rhetoric of Chrysostom and others, the
theological position that political achievement was some kind of index of
divine favour was shortly to receive a searching examination in the work
of Augustine of Hippo. At the end of the second century, Tertullian felt
obliged to counter claims that the political success of pagan Rome was to
be attributed to her eminence in piety;[18] after the sack of Rome by Alaric
in 410, Augustine had to face accusations that her defeat was the result of
the decline in that piety under the baleful influence of the Christian
Church. It has been argued that this event helped Augustine to reject the
Eusebian understanding of the "Christian" Roman empire and articulate in
his later works an approach more consonant with his own fundamental
theology, that only as recorded in scripture can history be interpreted with
confidence for marks of God's election and judgment, while post-biblical
history remains subject to inherent ambiguity.[19]

In Augustine's *De civitate dei*, these themes find their definitive
expression in the distinction between the two cities, of earth and heaven, in
terms of two "loves", we might say two orientations, to God and to self,
which cannot be stabilized in terms of specific human societies and
political entities. Thus while Israel before Christ, and the Church since
Christ, can be associated with the city of God over against the nations who
comprise the city of earth, it remains the case that first Israel and then the
Church nonetheless comprehend within themselves the division between
the two loves and therefore the two cities.[20] The Church, as Augustine had
learnt to stress against the Donatists, is a "mixed body" of saints and
sinners, elect and reprobate, those bound for heaven and those heading to
hell. In the great historical panorama of *De civitate dei*, the earthly success
and the earthly sufferings of the Church have no ultimate function at all as
indicators of divine grace; God's purposes cannot be "read off" the
fluctuating outcomes of human history. If anything, it more naturally

belongs to the adherents of the city of God to be persecuted by the citizens of earth, so that if for a while they live in prosperity and peace, they should be grateful but certainly not see in such circumstances some sort of divinely willed and enduring dispensation.[21]

We can therefore regard Augustine's later thought as a highly significant attempt to maintain the claim of the restoration in Christ of God's purpose of grace through the life of the Church, whilst resisting any facile account of the division of history in which the numerical and political successes of the Church are evident signs of divine favour. Yet Augustine's sustained reservation of theological judgment in relation to the Church's fortunes in human history found only limited and distorted echoes in subsequent medieval thought, even when it outwardly strove to be most faithful to him.[22] Moreover, Augustine's case can be considered as emblematic for one of the themes of this chapter as a whole, in that while he shows a high degree of ambivalence with regard to the question of how far the gracious purpose of God in the Church can be deduced from its career in history, there is no equivocation at all as to the assumption that God's prophesied punishment of "old" Israel can most certainly be discerned from its historical condition. Abraham's blessing of Isaac (Gen. 27:27-29) finds evident fulfilment in the Church's power over the Jews, for instance: Christ "is Lord over His brethren, since His people have dominion over the Jews."[23] In this case at least, we can discern theological truth directly from contemporary political relationships.

The weakening of certainty about the manifestation of promised salvation in the political ascendancy of the Church, then, seems to be balanced by an unbending conviction that predicted judgment is being acted out in the political humiliation of the Jewish people. The multiple dimensions of Augustine's theological vision somehow seem to shrink into something much cruder when dealing with contemporary Judaism— an asymmetry that will persist in the Western Middle Ages. Thus if Augustine allows that the city of earth and the love of self remain operative within the Christian Church as they were in ancient Israel, for him in continuing Israel there can be no question of any trace left of the city of God, of any enduring ambivalence. At one level, the Judaism that disdains Christ represents paradigmatically the rejected "other" within the history of the city of God;[24] yet given that the Church, like Israel once, contains this other within its own historical life, even the negative dignity of signifying divine rejection seems only loosely attributable to post-biblical Judaism.

What purpose, then, does enduring Israel serve in the scheme of human history? Here as in other, more central areas of his theology, Augustine's thinking shows evidence of shifts and developments over the course of his life, but his most influential contribution was his account of continuing Jewish existence as being for the sake of *testimonium veritatis*, "witness to the truth".[25] For Augustine, it is through the scattering of the Jews, not the *pax Romana*, that God prepared the way for the spread of the Christian gospel, so that throughout the world there would be people, hostile to the Church and therefore unimpeachable witnesses, bearing the written texts that prove Jesus to have been Christ and Son of God through his evident fulfilment of divine prophecy.[26] It is because of this providential purpose in relation to the Church's mission, Augustine suggests, that God did not annihilate unbelieving Israel—as standard Christian polemic might be expected to require—but rather preserved it in a state of exile and political powerlessness.

In *De civitate dei*, Augustine appeals to Ps. 59:12 as a scriptural key for understanding the ways of God in this matter: "Slay them not, lest at any time they forget your law; scatter them in your might."[27] This position was repeatedly invoked in the Western Middle Ages to justify a degree of both protection for and measured discrimination against Jewish minorities.[28] Augustine's own view of history as the arena for the continual encounter between the two cities, in which to any human eye they are mingled inextricably until the day of judgment, so that one could never expect before then to see the city of God in its purity, allowed him to be content with such an explanation for the endurance of Israel even after the newness of Christ was spreading through all the world. It is at least plausible, therefore, that when expectations ran high of an imminent resolution to such ambivalence, through decisive reform of Christian society or the return of Christ to earth, the Augustinian case for Jewish preservation was liable to be discarded along with the Augustinian reserve about the eschatological interpretation of present history, and the demand consequently made on Jewish populations to be baptized or to leave. It may well be the case that the rise in such expectations was one of the factors in the increasingly determined attempts to end the Jewish presence in Christian Europe, if possible through widespread conversion but if not through mass expulsions, in the later Middle Ages and then again in the sixteenth century.[29]

Into the Middle Ages: Challenges to Christendom

The force of Augustine's theological critique of the Eusebian reading of the division of history was weakened if not entirely lost within the narrowing theological and political horizons of the early Middle Ages in the West. The tension between secular and spiritual history that he had magisterially delineated in *De civitate dei* could not be sustained in the emerging forms of understanding represented by Gregory the Great in Rome and Isidore of Seville in Spain.[30] Nonetheless, while his teaching about Jewish witness survived the loss of this intellectual context to influence both thinking and policy throughout the Middle Ages, actual events inevitably coloured the way in which the manifestation of God's judgment in history continued to be interpreted.

To begin with, it might be expected that the political disintegration of the Christian empire in the West in the early Middle Ages would have rendered any straightforwardly triumphalist account of the Church's progress in history somewhat implausible. Yet as late as the seventh century we can find an anti-Jewish author such as Julian of Toledo arguing that the psalmist's vision of the messianic reign "from shore to shore" (Ps. 72:8) has achieved reality in Christianity's extension throughout the world; moreover, he asks, is it not the case that any who are still opposed to Christ are "oppressed and bowed down to the ground, while the Christian peoples grow strong," as befits those who inherit Jacob's deathbed promise to the lion of Judah?[31] Concern, from as early as Gregory the Great, to prohibit the owning by Jews of Christian slaves demonstrates the powerful connection between divine fulfilment of prophecy and human political policy with regard to Jewish subordination in Western Christendom.[32]

Developments whose origins lay outside the reach of Western Christendom presented a still more fundamental challenge to conventional explications of the people claim and judgment. The dramatic rise of the Islamic empire and its extension into the Western "Christian" lands of North Africa, Italy and Spain posed some disturbing questions: if the geographical spread and political success of Christianity in its early years proved it to be favoured by God, then Jews could legitimately ask whether the same criteria indicated that Islam was now his preferred form of religion.[33] Augustine had seen in Christian "dominion" over Jews a sign of prophetic fulfilment; what about the reality now of Muslim "dominion" over Christians? Muslims themselves regarded their political supremacy as evidence of divine election, just as Christians had done in the fourth century.[34] It is hardly surprising that Moses Maimonides could confidently tell his Jewish contemporaries in the twelfth century that the claims of Islam and Christianity effectively cancelled each other out.[35] In his account of the Barcelona disputation in 1263, Moses Nahmanides, representing the Jews, shows how dangerously double-edged Christian claims of decisive prophetic fulfilment in history had become: according to Nahmanides, the non-fulfilment of scriptural prophecies in Christ and his followers is confirmed by the fact that "now the worshippers of Mohammed have greater power than they."[36]

We also begin to hear, from the Jewish side, the explicit rejection of the idea that visible success can tell us anything about God's election. In the ninth century, Bodo-Eleazar, a deacon who converted to Judaism, redeployed Christian polemic against riches and the transience of earthly power to undermine the Christian presentation of a providential division of history between successful Church and impoverished Israel. In the twelfth, Judah Halevi argued that Israel's present suffering is actually the real sign of being chosen by God, elected to fulfil the vocation of God's suffering servant from Isaiah 53 and to be the heart of God's messianic purpose for human history as a whole.[37] Nonetheless, the idea that God's blessing of the Church is made manifest in particular contemporary historical events and achievements continues to recur in Western Christianity, not least around the time of the First Crusade, here again in clear tandem with an interpretation of Jewish powerlessness and exile as the fulfilment of divine judgment.[38] Yet undoubtedly the fluctuating political fortunes of the various successor states to Constantine's Christian empire, the enduring power of Islam as an alternative claimant to the fulfilment of prophetic horizons and at least partial awareness of Jewish counterarguments meant that the division of history, as the evident demonstration of the transfer of God's election from old Israel to the Church, became a more problematic topic for Christian writers in the period 1050-1300, the focus of this chapter and to which we now turn.

The Division of History in Medieval Exegesis and Visual Art

As already mentioned in connection with Augustine, greater reserve in making claims about the direct fulfilment of divine promise in the public history of the Church was not necessarily accompanied by increased caution in the assertion of the visibility of divine judgment in the history of Israel since Christ's passion. In the latter case, Christianity continued to assert very clearly that the social and political status of Judaism demonstrated its condition before God as rejected, subject to divine wrath and called to yield to the Church.[39] We can see this reflected in two particular pieces of evidence, one literary and one visual.

The literary evidence relates to the cardinal significance for Christian writers of the exegesis of Gen. 49:10, where the Latin Vulgate text could be rendered: "The sceptre shall not be taken away from Judah, nor the ruler from his thigh, until the one who is to be sent shall come, and he will be the hope of the nations."[40] Already in Justin Martyr, we find this text cited as the first proof from scripture that Jesus is the one foretold by the prophets: its clear implication, according to Justin, is that the sceptre will only depart from Judah when the promised Messiah comes, in other words, from that time on Judah will no longer have a kingly ruler; Judah ceased to have such a ruler soon after the death of Jesus; therefore Jesus must have been the promised Messiah.[41] Jewish defeat, exile and powerlessness become a vital premise for an exegetical argument demonstrating that Jesus is the Christ. It is not easy to convey in a modern context the apparent invincibility of this argument for ancient and medieval Christian polemicists. Their Jewish counterparts took issue with crucial details of translation and interpretation on which the argument relied,[42] yet its power for Christians derived at least in part from the way that it meshed with the cardinal judgment about the division of history; it provided a scriptural locus for the idea that the political disempowerment of the Jews was directly related to the coming of "their" Messiah, who has associated the Gentile nations with his sovereign rule because of Jewish unbelief. It also seemed to them to provide irrefutable proof for two vital points: first, the Messiah had already come, because the sceptre had clearly departed from Judah, and therefore Jewish claims to be still expecting him were obviously, wilfully misguided; and second, there could be no possible restoration of Jewish sovereignty or political power after the coming of Christ, because that would contradict the clear word of God in scripture.

We have just referred to the conversion to Judaism of the deacon Bodo-Eleazar; in a bid to persuade him to return to the Church, Paul Alvarus wrote him a sequence of letters in which he begins his case by appealing to Gen. 49:10 as a text that by itself clearly invalidates Judaism with its continuing messianic expectation, given the absence of any king descended from Judah since the time of Christ.[43] At the beginning of the eleventh century, Fulbert of Chartres repeatedly invoked the same text in his short treatise against the Jews.[44] Suggestions that in fact there was a Jewish kingdom in the distant East gained new credibility with the conversion of the Khazars to Judaism in the ninth century, although Christian polemicists were not slow to list reasons as to why this apparent counterexample was not in fact relevant.[45] As with the attempted rebuilding of the temple in the fourth century, however, their need to maintain the physical actuality of Jewish landlessness and powerlessness for the sake of the truth of theology cannot be underestimated, and indicates the oversimplification involved in trying to connect Christian anti-Judaism to the residue of an anti-historical and anti-physical dualism.

For the mainstream medieval Christian tradition, the Jewish "negative" of
the division of history was reflected directly in the actual circumstances of
contemporary Jews. It was taken for granted that the Church could only be
the people of God because the Jews had ceased to be; and God had made it
clear that this was the case by ensuring their exile and loss of political
sovereignty in perpetuity.

This same set of beliefs finds particularly striking expression in the
field of visual art in the depiction, common from the ninth century
onwards, of Ecclesia and Synagoga as two women, often in relation to the
cross.[46] The image allows the representation of old Israel's refusal to
accept the crucified Christ as her Messiah, of her loss of divine election
and of the end of her temporal power as dimensions of a single moment in
the history of salvation, inversely mirrored by the Church's recognition of
Christ as Lord and consequent reception of divine blessing. Synagoga's
staff is broken; Ecclesia bears a triumphant standard. As we might expect,
the extent to which God's blessing of the Church is manifest in political
power is to some degree ambiguous, although it is certainly latent in most
images.[47] Yet the linkage in the case of the Jewish figure between loss of
spiritual favour and loss of land and power is absolutely fundamental to
the iconography. In most cases, the veiling or blinding of Synagoga as she
turns away from the cross indicates she has henceforth ceased to be able to
receive divine revelation and therefore exist as the people of God, while
the removal of her crown and the breaking of her standard underline the
point that such spiritual blindness leads immediately to the political
humiliation that characterizes the Jewish people from the sack of
Jerusalem by the Romans to the observer's own time.

While occasionally it is angels who administer reward and
punishment,[48] it is sometimes Christ himself. In perhaps the most extreme
and grotesque development of this tradition, the so-called "Living Cross",
hands reach out from each end of the horizontal bar of Jesus' cross, on the
right to bless and crown Ecclesia, and on the left to strike Synagoga a
deadly wound with a great sword.[49] Other images focus rather on the
domination of Jews by Christians, with Synagoga lying on the ground at
the feet of triumphant Ecclesia, or, in one fifteenth-century example, the
two women riding towards each other in a lopsided joust in which the utter
defeat of Synagoga is the inevitable result.[50] The latent aggression of many
of these images, intensifying in the later Middle Ages, insinuates a
powerful connection between actual violence against the contemporary
adherents of Synagoga and the passion of Christ, viewed as a scene where
Jewish rejection of Jesus is inseparable from Jewish suffering of
violence.[51] Jewish unbelief means perpetual susceptibility to and

defencelessness against violent aggression. The sword that kills a Jew here and now can be seen as the sword that grows directly from the cross, expressing the deadly power of Christ's passion.

In conclusion, then, the Christian world became, at various points in the millennium we call the Middle Ages, less sure of the direct manifestation of God's promised blessing in its own historical fortunes. Yet literary and artistic evidence alike suggest that it remained utterly certain that the contrast between those fortunes and the fortunes of Judaism, exemplified by the powerlessness of actual Jews within the boundaries of Christendom itself, was an irrefutable demonstration of the transfer of divine election from Synagoga to Ecclesia. The division of blessing and punishment in the concrete conditions of Christianity and Judaism remained the irremovable mark of God's judgment within history. This emerging asymmetry in the articulation of the people judgment, scarcely evident in Christian sources before Augustine, needs to be recognized as a highly significant shift within the premises of the classic framework set out in the previous chapter. Arguably, it was a critical adaptation in the face of the Church's political failures that allowed vital elements of that framework to persist into the second half of the twentieth century, when Christian writers of unimpeachable scholarly credentials who would be wary of simplistically triumphalist readings of Church history continued to assert that Jewish exile from the land and political powerlessness were the consequence of divine judgment.[52]

Shift in the People Claim:
Restoration beyond Earthly Change

The asymmetry in interpretation of the people judgment that comes into view during the Middle Ages invites an important question: if the chosenness of Christ's Church is not in fact evident from numerical growth, spiritual vitality and historical influence, is it still evident at all? And if the blessing of the Church is not deducible from its historical circumstances, what then sustains the plausibility of the people claim of restoration in Christ? One aspect of theological development that marks the period that is the primary focus for this chapter, 1050-1300, is the emergence of a way of understanding salvation that proposes a "reasoned" affirmation of human restoration in Christ without appeal to the contested evidence of public, terrestrial history. This can be seen as a further adaptation to challenging realities, and one bound up again with the three-dimensional interaction between Judaism, anti-Judaism and Christian theology. The second section of the chapter seeks to outline that process and provides one example of how major developments in Christian theology have proceeded in part from unacknowledged concession to the force of Jewish critique—a pattern we will see again in chapter three.

Gilbert Crispin: A Transitional Text

The *Disputatio Judei et Christiani* of Gilbert Crispin, abbot of Westminster, is worth dwelling on for a number of reasons. To begin with, Gilbert's work, probably written in the last decade of the eleventh century, is one of the medieval texts that can most plausibly claim to represent in literary form an actual dialogue between a Christian and a Jew conducted with a degree of mutual courtesy and respect.[53] We see, for instance, Jewish puzzlement as to how Christians can claim the fulfilment of messianic prophecy to have taken place in a world where the promised reign of messianic peace is so demonstrably absent. The twelfth-century Jewish writer Joseph Kimhi expresses this objection with particular clarity:

> You claim that Jesus saved the world from the day he came, but he accomplished nothing which can actually be seen. Scripture says: *In anguish shall you eat of it* (Gen. 3:17) *and in pain shall you bear children* (Gen. 3:16), and it is so to this day. That which is manifest has not been remedied and you say it has been remedied.[54]

Gilbert's Jewish interlocutor appeals, not to Genesis 3, but instead to one of the classic messianic passages in Hebrew scripture, Isa. 2:2-4, posing a series of searching questions that arise from it. Where in the world, he inquires, are the nations saying "Let us go up to the mountain of the Lord and the house of the God of Jacob"? Where do we see evidence that military forces are beating their swords into ploughshares? And how could it possibly be asserted that nation is not lifting up sword against nation any more? Indeed, a state of perpetual war prevails in our own time, he says, with even children forced into combat and the manufacture of weapons unable to keep pace with demand.[55] Therefore it is not "the last days"; therefore the Messiah has not come. Now more then ever, history resists Christian claims about scriptural fulfilment.

In the late eleventh century, with the First Crusade around the corner, it must have been a line of argument carrying some force, but the Christian in Gilbert's dialogue is not short of things to say in reply. Two features of his response are particularly notable. First, he draws on allegorical exegesis to argue that the achievement of interior peace is a far greater achievement than the simple cessation of lethal hostilities, and on the vitality of contemporary religious expression to assert that there is clear evidence of Christianity bringing about such inward transformation in the contemporary conversion of the rich and powerful to lives of poverty and pilgrimage, with some even becoming hermits.[56] Secondly, he sketches out a periodization of Church history in which at the beginning of the "last days" spoken of in Isa. 2:2, that is, in the early centuries of the Church, peace on earth was indeed established in fulfilment of biblical prophecy, with even kings following the teaching of Christ about love for neighbour and enemy. Yet other parts of scripture foretell, the Christian says, a time of tribulation towards the end of the last days, before the final consummation, and that is what is being experienced now. Hence Christians should not come to doubt the fulfilment of prophecy just because the promise of peace on earth seems further away in the present than it did in earlier ages of the Church.[57]

Gilbert's complicated and at times tortuous response to the Jew's simple and striking questions indicates both the unwillingness of Christian theology to abandon the direct inscription in post-biblical history of prophetic fulfilment and also a recognition that articulating that inscription had become a less than straightforward task. Moreover, the defences on which Gilbert falls back, an appeal to the frequency of startling conversion and an assertion of the imminence of the end of the world, could hardly be sustainable or convincing in the longer term. Yet there are hints elsewhere in the dialogue of a rather different approach. While in the passage just referred to the Christian keeps exegesis at the forefront of his answer, a few pages later we find him saying that he will leave scriptural evidence aside for a moment and appeal instead to "the greatest necessity and reason" ("necessitas quoque summa et ratio").[58] The occasion for the proposal of this alternative, "rational" strategy is the Jew's objection to the claim that God has become human. Although he also appeals to scripture in responding to the Jew on this point, the Christian develops a "rational" argument which he invites his partner to judge "rationally." The argument itself begins with the universal guilt of the descendants of Adam, requiring eternal punishment for every one of them in hell. The only way this could be prevented was for one of them, a human being, to make appropriate restitution to God. To the person who made such restitution would be owed the service of the rest of humanity. Yet we are to serve no one except God. Therefore it was necessary for God to become human, to make the necessary restitution, defeat the power of the devil, rescue us from hell and become our Lord.[59]

The Appeal to Reason in Anselm of Canterbury
and Odo of Tournai

Gilbert's attempt to appeal to "the greatest necessity and reason" in articulating an argument for the incarnation that is not overtly grounded in contested scripture is at one level a relatively minor example of a much more widespread development during this phase of the Middle Ages. Self-conscious attention to arguments based on reason rather than scripture became a staple part of Jewish-Christian theological exchange in Western Europe from the twelfth century on, although just what reason meant in such contexts and how far it proceeded in total abstraction from interpretive strategies are more difficult matters.[60] Gilbert's Jew in fact sticks to the exegetical points raised by the Christian in his own subsequent interventions, but Jewish writers were, if anything, ahead of Christian theologians in using this approach because of their greater contact with the Islamic world. In the tenth century, a Spanish Muslim reported with shock and disapproval on the "philosophers' assemblies" he had encountered in Baghdad. In the heart of the Islamic world, he wrote, Muslims of different sects, Zoroastrians, Jews and Christians, together with those doubting any sort of system of revealed religion, met together for open discussion with just one condition: "Each one of us shall use arguments exclusively derived from human reason."[61] In less radical circles, the appeal to reason would tend to mean the assertion of a unique compatibility between one religion's distinctive claims and the universal standards of human rationality, which often meant in practice the particular norms and principles of argument identified within the corpus of ancient philosophy as this was received in the medieval world.

The deployment of reason in order to present an evaluation of the competing claims of different religions is evident in the work of the tenth-century Jewish writer Saadia Gaon.[62] Saadia commented on Islam and Christianity as part of the process of considering various religious claims against the standards of philosophical reason, concluding that Islam and Christianity were severely defective and Judaism in essential harmony with it. In the twelfth century, another Jewish writer, Judah Halevi, provided a fictional dramatization of the debate between religions in his *Kuzari*, which rehearses, via lengthy theological dialogue, the conversion of the King of the Khazars to Judaism. The Khazari's grounds for rejecting the advocate of Christianity are instructive:

> I see here no logical conclusion; nay, logic rejects most of what thou sayest. . . . As for me, I cannot accept these things, because they come upon me suddenly, not having grown up in them.[63]

From the twelfth century onwards, Jews in Western Europe, in the context of an overwhelmingly Christian culture, began to use arguments against Christian doctrine that drew on the philosophical traditions that all three religions appropriated from the ancient world.[64] These criticisms appealing to reason focused especially on Christian claims regarding Trinity and incarnation.[65] Later in the Middle Ages, the Virgin Birth and transubstantiation would also be targets for the same kind of rational refutation, which itself mirrored the activity of Christian anti-Jewish polemicists.[66]

As well as reflecting this wider phenomenon, Gilbert's argument about the "rationality" of the incarnation also has clear affinities with the much more famous work of his friend and contemporary, Anselm of Canterbury's *Cur deus homo*. As one might expect, Anselm develops his "necessary reasons" for the incarnation of God with far greater rigour and ultimate simplicity than Gilbert, seeking to work from the narrowest range of basic assumptions via strict inferences to the final conclusion. By focusing exclusively on the requirement for appropriate restitution if all humanity is not to be condemned to hell, Anselm avoids the need to bring in Gilbert's argument about serving the saviour or defeating the devil: instead, he sets out the argument that since only a human can make restitution for human sin against God, and only God can make restitution of sufficient value to compensate for injury done to God, therefore only the God-man can make the required restitution for humanity and open the way to communion with God and eternal life.

The extent to which Anselm himself was concerned to answer distinctively Jewish objections to teaching about Christ remains debated by commentators,[67] but it is certainly plausible to suggest that at least one catalyst for Anselm's reflections may have been growing awareness, quite possibly via contact with Gilbert Crispin himself, of such Jewish objections as are eloquently voiced by Joseph Kimhi:

> The great and mighty God Whom no eye has seen, Who has neither form nor image, Who said, 'For man may not see Me and live' (Exod. 33:20)—how shall I believe that this great and inaccessible *Deus absconditus* needlessly entered the womb of a woman, the filthy, foul bowels of a female, compelling the living God to be born of a woman, a child without knowledge or understanding . . .[68]

It is to the refutation of the charge that all this happened "needlessly" that Anselm will particularly devote himself. It is further worthy of note that the ending of the *Cur deus homo* explicitly draws attention to the potential relevance of the arguments it contains for attempts to engage Jews in theological debate. Boso, his dialogue partner, congratulates Anselm,

> For you prove that God became man out of necessity in such a way that, even if the few things which you have taken from our books were removed (such as what you said about the three persons of God and about Adam) you could satisfy not only the Jews but also the pagans with reason alone.[69]

There seems to be an implicit recognition here that appeals to "our books," despite the fact that they were in theory the Jews' books too, rarely succeeded in persuading Jewish representatives in debate, not least because Christian exegesis relied on a doctrinal framework for interpretation (including the Trinity and original sin) that they simply rejected.

Gilbert's "rational" argument about the incarnation, with its parallels to Anselm's treatment, appears in his dialogue at a certain remove from the exegetical response to the Jewish objection regarding non-fulfilment of messianic promises in history. We find the first clear evidence of the deployment of the Anselmian argument to provide a response based on reason to this point shortly afterwards, in the *Disputation with the Jew, Leo, concerning the Advent of Christ* by Odo of Tournai.[70] The process of theological exchange indicated by Odo in the Prologue is itself instructive: if, as we have just suggested, Anselm was prompted by Gilbert's contact with an articulate Jew to develop a rational argument for the incarnation to be used more generally within Christian theology, Odo tells us how he first rehearsed such an argument in the context of a talk to some monks and then subsequently used it in debate with a Jew.[71]

The starting point of the dialogue itself is historical non-fulfilment: "Tell me, bishop," Leo asks, "what benefit did the coming of your Christ confer upon the world?" Odo asks him what benefits he expects from the Messiah, and Leo replies:

> Whatever we read in the prophets, namely that all kingdoms will be subjected to us through him; that we will have perpetual peace under him; that we shall be gathered from all kingdoms into Jerusalem; that Jerusalem will have dominion over all kingdoms; and, all other things which the prophets happily enumerate. Since we do not see all these things fulfilled in your Christ, we wonder what you expect from him?[72]

It is essentially the same objection we found in Joseph Kimhi and again in Gilbert Crispin, but rather than seeking to "save" the argument for historical fulfilment as Gilbert does, Odo simply rules out history as irrelevant:

> We expect the kingdom of heaven through Christ, and we await that felicity which you hope will be earthly, but which through Christ we hope will be heavenly.

Leo replies that actually Jews hope for both earthly and heavenly blessing, but continues to press his point: even the forgiveness of all sins, which Christians claim to come from Christ, should lead directly to beatitude, but there is no evidence at all of this. "What, then, does your Christ do?" he asks.[73] It is at this point in the dialogue that Odo begins to manoeuvre the discussion around to his favoured ground of the Anselmian "reasons" for the incarnation. Just because satisfaction for sin has been made does not mean that the punishment is immediately lifted and erstwhile sinners at once admitted to glory; it is only right that they should have to wait. Still, it was necessary for the divine-human Christ to come into the world to make that satisfaction so that we can have the hope of glory. The bulk of the remainder of the dialogue consists in Odo's rehearsal of arguments similar to Gilbert's and Anselm's as to why this should be so. The arguments, however, whatever their merits, presuppose the removal of Christian claims about the newness of salvation beyond public history, indeed in a certain sense outside unfolding time. Salvation relates to what Christ did long ago and to what he will thereby do for each of the faithful at the end of time.

Necessary Reason and Historical Actuality

The price of Odo's deployment of a new degree of rational rigour, then, in setting out Christian claims for Christ as saviour is actually an intensification of the difficulty identified by Joseph Kimhi in the passage quoted at the beginning of this section: "You claim that Jesus saved the world from the day he came, but he accomplished nothing which can actually be seen." The more Christian debaters tended to retreat from strong claims about prophetic fulfilment in the blessing of the Christian Church within the division of history and to appeal instead, with Odo, to an exclusive focus on heavenly benefits that could only be actually realized in terms of life after death, the more sharply they were criticized by their Jewish counterparts for occupying ground that was both unassailable and indefensible because of its lack of any purchase on shared, historical reality. A century and a half after Odo, at the most revealing of all the staged disputations of the later Middle Ages, the

Jewish spokesman Nahmanides comments rather acidly on Christian claims about redemption from sin achieved through Christ leading to deliverance from hell and the attainment of heaven: "They say in our land, 'He who wishes to tell lies should cite evidence that is too far away to be checked.'"[74] Yet medieval Christians were clearly by this stage wary of repeating the kind of claims that could be checked—routinely made by their predecessors in the first millennium—regarding the fulfilment of prophecy in the earthly progress and experience of the Church.

Jewish anti-Christian writing suggests that, under pressure, even the assertion that we found in Gilbert Crispin of the transformation of individual lives through the grace of Christ tended to weaken. In Joseph Kimhi's dialogue, while the Christian and the Jew initially argue about which community shows better evidence of good works, the Christian eventually brings this passage of the dialogue to an end by declaring the matter irrelevant:

> All the good deeds to which you referred will do you no good since you do not believe that Jesus became incarnate through Mary in order to save the world. Works follow faith but faith does not follow works. Even though there is evil-doing among the Christians, they have sound faith so that they will fully repent and be received by the Creator by virtue of the faith which they profess.[75]

The Christian message to Jews appeared to come down to the demand for intellectual assent to the proposition that in Christ God had brought about the fulfilment of messianic prophecy, but in such a way that the results of this remained wholly invisible and inaccessible even to the one giving the assent until after death. As Profiat Duran puts it sarcastically in his letter from the late fourteenth century to a friend who had converted to Christianity,

> Faith alone goes up to heaven. Those who deny this go to hell. Also Scripture says therefore: "The just shall live by faith" (Hab. 2:4), if the Hebrew word does indeed mean that which thou and thy teachers wish to understand by it.[76]

Although the rational, Anselmian arguments for the achievement of salvation through Christ may have been no more persuasive to Jews than the earlier historical and exegetical ones, it is certainly possible to conclude from this evidence that is was not loss of contact with Judaism that fostered the spiritualization of Christianity and its dissociation (in some strands) of history from theological purpose. Rather, the renewed exposure of Western Christianity to Judaism and its critique of Christian claims within the pivotal period 1050-1300 contributed directly to a tendency to foreground a gospel of "spiritual" redemption and set far less store by the location of prophetic fulfilment within the present history of the Church than had been customary in the first millennium.

One clear danger for Christian theology here was the loss of any kind of foothold for proclaimed redemption in shared, historical reality, for all Anselm's intention of vindicating the gospel of the Word made flesh. A version of this theological vertigo seems to have been experienced by at least one twelfth-century figure. There is a rather curious passage in Herbert of Bosham's life of Thomas Beckett where he reflects on the possibility that God has not yet become incarnate.[77] Smalley, who drew attention to Herbert's proficiency as a Hebraist, suggested that Herbert had been impressed by Jewish arguments that the Messiah had not arrived.[78] Yet the case in fact appears rather more complex. Herbert is absolutely confident that the Jews are wrong, for they are expecting a mere man to come as the Messiah, while the Church knows that God must become incarnate for humanity to be saved—as Anselm claimed to have demonstrated. Herbert's doubt is decidedly post-Anselmian, so to speak. He is sure about the absolute necessity of the incarnation; yet he allows a shade of doubt to touch the claim that the incarnation can be reliably identified with a specific event in the past, in order to argue that even were this claim ultimately shown to be false, faithful adherence to it would nonetheless be commendable. Belief in incarnation as a kind of necessary theological principle appears here to float free from belief that the Word became flesh at any particular point in time, which has become somehow a secondary matter.

There is perhaps a parallel here with the debate rehearsed in the work of Herbert's Spanish contemporary Petrus Alfonsi, a convert from Judaism, in whose dialogical work the representative of his pre-Christian, Jewish self, "Moses", concedes that "the deity *could* unite with a human being" but demands proof from "Peter" that this has actually taken place.[79] In Herbert's case, the wider context for these reflections is consideration of eucharistic faith, and Herbert does acknowledge that he had at one time real doubts about transubstantiation, to the point of anxiety ridden dreams about a chalice with whirling hosts, which the holy archbishop wisely interpreted to him as the image of his own uncertainties. The critical point, however, remains analogous across both cases: one can accept that God can change bread into the body of Christ, one can accept that God must become human—but how can one know that this bread is God's body, or that Jesus of Nazareth was the incarnate Word? Anselm's argument may or may not show that it is necessary for God to become human; it cannot, however, by itself establish that God *has* become human, let alone tell us which human he became. The "necessity" to which Luke appeals in his Gospel and Acts, as a necessity of scriptural fulfilment, is an attempt to say that it had to happen like this, in this way. The "necessity" of (philosophical) reason to which Gilbert, Anselm and Odo appeal can only prove that the Word should be made flesh at some time in history; of its nature, it cannot say anything about *which* time was (or will be) the time of the incarnate Word. Herbert evidently recovered the theological balance shared by his theological mentors—but that was because the scripture claim of fulfilment in Christ remained for them wholly unchallenged, and the elaboration of this claim via allegorical exegesis, as developed in the early centuries and acknowledged by all in Christendom to be wholly compelling, was more than sufficient to establish that the "abstract" necessity of the God-human had found its concrete historical actualization in Jesus Christ.

Questions from the Covenant Judgment: Comprehending the Law

The covenant judgment of the displacement of Torah contained within it the implication that the Law given to Moses did at one (past) time hold a central place and purpose within God's work of revelation and redemption. It was a point spelt out in particular in confrontation with Gnosticizing voices in the early Christian movement. Yet Christian theology operating from the classic framework had to face some potentially challenging questions about Torah's place and purpose, such as why things had changed with the coming of Christ and what continuing value there was in the reading of the Law as canonical scripture in the life of the Church. We noted in the first chapter that the legacy of the New Testament in general and Paul in particular was a set of apparently divergent lines of thinking in relation to the original purpose and enduring significance of the Mosaic Law. Justin Martyr's careful harmonization of that legacy in resistance to both Judaizing and Gnosticizing elements within the Christianity of his day contributed to an emerging theological consensus in the Catholic Church that continued to have normative status during the Middle Ages and beyond. Yet the struggle to comprehend the Mosaic Law within the theological hermeneutics of Christianity clearly troubled many Christian thinkers in the period 1050-1300, in particular in the second half of that period when the intellectual culture of Western Christendom is generally characterized as "scholastic". The narrative character of the Christian gospel, as a telling of what God did, could readily embrace both historical and prophetic texts from the Old Testament as giving depth and perspective to its central story of incarnation, death and resurrection.[80] The detailed precepts of the Law could not be accommodated so easily by the same strategies, however: they did not obviously "advance" the story of creation and salvation, while the assertion that through their allegorical meanings they carried a hidden prophetic burden might prompt questions as to why that burden needed to be conveyed in such an oblique manner.

Once again, internal questioning on this issue was intertwined both with external criticism from Jewish sources and also with reasserting the force of anti-Judaism in response to Jewish attacks on Christian theology's coherence. Ralph of Flaix, a twelfth-century Benedictine monk, gives as the occasion for the composition of his influential commentary on Leviticus the discussions that were taking place within his monastery "concerning the arguments of the Jews" ("de iudeorum contionibus") and causing some of the weaker brethren to waver.[81] In the thirteenth century, Robert Grosseteste refers in the opening section of his work *De cessatione legalium* to some people's faith being shaken by questions about the continuing observance of "sacraments of the old law."[82] This suggests that Trypho's opening question to Justin still had the potential to trouble believers more than a thousand years later: how can Christians believe that the Law comes from God and yet not keep it in its entirety? In the fifth-century dialogue between a Christian and a Jew composed by Evagrius, the Jew wants to know first and foremost why Christians do not observe the commands to Moses about circumcision, Sabbath observance and clean and unclean foods; once satisfied on these matters, he promptly, if unrealistically, asks to be baptized.[83]

This repeated representation of Jewish puzzlement at Christian regard for Torah as scripture without actually doing what it says is likely to be in accordance with reality. It is the first question on the lips of Gilbert Crispin's Jewish interlocutor, while the short dialogue within Peter Damian's eleventh-century anti-Jewish treatise is wholly given over to explaining why despite Jesus fulfilling and not abolishing the Law Christians nevertheless are not bound by its instruction on various matters.[84] In the purportedly autobiographical account of the conversion to Christianity of Herman-Judah from the twelfth century, the same point about apparently arbitrary inconsistency in keeping Torah forms the initial focus for Herman-Judah's attack (while still a Jew) on Christianity in public debate, although it is also interesting that the reported response (from Rupert of Deutz) does not address it directly.[85]

The following section of this chapter endeavours to demonstrate in more detail the importance of the three-dimensional process of interaction between Christian theology, the encounter with Judaism and Christianity's self-legitimation through anti-Judaism in relation to the concerted effort during this period to comprehend the purpose of Law within the framework of Christian thought. The outcome of this effort is perhaps not so readily identifiable as in the two preceding sections. It certainly generates, in the work of Thomas Aquinas, a level of intellectual sophistication in formulating and responding to questions raised by the covenant judgment that is in itself a remarkable theological achievement. Beyond the impasse discernible even here in the comprehension of Torah within Christian theological hermeneutics, Aquinas' recourse to the theme of a history of progressive perfection in which the Law has its place and the incarnation is the final word can be seen to prepare the way for the much more fundamental questioning of the centrality of the concept of fulfilment in early modernity, and the corresponding foregrounding of historical development.

Can God's Law Change?

As was emphasized in the discussion of the *Dialogue with Trypho*, Christian responses to the Jewish challenge about the Law tried to maintain both that the Law was good and God-given (against Gnosticizing tendencies) *and* that it is no longer to be observed as God's Law (against Judaizing tendencies). If, however, we turn for a moment away from theological writing to the understanding expressed and conveyed in Christian art, which may have been closer to popular thinking in the Middle Ages, we can see an inclination to resolve this tension by effectively abandoning the original goodness of the Mosaic Torah or at least the clear distinction between the evaluation of the Law before and after Christ. For instance, in depictions of the Ecclesia-Synagoga pairing already referred to, Synagoga often clings onto the tablets of the Law as she turns away from Christ, and in one case a torn (Torah) scroll lies alongside her while Christ holds aloft his own book (the New Testament?).[86] One could readily infer that adherence to the Mosaic Law constitutes, as such, resistance to Christ and rejection of God's will. The replacement of Synagoga in another painting with Moses implies even more strongly that the negative evaluation of Torah observing Judaism after the coming of Christ (as constituting hostility to God's Son) is extended back retrospectively to apply to its very first origins at Sinai.[87]

We seem to find in such visual art a version of the claim in the second-century Epistle of Barnabas that the Sinai covenant was broken and lost by Israel before they even received the Law—because of their idolatry around the Golden Calf—rather than the theological framework of Justin and Irenaeus in which the old covenant as a true if imperfect relationship between Israel and God lasts until the death of Christ on the cross.[88] Given Church teaching that observance of the Law by converted Jews was forbidden, it is not surprising that ordinary Christians failed to distinguish between such observance before Christ as obedience to God and such observance after Christ as disobedience against God. In another, related form of medieval iconography, in which the drama of salvation is represented visually through a sequence of scenes divided by the tree of life, the equation of Law and the Judaism that kept the Law even before Christ with sin and divine rejection becomes still more explicit. In this genre, brought to a kind of culmination in the work of the elder and younger Cranachs, Synagoga embracing the Law is associated on one half of the picture with Eve, the original sinner, and thence with the sequence of sin, death, judgment and hell. Facing her on the other side stands Christ's Ecclesia, linked in pre-Reformation works to Mary, and leading the way to grace, righteousness and eternal life.[89] Moses and Torah are located on the same side of the theological history as sin and death, part of a single nexus under divine wrath, and separated from the other side, the offer of life in Christ foreshadowed in Old Testament prophecy and now received by the faithful in the Church.

Clearly, such one-dimensional evaluation of the Mosaic Law could not be expressed without qualification in orthodox Christian theological discourse, which was bound to give some sort of positive account of its divine origin. The Torah—including its problematic commandments—could not be filleted out from the Christian canon as having no providential value and no reference to Christ. What kind of value, however, and what kind of reference should be ascribed to it? These were questions that Christianity had always been obliged to answer as soon as it began to articulate the covenant judgment about the displacement of the Law. Increased engagement with an articulate Judaism in the period 1050-1300 now subjected this judgment to renewed scrutiny.

Already in the work of Saadia Gaon, Christian claims about the "abrogation" of the Law prompt a lengthy discussion that combines exegetical with more abstract and logical arguments.[90] Saadia is aware of detailed arguments on the side of both Judaism and Christianity relating to the possibility of a divinely given Law being subsequently abrogated, with Jewish defences of the Law attempting to demonstrate that there is a logical incoherence in the notion. He nonetheless frames his treatment of this topic with more straightforwardly exegetical issues, beginning with scriptural passages that indicate that the Law is to be observed by Israel in perpetuity, and ending by rejecting Christian exegesis of passages from the Jewish Bible to suggest the contrary. The section finishes with consideration of Jer. 31:31, the verse that we identified in chapter one as a critical locus for reflection on the place of Torah both in Paul and, most explicitly, in Hebrews, and which was thereafter treated as axiomatic by Christian thinkers for demonstrating the provisional and temporary nature of the covenant at Sinai. Saadia mentions his own response to Christian use of this verse, one presumably given in actual debate:

> To these I said, "Why don't you look at what follows this verse, where it is explicitly stated that this new covenant that was mentioned before was the Torah itself?"[91]

He proceeds to cite Jer. 31:33 to prove his point.

The more "rational" arguments that Saadia discusses tend to focus on the idea that a God given law must be perfect and enduring insofar as it is an expression of God's will which necessarily does not change. The idea that the Christian judgment regarding the displacement of Torah implied a certain mutability in the divine will clearly troubled Gilbert Crispin, whose Jewish interlocutor raises an objection along these lines; moreover, when he later composed a dialogue with a wholly fictional "pagan", who only has respect for reason and not Christian authorities such as scripture, the pagan uses it as a component in his case against Christianity.[92]

Three Themes from the Patristic Legacy

The legacy of the patristic period to the Western Christian theologians of the twelfth and thirteenth centuries included three themes especially relevant for responding to such challenges from contemporary Judaism. The first was the theme of providential contradictoriness within the Old Testament generally. The second was the theme of a natural or rational law intrinsic to humanity as such prior to any particular divine revelation and binding on all people for all time. The third was the theme of a progression in divine revelation from less perfect forms of divine communication to the perfect one in the incarnation. Jewish-Christian exchanges in this period acted as a catalyst for developments in Christian thinking that found limitations in both the first and second themes— without simply rejecting either of them—and placed more direct weight on the third. This constitutes an important development in how Christian theology made sense of the Law in its Bible and of the Law's continuing practitioners in ongoing history. It also marked the beginning of a long-term shift in emphasis away from the idea of fulfilment and towards the idea of development as pivotal for Christian self-understanding and self-legitimation in the face of enduring Judaism, a shift only completed in modernity.

The first theme of providential contradictions within the text of the Old Testament is associated particularly with the work of Origen, Latin translations of whose work continued to exercise an immense degree of influence on the medieval understanding of the Bible, to say nothing of the mediation of his approach through Ambrose, Augustine and Gregory the Great. As was mentioned in passing in chapter one, Origen played a vital part in developing and applying the interpretive framework that legitimated (in Christian eyes) the judgment that Judaism had been by its faithlessness dispossessed of its own scriptures, which were now faithfully interpreted only in the life of the Church. As part of that task, Origen commented at length on the legal passages of the Pentateuch, identifying multiple contradictions between different passages and intrinsic absurdities within them to argue that many precepts were never intended to be literally obeyed but were rather given by God as cryptic figures of the coming of Christ.[93] The assertion that the Law is inherently contradictory and defective, incapable of being kept in its "literal" sense, became a standard part of the Christian anti-Jewish armoury in the next millennium. It still formed the heart of Gilbert Crispin's response to the Jewish question of why Christians do not keep the whole Law and remained the guiding principle for the commentary on Leviticus by Ralph of Flaix referred to above.[94] It was integral to the Christian charge that Jewish approaches to scripture bore the marks of a wilful and sinful carnality, one expression of the scripture judgment of interpretive blindness.[95]

This first theme, however, sat increasingly uncomfortably with significant trends within biblical exegesis as such and also within wider medieval culture. Christian exegesis in the twelfth and thirteenth centuries began to identify its position more consistently with another strand of patristic theology, one confident that every passage in the Bible possessed a literal meaning, which acted as the foundation (in Gregory the Great's famous architectural metaphor) for the spiritual sense (variously subdivided into two or three further senses).[96] A way of thinking about Mosaic Law which relied on demonstrating the absence of a literal meaning and a literal reason for some commandments seemed out of step with this growing consensus.

Moreover, medieval European culture in the twelfth and thirteenth centuries was wanting to place at its heart reason, order and, increasingly, law as their institutional embodiment; so why would God give his people a law that expressed neither divine reason nor divine order but constituted instead a prolonged series of riddles, intrinsically indecipherable for the next thousand or more years—unless God was, after all, somehow capricious or inconsistent, or indeed unless there were two Gods, one less than good and less than all powerful? Such thoughts, like an excessively one-dimensional view of the Law as the agent of sin and Satan, raised again in the medieval context the spectre of that metaphysical dualism against which early Christianity had repeatedly fought to define itself. Such dualism, present in many forms of second-century Christian Gnosticism and in the Manichaeism that attracted Augustine of Hippo for a time, found new vitality in the success—political as well as religious—of the Cathar movement in the twelfth and thirteenth centuries.[97] Catholic concern in the face of this reviving threat may well have played a part in rendering the Origenistic approach to the Law, for so long a staple of spiritual reading as well as of anti-Jewish polemic, less and less attractive as the dominant account of God's purpose in his dealings with Israel through the Sinai covenant.[98]

The second element from the patristic legacy that had a direct bearing on this subject was the concept of natural law, which became the focus of a great deal of interest and theological development in the twelfth and thirteenth centuries.[99] Rom. 2:14-16 appeared to provide an unimpeachable warrant for the deployment of this idea from ancient philosophy in the context of Christian theology, and for setting the law of nature as a third law alongside the law of Moses and the new law of Christ—indeed, it would be better to say setting it first, as something given by God in creation and to which the laws of Moses and Christ must necessarily appear as additions or perfections. We commented earlier in the chapter on the idea of "reason" as providing a neutral term of comparison between different religions; given the centrality of law to Jewish self-understanding and also, perhaps increasingly, to Christian theological discourse, weighing these two "competing" laws against the natural law of reason was a predictable extension of the new focus on rationality in Jewish-Christian exchanges. This is what we find in Peter Abelard's twelfth-century text, *Dialogue of a Philosopher with a Jew, and a Christian*.[100] In this work, which Abelard presents as the account of a dream involving three anonymous characters, the Philosopher interviews first a Jew and then—at much greater length—a Christian, as he seeks to find a way to make sure the salvation of his soul in the same context of conflicting religious claims that troubled the Spanish Muslim referred to earlier who discovered the intellectual pluralism of tenth-century Baghdad.[101] Law is the principal connecting theme of the dialogue: the Philosopher holds to the natural, unwritten law only, and wants to know from the Jew and then the Christian why he should add to or exchange for this a revealed, written law.[102] The work is particularly interesting from our perspective because through his dialogue Abelard begins to dramatize the tension already identified in Justin's use of the natural law to relativize the Mosaic Law: if the unchanging and universal law of nature is the criterion by which revelation must be judged in the case of Moses, then what can be the function of *any* revelation that happens within history? How can it be truly new, rather than an illustration of perpetual truth?

In the first part of the dialogue, the Philosopher uses many of the arguments that could be found in standard Christian writing on Judaism (and indeed are in some cases borrowed from Abelard's own exegetical writings on the New Testament) in order to reject any binding force for the Mosaic Law.[103] These would include the argument that there were righteous people before Moses, and therefore as the Law cannot have been necessary before Moses neither is it necessary now. The Philosopher is also adamant that in the Mosaic Law there are only earthly, physical rewards for obedience and that such things cannot provide the goal for ethical activity, which is in any case defined as good or bad by the interior intention, not the external act.[104] Yet while the Christian, when it is his turn to make an initial presentation to the Philosopher, is very clear about the superiority of the new Law of Christ to the old Law of Moses,[105] he struggles to express in the course of the exchanges in precisely what way this law transcends the law of nature to which the Philosopher already adheres. In the first part of the work, the Philosopher had already defined the natural law as love of God and neighbour, while rejecting the Jew's claim that love of neighbour is taught by the Law of Moses. That fits well with the conviction expressed elsewhere by Abelard that pagan philosophers who followed the natural law were thereby more justified before God than Jews keeping the written Torah.[106] The dialogue in this part is much more respectful and irenic, yet this only underlines the sense that while at least the issues were clear in confronting the Law of Moses with the natural law, setting the Law of Christ against the law of natural reason may yield few sharp distinctions.

The Christian and the Philosopher in Abelard's *Dialogue* agree that the vital task is to identify the supreme good—but that in itself is a topic that reaches back to the early days of Greek philosophy, and the Christian finds it very difficult to come up with an account of the supreme good to function as the orienting principle for his "new" law that was not already discussed as an option in the philosophical tradition.[107] Even the vision of God as the supreme good is not a new idea with Christianity. The Christian is left with the explication of union with God in terms of resurrection, a notion with which the Philosopher has predictable problems. So the dialogue ends with something of an impasse (whether or not this is the ending that Abelard intended). The Christian, having defined his own position as possessing a superior law to the Jew, is hard pressed to explain what is really new about this law after all, given its general conformity to philosophical traditions regarding the natural law. Although this nowhere becomes explicit in the dialogue, as the Philosopher is deferential to the Christian where he was adversarial to the Jew, it is not difficult to see that the "rational" arguments used to reject the particularity of the Mosaic Law by the Philosopher (as by the "Christian" Abelard elsewhere) could quite easily be transferred as grounds for rejecting the comparable particularity of the Christian "law", as also not universal in time and also excessively linked to the external and the physical. So just as Christians like Justin split the old Law of Moses into those commands that are enduring and natural, and those that are transient and particular, the Philosopher distinguishes between different parts of the Christians' new law, with baptism replacing circumcision as a prime example of a "non-universal" component.[108] The "newness" of this new law turns out, it would seem, to add nothing permanent and binding to the natural law explicated and respected by the ancient pre-Christian philosophers.

The Intervention of Maimonides

If excessive reliance on the patristic theme of the contradictory nature of the Mosaic Law appeared to leave too wide an opening towards dualistic heresy, then too much emphasis on natural law as the dominant idea for reflecting on scripture's commandments could narrow the gap between Christianity and the best of pagan philosophy apparently to vanishing point. In a moment, we will consider the extent to which Aquinas achieved a synthesis of Christian thinking about the Law in the *Summa theologiae* that avoided both of these dangers through developing the vital role of the third theme that was also mentioned as part of the inheritance from Patristic Christianity, that of a progression towards perfection in divine revelation. First, however, it is important to note a decisive intervention in Christian debates about the "old Law" by a Jewish author. Moses Maimonides' *Guide for the Perplexed* was translated into Latin around 1220 and was already being used by Christian theologians in the later part of the same decade.[109] His work served as a catalyst in moving Christian treatments of the Mosaic Law beyond the impasse we have just noted. Here we encounter perhaps for the first time a different kind of Jewish-Christian theological exchange: an exchange arising not from face-to-face encounters, friendly or hostile, "staged" or informal, but from the careful reading of the other's theological texts. It is a significant moment.

Maimonides was not conveying an agreed Jewish position about the Torah in his *Guide*, although his thirteenth-century Christian readers probably had no means of knowing that. Attention to reason—and the ancient philosophical texts thought to embody it—had already occasioned similar questions within Judaism to those we can discern in Abelard, and the relation between Torah and reason remained a controversial topic in medieval Jewish thought. Saadia, for instance, had argued against those who deemed natural law alone sufficient that there was a need for divine law; he also divided divine law into two categories, "rational" precepts and "revelational" precepts.[110] His discussion in turn reflected debates within Islam, which had its own processes of questioning about divine law. Maimonides, like other later Jewish thinkers influenced by Aristotle, rejected this attempt to establish a distinction within the Torah, developing a position more akin to that of Josephus in the first century CE, according to whom the whole law has as its aim the moral formation of the Jewish community.[111] For Maimonides, the Torah is not natural as such, but it is always related to natural ends.[112] It is fundamental to his treatment of it as divinely given that "no intelligent person can assume that any of the actions of God can be in vain, purposeless, or unimportant."[113]

On the basis of this theological principle, Maimonides concludes that there must be a reason for every command of the Torah, even if, in a few cases, it is not clear to us at the moment. This reason relates primarily not to the universal moral law of nature, but to God's will for the human flourishing of his people. "The general object of the Law is twofold: the well-being of the soul, and the well-being of the body"—the former requiring right thinking (knowledge), the latter right acting (ethics and politics).[114] In the *Guide*, Maimonides is confident that he can relate (almost) every precept of Torah to this twofold aim, and he relies in doing so on his presumed knowledge of the ancient paganism (the religion of the Sabeans) by which Israel found itself surrounded:

> I say that my knowledge of the belief, practice, and worship of the Sabeans has given me an insight into many of the divine precepts, and has led me to know their reason.[115]

Even apparently obscure commandments—against marring the corners of the beard or wearing garments of mixed linen and wool—can be explained as ways in which God sought to protect his people, by ensuring their utter distinctness from the nations around them, from lapsing into idolatry, whose abolition was "the principal purpose of the whole law."[116]

Why should Maimonides' treatment of Torah have been so appealing from such an early stage to Christian theologians, with whose general approach to the Law he would hardly have been in sympathy? What he offered them was a way of construing the Law as rational—against the characterization of it as intrinsically irrational stemming from Origen—but without threatening to collapse it into the natural and universal law of reason, which could ultimately undermine the whole edifice of traditional Christian doctrine, as the discussion of Abelard suggested. Furthermore, in the hands of Christian thinkers, Maimonides' detailed justification of individual commands in terms of the need to separate Israel from ancient "Sabean" paganism and its associated practices could actually support the covenant judgment about the displacement of Torah: it once had a valuable, providential function but is now for the most part obsolete as a set of practical injunctions. Christian theologians took the historically conditioned rationality that Maimonides attributed to the Law and found in it confirmation of the Law's historical relativity and hence, in the time of the Church, redundancy.

Aquinas on the Law, History and Perfection

As Smalley has demonstrated, the reception of Maimonides' work into Christian theology in the thirteenth century was not a straightforward affair, but it was already well-advanced when we come to consider Aquinas.[117] In his great treatise on law at *Summa theologiae* I-II.90-109, we find a complex interweaving of all the major strands of thought about the Law considered so far in this section.[118] Aquinas accepts that natural law is a crucial concept for Christian theology, but one that needs to be related to divine law. He argues for a clear rationality in the Law of the Old Testament, even in its most apparently obscure parts, which can be explicated along the lines indicated by Maimonides, as conditioned by a historical need for moral formation and the avoidance of idolatry. Yet Aquinas will use Maimonides' work in a way quite contrary to Maimonides' own intention to underscore the limitation of the Mosaic Law in history, and therefore to reinforce the relevance to this topic of the third strand referred to from the Christian Fathers. For Aquinas the overriding argument is that the Law belonged to a providential phase in divine revelation, but an imperfect and passing one, pointing to the perfect and eternal which has now come. In this way Aquinas will preserve the basic thrust of Origen on the Law—that it always pointed and still points today to Christ—without sharing his attribution of irrationality to it or (by implication) its divine author.

Having defined the nature and purpose of law in question 90, in question 91 Aquinas turns his attention to the different kinds of law, carefully distinguishing the eternal, natural, human and divine. In article 4, in the light of the comprehensive roles of natural and human law that he has set out, he addresses directly the question that Abelard's dialogue appeared to raise and that Saadia Gaon confronted: "Whether any divine law was necessary." Aquinas, unlike Abelard's Christian, presents a clear and full answer about the newness that has been given through divine revelation and its relationship to the constant features of the human condition. First, he argues, it is necessary because human beings are ordered towards an end—eternal blessedness—that exceeds "the measure of their natural faculty," and this is something that a law based on human nature as it appears to human creatures cannot take into account. This line of argument is clearly rooted in Aquinas' dynamic theological anthropology and provides perhaps the strongest argument for his position. Still, he adds three more arguments to strengthen his case as to why natural and human law alone would not be adequate for us: the inherent uncertainty of human knowledge leaves us unsure about what to do and what not to do; growth in virtue requires precise judgment about interior affections and motivations as well as external actions; human law has to leave many areas of wrongdoing without prohibitions and punishments, since it serves as a practical framework for social and political existence.

Having established the need for divine law alongside the existence of natural law in article 4 of question 91, in article 5 Aquinas poses the question "Whether the divine law is only one." He rightly senses an important dilemma again here: if the law is one, then the newness of the Christian dispensation seems undermined, but if there are two wholly separate laws, then the door is potentially opened to some kind of dualism.[119] To resolve the dilemma, Aquinas appeals, as he does frequently elsewhere in this section, to Gal. 3:23-26, one of the Pauline passages where the Law is clearly assigned a role that is both providential and limited. It is a text that forms the definitive locus for a linkage between a Christian account of the Mosaic Law and the more general teaching about progressive revelation developed by early Christianity:

> Now before faith came, we were imprisoned and guarded under the law
> until faith would be revealed. Therefore the law was our disciplinarian

[*paidagogos*] until Christ came, so that we might be justified by faith. But now that faith has come, we are no longer subject to a disciplinarian, for in Christ Jesus you are all children of God through faith.

Aquinas explains that there is only one divine law, but it appears in two forms: one imperfect, corresponding to the child under the disciplinarian, and the other perfect, for the adult who no longer needs him. In what way, then, is the new law more perfect than the old? Aquinas' first answer goes back to Augustine and also appears in Abelard: the new law relates to "intelligible and heavenly good," the old law to "perceptible and earthly good." His second relates to one of his reasons for needing a divine law: the new law orders interior acts, not just external actions. His third also draws on Augustine: the motivation for obedience to the old law was primarily fear of punishment, but in the new law it is "the love which is poured out in our hearts through the grace of Christ, which is bestowed in the new law, but was only prefigured in the old law."

It is worth noting some of the tensions that still persist in Aquinas' very careful and coherent account at this point. The reasons given in article 5 as to why the new version of the divine law is more perfect than the old leave a question as to whether the old law really is divine law at all, in the light of Aquinas' own response to article 4. In article 5, he insists, with Abelard and Augustine, that the old law points only to inner-worldly good; but in article 4, his first and theologically strongest argument for the need for divine law is that it orients humanity towards the transcendent end of eternal blessedness. If the old law does not do this, in what sense is it divine law at all? Similarly, in article 5, it is only the new law that attends to interior acts; but in article 4, the regulation of interior life was one of the purposes of divine rather than human law.

The question raised here is approached most directly in question 98, article 2, "Whether the old law was from God." The first two objections directly recall the arguments mentioned in connection with Saadia's discussion of the abrogation of the law: God's work cannot be imperfect, and God's work cannot be temporary or provisional. In his response, Aquinas draws again on Gal. 3:23-26, but he also makes clear the fundamentally trinitarian pattern of his own theology. The proof for Aquinas that the Law was given by the Father is that it leads to Christ, the Son, and it does so, according to him, in two ways: first, by bearing witness to Christ, i.e. through its spiritual meaning, as Justin and then still more thoroughly Origen had taught; and secondly, by keeping Israel away from idolatry, in service of the one God until the coming of Christ. It is in connection with this second "way" of ordering humanity towards Christ that Aquinas will use Maimonides, sometimes naming him and sometimes not.[120] Where Aquinas differs from the older Origenist view of the incoherence of the Law is that there is no sense that these are two alternative ways to consider the commandments, or that one (figural meaning) only starts where the other (rational sense) fails. Rather, the Law as a whole is motivated throughout by both factors, whether or not they can be easily identified in every individual example.[121]

Aquinas' approach, then, vindicates the Mosaic Torah as the work of God but only insofar as it leads towards the one cardinal divine act of the incarnation. His theology will not allow any sense in which the Torah is from God independently of its relatedness to the coming of Christ. This applies above all to what Aquinas calls the "ceremonial" precepts, whose primary purpose is to prefigure the incarnate Word.[122] So Torah is divine law first and foremost in that it prepares the way for and points towards the perfect divine law in Christ, rather than in that it contains a limited portion of that law (as the stress on perfect / imperfect language might lead one to infer). The unity of the divine law, like the unity of the Christian canon itself in pre-modern theology, is at root a figural unity—the old law prefigures the new—and not a unity ultimately dependent on common form or content.

Just how starkly Aquinas maintains the Pauline antitheses of letter and spirit, law and grace within his presentation becomes clear in the final questions of the section, when he turns directly to consider the nature of the new law of Christ. In the very first article on the new law, question 106 article 1, "Whether the new law is a written law," Aquinas argues, much more clearly than either Justin Martyr or Peter Abelard had done, that the "new law" is not in the first place a written document as such, i.e. not the New Testament, but "that grace of the Holy Spirit that is given to Christ's faithful." Here Aquinas strikes a strongly Augustinian—and indeed ultimately Pauline—note whereby the contrast is not between one set of precepts and another, one text and another, but between law and grace. The equation here of the new law with grace enables us to understand more clearly the vital point in question 91 article 4 that divine law is needed to orient humanity towards its transcendent end. Yet it puts still further pressure on Aquinas' insistence that there is indeed just one divine law, of which the text of the Mosaic law is one, less perfect version, and the grace of Christ in the heart of the believer another, final, complete and unsurpassable. Are not these two things different in kind?

Aquinas returns to this point with question 107, article 1, "Whether the new law is other than the old law," and uses a distinction for his response; according to its fundamental aim—now defined as "that human beings should be subject to God"—the new law is not other than the old, but insofar as it orders things more effectively, indeed perfectly, to achieve this aim, it is different. While such unity of purpose certainly strengthens Aquinas' case for the oneness of the divine law, it remains the case that as soon as Aquinas tells us *how* the new law brings subjection to God—through grace and the Holy Spirit—what he describes appears to have no direct parallel at all in the old law, except insofar as its provisions function as figures of this. This brings us back to the point we reached in our consideration of the people claim and judgment earlier in the chapter: it was the scripture claim of fulfilment in Christ and the corresponding judgment, the interpretive blindness of those who would not acknowledge the authority of a comprehensive Christological reading, which allowed medieval Christian theologians to maintain the tensions we have been tracing.

Aquinas' synthesis on divine law reflects in a particularly striking way the re-examination of the patristic legacy on Mosaic Torah precipitated in part by renewed contact with Jewish culture in medieval Christendom from the later eleventh century. The twelfth-century responses of Ralph of Flaix on the one hand and Abelard on the other showed the limitations in this context of both the theme of providential contradictoriness in the Old Testament and the theme of universal natural law that were part of that legacy. By focusing instead on the theme of progress towards perfection in divine revelation, Aquinas offered, with Maimonides' unwitting assistance, a more thoroughly "historicized" reading of Torah than any of his predecessors. This was, indeed, a significant development in the way that Christian theology struggled to articulate with coherence the issues bound up with the covenant judgment of displacement of Torah in the classic framework. Nonetheless, the confidence he shared with those predecessors in the figural reading of the entire Old Testament ensured the unquestioned continuation of Mosaic Law as a highly valued presence in the Church's scriptures and the Christian culture interwoven with them.

Questions from the Covenant Claim: What Kind of Eschatological Horizon?

The classic framework placed those who accepted it between the new thing that God had done in the first coming of God's Son in Jesus of Nazareth and the second coming of the same Son at the end of time. The claim that God had made a new covenant in Christ was interpreted in this framework as an assertion that a new era of history had begun with the incarnation of the Word; indeed, time itself was reckoned from this pivotal event. Was this present time, however, the last era of history? Could there be another new stage in the covenant history of God and God's people? Should Christians be expecting things to change yet again as part of the ultimate fulfilment of God's purposes in time? If the covenant judgment tended to prompt questions about how to interpret the Church's present in relation to the past history of ancient Israel, the covenant claim could generate questioning about how to understand the present in relation to the coming future, and this is the subject for the final section of the chapter. As we saw in the case of Gilbert Crispin, medieval Christians were inclined to place themselves towards the end of a curve of steady decline in spiritual and moral terms stretching from the first glorious centuries of the Church to the last days. This was not, however, universally the case. Expectations of a future horizon of renewal in God's dealings with God's people between the new covenant in Christ and his coming in glory as judge of the world proved surprisingly resilient in the Western Middle Ages, given how prone they were to attract suspicion if not outright hostility from the institutional Church. Here again we find evidence for the three-dimensional process that we have traced in the previous sections: in this period, the encounter with Judaism, as real presence and imagined other, is inextricably bound up with the "internal" debate in Christian theology about eschatological horizons.

Joachim of Fiore and the Revival of Millenarianism

That debate about whether decisive, God-inspired change is to be expected in the future earthly time of Christ's Church briefly surfaces in the text that we have just been discussing, Aquinas' treatment of law in *Summa theologiae* I-II. Question 106, article 4, asks: "Whether the new law is to last until the end of the world." At one level, the question is the outcome of the internal logic of Aquinas' treatment of law. If new law succeeds old as more perfect (remembering Aquinas' reliance on Gal. 3:23-26), how can one be certain that there is not a still more perfect version of divine law still to come? If much of the Mosaic Law (following Maimonides) is explicable in terms of a contextualizing, historical rationality, is it possible that the new law also relates to particular historical circumstances that are not, of necessity, immutable? Certainly, the virtual equation of the new law with grace, and not with specific prescriptions, might be motivated at one level by Aquinas' awareness of the need to render such questions less compelling, through presenting the new law as fundamentally different in kind from the old—and therefore intrinsically immune to any subsequent historical perfection. The question at q. 106 art. 4 was also, though, precipitated by external factors: the teaching of Joachim of Fiore from the end of the twelfth century, and the subsequent spread of his writings and dissemination of his ideas, which would have perhaps their greatest impact among the movement of Franciscan "Spirituals" after Thomas's death.[123] Indeed, the specific objections presented at the start of the article clearly relate at least to popularized versions of Joachite views, if not to the writings of Joachim himself.[124]

Joachim of Fiore stood within a long tradition of millenarian thinking in Christianity, a tradition that has always tended to exist on the boundaries of authorized, orthodox thinking. Christian millenarianism finds its point of departure in the reign of the saints on earth for a thousand years prophesied in Revelation chapter 20, which was evidently interpreted as a future stage within earthly history by much of second-century Christianity. The final pages of Irenaeus' great work *Adversus haereses*, a milestone in the development of early Christian theology, are missing from most manuscript copies and the first printed editions. In these pages, Irenaeus fully shares the premise of the medieval Jewish writers discussed in this chapter that not all of the prophecies of the Bible about the messianic age have been fulfilled, yet without abandoning the scripture claim of fulfilment in Christ. According to Irenaeus, there will still need to be a final chapter of earthly history in which there is a consummation of prophetic fulfilment, after the division of history is over, in a divine reign of unmitigated blessing for Christ's followers.

> For God is rich in all things, and all things are His. It is fitting, therefore, that the creation itself, being restored to its primeval condition, should without restraint be under the dominion of the righteous. [125]

Here Irenaeus cites Rom. 8:19-21. In the following chapters, he offers a detailed exegesis of various prophetic texts and rejects the idea—evidently to be found already in much Christian teaching of the time—that such texts have a purely spiritual meaning. Jerusalem itself will be "rebuilt after the pattern of the Jerusalem above," in fulfilment of all the prophecies of her restoration, a belief also shared by Justin Martyr and those Justin described as "right-minded Christians."[126] The writer of Revelation had deployed the language of the book of the prophet Isaiah about a new heaven and a new earth, and Irenaeus turns to this in summarizing his argument:

> For since there are real men, so must there also be a real establishment (*plantationem*), that they vanish not away among non-existent things, but progress among those things that have an actual existence. . . . But when

> this [present] fashion [of things] passes away, and man has been renewed, and flourishes in an incorruptible state, so as to preclude the possibility of becoming old, [then] there shall be the new heaven and the new earth, in which the new man shall remain [continually], always holding fresh converse with God.[127]

It would be a mistake to consider that millenarian thinking simply disappeared from the Church between the second century and the twelfth, and Joachim of Fiore is only a small part of the story of its widespread impact in the later Middle Ages.[128] Nonetheless, he remains a significant figure in articulating a broadly millenarian viewpoint from within the high culture of Latin Christianity. His theology brings together traditional Christian theological hermeneutics of the letter and the spirit with a trinitarian approach to sacred history, leading to an enduring tension between a twofold and a threefold pattern in his thought. It has been argued that Joachim held clearly to the old and the new covenants as two "dispensations" within history, the new covenant enduring until the end of time; but overlapping with those two dispensations, he also interpreted history in terms of three "*status*" ("states" or "conditions") corresponding to the three persons of the Trinity.[129] In intertwining these two approaches, he transposed the figural technique of reading the Old Testament to render the events of the New Testament also figures of new things to come, and hence opened up the question (whatever his own views on the matter) of whether the revelation given in the incarnation was indeed perfect and complete, or itself a stage in a process still awaiting its final consummation in time through the fuller manifestation of the Holy Spirit. He seems to have expected a transition from the *status* of the Son to the *status* of the Spirit to occur (or begin to occur) in the near future, a transition that would have unspecified implications for the institutional life of the Church. It was, of course, precisely as others began to specify just what those implications might be (an end to priestly power, sacramental practice, ecclesial wealth?) that his ideas moved from the plane of pious speculation to the arena of social and religious upheaval. A technical point in his teaching about the Trinity was formally censured at the Fourth Lateran Council in 1215, but nothing was said about his trinitarian conception of history as such.

At one level, then, Joachim's own theology, understood on its own terms rather than through the lens of subsequent controversy, is hardly relevant to the objections that Thomas Aquinas raises and answers at *Summa theologiae* I-II q. 106 art. 4. Joachim did not expect a new law that would supersede the law of Christ; rather, he anticipated a future fulfilment within history of the work of Christ on earth through a renewed outpouring of the Spirit. Yet Aquinas was right to sense that Joachim represented a theological voice that spoke against his own presentation of history and law. It is surely not accidental that Joachim's biographer recalled (however enigmatically) the focus of his subject's first direct divine revelation as being the "twofold law": while the law was for Joachim himself never more than twofold, still the way he came to read the two together as mutually illuminating of one another, rather than the new and perfect simply shedding a one-directional light on the old and less perfect, generated a third term of historical expectation that led him to reopen the ancient stream of Christian millenarianism.[130] For Aquinas, there could be no such "new thing" between the time of the apostles (who according to his response in the article possessed the grace of the Holy Spirit more abundantly than anyone since) and Christ's return to judge the world and end its story. The progress of revelation reached its perfection at the time of Christ; since then, we are always looking back to the newness that entered history at that point, and forward only to the end of history at the final judgment. Joachim, on the other hand, accepted that the divine purpose for the earth and its trinitarian indwelling had not reached completion in our present condition, and he therefore concluded that we should expect some decisive further movement towards it at a particular point in history. Newness still lay ahead of us in history, and not only beyond its limit. It was not so much a matter for him of replacing the new law of the Spirit, as of that law finding its ultimate consummation in a "real establishment" among "real men," to recall Irenaeus, prior to the termination of this creation's time.

Christian Hope and Jewish Presence

What is particularly interesting from the point of view of this study is the association made by many Christian voices between millenarian speculation within Christianity and the outside other of "unbelieving" Judaism. Already in the third century, Origen regarded Christian believers in a coming earthly reign of Christ, such as Irenaeus, as understanding scripture "in a Jewish sense"; in the fourth, Jerome associates the same tradition of thinking with "Jewish error."[131] Over a thousand years later, the Augsburg Confession refers to such tendencies among Christians as "Jewish opinions," and the Confessio Helvetica Posterior calls them "Jewish dreams."[132] It may or may not have been any more than a polemical extension of this linkage when one of Joachim's contemporary opponents accused him of being a Jew who had failed to leave behind his

Judaism: "The person came from Jews, from Judaism, which he does not yet appear to have really vomited out."[133]

The connections between Christian millenarianism and continuing Judaism are more than merely polemical or autobiographical. As already noted, millenarians accepted, like Jews, that there was a distinctive "surplus" to scriptural prophecy awaiting fulfilment in terms of dramatic changes that would have visible, political implications in future history. Moreover, the period 1050-1300 saw a flourishing of intra-Jewish debates about the Messiah and periodic messianic movements within Judaism itself,[134] while the second half of the Middle Ages also witnessed all manner of apocalyptic speculation, learned and popular, in Western Christendom. It is entirely plausible that eschatological expectations on both sides were shaped by and responded to each other in a subtle but also dangerous rhythm of interplay, with escalating fears and frustrations on the Christian side contributing to the deeper and darker hostility that many scholars have identified towards Jews in the later Middle Ages.[135] There are also intriguing parallels between specifically Joachite speculation and some strands of Jewish messianic thought in the Middle Ages, although no evidence of any direct mutual influence.[136] Millenarian speculation was only one expression of a wider current with alarming potential to act as a catalyst in the rupturing of the present order. Yet while all pre-modern Christian eschatology had to find some kind of place for the Jews in the final achievement of God's purposes, some millenarians, from Justin and Irenaeus onwards, tended to give them a vital and active role in this regard, and moreover one that could be linked geographically to the Holy Land itself. The castigation of such ideas as "Jewish opinions," therefore, amounts to more than the usual name calling of theological polemics.

Learned Christians in the Middle Ages could not help but be aware of Paul's words in Romans 11 that "a hardening has come upon part of Israel, until the full number of the Gentiles has come in. And so all Israel will be saved" (Rom. 11:25b-26a). Reading this text alongside other parts of the New Testament, most importantly its final book, Revelation, confirmed the traditional position that continuing Judaism still had a vital part to play in the apocalyptic drama that would have to unfold before the end of this age and the beginning of the age to come. Commentators differed on details, but were agreed that some kind of large-scale and public conversion of Jews to Christian faith would be an integral part of that drama—as Jewish writers were sure that divine vengeance on Christians, or their recognition of the truth of Judaism, or indeed something of both, would come with the advent of the Messiah.

Many Christian writers in the Middle Ages anticipated a diabolical collusion of Jews with the Anti-Christ in the last days, reinforcing the belief in an intimate connection between Judaism in the here and now and the ever-present activity of the Devil that can be traced back at least as far as John Chrysostom. Yet this was not the only view. Honorius Augustodunensis, for instance, sketched out a rather different vision in the twelfth century, in which the converted Synagoga will take a leading role in combating and defeating the work of the Anti-Christ and bringing about the mass conversion of the un-baptized Gentiles.[137] Aelred of Rievaulx looked forward to the mutual embrace of Jews and Gentiles within the life of the Church in the last days, remarkably finding a figure of this in Luke's account of Jesus' visit to the temple at the age of 12 and identifying Mary as a type of the Jews who will finally receive Christ again.[138] For these writers, we might say, the coming renewal of the Church would be achieved through the acceptance of the Jews into the one (Christian) people of God, thereby bringing an end to the division of history between Christian Church and Jewish Israel, the people judgment of the classic framework.

The specific question for millenarian Christian thinkers was whether the conversion of the Jews would take place only at the end of the millennial reign of the saints and immediately prior to the final judgment, or whether it would precede and indeed inaugurate that reign. Joachim was clear that the second of these views was the correct one: at the end of the sixth age (the seventh being the millennium prophesied in Revelation), "there is a union of the Gentile and the Hebrew people, and there will be one fold and one shepherd."[139] Given his anticipation that this point was now close at hand, it is not surprising that he wanted to prepare both the Jews themselves and his fellow Christians for their imminent reconciliation in Christ, prompting the writing of his *Exhortatorium Judeorum*.[140] Moreover, those subsequently showing the influence of his thought made explicit the conclusion that the appropriate geographical focus for this renewal of the people of God would be Jerusalem and the Holy Land; Bonaventure, who supervised the suppression of Joachim's most ardent disciples in the Franciscan Order, nonetheless looked forward to a (further) fulfilment of Isa. 2:3, traditionally deemed accomplished in the work of the Church, in "a rebuilding of divine worship and a restoration of the city."[141] For Joachim and those who continued his approach, reference to the Jews in understanding history yet to come was not only required because Jewish unbelief was an outstanding "problem" requiring some kind of final resolution. The new things that still lay ahead in the purposes of God required the acceptance by old Israel of Christ—

not just for the sake of Israel, but for the sake of the (now imperfect) Church.

By contrast, the present for Thomas Aquinas, as indeed for Gilbert Crispin in his reply to the question about the non-fulfilment of prophecy, was viewed as a late point in the slow ebbing-away of the Church from the high-water mark of primitive Christianity, with the terrible tribulations of the book of Revelation standing somewhere between that passing position and the return of Christ in majesty to judge the world. In this context, the enduring suffering of "old" Israel was deemed to constitute an important if reluctant witness to the newness of an ever-aging Church. Aquinas' own writings elsewhere crystallize two important developments in Christian understanding of Judaism that become increasingly influential in the later Middle Ages: Jews being treated as falling somewhere between heresy and infidelity, and therefore potentially within the scope of the Church's own disciplinary apparatus as well as within a general taxonomy of its enemies; and the Jewish elders who demanded the crucifixion of Jesus doing so in full awareness that he was the promised Messiah and therefore not being excused by ignorance in putting to death the Son of God.[142] Aquinas' use of Maimonides' analysis of Torah also, however, undermined still further the rationale for the Augustinian injunction "Slay them not"—that continuing Judaism taught the world the literal meaning of the revelation whose spiritual sense was now made manifest in Christ. As Cohen summarizes it,

> For Augustine, the Jew served that instructive purpose because he continued to observe and to embody the literal sense of the Old Testament; thus could Bernard of Clairvaux dub the Jews "living letters of the law." For Aquinas, however, Jewish observance of the Mosaic commandments now amounts to nothing less than a repudiation of their literal sense, which limited their appropriateness to a particular period in the past.[143]

With that crucial shift in perspective, the apparent antiquity of Judaism was diagnosed as a feeble cover for wilful disobedience in the present, a judgment supported by Pope Gregory IX's denunciation of the Talmud as "another law" from the original Mosaic Torah.[144] In the course of the thirteenth century, Christians had become much more widely aware of the post-biblical literature—Mishnah, Talmud and Midrash—that informed the living culture of contemporary Judaism, as a result of which it was no longer so easy for them to regard it as a kind of living fossil from the pre-Christian era of the Old Testament.[145] The theological shift here left the door open to a change in practical policy, from the protection of deliberately marginalized Jewish groups that had broadly characterized

Western Christendom until the thirteenth century to attempts to remove Jewish populations in their entirety from Christian lands. This change, while never universally agreed, let alone achieved, culminated in the expulsions from Spain—the area with the largest and best established communities—of Jews along with Muslims refusing to convert to Christianity in 1492. The theological attempt to bring reason to bear on the defence of the incarnation on the one hand and on the other on the place of the Books of Moses in Christian understanding came close to locking Judaism into a completed phase of history irrelevant to the Christian, spiritual present, and leaving living Jews with no position in Christian thought or polity except as one group among many of the Church's enemies, the disobedient and faithless.

Yet this could never quite be the whole story about Israel according to the flesh for pre-modern Christianity. There remained an inextricable bond between Jewish presence and Christian hope because of the hermeneutic of history that had been generated from the accepted reading of scripture. Whichever view commentators took about the interpretation of Revelation, it remained the case that God had not finished with the Jewish people yet—and that their salvation was ultimately a pre-condition for the liberation of all creation from its bondage, and indeed would create some kind of new "stage" (however momentary) in the course of the Church through history. Millenarians such as Joachim of Fiore might remain marginal figures in expecting decisive spiritual transformation before the final judgment, but Aquinas and the rest of the orthodox mainstream also accepted that there were biblical prophecies yet to be fulfilled in the time of earthly history, and that these prophecies pertained in part to the endurance of the Jewish people, whose destiny still remained within the purposes of God and the scriptural story of promise and fulfilment. This was certainly not the least important way in which the scripture claim from the classic framework and its detailed explication in the hermeneutical tradition of pre-modern Christianity helped to preserve a continuing place, however marginal, for Jewish people within both Christian theological discourse and avowedly Christian societies throughout the vicissitudes of the Western Middle Ages and the shifts and questions we have identified in relation to other elements of that framework. The interpretation of scripture was assumed to require a role for the Jews in future history as prophesied and providentially guided by God—a history which could not be wholly detached either from the past history recounted in canonical scripture (including the giving of the Law at Sinai), or from the present if problematic reality of Jewish communities within Western Christendom.

Notes

[1] So for instance Ruether, *Faith and Fratricide*; Soulen, *God of Israel*, e.g. 57. Cf. the comments of Cohen, *Living Letters*, 5.

[2] Thus Baron asserted that, from the fifth century on, "all Judeo-Christian debates were mere variations on old themes" (Salo Wittmeyer Baron, *A Social and Religious History of the Jews*, 2nd ed. [New York: Columbia University Press, 1957], 5:110). On the Western medieval literature generally, see the comprehensive survey of Bernhard Blumenkranz, *Les auteurs chrétiens latins du moyen age sur les Juifs et le judaïsme* (Paris: Mouton, 1963), and the more recent brief monograph of Gilbert Dahan, *The Christian Polemic against the Jews in the Middle Ages*, trans. Jody Gladding (Notre Dame: University of Notre Dame, 1998).

[3] See for instance the classic works of Charles Homer Haskins, *The Renaissance of the Twelfth Century* (Cambridge: Harvard University Press, 1927) and Marie-Dominique Chenu, *La théologie au douzième siècle* (Paris: J. Vrin, 1957), and also the papers collected in Robert L. Benson and Giles Constable, eds., *Renaissance and Renewal in the Twelfth Century* (Cambridge: Harvard University Press, 1982).

[4] E.g. R. I. Moore, *The Formation of a Persecuting Society: Power and Deviance in Western Europe, 950-1250* (Oxford: Blackwell, 1987); Robert Chazan, *European Jewry and the First Crusade* (Berkeley: University of California Press, 1987); Gavin I. Langmuir, *History, Religion, and Antisemitism* (Berkeley: University of California Press, 1990); Anna Sapir Abulafia, *Christians and Jews in the Twelfth-century Renaissance* (London: Routledge, 1995). See also the review article by Anna Sapir Abulafia, "From Northern Europe to Southern Europe and from the General to the Particular: Recent Research on Jewish-Christian Coexistence in Medieval Europe," *Journal of Medieval History* 23:2 (1997): 179-90.

[5] Cyprian of Carthage, *Three Books of Testimonies against the Jews*, Ante-Nicene Christian Library, vol. 12, part 2 (Edinburgh: T & T Clark, 1869).

[6] See Cyprian's comments in the introduction to the *Testimonies*, 78-79; compare the opening of Book III (130).

[7] Cyprian, *Testimonies*, 85.

[8] Flavius Josephus, *Against Apion*, trans. H. St. J. Thackery, Loeb Classical Library, vol. 186 (Cambridge: Harvard University Press, 1926), II.125-134. Tertullian also appeals to the exile of the Jews as showing God has "transferred" his grace to a new people; see his *Apology*, trans. T. R. Glover, Loeb Classical Library, vol. 250 (Cambridge: Harvard University Press, 1931), XXI.4-6.

[9] Cyprian, *Testimonies*, 91-92.

[10] Timothy D. Barnes, *Constantine and Eusebius* (Cambridge: Harvard University Press, 1981), 249; cf. also R. A. Markus, *Saeculum: History and Society in the Theology of St Augustine* (Cambridge: Cambridge University Press, 1970), 47-50.

[11] Markus, *Saeculum*, 27-30.

¹² For a review of Julian's policy toward the Jews, see Simon, *Verus Israel*, 111-115.

¹³ Robert L. Wilken, *The Land Called Holy: Palestine in Christian History and Thought* (New Haven: Yale University Press, 1992), 65-101.

¹⁴ John Chrysostom, Discourse V, in *Discourses against Judaizing Christians*, trans. Paul W. Harkins, Fathers of the Church, vol. 68 (Washington DC: Catholic University of America, 1979), 97-145.

¹⁵ John Chrysostom, Discourse V.I.7, *Discourses*, 100.

¹⁶ John Chrysostom, Discourse V.XI.9, *Discourses*,139-40.

¹⁷ Cassiodorus, *Historia tripartita* VI.XLIII (PL 69:1059; my translation).

¹⁸ Tertullian, *Apology* XXV-XXVI.

¹⁹ Markus, *Saeculum*.

²⁰ E.g. Augustine of Hippo, *The City of God against the Pagans*, ed. and trans. R. W. Dyson (Cambridge: Cambridge University Press, 1998) XV.2 (on Jerusalem as symbol of both heavenly and earthly cities), XVI.35 (the pattern of the two sons in the patriarchal narratives), XVIII.49 (Judas among the twelve, wicked and good within the Church).

²¹ Cf. Serge Lancel, *St Augustine*, trans. Antonia Nevill (London: SCM, 2002), 391-412.

²² See e.g. Markus's analysis of Otto of Freising's twelfth-century account of Augustine's two cities, in *Saeculum*, 164-65.

²³ Augustine, *City of God* XVI.37.

²⁴ Cf. Augustine, *City of God* XVI.42 and XVII.7.

²⁵ For an overview and analysis of the relevant textual material, see Cohen, *Living Letters*, 24-41.

²⁶ Augustine, *City of God* XVIII.46-47; cf. Markus, *Saeculum*, 52-53.

²⁷ Cohen, *Living Letters*, 32-33, citing Augustine, *City of God*, XVIII.46.

²⁸ Solomon Grayzel, "The Papal Bull *Sicut Judeis*," in *Essential Papers*, ed. Cohen, 231-259; cf. Dahan, *Christian Polemic*, 14-16.

²⁹ Jeremy Cohen, in *The Friars and the Jews: The Evolution of Medieval Anti-Judaism* (Ithaca: Cornell University Press, 1982), argued for a significant tension "between two different ideological tendencies [regarding Judaism], that of Augustine and that of the friars" (244), with the latter providing theological justification for the growth of practical anti-Judaism in the later Middle Ages; but note the reservations about this thesis expressed by Robert Chazan, *Daggers of Faith: Thirteenth-century Christian Missionizing and Jewish Response* (Berkeley: University of California Press, 1989), 170-81. For the application of Cohen's ideas to the sixteenth century, see John Edwards, *The Jews in Christian Europe, 1400-1700* (London: Routledge, 1991), 58-74.

³⁰ Cf. Markus, *Saeculum*, 161-63, and *The End of Ancient Christianity* (Cambridge: Cambridge University Press, 1990); Cohen, *Living Letters*, 67-71.

³¹ Julian of Toledo, *De comprobatione aetatis sextae* I.18 (PL 96:551-52; my translation). The reference to Psalm 72 comes earlier, at I.14 (PL 96:549-50).

³² Cohen, *Living Letters*, 78.

[33] Cf. Isaac Troki, *Faith Strengthened*, trans. Moses Mocatta (New York: Ktav, 1970) I.III-V (17-22), where the success of Islam is repeatedly deployed in refuting Christian anti-Jewish arguments.

[34] Baron, *Social and Religious History*, 5:99.

[35] "Epistle to Yemen," in *Epistles of Maimonides: Crisis and Leadership*, trans. Abraham Halkin (Philadelphia: Jewish Publication Society, 1993), 98-99.

[36] Nahmanides, *Vikuah*, in *Judaism on Trial: Jewish-Christian Disputations in the Middle Ages*, ed. Hyam Maccoby (London: Littman Library Of Jewish Civilization, 1993), 120-122.

[37] Judah Halevi, *The Kuzari: An Argument for the Faith of Israel*, trans. Hartwig Hirschfeld (New York: Schocken, 1964), 106-11; on Bodo-Eleazar, see Bernhard Blumenkranz, "The Roman Church and the Jews," reprinted in *Essential Papers*, ed. Cohen, 223-24.

[38] Cf. Beryl Smalley, *The Study of the Bible in the Middle Ages*, 3rd ed. (Oxford: Blackwell, 1983), xi, and, on contemporary Jewish responses to this development, Robert Chazan, "May-June 1096," in *Yale Companion to Jewish Writing and Thought in German Culture, 1096-1996*, ed. Sander L. Gilman and Jack Zipes (New Haven: Yale University Press, 1997), 1-7.

[39] E.g. Petrus Alfonsi, *Dialogi* II, PL 157:567-581; Peter Abelard, *Dialogue of a Philosopher with a Jew, and a Christian*, trans. Pierre J. Payer (Toronto: Pontifical Institute for Mediaeval Studies, 1979), 38-39.

[40] "Non auferetur sceptrum de Iuda, et dux de femore eius, donec veniat qui mittendus est, et ipse erit expectatio gentium."

[41] Justin, *First Apology* XXXII (173).

[42] Cf. Blumenkranz, "Roman Church," 222-23.

[43] Blumenkranz, *Auteurs chrétiens*, 184-186.

[44] Fulbert of Chartres, *Tractatus contra Iudaeos*, PL 141:305-18.

[45] Cf. Blumenkranz, *Auteurs chrétiens*, 192-93, 211.

[46] Heinz Schreckenberg, *The Jews in Christian Art: An Illustrated History*, trans. J. Bowden (New York: Continuum, 1996), chapter III, "Ecclesia versus Synagoga. The Dispute between the Two Allegorical Personifications and their Reconciliation," 31-74.

[47] Although Ephraim Radner, in *The End of the Church: A Pneumatology of Christian Division in the West* (Grand Rapids: Eerdmans, 1998), 42-43, argues that some images indicate the Church's sharing in the woundedness of Christ, the implicit ecclesiology of most examples is strikingly triumphalist.

[48] E.g. Schreckenberg, *Jews in Christian Art*, 42, 51, 56.

[49] For an example of Christ himself blessing Ecclesia and pushing away Synagoga, see Schreckenberg, *Jews in Christian Art*, 35; on the 'Living Cross,' 64-66 and plates 5 and 6.

[50] E.g. Schreckenberg, *Jews in Christian Art*, 42, 53 and 61.

[51] In at least one example from the early fifteenth century, Synagoga is depicted as wearing the Jewish ring on her clothing that became common in the later Middle Ages, making explicit her identification with contemporary Jews (Schreckenberg, *Jews in Christian Art*, 60).

---

[52] Klein, *Anti-Judaism*, 92-126, citing e.g. Georg Fohrer, Michael Schmaus, Walther Zimmerli and Pierre Benoit.

[53] Gilbert Crispin, *Disputatio Iudei et Christiani*, in *The Works of Gilbert Crispin, Abbot of Westminster*, ed. Anna Sapir Abulafia and G. R. Evans (London: British Academy, 1986). On the context for Gilbert's work, see the editors' Introduction, xxi-xxx.

[54] Joseph Kimhi, *The Book of the Covenant*, trans. Frank Talmage (Toronto: Pontifical Institute of Mediaeval Studies, 1972), 30-31.

[55] Gilbert Crispin, *Disputatio Iudei et Christiani* 42-45 (17).

[56] Gilbert Crispin, *Disputatio Iudei et Christiani* 59-61 (21-22). This line of argument is unlikely to have impressed a medieval Jew; Christian asceticism is regarded in an unfavourable light as abandoning responsibilities to the neighbour and certainly not excusing the failure of the "Christian" majority to follow Christ's teaching e.g. in Kimhi, *Book of the Covenant*, 35 (and see also the further references given in note 21 ad loc.).

[57] Gilbert Crispin, *Disputatio Iudei et Christiani* 66-70 (23-24).

[58] Gilbert Crispin, *Disputatio Iudei et Christiani* 90 (30).

[59] Gilbert Crispin, *Disputatio Iudei et Christiani* 93-103 (31-35).

[60] Cf. Daniel J. Lasker, *Jewish Philosophical Polemics against Christianity in the Middle Ages* (New York: Ktav, 1977), 25-43; Abulafia, *Christians and Jews*.

[61] Baron, *Social and Religious History*, 5:83.

[62] On Saadia's treatment of Christianity, see Hans Joachim Schoeps, *The Jewish-Christian Argument: A History of Theologies in Conflict*, trans. David E. Green (London: Faber, 1965), 58-63; for a more detailed analysis of his philosophical and apologetic writing, see Colette Sirat, *A History of Jewish Philosophy in the Middle Ages* (Cambridge: Cambridge University Press, 1985), 18-36. The most important primary text is Saadia Gaon, *The Book of Beliefs and Opinions*, trans. Samuel Rosenblatt (New Haven: Yale University Press, 1948).

[63] Judah Halevi, *Kuzari*, 42.

[64] Lasker, *Jewish Philosophical Polemics*.

[65] For some examples, see Kimhi, *Book of the Covenant*, 38-39; Lasker, *Jewish Philosophical Polemics*, 48 and 121.

[66] Lasker, *Jewish Philosophical Polemics*, 135-59; Dahan, *Christian Polemic*, 97-104.

[67] See, for instance, R. W. Southern, *Saint Anselm: A Portrait in a Landscape* (Cambridge: Cambridge University Press, 1990), 197-202; Abulafia, *Christians and Jews*, 42-46; F. B. A. Asiedu, "Anselm and the Unbelievers: Pagans, Jews, and Christians in the *Cur deus homo*," *Theological Studies* 62.3 (September 2001): 530-548.

[68] Kimhi, *Book of the Covenant*, 36.

[69] Anselm of Canterbury, *Cur deus homo*, ed. F. S. Schmitt (Bonn: Hanstein, 1929), II.XXII (65.26-29); I am following the slightly amended translation of Abulafia given in *Christians and Jews*, 43.

[70] Odo of Tournai, *A Disputation with the Jew, Leo*, in *On Original Sin and A Disputation with the Jew, Leo, concerning the Advent of the Son of God: Two*

Theological Treatises, trans. Irven M. Resnick (Philadelphia: University of Philadelphia Press, 1994). There is also a suggestion of Anselmian influence in Guibert of Nogent, *Tractatus de incarnatione contra Judaeos*, PL 156:489-528; see especially III.III (509), and the comments of Dahan, *Christian Polemic*, 74-75.

[71] Odo of Tournai, *Disputation with Leo*, 85.

[72] Odo of Tournai, *Disputation with Leo*, 85.

[73] Odo of Tournai, *Disputation with Leo*, 86.

[74] Nahmanides, *Vikuah*, 118.

[75] Kimhi, *Book of the Covenant*, 35-36.

[76] Profiat Duran, "Be Not Like unto Thy Fathers," in *Disputation and Dialogue: Readings in the Jewish-Christian Encounter*, ed. Frank Ephraim Talmage (New York: Ktav, 1975), 120.

[77] Herbert of Bosham, *Vita sancti Thomae, archiepiscopi et martyris*, in *Materials for the History of Thomas Becket, Archbishop of Canterbury*, vol. 3, ed. James Craigie Robertson (London: Longman, 1877), 212-215.

[78] Smalley, *Study of the Bible*, 192. On Herbert as a Hebraist, see also Jeremy Cohen, "Scholarship and Intolerance in the Medieval Academy: The Study and Evaluation of Judaism in European Christendom," in *Essential Papers*, ed. Cohen, 319-321.

[79] Petrus Alfonsi, *Dialogi*, PL 157:618, as cited in Cohen, *Living Letters*, 208.

[80] The close relationship between the narrative shape of pre-modern theology and the practice of typological exegesis is stressed by Hans W. Frei, *The Eclipse of Biblical Narrative: A Study in Eighteenth and Nineteenth Century Hermeneutics* (New Haven: Yale University Press, 1974); see especially chapter 2, "Precritical Interpretation of Biblical Narrative," 17-50.

[81] Beryl Smalley, "Ralph of Flaix on Leviticus," *Studies in Medieval Thought and Learning: From Abelard to Wyclif* (London: Hambledon, 1981), 49-96; see especially 66-67.

[82] Robert Grosseteste, *De cessatione legalium*, ed. Richard C. Dales and Edward B. King, (London: British Academy, 1986), I.1.

[83] Evagrius, *Altercatio inter Theophilum Christianum et Simonem Judaeum*, PL 20:1165-82, e.g. 1172-74 (circumcision) and 1179-80 (Sabbath and dietary laws).

[84] Peter Damian, *Dialogus inter Judaeum requirentem, et Christianum e contrario repsondentem*, PL 145:57-68; Gilbert Crispin, *Disputatio Iudei et Christiani* 11-14 (10-11).

[85] Herman-Judah, "A Translation of Herman-Judah's *Short Account of His Own Conversion*," in *Conversion and Text: The Cases of Augustine of Hippo, Herman-Judah, and Constantine Tsatsos*, by Karl F. Morrison (Charlottesville: University Press of Virginia, 1992), 82-85.

[86] Schreckenberg, *Jews in Christian Art*, 53.

[87] Schreckenberg, *Jews in Christian Art*, 63.

[88] *Epistle of Barnabas* 4.6-8, in *The Apostolic Fathers in English*, trans. and ed. Michael W. Holmes, 3rd ed. (Grand Rapids: Baker Academic, 2006), 180.

[89] Schreckenberg, *Jews in Christian Art*, 119-124. Traces of this pattern of association can also be found in images of Ecclesia and Synagoga before the cross;

see for example 33 and in particular the late medieval representations of the "Living Cross," plates 5-6.

[90] Saadia, *Book of Beliefs* III.VII-VIII (157-167).

[91] Saadia, *Book of Beliefs* III.VIII (167).

[92] Gilbert Crispin, *Disputatio Iudei et Christiani* 11-14 (10-11), 32 (15); "Continuation of the *Disputatio Iudei et Christiani*" 22 (59); *Disputatio cum gentili* 11-14 (64-65). Cf. also Guibert of Nogent, *Tractatus contra Judaeos* III.VI, PL 156:518-521.

[93] Beryl Smalley, "William of Auverge, John of La Rochelle and St Thomas Aquinas on the Old Law," in *Studies in Medieval Thought*, 121-81; see especially 122-23. On Origen's influence on medieval exegesis in the West more generally, see Henri de Lubac, *Medieval Exegesis: The Four Senses of Scripture*, trans. Mark Sebanc, 2 vols. (Edinburgh: T & T Clark, 1998-2000), especially vol. 1, 161-224.

[94] Gilbert Crispin, *Disputatio Iudei et Christiani* 15-31 (11-15); Smalley, "Ralph of Flaix."

[95] E.g. Petrus Alfonsi, *Dialogi*, PL 157:540B-C.

[96] Smalley, *Study of the Bible*. On the senses of Scripture in medieval Christian theology, see de Lubac, *Medieval Exegesis*.

[97] See the overview in Malcolm Lambert, *Medieval Heresy: Popular Movements from the Gregorian Reform to the Reformation*, 2nd ed. (Oxford: Blackwell, 1992), 105-46.

[98] Cf. Smalley, "William of Auvergne," 132.

[99] Cf. John Mahoney, *The Making of Moral Theology: A Study of the Roman Catholic Tradition* (Oxford: Oxford University Press, 1987), especially 72-115; Jean Porter, *Natural and Divine Law: Reclaiming the Tradition for Christian Ethics* (Grand Rapids: Eerdmans, 1999).

[100] Abelard, *Dialogue of a Philosopher*. On the background to Abelard's thought, see Peter Dronke, ed., *A History of Twelfth-century Western Philosophy* (Cambridge: Cambridge University Press, 1988). In the ninth century, Walafrid Strabo had sketched a brief comparison regarding motivations for obeying the moral law for philosophers, Jews and Christians (Blumenkranz, *Auteurs chrétiens*, 194).

[101] The "dream" motif makes it clear that Abelard is not claiming that his dialogue relates directly to the contemporary realities of Jewish-Christian discussions, although Dahan mentions a rather peculiar piece of evidence regarding Abelard's engagement in a formal debate (*Christian Polemic*, 23). It may also be noted that Abelard seems to show a greater awareness of the profound constraints within which Jews were increasingly forced to live than other Christian authors (*Dialogue of a Philosopher*, 32-33).

[102] Abelard, *Dialogue of a Philosopher*, 19-23.

[103] Payer notes parallels between the arguments of the Philosopher and other texts by Abelard himself; e.g. Abelard, *Dialogue of a Philosopher*, 35-39.

[104] Abelard, *Dialogue of a Philosopher*, 65-71.

[105] Abelard, *Dialogue of a Philosopher*, 74-75.

[106] Abelard, *Dialogue of a Philosopher*, 36 and 56; cf. *Peter Abelard's Ethics: An Edition with Introduction, English Translation and Notes*, ed. D. E. Luscombe (Oxford: Clarendon, 1971), 18.

[107] E.g. Abelard, *Dialogue of a Philosopher*, 133-135.

[108] Abelard, *Dialogue of a Philosopher*, 120.

[109] Smalley, "William of Auvergne," 135-36; Moses Maimonides, *The Guide for the Perplexed*, trans. M. Friedländer, 2nd ed. (New York: Dover, 1956).

[110] Cf. Daniel H. Frank, Oliver Leaman and Charles H. Manekin, eds., *The Jewish Philosophy Reader* (London: Routledge, 2000), 165-81; Saadai Gaon, *Book of Beliefs and Opinions*, III.I-IV (137-147).

[111] Cf. Josephus, *Against Apion*, II.170-174.

[112] Maimonides, *Guide*, II.XL (233).

[113] Maimonides, *Guide*, III.XXV (307).

[114] Maimonides, *Guide*, III.XXVII (312-315).

[115] Maimonides, *Guide*, III.XXIX (318).

[116] Maimonides, *Guide* III.XXIX (317); cf. III.XXXXVII (335) on the particular commandments mentioned.

[117] Smalley, "William of Auvergne." For a review of different approaches to Aquinas on law in modern theology and philosophy, see Fergus Kerr, *After Aquinas: Versions of Thomism* (Oxford: Blackwell, 2002), 97-113.

[118] Thomas Aquinas, *Summa theologiae*, ed. Petrus Caramellus, 3 vols. (Turin: Marietti, 1948-50); translations are my own.

[119] It is noteworthy that the very first article in the question "Concerning the old law" (I-II.98) is "Whether the old law was good."

[120] E.g. *Summa theologiae* I-II q. 102 "On the reasons for the ceremonial precepts," a. 3 ad 4 & 11; a. 4 ad 2 & 7; a. 6 ad 4; a. 6 ad 1, 5, 6, 8 & 9.

[121] Cf. Aquinas, *Summa theologiae* I-II q. 102 a. 2, response.

[122] Aquinas, *Summa theologiae* I-II q. 102 a. 1 and q. 104 a. 2 (which contrasts them with "judicial" precepts which have only a secondary figural function).

[123] Cf. Lambert, *Medieval Heresy*, 189-214.

[124] Jürgen Moltmann reviews the objections and Aquinas' responses in relation to his own theological viewpoint in "Christian Hope—Messianic or Transcendent? A Theological Conversation with Joachim of Fiore and Thomas Aquinas," in *History and the Triune God: Contributions to Trinitarian Theology*, trans. John Bowden (London: SCM, 1991), 91-109.

[125] Irenaeus of Lyons, *Adversus haereses* V.XXXII, in Ante-Nicene Fathers, vol. 1 (Grand Rapids: Eerdmans, 1985), 560.

[126] Irenaeus, *Adversus haereses* V.XXXV (565-66); cf. Justin, *Dialogue with Trypho* LXXX (239).

[127] Irenaeus, *Adversus haereses* V.XXXVI (566-67).

[128] Cf. Norman Cohn, *The Pursuit of the Millennium: Revolutionary Millenarians and Mystical Anarchists of the Middle Ages* (London: Pimlico, 1993).

[129] Marjorie Reeves, *The Influence of Prophecy in the Later Middle Ages: A Study in Joachimism* (Oxford: Clarendon, 1969); Marjorie Reeves and Beatrice Hirsh-Reich, *The "Figurae" of Joachim of Fiore* (Oxford: Clarendon, 1972).

[130] Robert E. Lerner, *The Feast of St Abraham: Medieval Millenarians and the Jews* (Philadelphia: University of Pennsylvania Press, 2001), 7 and 29-30.

[131] On Origen, see Wilken, *Land Called Holy*, 75-77; for Jerome's comment ("Judaicum . . . errorem"), see his *Commentariorum in Isaiam libri octo et decem*, PL 24:628.

[132] Jürgen Moltmann, *The Coming of God: Christian Eschatology*, trans. Margaret Kohl (London: SCM, 1996), 155.

[133] Geoffrey of Auxerre, cited in Reeves, *Influence of Prophecy*, 14-15. Lerner is inclined to allow the possibility that Joachim may indeed have been Jewish by birth (*Feast of St Abraham*, 24-28).

[134] Baron, *Social and Religious History* 5, chapter XXV; Gershom Scholem, *The Messianic Idea in Judaism and Other Essays on Jewish Spirituality* (New York: Schocken, 1995), 1-48. For Maimonides' involvement in these debates, see especially his "Epistle to Yemen" (text with discussion in *Epistles of Maimonides*, 93-207), and the extracts assembled in Moses Maimonides, *Ethical Writings of Maimonides*, ed. Raymond L. Weiss and Charles Butterworth (New York: Dover, 1983), 165-82.

[135] See Yuval, *Two Nations*, especially 257-95.

[136] Cf. Gershom Scholem, *Major Trends in Jewish Mysticism*, 3rd ed. (New York: Schocken, 1995), 178-79.

[137] Jeremy Cohen, "*Synagoga conversa*: Honorius Augustodunensis, the Song of Songs, and Christianity's 'Eschatological Jew'," *Speculum* 79 (2004): 309-40.

[138] Aelred of Rievaulx, "Jesus at the Age of Twelve," in *Aelred of Rievaulx: Treatises and Pastoral Prayer* (Kalamazoo: Cistercian Publications, 1971). I am indebted to Jennifer Harris for drawing my attention to this reference. One might compare Joachim's reading of the same passage; cf. Lerner, *Feast of St Abraham*, 38.

[139] Quoted in Lerner, *Feast of St Abraham*, 24.

[140] Joachim of Fiore, *Adversus Iudeos*, ed. Arsenio Frugoni (Rome: Istituto Storico Italiano per il Medio Evo, 1957); cf. 3, 76-83, 95-96. On this work (and its title), see Lerner, *Feast of St Abraham*, 33-37.

[141] Lerner, *Feast of St Abraham*, 51.

[142] Cohen, *Living Letters*, 368-75.

[143] Cohen, *Living Letters*, 388.

[144] Cohen, *Living Letters*, 321-25.

[145] Cf. Cohen, *Friars and the Jews*, in particular 51-76, and Chazan, *Daggers of Faith*, 67-85. The earlier work of a Jewish convert to Christianity in the twelfth century, Petrus Alfonsi, was arguably a significant precursor here; see the discussion in John Tolan, *Petrus Alfonsi and His Medieval Readers* (Gainesville: University Press of Florida, 1993), 12-41.

CHAPTER THREE

MODERNITY:
AGAINST FULFILMENT

The previous chapter sought to show how the classic framework for understanding the newness of Christ in relation to the endurance of Israel was at once adapted, questioned and sustained during the Western Middle Ages through the process of interaction between Christian theological thinking, encounters with Judaism and the perpetuation of Christian anti-Judaism. A recurring theme was the contribution of the scripture claim and judgment (fulfilment in Christ / interpretive blindness), secured by the tradition of allegorical interpretation, in preventing any deep rupture between history and grace, flesh and spirit, despite the tensions and questions. Yet one aspect of the remarkable series of changes in Western Christian culture between the 16th and the 18th centuries was the effective abandonment of the traditional formulation of that claim by some influential voices, who instead developed alternative strategies for defending claims about the supremacy of Christ against their perceived critics, including contemporary Jews. Such a move required restatement of the primary subject of Christian theology, the newness of the good news proclaimed about Jesus Christ. The beginnings of such restatement nonetheless remained bound up with accounts of "old" Judaism, as the initial hypothesis proposed at the end of the Introduction suggested. Indeed, while they required revision of the judgments from the classic framework that we have argued perpetuate the intellectual tradition of anti-Judaism in Christianity, they also reinstated them for a changed culture.

How all this comes to be the case is a complex story, bound up with the wider history of biblical interpretation.[1] The intention of the chapter is certainly not to provide an exhaustive study of that history, but rather to highlight its participation in the three-dimensional process we have been examining in the two chapters so far: the interaction between changes within Christian theology, exchanges between Jews and Christians and the persisting Christian conception of Judaism as its original and hostile "other". At the end of the sixteenth century, Isaac Troki, a Karaite scholar familiar with Christian communities associated with the Radical Reformation, provides a case of intra-religious polemic meeting inter-religious polemic. With the great philosopher Baruch Spinoza, a further step is taken as such inter-religious polemic is brought into the service of a sceptical critique of the truth claims of religion as such, including claims about scriptural fulfilment. Philippus van Limborch and Issac Orobio de Castro, a Christian and a Jew who benefited like Spinoza from the relative tolerance of the Dutch Republic in the seventeenth century, agreed on the need to counter Spinoza's anti-theological arguments. They also explored new territory in their literary exchanges as Limborch strove to articulate the claim of the Christian gospel for a Jewish interlocutor without appealing to any of the strategies we discussed in the previous chapter in relation to pre-modernity. In all these cases, the importance of the Protestant Reformation in challenging the accepted relationship between scriptural interpretation and ecclesial tradition is evident.

By the early eighteenth century, the choices for those "moderns" who would abandon the scripture claim in its classic form of fulfilment in Christ are becoming clearer. On the one hand there is the path marked by Spinoza, the path of religious relativism. On the other hand there is the path marked by Limborch's friend, John Locke, the path of historical superiority, in which the scripture claim is re-conceived as the assertion that the New Testament provides evidence for the historical superiority of Jesus and the religion he founded. This signals the replacement for some leading Christian thinkers of newness as prophetic fulfilment by newness as the summit of gradual revelation through history. What had been a subordinate strand in the theological understanding of Christian newness in medieval thinking (though we noted its increased prominence in Aquinas' treatment of the Mosaic Law) now becomes the dominant one. Despite this dismantling of a cardinal part of the classic framework, anti-Judaism nonetheless remained integral to the theological enterprise for those who followed the path of historical superiority. Indeed, Christianity now understood as the decisive culmination of a historical process needed to keep proving that Judaism's place in history was finished. For "modern" theology, that place was finished already with the earliest proclamation of the good news about Jesus of Nazareth, and hence Judaism's survival into the present day is less a testimony to the strangely wise ways of divine providence (as it had been for Augustine and his successors) than a monument to human stubbornness and un-reason that would be better taken down and cleared away.

"Scripture Alone" and the Scripture Claim

The interpretation of scripture was perhaps the most obvious site for deliberate Jewish-Christian exchanges from earliest times. In order to provide some background for understanding how such exchanges in the seventeenth century contributed to the destabilization of the classic framework and the beginning of "modern", liberal Christian theology, this section considers some relevant developments in the later Middle Ages before briefly reviewing how the *sola scriptura* motto of the Reformation altered the basic terms of such exchanges for Protestant Christians. Isaac Troki as a Jewish critic of Christianity is particularly alert to some of the emerging dilemmas for Protestant polemicists in sustaining the scripture claim of fulfilment in Christ and its corresponding judgment of interpretive blindness on the part of Jews.

Two Medieval Developments

Exegesis may not seem a promising area for examining the dynamic character of Jewish-Christian exchange and its contribution to theological development. One can easily gain the impression that here at least very little changes in Christian theological engagement with Judaism between the second century and the early modern era. If, for instance, we compare Justin's dialogue, written more than a thousand years earlier, with perhaps the most illuminating of the many "official" disputations of the Middle Ages, that held at Barcelona in 1263, we can immediately identify a common handful of biblical passages, with standard Christological readings being reproduced on the Christian side and rejected on the Jewish side across the intervening millennium.[2] The assembling of thematically organized sequences of biblical texts, with varying amounts of commentary, remained the dominant form of medieval Christian anti-Jewish literature, and not one prone to significant innovation.[3] Images in art of Jewish-Christian debates where representatives point at the scriptures they hold also witness to the way that theological exchange tended to circle around the exegesis of a limited number of passages that would have been very familiar to the learned contributors on both sides.[4] Yet while the apparently interminable recycling of interpretive arguments is certainly one feature of the extant literature, as it doubtless was of oral discussions, it would be a mistake to imagine that the post-eleventh century developments in Jewish-Christian exchange noted in the previous chapter left the area of biblical exegesis wholly unaffected. Two developments in particular are worth underlining. Both of these are

already evident in the *Book of the Covenant* by Joseph Kimhi from
Narbonne in the twelfth century, where we see them from the Jewish side,
at once anticipating and mirroring parallel Christian responses.

The first is that Jewish writers are using the growing tradition of *peshat*
interpretation to place the texts appealed to by Christian interlocutors back
into their literary and (alleged) historical context in order to undermine the
plausibility of Christological interpretation.[5] This insistence on recourse to
precise context in inter-religious debate about passages from holy texts is
also evident in Jewish responses to Islam, for instance in Moses
Maimonides' *Epistle to Yemen*.[6] It is possible that Jewish exegesis in
France in particular became more consciously and rigorously attentive to
contextual and historical meaning because of the need to counter the
power of "spiritual" interpretation as represented in the oral, visual and
literary expressions of the dominant culture of Christendom. Such exegesis
was then deployed in polemical engagement with Christianity by figures
such as Joseph Kimhi. In turn, Western Christian exegesis, certainly with
some assistance from and perhaps partly in response to these Jewish
approaches of which Christian scholars were newly aware, became more
rigorous in the twelfth and thirteenth centuries in explicating the literal
sense of scripture as the foundation for Church doctrine, relating the
meaning of individual verses to the interpretation of wider units and their
supposed historical origins.[7]

In the contested field of exegesis, Christian and Jewish intellectual
cultures in Western Europe competed with one another in developing
technologies of scholarly reading. Certainly, clarifying the "literal" sense
and, where appropriate, drawing on a knowledge of the Hebrew language
and of Jewish interpretive traditions came to be considered an important
task for Christian theology in the course of the twelfth century, although
any suggestion that this might lead to questioning of standard
Christological interpretations (e.g. in the case of Isa. 7:14-16) was firmly
rejected.[8] Nonetheless, the long-term continuities of pre-modern biblical
interpretation in Christian theology should not be underestimated. It has
been powerfully argued that the fundamental (and related) assumptions of
direct anticipations of the New Testament in the Old and of the presence
of literal and spiritual meanings throughout shape the hermeneutics at the
heart of mainstream Christian doctrine from the second century until at
least after the first generation of the Protestant Reformation.[9]

The second development that we can see already in Joseph Kimhi is
the extension of exegetical attention on both sides beyond the notionally
common texts of the Jewish Bible / Old Testament, to the later literature in
the light of which those texts were interpreted: the New Testament in the

case of Christianity, Talmud and Midrash in the case of Judaism. We commented briefly on growing Christian awareness of post-biblical Jewish texts from the twelfth century onwards at the end of the previous chapter. Increasing realization that the classic "fulfilment" texts that had come down from Justin and others were never likely to convince their learned Jewish interlocutors may have played its part in prompting this shift on the Christian side, which begins in the twelfth century but becomes much more significant in the thirteenth, when there is a sustained effort to use post-biblical Jewish writings to find evidence of Christianity's claims.[10] It was noted at the start of this section that the Barcelona Disputation rehearses exegetical arguments about particular verses of the Christian Old Testament that go back to Justin's *Dialogue with Trypho*; but the chief Christian speaker in the disputation, Fray Paul, himself a convert from Judaism, is quick to move beyond these standard opening gambits to the new style of argument based on material from the Talmud and Midrash in order to secure his points.[11]

Even before Christian anti-Jewish polemicists started to be interested in Jewish writings subsequent to the Hebrew scriptures, however, Jewish scholars in the West were beginning to read the texts of the Christian New Testament for themselves, something for which there is no evidence in earlier writers from the Muslim world such as Saadia Gaon. By engaging with the New Testament, Joseph Kimhi could move beyond a defensive posture with regard to Christianity that simply problematized the presumed "fit" between Old Testament texts and Christian claims about fulfilment. He could suggest that there are actually inconsistencies between the Church's current teaching and the New Testament documents that were its purported sources.[12] Such challenges from Jewish teachers may have played a part in stimulating Christian theologians in the emerging scholastic milieu of the twelfth century to provide careful theological narrations of biblical history in its entirety, overviews of God's work that sought to demonstrate its Christologically focused coherence and were intended to serve as text books for the emerging university curriculum in theology.[13]

Hopes of Conversion from Renaissance to Reformation

We have sketched in outline how the increase in Jewish-Christian exchange in Western Europe during the twelfth and thirteenth centuries both challenged the scripture claim and judgment from the classic framework and also stimulated their ever more systematic articulation in Christian theology. Concern to vindicate Christianity's negative evaluation of continuing Judaism and, if possible, win converts from it to the Church, remained primary motivations for Christians to engage self-consciously in contact with Jews and Jewish culture throughout the period we are considering in this chapter. Renaissance scholars in the fifteenth century recovered a knowledge of Hebrew unparalleled in Christian circles since the early centuries of Christianity; "trilingual man", fluent in Latin, Greek and Hebrew, became the humanist ideal in the sixteenth.[14] Yet such knowledge, geared primarily to the understanding of the Christian Old Testament, did not initiate any great reassessment of the relationship between Judaism and Christianity. Johannes Reuchlin, a prominent German humanist, found himself involved in a trial for heresy in 1513 because of his well-known interest in Jewish traditions of Kabbala and his opposition to the latest round of measures to destroy post-biblical Jewish books and manuscripts. On both counts, he was an object of intense suspicion among traditionalist Catholic clergy on the eve of the Protestant Reformation. Yet Reuchlin sought to address, in admittedly more irenic fashion, the same task that Fray Paul had attempted at the Barcelona disputation in the thirteenth century: to convince Jews of the truth of Christianity on the basis of their traditional texts (in his case including Kabbalistic material), in the hope of moving beyond the exegetical impasse encountered when the territory was restricted to the Old Testament alone. His fictional dialogue, *De verbo mirifico*, set in antiquity as a conversation between a pagan philosopher, a Jew and a Christian, ended with the Jewish interlocutor repenting and receiving baptism, in contrast to the resoluteness of the Jewish participants in most Christian dialogue texts from Justin to Abelard and beyond.[15]

The scripture judgment of interpretive blindness on the part of Jews existed in some tension with pious hopes for converting Jews through discussion of common scriptures. How to negotiate that tension seems to have been one of the issues in the controversy around Reuchlin: could interpretive blindness be circumvented by appeal to a different set of texts respected by Jews, or was it better to ban all such non-scriptural texts as directly contributing to the perpetuation of that blindness? It is possible to interpret Martin Luther's two most famous texts about Jews and Judaism as reflecting in part the same oscillation between the desire to overcome Judaism's perceived interpretive blindness through better theological exchange and the concern to police its supposedly pernicious influence by suppressing such exchange altogether. Optimism about the possibility of persuading Jews of the truth of Christianity, now purged of its inherited errors and excesses, seems to have fired Martin Luther in the early years of the Reformation, as reflected in his tract from 1523, "That Jesus Christ

Was Born a Jew." Subsequently, however, perhaps partly influenced by disappointments on a number of fronts, Luther composed some of the most bitter anti-Jewish literature ever written by a major Christian theologian and advocated a persecutory regime whose severity considerably exceeded anything that had previously existed or would exist until Nazism.[16] His tract "On the Jews and their Lies," published two decades later in 1543, appears to have been triggered by his reading of a Jewish literary representation of Jewish-Christian dialogue, and in it he specifically objects to any attempt to discuss the exegesis of shared scriptures with Jews, insisting that Christians need only observe the Jews' political humiliation to know their error.[17] The transparency of the people judgment, in terms of the classic framework, should be sufficient according to Luther to rule out any deliberate exchange with Jews on the part of Christians.

Luther's identification of a resemblance between Jesus' and Paul's Jewish opponents in the New Testament and the current Catholic opposition to the Protestant Reformation was hardly calculated to make relations with Jews in the present any more productive. Catholics were happy to repay such polemic in kind and accuse their Protestant adversaries of membership in "the synagogue of Satan, the antichrist."[18] Indeed, the link between Judaism and Christian heresy had already been made in the fifteenth century, in the context of the controversy about the teachings of Jan Hus and then perhaps more significantly in Spain in the wake of increasing pressure on the large Jewish community there to conform to the Catholic Church, pressure that culminated in the order for the expulsion of all Jews and Muslims who refused to convert to Christianity in 1492. The institution of the Spanish Inquisition, specifically to deal with the issue of Jews whose apparent conversion to Christianity might not preclude continuing Jewish beliefs and practices, gave official expression to the treatment of Judaism as a kind of deviancy from Christianity, to be punished in the same way as other heretical tendencies, for which we saw Aquinas paving the way in the final section of the previous chapter. It was not such a distant step from this to the view, also originating in Catholic Spain, that ethnic Jews within the Church were some kind of potential fifth column infiltrating the pure faith with heresy—including Protestantism.[19]

Isaac Troki and the Appeal to "Scripture Alone"

What kind of effect did the changes associated with the sixteenth-century Protestant Reformation have on Jewish writing about Christianity in relation to the scripture claim and judgment of the classic framework? How did the principle of *sola scriptura* ("scripture alone") alter the terms of exchange between Judaism and Christianity? In order to suggest some initial answers to this question, we will look briefly at a text by Isaac ben Abraham of Troki, known in English translation as *Faith Strengthened*. It was composed towards the end of his life, shortly before his death in 1594. Although Troki was a Karaite, a group who were separated from mainstream Rabbinic Judaism, there is nothing in *Faith Strengthened* that could not have been shared by Troki's non-Karaite Jewish neighbours.

Theological issues aside, the Protestant Reformation influenced Troki's work most immediately in terms of the context in which he lived in sixteenth-century Lithuania. An unintended but in the long run far-reaching effect of the upheavals associated with the Protestant Reformation was the emergence of societies where far greater de facto toleration of religious diversity existed than had hitherto been the case. In subsequent sections of this chapter attention will focus on the Dutch Republic in the seventeenth century, perhaps the most important example of this development. It is not the only one, however. One of the factors in Luther's violent polemic against the Jews had probably been his fear that in the relatively open exchanges taking place between Jews and Christians in areas such as Bohemia Christians might be weakened in their Reformation faith.[20] A significant locus for such exchange by the end of the sixteenth century was Poland and Lithuania. Mass expulsion of Jewish populations from Western European countries in the later fifteenth and early sixteenth centuries led to extensive Jewish immigration there, although there had been significant communities before then, with a measure of legal recognition and protection after 1400.[21] Crucially, adherents of more radical interpretations of Reformation doctrine than people like Luther were prepared to countenance were also finding a relatively safe place of refuge in the same territories in the mid-sixteenth century. Political events placed Jews alongside dissident Christians in the context where Troki lived and worked and afforded opportunities for relatively open discussion with Orthodox, Roman Catholic and mainstream Protestant Christians as well.

It is because of this new, post-Reformation situation that we can observe in Troki's work the coming together of Jewish objections to Christianity with the internal Christian critique of traditional doctrine by groups from the Radical Reformation. Troki was able to use the resources of the latter, in particular their anti-trinitarian readings of the New Testament, to compose perhaps the most comprehensive Jewish refutation of Christianity from the pre-modern period. On the other hand, anti-trinitarian Christians were beginning to experiment with a return to partial observance of Jewish Torah—precisely the feared scenario of Jewish contact encouraging Christian doctrinal unorthodoxy and re-engagement with Torah practices that helped to precipitate Luther's terrible denunciations. Troki's arguments would also, however, have less direct effects on Christianity in Western Europe. Translated into Latin in 1665 with an extensive refutation in order to assist Christian writers in addressing Jewish criticism, they would be recycled in turn in the eighteenth century by such Enlightenment thinkers as Voltaire in the cause of undermining the authority of all revealed religion, Judaism as well as Christianity.[22]

Faith Strengthened clearly aims at a comprehensive, rather than merely ad hoc, treatment of the issues raised by Christianity for Jews. The first eight chapters of Part I rehearse Christian objections to Judaism and seek to show how misconceived they are. Chapters IX-XLII then work through every text from the Jewish Bible which Troki is aware of Christians presenting as prophecy fulfilled in Christ and his Church, in order to show that a proper reading of the passages in question cannot support the Christian interpretation. In general, Troki uses precisely the same strategy as Joseph Kimhi: a careful exegesis of the passage, attending to the Hebrew and to the original literary and historical context, is considered sufficient to show the implausibility of what the Christians allege. As Troki reports himself saying to some Christian disputants,

> You Christians are accustomed to establish your objections to our faith, and the evidences of your faith, on detached biblical passages, without regard to the leading idea, and with the preceding and subsequent words of the text, nor do you make unbiased comparisons with the parallel sayings of other prophets.[23]

He makes the same point to Jews who might be engaged in argument with Christian scholars while commenting on Gen. 22:18:

> Here again, we have to treat with a palpable fallacy, because the Christians generally argue in favour of their religion from detached portions of the prophecies, without going deeply into the subject and studying the context.[24]

Yet while, from the Jewish side, Troki is remarkable chiefly for the attempted comprehensiveness and rigour of his approach, which is still recognizably continuous with the work of Joseph Kimhi some four centuries earlier, it is important to recognize how differently these criticisms might be received and answered in an early modern Protestant context rather than a medieval Catholic one. A foundational principle of the Protestant Reformation was *sola scriptura*: doctrine must be based on scripture alone, that is, on its primary, clear meaning, and, where matters are unclear, scripture is to be interpreted by scripture, in other words, by other relevant passages where matters are clearer.[25] Whereas a medieval Catholic could appeal to the teaching of the Church as the "frame" within which scripture is to be read, and within which it finds coherence, such an appeal is much more difficult if not altogether impossible for a Protestant thinker. It was along such lines that one of the pioneers of Christian biblical scholarship, the French Roman Catholic Richard Simon, would argue some seven decades later for Catholicism as the necessary support for serious study of the Bible. He wrote in the preface to his *Histoire critique du Vieux Testament*,

> if the rule of faith is divorced from the rule of fact, in other words, if the Scriptures are unaccompanied by Tradition, one can be sure of scarcely anything in religion.[26]

In a context where *sola scriptura* obtained as a basic axiom for theological debate, Troki could pursue with new force traditional Jewish arguments that Christians must abandon their claims about prophetic fulfilment, on the grounds that the kind of literal, contextual reading of scripture urged by the Reformers (with an expectation of subverting established Catholic interpretation of the New Testament) could not provide convincing exegetical foundations for it. If that was indeed the case, then Christians, or at least Protestant Christians, were faced with the dilemma either of diluting claims to newness (perhaps like the groups who effectively abandoned the covenant judgment and advocated a partial return to Torah), or of reinterpreting them as something other than fulfilment of prophecy. As we will see later, it is this second strategy that came to prevail in liberal strands of Protestant Christian modernity.

Troki reaffirms the medieval Jewish case that one cannot project forward from any text of the Jewish Bible to Jesus of Nazareth and the Christian Church. He also rearticulates the position that there exists a messianic "surplus" in the Hebrew scriptures that remains unfulfilled in the supposedly Christian era and points forward to a very different kind of Messiah from the crucified God of Christian teaching: a historical, political leader who will help to initiate the reign of God on earth.[27] Here again, there were potentially new difficulties for Protestant thinkers in trying to maintain the correspondence between Old Testament prophecy and the *novum* of Jesus Christ. Medieval theologians could take for granted the two senses of scripture, literal and spiritual, operative in every biblical text, and could therefore read every apparently "literal" prediction of messianic time in the Hebrew prophets as a "spiritual" statement about life in Christ, in this world or the next, as we saw in the previous chapter. This, however, became a rather more problematic hermeneutical strategy for the Reformers, with their strong emphasis on the plain meaning of the text. What were Christians to make of the messianic surplus arguably left over by a literal reading of the Hebrew prophets that did not resort to the idea of spiritual meaning in confronting apparently inconvenient passages?

This was a theological question with potentially explosive ecclesial and political answers. We might recall how Aquinas argued against Joachim of Fiore that no further "newness" lies ahead for the Christian Church, and how quick church leaders were to level accusations of Judaizing against any kind of millenarian expectations within their own ranks.[28] In 1525, Luther invoked the force of arms to crush the Peasants' Revolt, which Thomas Müntzer was seeking to strengthen with his apocalyptic theology, raising expectations of the kingdom of heaven coming on earth. In the mid-seventeenth century, radical Protestant groups in the wake of the English revolution came to believe that the still unrealized newness prophesied in the Old Testament for human history was about to break out, not through patient and passive waiting but through the decisive action of the elect.[29] The distance between such movements within Christian culture and recurrent Jewish messianic expectations outside it might not appear so very great. The parallels between, for instance, James Nayler, the early Quaker leader who rode into Bristol on a Donkey in 1656, and Sabbatai Zvi, who announced himself to fellow Jews as the Messiah in 1665, were not lost on some contemporaries.[30]

Troki's artful defence in Part I of *Faith Strengthened* of Judaism against Christian polemic is, however, less immediately important for our purposes at this stage than his direct attack on Christianity in Part II. Here he works through the New Testament book by book in order to highlight inconsistencies, both between the biblical text and Christian doctrine (for instance on the Trinity) and between different New Testament documents. What is particularly interesting to observe here is the use of the historical criticism being developed by humanist scholarship to foster a sceptical attitude towards the identification of a particular set of texts as possessing unique authority. Troki only intended by his application of such techniques to undermine the claims of the New Testament; as we will see shortly, Spinoza used essentially the same strategy to subvert the authority of any scripture, beginning with the Jewish Bible. Troki is able, for

instance, to comment extensively on both the contradictions between
Matthew and Luke's genealogies at the beginning of their Gospels and the
inconsistencies in the accounts of the passion at the Gospels' end.[31] His
conclusion is that such an evidently historically unreliable collection of
documents—written well after the events themselves—cannot feasibly be
regarded as divine revelation.[32]

In this respect as in others, Troki is continuing earlier Jewish traditions
of writing against Christianity,[33] but the concise and forceful manner in
which he assembles his case anticipates the sceptical critique of both
Judaism and Christianity that emerges in the next century. Having listed
what we would call the "Synoptic parallels" for the story of the woman
anointing Jesus at Bethany, and noted the Johannine equivalent, Troki
comments:

> These extracts, from the several books of the New Testament, are curious
> specimens of the want of agreement between the several authors, who of
> necessity would have been in perfect unanimity, had they been under the
> influence of divine inspiration.[34]

As well as anticipating the emergence of the new historical biblical
criticism in the following century, Troki's acuity on such points is also
directly relevant to Christian claims of prophetic fulfilment. For although
such claims, as we have said, were extended into the history of the Church,
the asserted foundation for them was always the detailed "matching"
between the narrative of the New Testament, above all the Gospels, and
particular texts from the Old Testament. Troki was not only undermining,
in a Protestant context that distrusted the authority of the Church and the
appeal to spiritual meaning, the plausibility of Christians using texts from
the Old Testament in this way. He was also beginning to ask the question
of whether the New Testament accounts could safely be regarded as the
starting-point for this exercise in the first place. If we cannot trust the
Gospels as a record of historical events, then how can we possibly justify
the scripture claim of fulfilment in Christ by identifying detailed
correspondences between their clearly unreliable accounts of his life and
particular texts lifted out of context from the Jewish Bible?

From "Scripture Alone" to Reason Alone

Isaac Troki believed in prophetic inspiration and accepted the
theological interpretation of history in terms of divine fulfilment: we have
seen and will see new things in history that correspond to the prophetic
"surplus" of old words and old deeds and as such disclose the redemptive

will of God. To that extent, he inhabited the same intellectual world as his Christian opponents, Western Catholic and Eastern Orthodox, Lutheran and Calvinist, trinitarian and anti-trinitarian, at the end of the sixteenth century; indeed, he and they alike inhabited an intellectual tradition continuous with (which is not to say unmodified since) the formation of the Jewish and Christian Bibles. He was carrying on an argument with contemporary Christians in Lithuania which took its parameters from that shared tradition, shaped by a common concept of prophecy, and focused on disagreement as to whether the Church's claims about Jesus Christ could be substantiated by an appeal to that traditional understanding of prophecy and newness in relation to scripture and history.

Yet the tools that Christian writers had been sharpening against Judaism and the comparable but different tools that Jewish writers such as Troki had been sharpening against Christianity in the pre-modern period were wielded together in modernity to cast doubt upon the most basic assumptions of the scriptural tradition in which writers of both religions had remained. Early Christian theologians had used the story of Samson tying pairs of foxes together by their tails as a figure of how Christianity made patent the mutually destructive implications of the pagan philosophical tradition. In the early Enlightenment, the inter-religious arguments of Judaism and Christianity were deployed in tandem to set out a philosophical attack on the very conception of newness as scriptural fulfilment that allowed Troki to engage contemporary Christians in theological dialogue. The Reformation divorce of scriptural interpretation from traditional authority seemed to have opened up a chasm into which all theological claims must ultimately fall, to be replaced by the deliberations of philosophical reason. Reason alone was pressing to take over from scripture alone, on the grounds that a reading of scripture that truly set aside all traditional prejudgments could only send the reader back to the authority of reason.

For Christians who accepted even partially the force of the philosophical attack on theological readings of scripture, the scripture claim of the classic framework and with it the framework itself needed radical reappraisal, as we shall see in the following section. The focus here, however, will be on the formulation of that attack in the *Tractatus theologico-politicus* of Baruch Spinoza and its participation in the dynamics of Jewish-Christian exchange. As with Troki, the political context is important here. Spinoza was writing in Holland in the second half of the seventeenth century. Following the decisive defeat of the Spanish after a protracted war, the Dutch Republic, and in particular Amsterdam, the major city of its most powerful province, Holland, had

emerged as a post-Reformation society where religious diversity found a
new measure of toleration. To that extent it was analogous to the Poland-
Lithuania of Isaac Troki, but unlike those territories the Dutch Republic
was beginning to achieve a dominant position in European trade and an
increasingly influential role in shaping its emerging culture. Beginning
from the later sixteenth century, it also experienced a significant level of
Jewish immigration, especially from the Iberian Peninsula. Many of these
Jews had outwardly conformed to Christianity to avoid persecution in
Spain and Portugal, but once arrived in the Netherlands some of them
began to practise Judaism again. Having experienced Iberian Catholicism,
and now renewed in their engagement with Judaism, they also had an
exceptionally high level of contact with their Protestant neighbours, with
at least some of whom they shared around the middle of the seventeenth
century a heightening of millenarian expectations that has intriguing
parallels with the thirteenth-century context discussed in the previous
chapter.[35] Spinoza's origins were with this distinctive grouping of
Sephardic Jews, but his own conformity to Judaism did not last very long:
in 1656, while still only 23 he was banned for life because of his
unorthodox views from the Jewish community, though not before he had
studied under some of its most learned teachers.[36] The *Tractatus*, his major
work on theological matters, united Jews with Christians in fierce criticism
when it was published in 1669-70.

Spinoza's First Move: From Inter-Religious Polemic to Sceptical Critique

Spinoza's *Tractatus* is a significant landmark in the history of modern
philosophy and theology. It was not without its influences and parallels,
but at least part of Spinoza's originality, it has been argued by Popkin, lay
in bringing together a Cartesian certainty about rational and philosophical
knowledge with the application of Cartesian doubt to the one area that
Descartes had sought to insulate from his inquiries—religion.[37] In order to
mount a sceptical critique against any sort of theological claim to
intellectual knowledge (and hence political power), Spinoza drew on and
developed earlier patterns of inter-religious polemic to challenge the most
basic assumptions of Jewish and Christian theology. Nor is his starting
point in the *Tractatus* at all accidental: the first chapter is entitled "Of
Prophecy," and the second "Of Prophets." Spinoza needed to eliminate the
theological understanding of history and truth in which these concepts
were determinative, in order to clear the way for his own anti-theological
vision, with its alternative historical teleology. In pursuing this task, he

showed a remarkable ability to deploy arguments with theological roots while at the same time cutting away at those roots themselves. Perhaps it was this strategy, as much as his radical conclusions, that was so disturbing to the religious leaders of his own time, Jewish and Christian, Catholic and Protestant.

Important features of Spinoza's approach are already apparent in the first chapter of the *Tractatus*. He explicitly invokes the Reformation slogan, *sola scriptura*[38]—but in order to rule out any kind of appeal to a wider theological framework or hermeneutical criterion in interpreting particular passages, something that the Reformers themselves took for granted. We could well compare Troki's use of "literal" interpretation to attack Christological use of the Hebrew scriptures and the new force, as noted above, of such traditional polemic in the Reformation context, but Spinoza is both more subtle and more radical in using this tactic. By showing that the literal reading of any one text, or even collection of texts, cannot be used to generate conclusively the theological claims of any of the competing religious groups of his time—Judaism no more than Catholicism or Lutheranism—he aims to undercut them all.

As the work progresses, Spinoza will use the restriction of exegetical argument to the "literal" sense in its historical and literary context, central to Jewish anti-Christian writing, to demonstrate the fragile theological foundations of Judaism itself, rooted in the reading of its scriptures. Troki had pointed out inconsistencies in the Gospels and argued that the degree of distance that existed between the events themselves and their written narration renders the New Testament writings unreliable as historical evidence. Spinoza applies the same kind of critical judgment to the Torah, famously arguing against the authorship of Moses and suggesting instead that the final version of the text as we have it was edited by Ezra, many centuries later. He also points out significant differences between the prophetic books and invokes the *sola scriptura* principle to resist any sort of harmonizing exegesis. In fact, Spinoza refrains from applying the same critical methodology so thoroughly to the New Testament that he deploys more systematically on the Old, perhaps in part in the hope of evading the censors in what was still, after all, a Christian country. Yet it is also the case that he hardly needs to do so: intelligent readers could make the application for themselves, while his attack on the theological authority of the Church's Old Testament is in itself sufficient to cast serious doubt on the doctrinal edifice raised upon it.

Spinoza uses themes in Jewish anti-Christian writing, including the insistence on arguing from the literal sense alone and the undermining of the New Testament's historical reliability, to turn the dilemmas for

Protestant theology that arise from Troki's work into dilemmas for any kind of traditional religious faith. He also invokes the heritage of Christian anti-Jewish writing. This is apparent in relatively superficial features, such as the disparaging use of the term "Pharisees" to refer to Judaism's rabbinic leaders since the second century CE.[39] It shows itself more significantly in Spinoza's repetition of the assertion, already found in the second-century *Epistle of Barnabas*, that the original covenant with Moses ended with the incident of the Golden Calf[40]—an assertion that Spinoza develops in a highly original commentary on Israel's history in the later chapters of the *Tractatus*, transforming it from a judgment about how God deals with God's people to an element in a human and political process that can be described in wholly naturalistic terms. Here again, a motif from inter-religious writing, in this case Christian polemic against Judaism, is deployed to make a negative point about one religion but then developed in an anti-religious and naturalistic way to implicate Christianity quite as much as Judaism insofar as it seeks to establish any claims to truth about reality or to authority in the state.

Spinoza's Second Move: From Changing Faith to Abiding Reason

Spinoza also invokes the familiar anti-Jewish claims that the Law of Moses only pertained to earthly rewards and punishments and that the destruction of the temple and exile from Jerusalem brought a definitive end to its relevance.[41] Yet while the point of such assertions in Christian writing was to make the Torah subordinate to God's definitive revelation in Christ—to the new Law—Spinoza uses them instead to relativize the teaching of the Old Testament to the natural and unchanging law of the divine decrees, as he calls them. Paul called the Law a *paidagogos*, a teacher and guide for the immature; for Spinoza, the Law is certainly that but so also, by implication, is any kind of historical, prophetic revelation, including Christianity. A crucial thesis of the first two chapters and their analysis of prophecy is that the prophets were distinguished by their ability to discern God's truth through the use of images and the faculty of the imagination. The truth that they discerned in this relatively unfocused and unreliable way, however, is no other than the same truth that can also be more universally and more adequately grasped by "natural knowledge"; indeed, scripture directs us towards this, as it "unreservedly commends the natural light and the natural divine law."[42] So while Spinoza seems to be giving biblical prophecy a distinct and honoured position, in fact he is relegating it to be a kind of *preparatio evangelii*—where the gospel is the good news of universal, natural reason.

The effect of the very first chapter of the *Tractatus*, "Of Prophecy," is already to undermine the theological claim of Israel's election, and not without some of the derogatory colouring of Christian anti-Jewish writing:

> But since natural knowledge is common to all men, it is not so highly prized, as I have already said, and particularly in the case of the Hebrews, who vaunted themselves above all men—indeed, despising all men, and consequently the sort of knowledge that is common to all men.[43]

The arrogance of Israel lies for Spinoza, then, not in its indifference to God's prophetic word, its great sin according to pre-modern Christianity, but in failing to realize that to have received the prophetic word as such is a distinction that makes no distinction, since it only points towards universal truths that can be known by any rational person. Indeed, they are known better by the use of reason independently of the "imaginative" route to truth supplied by prophecy. Again, Spinoza never draws the obvious parallel with the claims to election and unique knowledge by the Christian Church, but his Christian readers were not slow to perceive it for themselves.

The point becomes clearer as the work unfolds. In chapter 5, Spinoza allows for the utility of scriptural narrative in inculcating virtue and obedience among "the common people." Yet he also states that the person who arrives through the use of reason at the truth of God's providential existence and the imperative of righteous living "is altogether blessed—indeed, more blessed than the multitude, because in addition to true beliefs he has a clear and distinct conception of God."[44] A familiar Cartesian epistemological concept is being invoked in order to justify Spinoza's alternative historical teleology—that we move, not from prophecy to prophecy's fulfilment, but from scriptural faith to non-scriptural reason. One of the arguments Spinoza gives for looking to scripture only for basic moral guidance, and not for knowledge about reality, is that it is "clear" about the former, but not about the latter.[45] Certainty in knowledge requires, in Descartes' philosophy, clarity in the apprehension of the object of knowledge, but Spinoza's reductively "literal" and contextual reading of the Bible shows it to be less than consistent and therefore less than clear in relation to the historic theological claims of Judaism and Christianity alike. Therefore theological knowledge must move beyond scripture to something clearer and more certain: the outcomes of natural reason. In chapter 12, Spinoza even appeals directly to one of the cardinal passages for Christianity's understanding of the always intended obsolescence of the Torah—Jer. 31:31—and to Paul's linkage of the Law to immaturity in order to argue that written revelation is just a stage on the way towards the fullness of knowledge that has no need for texts: "To the early Jews religion was transmitted in the form of written law because at that time they were just like children."[46]

It is in one of Spinoza's longer notes to the text, first added from his manuscripts to the French translation of 1678, that we find his alternative teleology of reason articulated most clearly. In a note to chapter 16, Spinoza writes:

> Furthermore, we have shown that the divine commandments appear to us as commandments or ordinances only as long as we do not know their cause. Once this is known, they cease to be commandments, and we embrace them as eternal truths, not as commandments; that is, obedience forthwith passes into love, which arises from true knowledge by the same necessity as light arises from the sun.[47]

In John's Gospel, Jesus had told his disciples that they had now become friends, not servants; in the first letter of John, we read that perfect love drives out fear. This originally Christian teaching that love is the fulfilment of law, itself intertwined with the confrontation with non-Jesus believing Judaism at the origins of the Christian Church, is here rehearsed and transposed to indicate the transcendence of historic Christianity just as much as Judaism. That which troubled Abelard about law—an unchanging law of nature which has always been true and was known already to the ancient philosophers—and that which troubled Aquinas a century later—a new law of the spirit and of love which would mark the end of the order of faith, sacraments and Church—come together in Spinoza's writing. The new law is the final stripping away of tradition's confusing layers to reveal the unchanging law in its original simplicity.

At the radical edges of theology after the Protestant Reformation, speculation about the unfolding of future history continued to germinate alongside attempts at the critical analysis of past history and its recording in the Bible. Spinoza would have had some familiarity with this tendency: the works of the French millenarian thinker Isaac La Peyrère had been printed in Holland, and we know that Spinoza owned a copy of his *Prae-Adamitae* and used it as a source for his arguments against the Mosaic authorship of the Pentateuch.[48] Certainly in the *Tractatus* there is a trace of the Joachite, millenarian tradition of a coming age that will burn away the dross of political and ecclesial institutions in the fire of the spirit and love. Yet what will be revealed in this new age will be, according to Spinoza, no new truth, but the same truth that has always existed and always will, the "eternal truths" now freed from the accretions of texts, ceremonies and narratives, as well as from the kind of religious bodies deriving authority from those things that had so emphatically rejected Spinoza and resisted the message he proclaimed. This aspect of his thinking seems to be clearly related to the "strand of millenarian ecumenical rationalism" that Sutcliffe describes in relation to Lodowijk Meyer, Spinoza's friend and ally.[49]

An English Parallel: Hobbes on Prophecy

It was the way that Spinoza was able to adopt themes from pre-modern theological discourse and adapt them to his anti-theological discourse of modernity that made him such a pivotal figure, and ultimately perhaps a more difficult and dangerous adversary for the theologians than his "Christian" contemporary in England, Thomas Hobbes. Hobbes also sought to undermine the political claims of theology by a radical reformulation of religion. Rather than arguing for toleration, however, Hobbes resolves the sceptical dilemmas of post-Reformation theology by arguing for the state as the source and arbiter of religious authority.[50]

In *Leviathan*, Hobbes like Spinoza effectively repudiates the capacity of prophecy to point to any sort of revelatory *novum*, not least by the second of his two essential criteria for true prophecy: "One is the doing of miracles, the other is the not teaching of any religion than that which is already established."[51] Newness can hardly be explicated as the fulfilment of prophecy on such an understanding. Hobbes's critique of traditional theology, like Spinoza's, deploys a kind of reductive hyper-literalism, but whereas Spinoza uses this strategy to argue that scripture only discloses basic moral guidance, and not intellectual knowledge, Hobbes is happy to advocate some startling positions on the basis of it, including the restoration of Jerusalem as the centre for God's future kingdom.[52] As in the *Tractatus*, early modern rationalism deploys motifs from medieval millenarianism, although *Leviathan* does not offer anything quite like Spinoza's provocative inversion of theological eschatology as teleological progress towards complete human knowledge of what is eternally the same. Still, Hobbes too played a part in creating a new intellectual climate in which the theologians, both Jewish and Christian, could no longer take for granted the consensus about the prophetic interpretation of history which had previously underpinned theological discourse not only within but also between the two faiths. The question of how those who accepted this breakdown of consensus might continue to defend their faith as divine revelation—against both the new anti-religious critique pioneered by

Spinoza and Hobbes, as well as the continuing inter-religious critique from other faiths—is the subject to which we now turn.

New Terms of Exchange: Limborch and Orobio

In 1687, the Dutch Remonstrant theologian Philippus van Limborch published a remarkable book, the *De veritate religionis Christianae amica collatio cum erudito Judaeo* ("A friendly conversation with a learned Jew about the truth of the Christian religion").[53] It comprises an exchange of texts between Limborch himself and the Jewish writer Isaac Orobio de Castro who, after a highly eventful life including imprisonment and torture at the hands of the Inquisition in Spain, had come to reside, like Limborch, in Amsterdam. There he renounced the Christianity to which he had earlier outwardly adhered and became a religiously devout Jew.[54] Although many of the arguments and counterarguments in it are very familiar from the previous history of Jewish-Christian theological exchanges, the book certainly constitutes a far more genuinely "friendly" encounter than can easily be found in any earlier period, not least in that each person represents himself, in his own words, in a common language, and without obvious fear of censorship or reprisals on the Jewish side.[55]

In Limborch's book we can discern something of how the general sceptical crisis about knowledge and the more specifically theological concern with the interpretation of scripture interact with Christian responses to Judaism in early modernity, with results that point the way towards some very significant alterations to the classic framework for Christian self-understanding in relation to Judaism. Both Orobio and Limborch had, independently, been among those religious leaders in the Netherlands who criticized and sought to refute Spinoza. Orobio devoted part of his *Certamen philosophicum* to the refutation of Spinoza's ideas, and in the *Amica collatio* itself he explicitly notes and dismisses Spinoza's case regarding the Mosaic authority of the Pentateuch.[56] Still, they were also both beneficiaries of the relatively extensive de facto religious tolerance of the Dutch Republic and certainly not at all in sympathy with the Calvinist religious conservatism that remained a powerful countervailing influence in Dutch public life. Moreover, Limborch's principles for biblical interpretation, expressed elsewhere, might have been broadly endorsed by both Orobio and Spinoza for their overt setting aside of any appeal to theological authority outside the text:

> From these things it appears what is the key by which the obscure meaning of Scripture is to be unlocked: viz. indubitably Scripture itself and right reason. . . . Right reason; in so far as it is no less from God than Scripture,

and is implanted in us as a light, by whose aid we can distinguish the true from the false.[57]

For Limborch, the essentials of Christian doctrine could nonetheless be established on this rigorous basis of the rational exegesis of scripture's literal meaning—and established moreover against the Jewish critique of Orobio. It is in Limborch's contribution to the *Amica collatio* that we can see the beginnings of an attempt to reckon with the perceived limitations of pre-modern accounts of Christian newness as prophetic fulfilment and to find fresh ways to articulate the original Christian claim.

Limborch's "New Method of Arguing" for Christian Truth

The "friendly" character of Limborch's answers to Orobio should not be taken to indicate a significant break from previous theological evaluations of Judaism in Christianity. Rather, Limborch might at one level be compared to earlier figures, such as Reuchlin, whose tolerant attitude towards Judaism cannot be separated from an expectation that, once the case for Christianity was presented to Jews in a clear and rational way, conversion could and should properly follow, with the assistance of God's grace. Having recalled Paul's assertion in Rom. 11:26 that "All Israel will be saved," Limborch continues:

> We still hope for such happy times, and wish with all our soul that Israel, after proper purifying of its soul, would prepare to recognize and revere its redeemer.[58]

Limborch regarded his exchange with Orobio as particularly important, and hence deserving of publication, because it modelled a fresh approach to Christian conversation with Jews, in which the case for Christianity was made in a respectful and non-polemical way on the basis of common ground and was therefore far more likely to succeed.[59] In this case, the common ground was to be provided by the Jewish scriptures and a method of rational argument that owed something to the epistemological debates in early modernity already touched on in this chapter. Limborch wanted to take his Jewish interlocutor's grounds for believing Moses was sent by God—his "criteria" for this theological judgment—and show that the case for judging Jesus Christ to have been sent by God, on the basis of the same criteria, is overwhelming.[60] While even in the mid-seventeenth century most Protestant theologians were content to recycle medieval Catholic arguments against Judaism, Limborch sought instead to apply the new kind of theological rationality represented by the passage quoted above on

biblical interpretation to the task of engaging with contemporary Jews. It
was an approach associated with such figures as fellow Dutchman Hugo
Grotius, whose *De veritate religionis Christianae* he singles out for
particular praise in the preface to the *Amica collatio*.[61] Certainly
Limborch's friend John Locke, whose contribution we shall be considering
at some length in the next section, agreed that Limborch's procedure in the
Amica collatio was unlike any previous Christian writing in this area.[62]
Indeed, Locke professed some disappointment when hearing of Orobio's
death soon after publication, as "it would not have been unsatisfactory to
have some confession of the truth in him while still alive"; he really
believed it was possible that his friend's arguments might have succeeded
in converting Orobio to Christianity. Limborch's approach was recognized
as a new "method of arguing," but it was pursued in the service of the
common task inherited from Justin, Anselm and Aquinas of "combating
the Jews" and their failure to acknowledge the truth of Christianity.[63]

    One effect of Limborch's new model for Christian engagement with
Jews was to focus the attention of the debate on the verification of
historical miracles. According to Limborch, God attested to the divine
missions of Moses and of Jesus by miracles, and it is not rational to accept
the miracles attesting to Moses and reject the miracles attesting to Jesus
when the evidence is even stronger for the latter than the former. Orobio
responds by developing further the sceptical arguments against the validity
of the New Testament evidence that we can already see clearly in Troki,
and appealing to the unbroken tradition of collective Jewish witness to
Sinai as a mode of verification for Mosaic claims that cannot be replicated
let alone surpassed in the case of Jesus. He also tries to show that
Limborch's argument for Christianity could be used equally legitimately
to argue for the truth of Islam, and he carefully presents, as a
counterweight to Limborch's argument that the Gospel writers had no
reason to tell anything other than the truth, the historical hypothesis that
early Christian writers could have had motivations for misrepresenting the
actual events, including the miraculous deeds so crucial for Christianity's
vindication according to Limborch.[64]

    The outcome of this shift of attention to the verification of historical
miracles seems to be, certainly with hindsight, a drift in the direction of
increasing scepticism for the unconvinced reader if not for the participants
themselves. The arguments produced by each participant to cast doubt on
the consistency of the historical beliefs held by the other might appear
more compelling than the arguments each uses to vindicate his own.
Certainly the *Amica collatio* was judged by some of its early readers to
amount to a case for religious scepticism, rather than a proof of Christian

faith, whatever the intention of the writers. Once again, religious apologetic feeds into anti-religious critique, one of the recurring themes of this chapter.[65]

The Abandonment of Christological Exegesis

Exhibiting his new "historical" method of argument to convince Jews about Christianity may have been Limborch's principal reason for publishing the *Amica collatio*, but it at least appears to begin on much more conventional territory, and territory closely implicated with the question of prophecy that is the focus for us here. The first, and much the briefest, text is by Orobio, in which he asks four short questions of his Christian friend: first, where it says in scripture that faith in the Messiah is necessary for salvation, and without it a person is damned; second, where it says in scripture that Israel's only way of salvation and restoration to divine favour is faith in a Messiah who has already come; third where it says in scripture that Israel is to be rejected and scattered among the nations because of its lack of faith in the Messiah, so that it ceases to be God's covenant people and is liable to eternal damnation; and fourth, where it says in scripture that the commandments of the Law, except for the "moral" ones, are a shadow of what was to come about through the Messiah, and that most things in the Law and the Prophets are to be explained in a mystical sense, with contempt for the literal meaning. Orobio frames his questions more sharply than many of his Jewish predecessors, with an eye for the paradox inherent in the standard Christian hermeneutic from Justin onward that the Old Testament is to be valued and preserved as a kind of witness to its own ever lengthening redundancy, but his concerns are familiar enough.

Yet if the *Amica collatio* begins on conventional territory, it quickly moves away from it. In his second submission, Orobio purports to be shocked by Limborch's response to his relatively standard opening gambit. He presumably expected Limborch to reply to his initial four questions with a list of Old Testament texts with Christological interpretations that he would then have demonstrated to be wrongly used by the Christians, through placing them back in literary and historical context, much as Troki and Kimhi and many others had done before him. Limborch, however, does not respond along such traditional lines. Instead, he begins from the principle that "Our faith should be fitted to the divine revelation,"[66] so that as long as the Messiah was only promised, it was only required to believe that he would come, and after he had been divinely revealed, it was then

required to believe in him. His reply to the first question lays the basis for
his response to the others:

> From what has been said it is clear that it was not necessary that God
> should have commanded or expressly said in the Old Testament that faith
> in the Messiah is absolutely necessary for the salvation of the human race,
> so that anyone who does not believe is damned. It is enough that God said
> he would send the Messiah, and then after that he fully made clear his own
> will through the Messiah, when he came into the world. Then from that
> time distinct and expressed faith in the Messiah was necessary.[67]

The Hebrew scriptures testify that God will at some point in the future
reveal the Messiah, and that when the Messiah comes, Israel should heed
his message. That is all that is needed, Limborch implies, to establish the
claims of Christianity and to show that Judaism has failed to be faithful to
its own purported foundations in rejecting the promised Messiah when he
came and was duly attested by God with miraculous signs. The specific
"proof texting" that Orobio demands is irrelevant in the light of the whole
shape of Israel's scriptural witness, which prophesies the coming of God's
new revelation through the Messiah without spelling out in what this new
revelation will actually consist. Hence Orobio's questions are simply
beside the point.

Perhaps Orobio was thrown by this unconventional response to his
relatively conventional opening move. Limborch seemed to be virtually
admitting the case that Jewish anti-Christian polemic had been making
since its beginnings, that no texts from the Jewish Bible directly
prophesied the ministry, teachings and death of Jesus of Nazareth, yet he
was still seeking to persuade Jews of Christianity's truth.[68] It is certainly
hard to imagine any pre-modern Christian theologian arguing for the kind
of understanding of prophetic fulfilment in Christ that Limborch appears
to be advocating. At the beginning of his second text, Orobio cites Calvin
himself as holding that faith in Christ has always been necessary.[69] In the
introduction to his third and final text, he claims that Limborch has indeed
effectively conceded the Jewish case about Old Testament prophecy, by
accepting the Jewish answers to each of his initial four questions—that
there is nowhere in Jewish scripture that points unambiguously to these
cardinal features of Christian doctrine.[70] Yet while Limborch is indeed
shifting the ground, he is not abandoning the battle.

There may well be an implicit concession in Limborch's approach that
the work of people like Troki is simply not answerable on its own terms in
the light of duly "Reformed" theological reason and its understanding of
scripture. For Limborch that does not entail a denial, however, of the

central claim of the Church that the Jewish scriptures find their fulfilment in Jesus Christ. Point for point correspondences between the text of the Old Testament and the events set out in the text of the New are not the only possible foundation for that theological claim. Rather, all that is necessary according to Limborch is that the Old Testament be read in its totality as a "messianic" text; that is, a text that, read rationally as a whole, as Limborch's hermeneutical principles prescribe, looks forward to the coming of a figure who will bring the definitive revelation of God. Jesus Christ then becomes the divinely (i.e. miraculously) attested fulfilment of the scriptures, which do not predict in any detail the life and teachings of the Messiah who is coming to fulfil them, since there is, for Limborch, no need for them to do so, but only to point towards him. Moreover, Jewish arguments that, as we have seen, go back at least to the eleventh century, about the observance of Torah in early Christianity, are readily dealt with by Limborch via his conception of stages in divine revelation: the new stage of God's revelation that arrived with Christ was still "immature" in the immediate apostolic period, so that for a transitional period the old forms of the Law were continued, until "given a decent burial" with the destruction of Jerusalem and the temple.[71]

Clarity and Certainty

Limborch offers a "post-medieval" defence of the Christian claim of prophetic fulfilment, separated from the kind of detailed exegetical correspondences that formed the contested subject matter for the greater part of Jewish-Christian polemical exchanges in the pre-modern period. Orobio's response shows affinities with themes from early modernity already discussed in this chapter. One of the key strategies he deploys, for instance, is to take the concept of clarity—important in different ways for Reformation hermeneutics and Cartesian epistemology—and turn it against the "enlightened" Limborch, who is still prepared to use the traditional Christian language of the newness of Christ "making clear" the shadows of the Law and the Prophets. Orobio mocks that assertion: from the very beginning, he points out, Christians (unlike Jews, in his view) have been unable to agree on the meaning of their "clear" revelation, with multiple heretical groupings springing up. Moreover, surely it can only be the *lack* of clarity in the Christian revelation that can have allowed the "papistical" Church to become saturated for so many centuries with idolatry, in a way that both Limborch and Orobio abhor.[72] By contrast with this dizzying confusion that in fact characterizes Christianity, the Israel's scriptures, far from requiring some kind of additional, clarifying revelation, are in fact perfectly clear and unambiguous; clear and unambiguous, amongst other things, about the nature of the Messiah who is to come as a political, historical ruler, judge and shepherd of his people.[73] Orobio praises millenarian forms of Christianity, including the English Fifth Monarchists of recent history, which acknowledge this evident messianic surplus of the scriptures as still outstanding and refuse to spiritualize it or postpone it until the day of judgment.[74] The only unclarity that Christian exegesis "solves" is the unclarity it has itself created by refusing to accept the plain meaning of such texts and insisting they must pertain to something to which they patently do not, the past life and death of Jesus of Nazareth and the subsequent history of the Christian Church.[75]

What is particularly interesting is how the debate about "clarity" becomes implicated in the Christian claim about newness. Commenting in his second text on his first question, about the need for salvation through faith in the Messiah, Orobio explains that he only asked it so that a Jew could consider the passages to which a Christian might direct him and consider their implications for himself,

> certain, that God has revealed most clearly everything which he foresaw to be simply and absolutely necessary for the salvation of his own people, lest they be deceived by the succession of times and the persuasion of the nations. This we believe pertains to the divine providence and love which he has always exercised with Israel, not just firmly, but with the utmost constancy.[76]

As Descartes confronted and rejected a deceitful deity in establishing the foundations of his epistemological certainty, so Orobio argues on theological grounds that a God who loves God's people must ensure that this people have clarity through divine revelation about what pertains to their salvation. If it was always God's plan to make belief in the Messiah necessary for salvation at some point in the future, God would have ensured this was clearly communicated to God's people in advance of the event. Limborch has conceded that central Christian doctrines were not so communicated in advance in the Hebrew scriptures, in which case either God is deceitful after all, or Israel is not obligated to accept these doctrines, indeed is obligated not to accept them.

Limborch's response brings us to the heart of the theological debate that opens up in this exchange. He shares Orobio's assumption that certainty of belief depends on clarity of evidence, although according to him God's witness to Christ is clear, through the miracles reliably recorded for us in the New Testament. To Orobio's argument that a loving

God would have "predicted" Jesus as the Christ and the substance of the Church's teaching to his beloved people if these things were going to be necessary for them in the future, Limborch's counterargument is:

> If God had already previously through the prophets clearly revealed the grace that was to be revealed through the Messiah, the Messiah could have revealed nothing new, and the prophet, by whose ministry God had revealed that grace, would have fulfilled a great part of the Messiah's office.[77]

The impasse here indicates the irreconcilable starting points of the two interlocutors: Limborch takes it for granted that the Messiah to whom the scriptures of Israel point is the bearer of a new revelation from God, while Orobio takes it for granted that he is not, but will rather be the restorer of the one original revelation to Moses.

Orobio shows perhaps a clearer grasp that this is the fundamental point at issue than Limborch, particularly in his third contribution, where he argues at some length that any prophet in the tradition of the Jewish scriptures must of necessity be one who speaks in accordance with the Law of Moses and calls for renewed faith in the God who gave that Law, not a new faith in himself.[78] Orobio defines fulfilment of prophecy—even when it pertains to the coming of another prophet, as with Deuteronomy 18:15-22, a favourite text with Christian writers on Judaism—as necessarily constrained by faithfulness to the one revelation of God to Moses. Limborch, by contrast, defines prophetic fulfilment as consisting in a new, subsequent revelation. It is hard to be confident as to whether he would wish to argue that the Old Testament made it clear that such a new revelation was going to be given; it seems to be enough for him, at least in the context of his debate with Orobio, to argue that the Old Testament made it clear that a Messiah was coming, and that when he came, Israel should heed his message. Given Jesus was attested as the Messiah by God, Israel was then obliged to heed his teaching, and to be open to the possibility that it could constitute a new, further revelation beyond the one given to Moses.

The Non-Predictability of the Christian Gospel

From the perspective of Christian theology, what emerges from Limborch's responses to Orobio is a recognition that the *novum* of the Christian Gospel actually requires the *non*-predictability of Jesus' life, death and resurrection, and the doctrines of the Church that arose in response to this, from the text of what Christians call the Old Testament.

At one level, Limborch can be understood as recovering something of the original Pauline interpretation of scripture, beyond the assertions about "proving" that Jesus was the Messiah from scripture that we find in Luke-Acts and which then became foundational for subsequent Christian tradition. All Limborch needs, in his own eyes, to demonstrate the truth of Christianity is two things: an acceptance of the Hebrew scriptures as divinely inspired and requiring a messianic reading, and an acceptance of the New Testament evidence about Jesus as attested by God through miraculous signs as Messiah.

Once that double acceptance has led to Christian faith and an initial understanding of the new revelation that has come through Christ, then one can reread the words of the Law and the Prophets and see how although they may have a literal fulfilment in the history of Israel,

> in a second and mystical sense they have been fulfilled in Christ our Lord, indeed in a most perfect way, with the sense of the letter received in its fullness.[79]

This rereading of the (thereby) Old Testament as fulfilled in Christ, however, is detached by Limborch from any kind of claim about the Hebrew scriptures containing texts that predicted the specifics of Jesus' life and the Church's teaching. At a stroke, that approach unravels the bulk of Jewish-Christian debate prior to this point. It leads to a much clearer and more rigorous assertion of the newness of the Christian Gospel. Yet it also leaves the "fit" between that Gospel and the Church's Old Testament looking somewhat precarious, once it is no longer anchored in any detailed exegesis of correspondences. That precariousness appears to reopen the question of the second-century "radical Paulines" such as Marcion: does the Church really need an "Old Testament" at all? Even if the Jewish Bible speaks of a general anticipation of a new work of God and can be read retrospectively as filled with spiritual meanings, could one not say much the same of some of the great works of pagan antiquity?

Miracles without Prophecy

We have already noted that Limborch's strategy for arguing with Orobio focuses attention on comparing the miracles of Moses and Christ, and the reliability of the evidence for establishing them. One effect of his weakening from the Christian side of the probative force of the argument from Old Testament prophecy is to place ever greater weight on the argument from miracles to demonstrate the truths of the Christian faith. Defences of Christianity in the early modern period tended to appeal to two supposedly indisputable foundations for validation of the Church's truth against unbelievers of all sorts, now including overt sceptics regarding any religious claims at all: the evident fulfilment of specific Old Testament texts in Christ and Christian history, and the miraculous attestation of Jesus as God's Messiah and Son—an approach summed up as "prophecy and miracles". Furthermore, some of the most intelligent defenders of orthodox Christianity regarded the argument from prophecy as the more primary and compelling of the two. According to Pascal, for instance,

> The most weighty proofs of Jesus are the prophecies. It is for them that God made most provision, for the event which fulfilled them is a miracle, continuing from the birth of the Church to the end.[80]

George Herbert, advising the "Country Parson" on how to debate with the doubters he is already likely to encounter in the English village of the earlier seventeenth century, recommends the appeal to prophecy as particularly immediate, and less prone to difficult questions about why we see no miracles today: "Now a Prophesie is a wonder sent to Posterity, lest they complaine of want of wonders."[81]

If the appeal to the demonstrative value of prophetic fulfilment was recognized as no longer intellectually effective, however, as the Jewish critique of Christianity had always maintained and Limborch as a Christian theologian appeared prepared to concede, that left the entire burden of proof for Christianity on the second half of the conventional twofold validation—miracles. Indeed, in the eighteenth century thinkers belonging to what Jonathan Israel calls the "moderate Enlightenment," who still adhered to Christianity in some form, placed increasingly exclusive reliance on the empirical evidence for biblical miracles in seeking to demonstrate the rationality of belief in revealed, and not just "natural", religion.[82] In retrospect, admitting the power of the Jewish theological critique of Christianity regarding the fulfilment of prophecy left Christian theology that was seeking to respond to the "radical Enlightenment" on its own ground of reason in a highly precarious position.

The End of Prophecy: From Locke to Collins

Limborch's exchanges with Orobio begin to sketch out both new possibilities and new dilemmas for Christian theology that puts to one side the scripture claim of fulfilment in Christ as this had been traditionally conceived in pre-modernity. In this section, our focus shifts to England—

though not without some important references back to the Dutch Republic, with which England had particularly close ties during the seventeenth century. In the work of John Locke and then still more overtly in Anthony Collins, prophecy becomes more marginal still for theological discourse than it had been in the case of Limborch, who accepted that specific predictions about Jesus from the Hebrew scriptures could not be compelling but was concerned to reformulate what it might mean to claim nonetheless that Jesus was the fulfilment of biblical prophecy. By the eighteenth century, a way of doing Christian theology is becoming visible that puts to one side the understanding of the gospel's newness in terms of prophetic fulfilment, an understanding intrinsic to what we have been calling the classic framework. Engagement with Jewish texts and disdain for Jewish life both have a significant role here, as once again Judaism and anti-Judaism shape crucial developments in Christian theology.

The Foundations of Reasonable Christianity

Limborch first met the English philosopher John Locke, in exile in the Netherlands, at the dissection of a lioness, and a significant friendship between them developed over the following years after Locke's stay in Amsterdam in the winter of 1683-84. Locke took a great interest in Limborch's literary debate with Orobio and in its progress towards publication; some of his comments about it have been noted already. In 1685, Locke wrote to Limborch asking to see again "those writings of your own and of Don Balthasar [i.e. Orobio] which you lent me some time ago."[83] What would become the *Amica collatio* was still a work in progress at this point; later on the same year, Limborch apologizes for not being able to send Locke his "response" to Orobio, probably referring at this stage to the second response in the final text.[84] When the book was finally ready for publication in 1687, Limborch sent Locke an unbound copy before even Orobio himself had seen the final, bound volume, and both men are fulsome in expressing their debts to one another in relation to it. Limborch explains that he wants Locke to be the first to receive the volume because of his editorial assistance, including supplying additional arguments; in responding to his friend's covering letter, Locke insists that "you could not have bestowed this volume on anyone else who could have longed for it as much, and found it as acceptable, as I."[85]

While Locke's praise of the *Amica collatio* may in part have been a matter of courtesy, it has been argued that his involvement with Limborch's project was a significant factor in moving him beyond a predominantly political concern with Judaism as a test case for religious tolerance in the modern state to a more traditionally theological desire to hasten Jewish conversions—which Locke, along with some other contemporary thinkers, appears to have eventually come to believe would result in their restoration to the land of Israel and the rebuilding of the temple.[86] Moreover, it is clear that his own major theological text, *The Reasonableness of Christianity as Delivered in the Scriptures*, published a few years later than the *Amica collatio* in 1695, shares much common ground with Limborch and with the approach of the *Amica collatio* in particular. Yet the immediate context for Locke's work is quite different. In the opening pages of the *Reasonableness of Christianity*, Locke presents himself as seeking a *via media* on the doctrine of salvation between two extremes, on the one hand those who considered "all *Adam's* Posterity doomed to Eternal Infinite Punishment for the Transgression of *Adam*" and on the other those who "made Jesus Christ nothing but the Restorer and Preacher of pure Natural Religion"; in other words, between conservative Calvinists and the emerging deists.[87]

The mediating position Locke proposes, based exclusively (so he claims) on scripture, is essentially that taken up by Limborch in his debate with Orobio: salvation now requires belief in Jesus as the Messiah expected by the Jews, because God has revealed that he is the Messiah through the attestation of miracles. Locke supplements the testimony of miracles in key passages not with the testimony of fulfilled prophecy, as was conventional, but by (variously) Jesus' own "profession" to be the Messiah, the "Good he did" and "the unblameable Life he led."[88] Particularly when commenting on specific New Testament texts that make explicit fulfilment claims, he is happy to assert the existence of detailed correspondences between Jesus' life and Old Testament prophecy,[89] yet this does not play the same part in his cumulative argument for the Messiahship of Jesus as the evidence of miracles and of Jesus' own life and teaching. One reason for this becomes clear in chapter X: Locke accepts, with Limborch, that such correspondences were only discernible, even for the first apostles, retrospectively, in the light of the resurrection, so that they could not plausibly be presented as having any kind of demonstrative power in making the case for Jesus as Messiah to those who had not already accepted this on other grounds.[90] They simply serve as an additional confirmation for those who believe. Indeed, in a reply to John Edwards, one of the fiercest critics of the *Reasonableness of Christianity*, Locke explicitly maintains that the kind of evidence for the gospel set out by the writer of the letter to the Hebrews, "by showing its correspondence with the Old Testament, and particularly with the economy of the Mosaical constitution," is only intended for those who already believe; this is quite distinct from what Jesus and the apostles "taught and required to be believed, to make men Christians."[91]

Locke's treatise, published anonymously, immediately generated a great deal of hostile opposition from those who saw themselves as defenders of the "orthodox" faith. On one level, this might seem surprising: for all his eminence as a philosopher, Locke does not even acknowledge the circulation of sceptical arguments about the historical plausibility of the New Testament, using the Gospels (including, crucially, John) and Acts to reconstruct the teaching and ministry of Christ and the first apostles, and even claiming, at one point, that Jesus' miracles "never were, nor could be denied by any of the Enemies or Opposers of Christianity"[92]—and this from a man who helped Limborch with the counterarguments to Orobio! Yet the effect of deploying the new "method of arguing" that he and Limborch had developed against Orobio in the rather different context of debate with the early deists was to bring to the surface what is already implicit in the *Amica collatio*: that some traditional Christian truths are deemed foundational for establishing faith, while others have at best a secondary and supplementary role.

There remains in Limborch a certain ambiguity about the extent to which the distinction between essential and non-essential doctrines is simply a strategic one, i.e. it concerns priority in the process by which an unbeliever comes to believe, rather than priority in theological significance as such. Thus in the *Amica collatio*, it is at least possible to read Limborch's insistence on the "minimal" affirmation of Jesus as the Messiah as the necessary pivot for Orobio to move from Judaism to Christianity, which transition having been made everything else in Christian doctrine—incarnation, Trinity, atonement—will follow in its turn. The *Reasonableness of Christianity*, however, is quite opaque about what, if anything, is to be added to this bare, fundamental affirmation of Christian faith. Moreover, Locke is quite explicit that everything else that might be claimed as pertaining to it, including traditional Christian doctrines hitherto shared by Catholics and Protestants alike, can only have at best a secondary and non-foundational status compared to the one "necessary" belief that Jesus is the Messiah. Thus in setting out his view that the essentials of Christianity can be derived from a reading of the Gospels and Acts alone, without recourse to the Epistles, he draws a clear distinction between "the Fundamental Articles of the Christian Faith," which are "necessary to Salvation," and the many other truths contained in the Bible, "which a good Christian may be wholly ignorant of, and so not believe."[93]

It was this apparent relegation of much traditional orthodox Church teaching to a secondary position that many of Locke's first readers found so alarming, and perhaps not without cause. It is at least arguable that while Locke is careful to leave a space for Christian doctrines beyond the Messiahship of Jesus, for his own part he preferred to leave it empty.[94] It is surely significant in this regard that when, in the penultimate chapter of the *Reasonableness of Christianity*, he directly addresses the question of what Jesus is other than "the Restorer and Preacher of Natural Religion"— or, in the terms, we have been using, what is the "new thing" that God has done in Christ—he seems to struggle to articulate a wholly convincing answer. Through Jesus, he claims, there have come about the following: the spread of belief in one God; knowledge of duty and virtue; reformation of "the outward forms of *Worshipping the Deity*"; the encouragement to lead a virtuous life through the clear presentation of the hope of life beyond death; and the promise of assistance in the moral task—"If we do what we can, he will give us his Spirit to help us to do what, and how we should."[95] What is particularly noteworthy for the purposes of the present study in Locke's catalogue is that while in his overview of the Christian *novum* he makes no reference at all to the Old Testament as prophecy, he does however make significant mention of the state of Judaism in the first century, as evidently incapable of being the means for promoting the worthy things just listed; hence the need for Jesus Christ and the Church.[96] In other words, the appeal to the Jewish scriptures as prophecy has been displaced by a form of theological argument that relies on a historical narrative including Jewish decline and intrinsic limitation in order to legitimate Christianity. We will return to this point in a moment.

The Dilemma of "Scripture Alone" in the New Christian Theology

The absence of any mention of the Old Testament as scripture in Locke's summary of God's purpose in sending Jesus confirms the marginal status of the argument from prophecy in Locke's earlier discussion of the New Testament evidence about belief in Jesus. There may be many retrospectively discernible correspondences, but these possess a confirmatory function only for the task of Christian theology, which must place itself on firmer foundations. We can already detect an emerging dilemma for "modern" Christian theology here. Limborch and Locke appealed to the Reformation principle of *sola scriptura*, but unlike the Reformers themselves the rejected "other" to scripture for them was not so much the edifice of Western Catholicism as any kind of theological presupposition or framework about scripture's meaning. So Locke begins the Preface to the *Reasonableness of Christianity*:

> The little Satisfaction and Consistency is to be found in most of the Systems of Divinity I have met with, made me betake my self to the sole Reading of Scripture (to which they all appeal) for the understanding the Christian Religion.[97]

And scripture is to be read, as he argues in the first chapter, according to

> the plain direct meaning of the words and phrases, such as they may be supposed to have had in the mouths of the Speakers . . . without such learned, artificial, and forced senses of them, as are sought out, and put upon them in most Systems of Divinity.[98]

There is an evident analogy between Locke's approach to the problems of theology in this treatise and his approach to knowledge in the *Essay concerning Human Understanding*, where he also distinguishes his work by "this Historical, plain Method."[99] Later on in the *Essay*, however, Locke notes how difficult it is to decide what the meaning of a biblical passage is beyond all reasonable doubt—a point that leads the author to praise the comparative simplicity and directness of divine communication in natural religion.[100] At least part of the problem for would-be rational theologians was that while their own preferred method of setting things out might be plain and direct, scripture itself did not necessarily appear to be written with this priority in mind. In what sense, then, did they really accept the *sola scriptura* of the Reformers? Was not their ultimate criterion in fact a form of rationality arrived at quite independently of scripture and revelation, and therefore never entirely at ease with them?

The exegetical practice of the Christian Bible itself—most importantly, the interpretation of Old Testament texts in the New—posed a particularly sharp version of this dilemma. The "plain direct meaning" of many New Testament passages was that at least selected portions of the Old Testament looked forward explicitly to critical events in the life of Christ and the history of the Church. Yet the "plain direct meaning of the words and phrases" of those Old Testament texts themselves, "such as they may be supposed to have had in the mouths of the [original] Speakers," did not in fact appear to have anything to do with the events of the New Testament in most cases. Kimhi and Troki were right in that regard, it would seem; at the very least, Locke shows no inclination to refute them, and in his relegation of such matters to the second division of the edifying but optional in Christian thought he implies an endorsement of their verdict that many contemporaries found highly alarming. But did that then make the New Testament authors actually mistaken? Troki certainly thought so, and argued the point at some length.[101] We have no reason to think that Limborch and Locke would have agreed, but they fail to provide any convincing counterarguments either. How could they have responded? Conceding to Troki and other Jewish critics the unreliability of the New Testament authors in interpreting—and even simply quoting—the Old would inevitably open up a whole gamut of questions about the historical reliability of the New Testament as such, on which Limborch and Locke were increasingly placing enormous theological weight, not least in their dependence on it for the supposedly unquestionable evidence for miracles. It would also prompt the sceptical question about the criterion for their criterion: why should the "plain direct meaning" of a biblical text be determinative for us, as Limborch and Locke insisted it must be, given that it clearly was not for the "authoritative" New Testament writers themselves in their approach to interpreting their own scriptures?

Troki concluded his section on biblical quotations in the New Testament with the observation that

> Many Christian commentators have lost their way, while attempting to reconcile those inconsistencies which we perceive in the New Testament, and they have found it necessary to assert, that it is not right to argue on these dubious matters.[102]

That loss of confidence is surely part of the background for Limborch's new "method of arguing" with Jews. Yet Locke's extension of Limborch's method into constructive theology pointed towards the potentially disastrous consequences of abandoning the traditional understanding of the first claim of the classic framework not only for any attempted continuation of pre-modern forms of Christian doctrine but also, as has just been suggested, for the "modern" theology of Limborch and Locke, with its attempt to make the "plain direct meaning" of scripture foundational. Was there any way in which the pre-modern Christian confidence in direct and detailed prophetic fulfilment could be sustained in the light of new approaches to biblical scholarship stemming ultimately from the Renaissance and humanism?

Christian Hebraism vs. Sceptical Deism

There had certainly been no shortage of effort in responding to the challenge of restating the Christological interpretation of the Old Testament in the light of new thinking: the seventeenth century had witnessed, alongside the developments already reviewed in this chapter, an enormous amount of scholarship being invested in Hebrew studies. This work was focused on the Old Testament but also engaged with post-biblical Judaism and fed into the composition of comparative histories which sought to fit the biblical narrative as a whole into a comprehensive chronology of human civilizations from the creation onwards. This tradition of Christian Hebraism had its roots in the work of Renaissance figures such as Reuchlin. Yet while the conscious, or at least public, motivation for such endeavour tended to be the defence of orthodox faith in the face of honest questioning and hostile critique, by the midpoint of the century it was clear that attempted scholarly resolutions of textual and historical problems relating to the Old Testament tended in practice to raise ever more troubling issues for traditional approaches.[103] Confidence in the potential of such work to contribute positively to current theological debate and vindicate conventional arguments from biblical prophecy in the face of increasingly overt scepticism ebbed away thereafter.

The tradition of Christian Hebraism had not entirely died, however, at the start of the eighteenth century, and another Dutchman, Willem Surenhuis can be seen as one of its last significant representatives.[104] Surenhuis' principal scholarly achievement was the publication of a complete Latin translation of the Mishnah, and drawing on the exceptional historical knowledge of Judaism that he had thereby gained, he published the *Biblos katalleges* in 1713. In this book he addressed directly the question of the use of Old Testament passages in the New, arguing that the "inconsistencies" highlighted by Troki and others—in textual accuracy as well as respect for the original context of quotations—were only inconsistencies by modern standards of interpretation. According to him, the approach of the New Testament writers to the interpretation of the sacred text of scripture was of a piece with that of the Jewish contributors to the Mishnah, who showed the same kinds of creative flexibility, ultimately governed by a precise set of rules, in their deployment of biblical passages. Spinoza and Locke alike had insisted that we read scripture in the light of its original context—linguistic, literary and historical. Surenhuis asked for the New Testament quotations to be read in *their* context, which was a particular—Jewish—context of biblical interpretation, within which they made perfect sense and were entirely legitimate and indeed consistent. In fact, Surenhuis explains the central purpose of the *Biblos katalleges* as a defence of the *integritas scripturae*—the wholeness and consistency of the Christian Bible.

Surenhuis was not a speculative theologian, and his belief in the divine inspiration of the Mishnah meant that his case for using it as a guide to reading the New Testament was not simply about historical context. That belief was, of course, idiosyncratic, if not indeed unique, and it was not difficult for Surenhuis' intended defence of scriptural consistency to be turned to more critical purposes—as was done by the English writer Anthony Collins, in his *Discourse of the Grounds and Reasons of the Christian Religion*, published in 1724.[105] Collins, a friend and disciple of Locke, had made precisely the transition for which Locke's critics feared he paved the way, to the overt rejection of the claims of institutional Christianity. In the *Discourse*, Collins makes the case for abandoning prophetic fulfilment claims rigorously and explicitly. As with Spinoza, familiarity with inter-religious polemic, in this case Jewish anti-Christian writings, of which Collins had clearly made a careful study, is put at the disposal of essentially anti-religious argumentation (insofar as religion is conceived as making binding intellectual and political claims).[106]

At first glance, Collins' argument proceeds from eminently respectable assumptions of traditional Christianity: the claim, foundational from the New Testament onwards, that "the truth of christianity depends . . . on antient revelations, which are contain'd in the Old Testament";[107] and the principle of Christian hermeneutics, clearly formulated in Thomas Aquinas, that doctrine must rest on the literal sense of scripture, while it is illustrated and confirmed by the spiritual sense.[108] From these two assumptions, Collins presents his orthodox Christian opponents with a dilemma: either the fulfilment of Old Testament prophecies in the New arises from the literal meaning of those prophecies, or they are instances of spiritual exegesis only. Yet it is agreed, Collins argues, that the relevant texts are

> sometimes, either not to be found in the *Old*, or not urg'd in the *New*, according to the literal and obvious sense, which they seem to bear in their suppos'd place in the *Old* . . . therefore not proofs according to scholastick rules.[109]

Responsible biblical scholarship means that we must take the second horn of the dilemma and admit that the fulfilment of prophecy is only ever a matter of spiritual interpretation. Yet if that is the case, then the fundamental truth of Christianity, with its fulfilment claims necessary to make sense of the assertion that Jesus is the Messiah, rests itself on no solid foundation, given that doctrinal truths cannot rely on spiritual exegesis alone.

It is at this point that Collins is able to deploy selected passages from Surenhuis in order to buttress his case that New Testament exegesis of the Old is indeed spiritual, or "mystical" through and through, and therefore cannot be used to establish doctrine.[110] Surenhuis' work also, however, serves other purposes for Collins. Shorn of its peculiar theological context, it becomes an argument for the historical relativization of the New Testament itself: it was written in a particular way for a particular situation which no longer obtains. Collins argues (with some plausibility) that while Jews in the apostolic period were sympathetic to the exegetical methods deployed in the New Testament writings, very soon afterwards they ceased to be, so that such methods have become an actual obstacle to persuading them to convert (as Limborch's procedure implicitly concedes).[111] What may have served a purpose once need have no binding force for the rest of time—as Aquinas argued in relation to the Mosaic Law.

There is also another dimension to Collins' use of Surenhuis that is harder to pin down. It seems likely that Collins enjoys drawing on prevalent anti-Judaism and perhaps also antisemitism in depicting the New Testament authors as essentially "rabbinic" in their outlook. For the overwhelming majority of Christians—unlike Surenhuis—the rabbis from the Mishnah to the present day stood for spiritual blindness and moral sclerosis. Moreover, if anything the divisions of the Reformation intensified such hostility, with each side accusing the other of identification with the faithless and rejected Jewish synagogue.[112] The residual Torah observance of primitive Christianity—along with the frequent working of miracles—was seen by many seventeenth-century Protestants as part of the immaturity of that period which was swiftly and providentially overcome. Did the New Testament exegesis of the Old also belong to that same immaturity, something we should have long outgrown? And in that case, was there any real substance left to a religion whose fundamental claim was about fulfilment, Jesus of Nazareth as the one anointed by God to bring about God's prophesied purpose?

After Prophecy: Newness as Historical Development

It is important to remember that most mainstream European Christianity in the eighteenth and nineteenth centuries continued, despite all of this debate, to maintain and defend as foundational for faith and theology the thoroughgoing Christological interpretation of scripture that had been developed by the early Fathers and still accepted by the great Reformers.[113] Yet the new availability to non-Jews of Jewish anti-Christian polemic, the continuation of the humanistic study of scripture and Christian origins in historical scholarship and the existence of overt religious scepticism in the public domain all rendered this increasingly hard to sustain, ultimately for much the same reasons that seventeenth-century figures such as Grotius, Limborch and Locke had sought alternative foundations for Christian truth. For those who accepted that the argument from prophecy, still so compelling in the eyes of Pascal and Herbert alike for their rather different audiences, could no longer be presented as possessing demonstrative value in an age that valued clarity and demanded direct evidence, the potential alternatives were also already largely set out in the seventeenth-century discussions, certainly as long as it was assumed that what has no demonstrative value for the unconvinced cannot take a foundational role in an intellectual enterprise. If the newness of Christianity could no longer be explicated as the fulfilment of prophecy to Israel, then either it should not be presented as a new thing at all, but simply as a variation on the ancient universal of religion; or it could be re-described in historical terms as a genuine and indeed decisive development relative in the first place to Judaism and then also to other religious varieties current both at its inception and subsequently. In the case of the second alternative, the interrelated pattern of claims and judgments recurs beyond the subversion of the classic framework by the loss of confidence in prophetic fulfilment. With it, the intertwining of Christian theology's development with exchanges with Judaism and rationalization of anti-Judaism is also evident, as we would expect from the basic hypothesis of this study, the inseparability of claims about Christian newness from the need to give some kind of account of Jewish persistence.

The Path of Religious Relativism

Spinoza paves the way for the formal articulation of the dilemma's first resolution, Christianity as a particular variation on the universal theme of religion, in eighteenth-century English deism and then in Continental Enlightenment thought.[114] If the essential and eternal truths about humanity, the world and God are knowable through rational reflection, as Spinoza maintained, then religions are simply the cultural embedding—and obscuring—of those truths in myth, instruction and ritual. As such, religions certainly serve a cultural, social and historical purpose, but they cannot convey any new truth to the truly rational person, while if there is to be some kind of "culmination" of history imagined at all, it could only be the total replacement of institutional religion with philosophical thought and the kind of human community expected to follow from that.

Within such very general parameters, there could be more and less positive estimates of the particular contribution of Christianity. The title of Matthew Tindal's work, *Christianity as Old as Creation: Or, The Gospel a Republication of the Religion of Nature*, shows an evident continuity

with the view of the deists noted in Locke's introduction to the
Reasonableness of Christianity, in which Christianity is (apparently)
valued as an especially pure form of the one original and eternal core of
religion.[115] Later Enlightenment figures, such as Reimarus in Germany,
begin to paint it in rather darker colours, picking up on Orobio's
suggestions in the *Amica collatio* that the apostles could have had their
own motives for falsifying the historical evidence about Jesus. There is
also the development of a historical narrative here, most famously in
Gibbon, but also with roots in Spinoza if not beyond, in which
Christianity's adoption of the "exclusive" claims of Judaism is actually
seen as precipitating a moral and religious decline from the tolerant
inclusiveness of non-Christian ancient philosophy. As with Spinoza
himself, such an approach borrows happily from Christian anti-Judaism
and Jewish writing against Christianity alike in order to tar both religions
with the brush of prejudice and irrationalism. Still, such overt hostility to
prevailing institutional religious forms could itself seem less than fair and
generous by the standards of some other Enlightenment thinkers.

One of the most memorable presentations of the view of Christianity as
one among many variations on the universal phenomenon of religion
comes in Gotthold Lessing's play *Nathan the Wise*. The approach is not
only conveyed through the (repeated) re-telling of Boccacio's parable of
the three rings,[116] but also more generally in the mixture of criticism
levelled in the course of the play against each of the claimants to final
religious authority, Christianity, Judaism and Islam, with the attribution of
positive qualities to at least some of the representatives of each. The
message is clear that any theological claim to truth or religious claim to
political authority must be treated with a high degree of scepticism if not
actual resistance, while the religions as such have been and still can be
forces for good in human history. The depiction of a Jewish hero in the
figure of Nathan himself has to be set against the Templar's speech that
presents the Jewish claim to election as the root of all religious fanaticism
and intolerance, quite in the line of the non-Christian intellectual anti-
Judaism of Spinoza, Gibbon and Reimarus:

> . . . But do you know the folk
> That was the first to carp at other tribes?
> Was first to call itself the chosen people?
> Suppose that I did not exactly hate,
> But for its pride was forced to scorn that folk:
> That pride it then passed on to Christians, Moslem,
> Which says their god alone is the true god![117]

For Lessing, religion can be valued only insofar as it abstains from theological or political claims—but what kind of religion is that? The inherent instability of an approach claiming to hold all religious claims within an equal tension is indicated by Lessing's affinity for Spinoza's philosophical transposition of the Joachite "eternal gospel".[118] However much cultured admiration there may be in Lessing's case for individual religious figures (not least his Jewish friend Moses Mendelssohn) and insistence on the continuing social necessity of institutional religion, the truly new in history can only be understood as a return of the eternal, the "necessary truths of reason" that will sweep away all excessive attachment to the "accidental truths of history" and with it the varieties of historical religion that have been known hitherto.

The Path of Historical Superiority

If religious relativism was one possible response to loss of confidence in the first claim of the classic framework and the traditions of figural and allegorical interpretation associated with it, there was also another path that could be pursued. If Spinoza points to the first in the later seventeenth century, Locke shows the way to the second. Locke might be regarded as the symbolic father of those forms of modern theology that wanted to avoid any foundational status for fulfilment claims whilst also maintaining the definitive "newness" of Christianity and thus preserving its theological claims to uniqueness and universality, against the (deist and Enlightenment) reduction of Christian faith to a particular variation on the general theme of religion. Inevitably, such newness now has to be explicated in comparative terms, as historical superiority: how Jesus and then the Church brought something radically and irreplaceably "new" into human history relative to what was already present in Judaism and Greco-Roman paganism and to other, later forms of religion such as Islam.

In refuting the historical relativism of the first approach, Locke chooses to meet it on its chosen ground of "objective" history in his affirmation of the significance of Jesus Christ, as we have seen in his treatment of this topic in chapter XV of the *Reasonableness of Christianity*. His narrative of historical development in religion and morals can be set against Gibbon's counter-narrative of decline—both being attributed to the influence of Christ and the Christian Church. This kind of approach to Christianity as an unsurpassable historical development, however, also necessarily spawned its own, internal dilemmas. How can absolute newness be legitimated by comparative historical study? How can the prospect be ruled out of a future religion (Lessing's eternal gospel, perhaps) that would achieve everything that Locke ascribes to the coming of Christ and more besides, thus being entitled to claim a place as Christianity's successor? Locke's point of resistance to the application of sceptical relativism to matters of religion by Spinoza and the deists seems to be inherently precarious, as the figure of Collins already suggests. If religions are to be evaluated for their relative "success" in teaching truth and morality, then all particular religions are already rendered subordinate to some kind of formulation of truth and morality transcending the doctrines of any particular religion, which can hardly be so very different from what Spinoza, Tindal and Lessing alike would have called natural religion or the religion of nature. Such a strategy, while seeking to "save" revealed religion, has already effectively conceded the superior authority of natural religion with the first move in its argument, and therefore cannot indefinitely resist relativizing the claims of any particular historical faith. The instability in such modern theology is the direct descendant of the instability discerned in the attempts of medieval thinkers such as Peter Abelard to make the case for the superiority of the new law against the old by appealing to the common standard of the natural, eternal law of reason.[119]

"Christianity without Judaism"

From the point of view of this study, however, what is perhaps more important to note is that such emphasis on the historical newness of Christianity relative to Judaism tended to leave the status of the Old Testament as something of a question mark, most immediately in terms of its foundational status for Christian theology. Locke's attempt to derive the essential truths of Christianity from the New Testament alone, and indeed from his inner canon of the Gospels and Acts, would convince few of its particular conclusions, but many would follow the same basic method. If the Old Testament is nonetheless retrospectively illuminating, as Locke and Limborch maintain, that still does not seem to render it authoritative canonical scripture in the same way as the New Testament. [120] Thomas Sherlock, who wrote against Anthony Collins in defence of what was perceived to be orthodoxy, is in complete agreement with the position that, even in the case of something as central as the resurrection of Jesus, particular prophecies can only confirm the truth of what has already been ascertained on other grounds; a general Christological reading of the Old Testament is something to which Christian theology may eventually proceed, but certainly not a point from which it may begin.[121]

Even this vestigial respect for comprehensive figural reading of the Christian Bible comes to be rejected by the rationalizing historical critics of the later eighteenth century, who fiercely oppose the retention of spiritual interpretation among the Pietists.[122] With that ancient anchorage of Christianity in the text of the Hebrew scriptures cut away, voices openly advocating the Old Testament's relegation from or at least demotion within the canon of Christian scripture begin to be heard for the first time since the early centuries, voices that would ultimately include two of the most influential figures for nineteenth- and earlier twentieth-century theology, Kant and Schleiermacher.[123] Nor was this disenchantment restricted to leading voices in German theology. In Victorian England, Baden Powell, professor of geometry at Oxford, published a book in 1858 entitled *Christianity without Judaism*, while the great novelists Dickens and Thackeray shared both a profound reverence for the New Testament and outright hostility to the Old.[124] The Old Testament, for Pascal the source of the most powerful arguments for the truth of Christianity, was being perceived as at best marginal, at worst a liability for the Church's faith in the context of the modern age.

At the same time, historical studies increasingly suggested the substantial continuity of the early Christian movement with its Jewish origins, material made much of by champions, such as Reimarus, of the position that Christianity is simply one variation on the universal. This virtually required the defenders of Christianity's historical superiority to minimize Christian debts to Judaism, especially first-century Judaism, and to portray it in the blackest colours possible, so that the brightness of the Christian *novum* could shine and avoid becoming obscured in the mists of historical relativism. This is a point we will consider in more detail in the following chapter.

The replacement of newness as prophetic fulfilment by newness as historical development did not only have implications for the evaluation of Israel's biblical past, however. With it, the continuation of inferior Judaism through history since the coming of Christ became something quite inexplicable, no longer susceptible of being interpreted as the activity of divine providence in preserving God's former people for *testimonium veritatis*, a testimony specifically to prophetic truth through their custodianship of the Hebrew scriptures, prior to the overcoming of the division of history with the conversion of "all Israel" in the last days. That eschatological horizon had also disappeared in modern theology. Schleiermacher went further than the letter to the Hebrews: no longer "growing old," Judaism was "long since dead," and "Those who wear its livery only sit lamenting around its mummy."[125] The interconnected negative evaluations of contemporary, first-century and Old Testament Judaism in some kinds of nineteenth-century theology and religious culture need to be understood in the context of the theological moves set out in the previous sections of this chapter, as deriving from fault lines within the position that re-described Christianity's newness in terms of intra-historical development. Those fault lines came under ever greater pressure from the constant need to prevent that position collapsing back into a view of Christianity itself as simply one religious variation amongst many. The path of historical superiority was always in danger of suddenly bending back into the broad path of religious relativism.

When certain strands in the Christianity of modernity, then, turned away from the Christologically focused prophetic relationship between the Old Testament and the New, thereby breaking decisively with pre-modern Christianity, they did not leave behind the problem of how to articulate the newness of the Christian good news in the light of the persistence of Judaism. Nor did they dissolve the pre-modern inheritance of anti-Judaism in Christian theology as the shadow of its claims about the gospel. In rephrasing the scripture claim of the traditional framework in terms of progressive revelation rather than prophetic fulfilment, the judgment of Jewish interpretive blindness was restated rather than removed. Much the same could be said of the covenant judgment and the people judgment, the displacement of Torah and the division of history, whose reformulation was now industriously supported with all the might of supposedly scientific historical scholarship. The effect of these shifts was to leave the "surd" of enduring Judaism in the present more perplexing than ever. The yearning for consistency could draw modern admirers of clear thinking towards more radical solutions than the pre-modern mainstream had ever contemplated, in which the disappearance of Judaism within history, and of the Old Testament as scripture within the Church, could be willed as the completion of the new thing Jesus began with his life and teachings in the first Christian century. It is against this background, necessarily coloured from our perspective by awareness of the Holocaust as a kind of violently distorted reflection of such apparently enlightened religious willing, that we can proceed in the following chapter to consider some of the ways in which the newness of Christ came to be re-described once again in relation to the endurance of Israel during the traumatic upheavals of the first half of the twentieth century.

Notes

1 Cf. the seminal work of Frei, *Eclipse of Biblical Narrative.*

2 For the thirteenth-century Barcelona Disputation, the *Vikuah*, the account of Nahmanides, the Jewish spokesman, can be used as one source (see *Judaism on Trial*, ed. Maccoby, 102-146). Compare, for instance: *Vikuah*, 105-106 with Justin, *Dialogue* LII (Gen. 49:10); *Vikuah*, 112-113 with *Dialogue* XIII-XIV (Is. 52:10ff); *Vikuah*, 135-37 with *Dialogue* XXXII-XXIII (Psalm 110).

3 See Dahan, *Christian Polemic*, 42-53.

4 For some examples, see Schreckenberg, *Jews in Christian Art*, 222-34.

5 Kimhi, *Book of the Covenant*, e.g. 28-30 (on Is. 9:5), and 43-45 (on Gen. 49:10). On the exegetical approach developed by Joseph Kimhi and its subsequent significance, see F. E. Talmage's monograph on Joseph's son, *David Kimhi: The Man and the Commentaries* (Cambridge: Harvard University Press, 1975).

6 *Epistles of Maimonides*, 107-111.

7 Smalley, *Study of the Bible.*

8 Cf. Smalley, *Study of the Bible*, 110-111 and 163 on the debate about Isaiah 7.14-16 within the twelfth-century Victorine school.

9 This continuity is an important theme in the very different work of both de Lubac, *Medieval Exegesis* and Frei, *Eclipse of Biblical Narrative*. Smalley herself recognizes that she underestimated this aspect in her earlier work, in the preface to the third edition of *Study of the Bible*, vii-viii.

10 Cohen, "Scholarship and Intolerance."

11 See the parallel Jewish and Christian accounts of the disputation in *Judaism on Trial*, ed. Maccoby, for instance 105-06 and 147-48.

12 Kimhi, *Book of the Covenant*, 31.

13 The most famous and influential example of such a work is Peter Comestor's *Historia scholastica*; see the comments of Smalley, in *Study of the Bible*, 214-15.

14 Manuel, *Broken Staff*, 13-36.

15 Cf. Edwards, *Jews in Christian Europe*, 43-54.

16 Marc Saperstein, *Moments of Crisis in Jewish-Christian Relations* (London: SCM, 1989), 34-35.

17 One can compare extracts from the two texts in *Disputation and Dialogue*, ed. Talmage, 33-36.

18 Radner, *End of the Church*, 124-125, and also 87-88. Cf. Edwards, *Jews in Christian Europe*, 57-63.

19 Saperstein, *Moments of Crisis*, 27-31; Rowan Williams, *Teresa of Avila* (London: Continuum, 2003), 15-24.

20 See Mark V. Edwards, "Against the Jews," in *Essential Papers*, ed. Cohen, 345-371.

21 Edwards, *Jews in Christian Europe*, 114-133.

22 On Voltaire's "Judeophobia," see Manuel, *Broken Staff*, 193-201.

23 Troki, *Faith Strengthened* I.XXV (133).

24 Troki, *Faith Strengthened* I.XIII (60).

[25] On the interconnection between epistemological debates within theology and philosophy in the sixteenth and seventeenth centuries stemming from the Reformation, see the classic study of Richard H. Popkin, *The History of Scepticism from Erasmus to Spinoza*, 2nd ed. (Berkeley: University of California Press, 1979).

[26] Quoted in Paul Hazard, *The European Mind, 1680-1715*, trans. J. Lewis May (Harmondsworth: Penguin, 1973), 223.

[27] Troki, *Faith Strengthened* I.I, I.VI. The latter chapter includes a helpful list of all the prophecies that Troki regards as clearly unfulfilled (32-38).

[28] See 91-107 above.

[29] Cf. Andrew Bradstock, *Faith in the Revolution: The Political Theologies of Müntzer and Winstanley* (London: SPCK, 1997).

[30] An engraving of them together is reproduced in Schreckenberg, *Jews in Christian Art*, 354.

[31] Troki, *Faith Strengthened* II.1, LVI.

[32] Cf. Troki, *Faith Strengthened*, Introduction to Part II (227-28).

[33] Cf. Schoeps, *Jewish-Christian Argument*, 76.

[34] Troki, *Faith Strengthened* II.XXIII (245-46).

[35] Adam Sutcliffe, *Judaism and Enlightenment* (Cambridge: Cambridge University Press, 2003), 104-112.

[36] The evidence for Spinoza's early intellectual and religious development is reviewed in Jonathan I. Israel, *Radical Enlightenment: Philosophy and the Making of Modernity, 1650-1750* (Oxford: Oxford University Press, 2001), 159-174.

[37] See Popkin, *History of Scepticism*, 229-48.

[38] Baruch Spinoza, *Tractatus theologico-politicus*, trans. Samuel Shirley (Leiden: Brill, 1989), 60. Compare the explicit attack on allegory later on (140-41).

[39] E.g. Spinoza, *Tractatus theologico-politicus*, 96, 98, 115.

[40] Spinoza, *Tractatus theologico-politicus*, 208; cf. *Epistle of Barnabas* 4.6-8 (180).

[41] Spinoza, *Tractatus theologico-politicus*, 113, 282.

[42] Spinoza, *Tractatus theologico-politicus*, 91.

[43] Spinoza, *Tractatus theologico-politicus*, 70.

[44] Spinoza, *Tractatus theologico-politicus*, 121.

[45] Spinoza, *Tractatus theologico-politicus*, 154.

[46] Spinoza, *Tractatus theologico-politicus*, 205.

[47] Spinoza, *Tractatus theologico-politicus*, 308.

[48] Cf. Popkin, *History of Scepticism*, 227-28.

[49] Sutcliffe, *Judaism and Enlightenment*, 124-28.

[50] Thomas Hobbes, *Leviathan*, ed. J. C. A. Gaskin (Oxford: Oxford University Press, 1998), e.g. III.XXXIII-XXXV, 251-77.

[51] Hobbes, *Leviathan*, III.XXXII (249).

[52] Hobbes, *Leviathan*, III.XXXVIII (307-08).

[53] Philippus van Limborch, *De veritate religionis Christianae amica collatio cum erudito Judaeo* (Gouda, 1687). Translations in the text are my own.

[54] On Orobio's life, see Yosef Kaplan, *From Christianity to Judaism: The Story of Isaac Orobio de Castro*, trans. Raphael Loewe (Oxford: Littman Library of Jewish

Civilization, 2004). The series of events leading up to the publication of the *Amica collatio* itself is reconstructed in Peter van Rooden and Jan Wim Wesselius, "The Early Enlightenment and Judaism: The 'Civil Dispute' between Philippus van Limborch and Isaac Orobio de Castro (1687)," *Studia Rosenthaliana* 21 (1987): 140-153.

[55] Cf. Schoeps, *Jewish-Christian Argument*, 88-90.

[56] Orobio, in Limborch, *Amica collatio*, "Tertium scriptum Judaei" IV.VII (143-144); cf. Israel, *Radical Enlightenment*, 307. The wider context of the reception of Spinoza's work is surveyed in Jonathan I. Israel, *The Dutch Republic: Its Rise, Greatness and Fall, 1477-1806* (Oxford: Clarendon, 1995), 916-925.

[57] Quoted from Limborch's *Theologia christiana* in Robert S. Franks, *The Work of Christ: A Historical Study of Christian Doctrine* (London: Nelson, 1962), 378-79.

[58] Limborch, *Amica collatio*, "Responsio ad secundum scriptum Judaei" II (27). Limborch also prays at the very end of this second "Responsio" for the removing of the veil from the hearts of the Jews so that they might join with the Christians in acknowledging Jesus Christ as the Lord (48).

[59] Limborch, *Amica collatio*, "Praefatio ad lectorem." Cf. Kaplan, *From Christianity to Judaism*, 272-73.

[60] E.g. Limborch, *Amica collatio*, "Responsio ad secundum scriptum Judaei" II.VI (41-48).

[61] Limborch, *Amica collatio*, "Praefatio ad lectorem" A3v; Van Rooden and Wesselius, "Early Enlightenment and Judaism."

[62] Kaplan follows Schoeps in underestimating the originality of Limborch's presentation in *From Christianity to Judaism*, e.g. 273 and 284-85.

[63] Both phrases are taken from Limborch's correspondence with John Locke immediately after the publication of the *Amica collatio*, printed in *The Correspondence of John Locke*, ed. E. S. de Beer, 8 vols (Oxford: Clarendon, 1976-89), vol. 3, letters 963-964. The quotation in the previous sentence is taken from letter 979 (301).

[64] Limborch, *Amica collatio*, "Tertium scriptum Judaei," IV.VII-VIII.

[65] Israel, *Radical Enlightenment*, 466.

[66] Limborch, *Amica collatio*, "Responsio ad primum scriptum Judaei," 3. Limborch's departure from previous traditions of Christian debate with Jews is rightly stressed in the analysis of the *Amica collatio* in Sutcliffe, *Judaism and Enlightenment*, 166-70.

[67] Limborch, *Amica collatio*, "Responsio ad primum scriptum Judaei," 3-4.

[68] Cf. Limborch, *Amica collatio*, "Tertium scriptum Judaei," 50.

[69] Limborch, *Amica collatio*, "Secundum scriptum Judaei," 6. Limborch himself simply replies that as a good Reformation Christian, Scripture is his only rule of faith, and not any human author—even Calvin ("Responsio ad secundum scriptum Judaei," I [17]).

[70] Limborch, *Amica collatio*, "Tertium scriptum Judaei," 49-50.

[71] Limborch, *Amica collatio*, "Responsio ad secundum scriptum Judaei" II (23-24), and IV (36-37). Limborch is here reflecting a line of thought that also features in Protestant anti-Catholic writing, which linked spiritual gifts and miracles along

with "the *Ceremonial Law* and *Mosaick* Rites" to the primitive age of the Church which was now surpassed; so John Edwards, writing in 1699, as quoted in Radner, *End of the Church*, 91-92.

[72] Limborch, *Amica collatio*, "Tertium scriptum Judaei" I.VII (57-59).

[73] Limborch, *Amica collatio*, "Secundum scriptum Judaei," 8.

[74] Limborch, *Amica collatio*, "Tertium scriptum Judaei," I.VI (57).

[75] Limborch, *Amica collatio*, "Tertium scriptum Judaei" I.XIII (64-66).

[76] Limborch, *Amica collatio*, "Secundum scriptum Judaei," 10.

[77] Limborch, *Amica collatio*, "Responsio ad secundum scriptum Judaei," I (20).

[78] Limborch, *Amica collatio*, "Tertium scriptum Judaei," III.VII-VIII (107-111); cf. "Primum scriptum Judaei," 14.

[79] Limborch, *Amica collatio*, "Responsio ad secundum scriptum Judaei," V (39).

[80] Pascal, *Pensées* 335 (in Blaise Pascal, *Pensées*, trans. A. J. Krailsheimer [Harmondsworth: Penguin, 1966], 130). Cf. Pascal, *Pensées* 321: "Any man can do what Mahomet did. For he performed no miracles and was not foretold. No man can do what Christ did" (127).

[81] George Herbert, *A Priest to the Temple or The Country Parson with Selected Poems*, ed. Ronald Blythe (Norwich: Canterbury Press, 2003), 81.

[82] Israel, *Radical Enlightenment*, 461-63.

[83] Locke, *Correspondence*, vol. 2, no. 810 (690).

[84] Locke, *Correspondence*, vol.2, no. 832 (743-44). Limborch's third and final response was only completed immediately before the work went to the printer.

[85] Locke, *Correspondence*, vol. 3, nos. 958-59 (258-60).

[86] Nabil I. Mahir, "John Locke and the Jews," *Journal of Ecclesiastical History* 44:1 (1993): 45-62.

[87] John Locke, *The Reasonableness of Christianity as Delivered in the Scriptures*, ed. John C. Higgins-Biddle (Oxford: Clarendon, 1999), 5.

[88] Locke, *Reasonableness of Christianity*, 22-23, 55, 89.

[89] E.g. Locke, *Reasonableness of Christianity*, 54-55, 76, 88-89.

[90] Locke, *Reasonableness of Christianity*, 88-89; he attributes the limited nature of such correspondences to Jesus' need to evade the attentions of the Jewish authorities for the duration of his public ministry (92), a point bound up with Locke's treatment of what is known in modern scholarship as the "messianic secret". This is a serious problem for Locke: if the one thing Jesus taught as necessary for salvation is belief in himself as Messiah, why was he so keen to keep his identity hidden from the general public?

[91] John Locke, *A Second Vindication of the Reasonableness of Christianity etc.*, in vol. 7 of *The Works of John Locke: A New Edition, Corrected* (London: Thomas Tegg, 1823), 253-54.

[92] Locke, *Reasonableness of Christianity*, 143; the claim is repeated, for good measure (146).

[93] Locke, *Reasonableness of Christianity*, chapter XV, 164-171; the quotations are from 165. Locke presents this question as specifically one about the interpretation of the New Testament Epistles; as already noted, he assumes that all the "necessary" doctrines of Christianity can be deduced from the Gospels and Acts.

[94] So William H. Trapnell, *The Treatment of Christian Doctrine by Philosophers of the Natural Light from Descartes to Berkeley* (Oxford: Voltaire Foundation, 1988), 123-63.

[95] Locke, *Reasonableness of Christianity*, 141-164; quotations from 159 and 163.

[96] Locke, *Reasonableness of Christianity*, e.g. 145-46 and 159-160.

[97] Locke, *Reasonableness of Christianity*, 3.

[98] Locke, *Reasonableness of Christianity*, 6.

[99] John Locke, *An Essay concerning Human Understanding*, ed. Peter H. Nidditch (Oxford: Clarendon, 1975) I.2 (44).

[100] Locke, *Essay* IX.23 (489-90).

[101] Troki, *Faith Strengthened*, 209-17.

[102] Troki, *Faith Strengthened*, 217.

[103] Sutcliffe, *Judaism and Enlightenment*, 23-41 and 58-78.

[104] Peter van Rooden, "The Amsterdam Translation of the Mishnah," in *Hebrew Study from Ezra to Ben-Yehuda*, ed. William Horbury (Edinburgh: T & T Clark, 1999), 257-67. The article is the main source for what follows in this paragraph.

[105] Anthony Collins, "Discourse of the Grounds and Reasons of the Christian Religion," in *Critics of the Bible, 1724-1873*, ed. John Drury (Cambridge: Cambridge University Press, 1989), 21-45. See also Frei, *Eclipse of Biblical Narrative*, 66-85.

[106] See Collins, "Discourse," 41, note b, for Collins listing of his Jewish sources.

[107] Collins, "Discourse," 26.

[108] Aquinas, *Summa theologiae* I q.1 a.10, especially the response to the first objection.

[109] Collins, "Discourse," 26-27.

[110] Collins, "Discourse," 31-39.

[111] Collins, "Discourse," 40-41.

[112] See 113 above.

[113] Cf. the comments of Jaroslav Pelikan, *Christian Doctrine and Modern Culture (since 1700)*, vol. 5 of *The Christian Tradition: A History of the Development of Doctrine* (Chicago: University of Chicago Press, 1989), 112-13.

[114] Even in the thirteenth century, William of Auvergne was aware of the opinion that Judaism, Christianity and Islam were equally valid versions of the same basic truths (Smalley, "William of Auvergne," 137). What had now changed, however, was both the level of confidence in the theological foundations for resisting such a view, and the cogency with which it could be overtly supported within the dominant culture.

[115] Matthew Tindal, *Christianity as Old as the Creation, 1730*, (New York: Garland, 1978).

[116] On the historical origins of the parable, see Iris Shagrir, "The Parable of the Three Rings: A Revision of Its History," *Journal of Medieval History* 23:2 (1997): 163-77.

[117] Gotthold Ephraim Lessing, *Nathan the Wise: A Dramatic Poem in Five Acts*, trans. Bayard Quincy Morgan (New York: Frederick Ungar, 1955) Act V, Scene II, lines 89-95.

[118] "The time will certainly come, the time of a new, eternal gospel, which is promised to us even in the primers of the New Covenant," quoted by Karl Barth in his chapter on Lessing in *Protestant Theology in the Nineteenth Century: Its Background and History* (London: SCM, 1972), 247. On the wider context for the transposition of Joachite themes in subsequent Western thought, see Karl Löwith, *Meaning in History: The Theological Implications of the Philosophy of History* (Chicago: University of Chicago Press, 1949).

[119] See 82-84 above.

[120] Locke refused to be scandalized by the suggestion of Jean Le Clerc that some portions of Scripture are more inspired than others; see Locke, *Correspondence*, vol. 2, no. 832 (746-51), from 1685.

[121] Thomas Sherlock, "Discourses on the Use and Intent of Prophecy," in *Critics of the Bible*, ed. Drury, 47-56.

[122] Frei, *Eclipse of Biblical Narrative*, e.g. 37-39.

[123] See Soulen, *God of Israel*, 57-80.

[124] Owen Chadwick, *The Victorian Church* (London: A. and C. Black, 1966), 1:553-54 and 532.

[125] Quotations from Pelikan, *Christian Doctrine*, 192, and Amos Elon, *The Pity of It All: A Portrait of Jews in Germany, 1743-1933* (London: Penguin, 2004), 76.

CHAPTER FOUR

AT THE END OF MODERNITY:
WHAT IS NEW?

The previous chapter explored how Jewish voices became a catalyst for the erosion of confidence in modern Christianity in the pre-modern understanding of Christ's fulfilment of scriptural prophecy. Christian intellectuals who could not see a way to combat that erosion yet at the same time wanted to resist the path of religious relativism were drawn instead to reformulate assertions of the historical superiority of the Christian religion. Although this characteristically modern theological paradigm emerged in the context of significant Jewish-Christian exchanges and required substantial restatement of the claims and judgments in the classic framework, it nonetheless replicated the dynamics of theological anti-Judaism in fresh ways. In particular, the displacement of the Law, the covenant judgment from that framework, was still identified as the decisive hinge which allowed the new faith to break out of the constricting chrysalis of the old. Moreover, the dominance of religious progress over scriptural fulfilment (with its eschatological horizons) as the model for Christian self-understanding left Jews, deemed to persist in outworn forms of religious life, with no share at all in God's continuing work in history, a transposition of the people judgment which medieval Christian theology could not have imagined.

By the end of the nineteenth century, the dismissal of Jews and Judaism from the theological present in such modern religious thinking increasingly contrasted with their growing participation in mainstream cultures in Western Europe following political emancipation. Christian theology could hardly remain insulated from the social tensions relating to this phenomenon. Antisemitic attitudes and language were becoming more prevalent, at an earlier stage most obviously in France rather than Germany, with the Dreyfus affair acting as a powerful catalyst for exposing this issue. There were influential conversions from Judaism to Christianity, perhaps most notably in the first few decades of the twentieth century. Clearly these reflected a variety of motivations, but often

assimilation and loss of distinctive religious traditions and belief among
Jews were at least part of the story.[1] Powerful new intellectual currents in
conscious opposition to the legacy of liberal modernity started to flow
strongly during the interwar years: revolutionary politics, cultural
modernism, psychology of the unconscious. Yet somehow also travelling
alongside those currents was the image of "the Jews" as an enduring social
problem, an image that eventually gave the antisemitic mentality of the
Nazis and the Third Reich a fearful plausibility to many people.

It is not easy to consider how Christian theology in the first half of the
twentieth century was shaped through all of this both by exchanges with
Judaism and by the perpetuation of anti-Judaism—the subject of this
chapter. Historical proximity and the sheer mass of evidence are part of
the challenge; the degree of arbitrariness in the selection of writers and
texts is inevitably even higher in what follows than in previous chapters.
Our awareness of the Holocaust perhaps also renders it difficult to be
attentive to what influential Christians in this period actually said in
relation to Jews and Judaism without immediately intruding judgments
about we think what they should have said, or could have said that might
have diminished the evil, or conversely without assimilating their meaning
to what we wish in retrospect they had meant at the time.

Nonetheless, in terms of tracing the vicissitudes of the framework that
was sketched in chapter one these five decades are of the greatest
importance. Ways of doing Christian theology that accepted the critique of
liberal progressivism were obliged to revisit the determining issue for that
framework since the beginning: the newness of the gospel and how this
was to be articulated in relation to continuing history. Moreover, at this
very point the persistence of Jews and Judaism shifted back towards the
centre of the Christian theological conception of continuing history, in a
movement that both replicated and resisted prevailing discourse about "the
Jews" in non-theological contexts, including avowed antisemitism. A vital
question thereby arose for Christian theology at the end of modernity: how
far does the conscious rejection of certain "modern" trajectories clear
space for the recovery of pre-modern discourse about Christian newness
and corresponding Jewish oldness (i.e. the classic framework with its
claims and judgments), and how far has there in fact been a rupture calling
for a more far-reaching and creative re-description? Attachment to the
covenant judgment in particular—the displacement of the Law—among
thinkers who were critically innovative in their approach to other aspects
of the framework means that none of the "after-modern" Christian
theological voices considered here gives an unequivocal response to this
question.[2]

Adolf von Harnack: Modern Theology on Jesus and Judaism

We begin by considering the work of Adolf von Harnack, one of the most influential figures in Protestant academic theology at the beginning of the twentieth century, as a way of linking the analysis of the present chapter to the conclusions of the previous one. Harnack continued and indeed brought to a kind of culmination the path of historical superiority that was described there as one response to the collapse of confidence in prophetic fulfilment as demonstration of the gospel. Yet he did so in a context where Judaism was in fact finding new levels of cultural flourishing; indeed, the strength of Jewish historical scholarship of Christian origins and its alternative reading of the texts was something Harnack had to confront directly. His work thereby makes transparent some of the implications and some of the contradictions to which "modern" theology might lead, not least in its need to distance Jesus from Judaism both past and present.

"The Question of What is New in Religion"

When he published the acclaimed series of lectures he had recently given in Berlin as *Das Wesen des Christentums* in 1900, Adolf von Harnack was approaching the peak of an immensely successful career.[3] Protestant theologians in pre-war Germany could enjoy a high public profile, but very few approached the eminence of Harnack.[4] He held an international reputation as a scholar of Christian origins and an exponent of Liberal Protestantism; the book appeared in English the following year under the title *What is Christianity?*[5] It reflected Harnack's well-developed position that the task of defining Christian teaching was best addressed by delegating it—at least in the first place—to the labour of scholarly history:

> History surely does not have the final word anywhere, but in the science of religion and of the Christian religion especially it has the first word everywhere.[6]

For Harnack, the value of historical study lay in vindicating Christian faith in the context of modernity via a twofold strategy: first, peeling back the manifold layers of historical development to identify the "essence" of this religion; and second, demonstrating that it is historically unique and therefore demanding of our allegiance here and now. His great multi-

volume work, the *History of Dogma*, attempted to show how the
development of traditional Christian doctrine had been significantly
contaminated by the influence of Greek speculation, in order that the
original message of Jesus could be received again in its purity by modern
people.[7] Such sustained historical study, Harnack believed, was the
necessary path to greater theological understanding and the renewal of the
contemporary church:

> Neither *exegesis* nor *dogmatics* will lead us to a healthy progress and to a
> purer comprehension of what is original and of value, but a better known
> *history*.[8]

In the lectures contained in *Das Wesen des Christentums*, he gave a
synoptic account of what he took to be the source of Christianity, "what is
original and of value," located in the life and teaching of Jesus and of his
greatest disciple, Paul, and then a summary overview of how that message
had fared in the vicissitudes of subsequent Christian history.

Harnack assumes at the outset that it is not possible in modernity to
demonstrate the truth of the Christian faith on the basis of argument from
prophecy; "the conviction that Old Testament prophecy was fulfilled in
Jesus' history had a disturbing effect on tradition," he notes in passing.[9]
Because the superiority of the Christian religion is expressed and argued
as a historical thesis, however, the need to relate that thesis to the
documents of the Old Testament, to the Judaism of the first century and, at
least obliquely, to the continuing Judaism of the present day was
inescapable. As was suggested in the final section of the previous chapter,
the replacement of the theological fulfilment claim by the historical
superiority claim needed a firm demarcation between Jesus of Nazareth
and the Judaism of his time if it were not to be a route after all into
religious relativism. The assertion of the newness of Christianity aside
from the scripture claim of fulfilment in Christ actually required an
intensification of the covenant and people judgments: the displacement of
Law (in favour of ethics) and the division of history (between the living
Church and moribund Judaism).

This is already apparent in the first lecture of *Das Wesen des
Christentums*, where Harnack explains to his audience that they will not
need to learn much about ancient Judaism in order to come to the
(historical) understanding he is offering them of the *Wesen*, the "essence,"
of Christianity; they will soon see that the connection between Jesus'
teaching and Judaism is "only a loose one."[10] In the third lecture, he then
addresses the question of newness directly in the context of Christian
origins: "What was new in the whole movement?" He begins his response

by alerting his audience to a wider context: "Gentlemen, the question of what is new in religion is not a question which is raised by those who live in it."[11] So who, then, is raising this question? "Jewish scholars," we are told[12]—with the clear inference that they are not among those who "live in" religion.

Before proceeding to look at Harnack's own answer to the question, we need to sketch in briefly the background to that remark about "Jewish scholars." For in the course of the nineteenth century, the nature of first-century Judaism and its relationship to Jesus and the early Christian movement had become a focus of intense attention among Jewish as well as Christian historians. Liberal Protestantism celebrated, with Harnack, the religion of Jesus, i.e. the religion taught and practised by Jesus, as the heart of Christianity. Recovering that religion through the shedding of prejudice and the labour of historical scholarship would, it was hoped, lead to a renewal of Christian life; in the USA, Walter Rauschenbusch felt confident it could lead to a recognition outside the institutional church of Jesus as one of the human race's "highest points, if not its crowning summit thus far"—and thought this was already happening among American Jews.[13] The Jewish community, however, was not so quick to be convinced, and those belonging to it who ventured to engage with Christianity on its home ground of New Testament studies saw things very differently. The great German scholar Abraham Geiger, for instance, argued that the Jesus who appeared from the Gospels after modern criticism had stripped away the accretions of later tradition belonged squarely within the history of Judaism: his teaching as thus reconstructed contained much that was fine but nothing that was new.[14] The point was made forcefully by the American Reform Rabbi Isaac Mayer Wise that this left liberal Christians struggling to find any decisive meaning in Jesus' death: contrary to their general belief, "Jesus did not die for an idea. He never advanced anything new to die for. He was not accused of saying or teaching anything original."[15]

Such denial of the originality of Jesus did more than inoculate Judaism against the evangelistic zeal of liberal Christians like Rauschenbusch. It struck at the very heart of the liberal Protestant theological project, which staked the defence of Christianity on its superiority and its superiority as an (ethical) religion on the superiority of (the historical) Jesus. If Jesus was simply one good Jew like and among many others, would not the proper end of liberal Protestantism as faithfulness to him be in fact conversion to Judaism? Exponents of liberal Judaism, engaged in its own version of purification via a return to origins, certainly tended to think so, and even dared to hope so. Franz Rosenzweig recalled a conversation with the great Jewish philosopher, Hermann Cohen, from around the time of World War I. Cohen, now over 70, still expressed his hope of living to see "the beginning of the Messianic time." Rosenzweig then comments that Cohen understood by that phrase

> the conversion of the Christians to "pure monotheism" of his Judaism, something which he thought he saw ripening in contemporary liberal Protestant theology.[16]

To secure his defence of Christianity against such Jewish counter-attack, therefore, Harnack needed to make it clear that Jesus was not simply one Jew like other Jews of his time and that he indeed inaugurated something decisively "new"—despite his initial response that this was not a significant question for genuinely religious people. He accepted, as a religious historian, that there was precedent for much if not all of what Jesus taught in the scriptural traditions of Judaism, but he maintained that in him "the spring of holiness" "burst through the rubbish which priests and theologians had heaped up to smother the true element in religion." The Pharisees may have used the same scriptural words as Jesus,

> But what was the result of their language? That the nation, in particular their own pupils, condemned the man who took the words seriously. All that they did was weak and because weak harmful.[17]

By contrast, Jesus backed those apparently identical words with the "power" of his "personality," and therefore they took effect and bore fruit; "That was what was new"—and what enabled the creation of "a new humanity opposed to the old."[18]

In this short stretch of text, Harnack offers a connected series of answers to his question about what was new with the Christian movement. First, he tells us that Jesus' "newness" is to be located in an activity strangely akin to that of a nineteenth-century religious liberal, who seeks to purify religion by stripping away the accretions of tradition and returning to the purity of origins; we might call this the newness of reform. Secondly, he asserts that Jesus' life expressed a union of teaching with personality that gave his teaching new power to convince and to transform. Here Harnack comes closer to the common liberal Protestant emphasis on the unique self-consciousness of Jesus as God's Son, a theme he will develop later in the lectures.[19] Thirdly, he claims that the acceptance of the teaching linked to this personality led to a new stage in human history, one that he characterizes in various ways through the course of the remaining lectures, in particular invoking its characteristics of universality and interiority.[20] In effect, we are being presented with a reworking of the covenant and people claims from the classic framework, but with the primary claim of newness now being expressed in terms of historical originality focused on the person / personality of Jesus, rather than via the comprehensive "matching and exceeding" exegetical pattern of prophetic fulfilment, long abandoned by self-consciously scientific scholarship.

One effect of this reworking is that each of the three interlocking components of Harnack's account of the *novum* of Jesus relies on a highly negative evaluation of Judaism. First-century Judaism was the ostensible subject, but, as we have already noted, Harnack's audience was left to make the implicit connections with the Judaism of their own time. If Jesus was a reformer, then Judaism was clearly in need of reform, and if he was ultimately rejected by Judaism, then Judaism was equally clearly not capable of reform. Similarly, if Jesus' religious personality could carry such unexampled conviction, then evidently the spirituality of his Jewish contemporaries was uninspiring to say the least. And if the new humanity he created rested on universality and interiority, then the "old" humanity of Judaism reflected by contrast particularism and a preoccupation with externals—and it belonged to the past.

Paul is of tremendous significance for Harnack because he alone realized all this at the outset with total clarity: "It was Paul who delivered the Christian religion from Judaism." It was Paul who, in the guiding metaphor of Harnack's book, stripped the "husk" of Judaism away from the "kernel" of Jesus' message.[21] Judaism was a stage in history that history left behind in the first Christian century, and, implicitly, those who still fail to grasp this render themselves irrelevant to history's progress.[22] It was entirely in keeping with the logic of this approach that Harnack should have rounded off the initial rebuttal of the question posed by contemporary Jewish scholars about originality with a purple passage contrasting their first-century forbears with his Jesus:

> They thought of God as a despot guarding the ceremonial observances in His household; he breathed in the presence of God. They saw Him only in His law, which they had converted into a labyrinth of dark defiles, blind alleys and secret passages; he saw and felt Him everywhere. They were in possession of a thousand of His commandments, and thought, therefore, they knew Him; he had one only, and that is why he knew Him. They had made this religion into an earthly trade, than which there is nothing more detestable; he proclaimed the living God and the soul's nobility.[23]

Marcion Again

Harnack's defence of the newness of Jesus against contemporary
Jewish scholars of Christian origins rested on a deeply negative picture of
the Judaism within which Jesus originated. The raising of "the question of
what is new in religion" by those scholars led him to make completely
explicit what we argued in the last chapter was always implicit in the
Enlightenment defence of Christianity via the path of historical
superiority. That sweeping judgment on ancient Judaism, bound up with
the recasting of the first claim of the classic framework in terms of
religious progress, was bound to raise the further question of the value for
"modern" Christian religion of the scriptures it shared with Judaism then
and now, and here again Harnack showed with resolute clarity the
destination towards which the path was leading.

In the second chapter, we noted how often Aquinas had recourse to the
metaphor of the *paidagogus* from Gal. 3:23-26 and the contrast between
less perfect and perfect to describe the relation of the old law to the new.
Yet Aquinas' figural understanding of reality meant that the less perfect
could not simply be dispensed with now that the new had come, however
problematic it might be to give a coherent account of its providential
purpose: it was a past that remained present, and thereby gave theological
significance, admittedly ambivalent, to those Jewish communities who by
their practices re-presented it. Moreover, despite his disagreements with
Joachim of Fiore, Aquinas shared with him and Christian theology
generally the assumption that the fulfilment of prophecy must include,
before the end of time, some kind of collective recognition by the Jewish
people (even if only a faithful remnant) of their Messiah, and hence an at
least limited reconciliation of Church and Judaism. The logic of Romans
9-11 in this regard was unquestioned. Jewish communities here and now
were not only a sign of the past of theological history, but also of its
future—and therefore a sign that had to endure.

With the abandonment in modernity of both prophetic fulfilment and
an eschatological narrative about the last days, these interpretive
connections were severed. Harnack was not afraid to contemplate the
implications of such a loss. Jewish irrelevance to the unfolding purposes of
God is taken for granted in his 1900 lectures, as we have seen.[24] In 1920,
with his book on Marcion, he proposed the revision of the Christian canon
as well, arguing that it was time for the Church to grow up and let go of its
"Old Testament" as scripture on a par with the New.

The rejection of the Old Testament in the second century was a mistake the
Greek Church rightly refused to make; the retention of it in the sixteenth

century was a fatal legacy which the Reformation could not avoid, but for Protestantism since the nineteenth century to continue to regard it as a canonical document is the result of a paralysis affecting religion and the church.[25]

He regarded this call for a restructured canon as nothing other than the logical conclusion of the Christocentric understanding of revelation clearly articulated by such founding figures for modern theology as Schleiermacher and Ritschl.

In Harnack's work, then, reformulating the scripture claim does not lead to a relinquishing of the scripture judgment of interpretive blindness on the part of continuing Judaism, but rather, as we have seen with the covenant and people judgments, to transposition and intensification. It is not so much for him that the Church has a uniquely authoritative understanding of the Hebrew scriptures as its Old Testament needing to be read alongside the New; instead, Christians are recognizing the redundancy of the Old Testament as scripture in the modern world, while religious Jews still fail to see this. The newness of Christ was demonstrated for him not by the fulfilment of scripture but by the contrast between the religion of Jesus and the religion of Judaism in terms of their transformative efficacy in human history. Such newness nevertheless still implied the terminal displacement of Torah observing Judaism as a now obsolescent form of religious practice, a strange and strictly meaningless survival from an earlier period that served no purpose whatsoever since the advent of "the new humanity opposed to the old." That particular reformulation of the covenant and people judgments, the displacement of Law and the division of history, left the Old Testament functioning only as a kind of "background" document for Christianity, interesting testimony to an earlier stratum of religious history. For Harnack, therefore, Christianity could—and should—live its gospel without needing to refer to the Jewish Bible as its own Old Testament; much less did it need to refer in any way to the continuing representatives of the Jewish people, as medieval Christianity somehow still did.

Jesus in History

Given the way that Harnack's case for Christianity in *Das Wesen des Christentums* was bound up with an overt and hostile engagement with Judaism both past and present, it is hardly surprising that it elicited a number of responses from Jewish scholars. One—sharply critical—was written by a liberal rabbi from Oppeln called Leo Baeck.[26] The assessment of Christianity that Baeck eventually developed in the 1920s and 1930s will be reviewed in the next chapter. In this early article, however, Baeck did not confront directly the theological construction that lay behind Harnack's work and its highly negative estimate of Judaism both past and, implicitly, present. Rather, it identified two "basic mistakes" in the book: "the apologetic purposefulness and then the disregard of Jewish literature and Jewish scholarship."[27]

Baeck was on particularly strong ground with the latter charge. According to Baeck (and it would be hard to disagree), Harnack did not even attempt to ground his picture of first-century Judaism in a serious analysis of relevant Jewish sources, and yet he used that picture as an essential "frame" in what purported to be a historical argument carrying academic authority. Baeck suggested that scholarly investigation into first-century Palestinian Judaism would in fact show its outstanding moral and spiritual quality. More specifically, he claimed that the historical Jesus of scholarly reconstruction would fit very well into this properly reconstructed Jewish context. Against Harnack's first statement of Jesus' "newness", first-century Judaism was not a degenerate religion in need of reform. Against his second, far from being a personality set apart by some sort of unique self-consciousness, Jesus was "a *thoroughly Jewish character*," "a genuinely Jewish personality," rooted in his particular place and time.[28] With that, the third element clearly fell away: because if Jesus belonged *within* Judaism, then the newness of the Christianity that subsequently emerged as a historical phenomenon had its source not in Jesus himself but in something else—and therefore that "new" Christianity was not, as Harnack and others like him wanted to think, the religion of Jesus, but actually something quite different. We will return to this issue in the next chapter. At this point, it is enough to note Baeck's argument that scholarly history could not be legitimately invoked to sustain Harnack's reformulation of the newness of Christ as the "originality" of the historical Jesus and the effects of his teaching.

Although the argument as thus framed has never entirely disappeared, it became increasingly marginal from the First World War onwards for the new theological movements that were eclipsing the liberal ascendancy.[29] In Germany during this period—and Germany remained very much at the forefront of Western theological development for the time being—a widespread reaction against various forms of "historicism" began to take hold. The idea that the critical study of history, conducted via a supposedly neutral and objective scholarly methodology, could lay the foundations for knowledge of what relates to humanity, in an analogous fashion to empirical investigations of natural science providing the basis for knowledge about the physical world, was consciously rejected by many figures who would become leading voices in the period between the wars. Such a rejection had many implications—including the need for Christian theologians who shared it to put aside the path of historical superiority we have traced from Locke to Harnack and find different ways to re-describe the newness they continued to wish to claim for the gospel of Jesus Christ at the end of modernity. At this crucial juncture, exchanges with Judaism and the ideology of anti-Judaism were once again shaping the development of Christian theology, as we will see in the remaining sections of this chapter.

Rosenzweig and Rosenstock-Huessy: Christianity beyond Judaism?

The correspondence between Eugen Rosenstock-Huessy and Franz Rosenzweig during the First World War discloses some of the dynamics of transition between modern and after-modern modes of Christian theological understanding in relation to Judaism and anti-Judaism. Jewish by birth and background, both writers agreed on the repudiation of nineteenth-century historicism in general and the kind of liberal theology associated with Harnack in particular but disagreed sharply not only in their decisions about conversion to Christianity but in their understanding of the relationship between Christianity and Judaism. Paradoxically, it is the self-consciously Jewish thinker, Rosenzweig, who emerges as more perceptive than his convert friend about the situation of Christianity at the end of modernity, and in particular the way in which Christian theology needs to face living Judaism as its "internal foe" more directly than it ever has before. In the final chapter of the book, we will return to Rosenzweig's insights and their profound congruence with the research into theological history that has been presented within it. At this point, however, Rosenzweig's place within that theological history is our primary concern.

New Thinking

Franz Rosenzweig is a major figure in the history of twentieth-century Judaism, with a considerable amount of his published writing directly concerning Christianity.[30] In common with others of his generation, Rosenzweig was beginning to reject the intellectual legacy of the nineteenth century before World War I turned such disillusion into an epochal shift. Brought up in a Jewish family who—unlike many of their friends and relations—resisted conversion to the state religion of Christianity, while keeping their own practice of faith to an apparent minimum, since 1908 he had been immersed in the study of modern German philosophy. By 1910 he was already becoming convinced that Hegelianism, the most plausible system to have emerged from that philosophy, was beset by internal contradictions that could only be escaped by an appeal to religious faith.[31] It was at this point that he became aware of Eugen Rosenstock-Huessy.[32]

Rosenstock-Huessy also came from a Jewish background but, like Rosenzweig's friend Rudolph Ehrenberg, had converted to Christianity. Rosenstock-Huessy's conversion was motivated by the same sense that Rosenzweig was reaching, that the secular philosophy of modernity had arrived at an irresolvable impasse requiring the recovery of religious revelation. For Rosenstock-Huessy, it was obvious that only Christianity contained the resources for that recovery. In 1913, Rosenzweig came more directly under Rosenstock-Huessy's influence when he became his pupil in constitutional law and, after a critical conversation with his mentor prolonged well into the night, he was "converted" from Hegelianism to religious faith. Rosenzweig decided to become a member of the Church, but he was clear that he would enter it as a Jew, not a pagan. So to prepare for his conversion to Christianity, he first went back to the faith of his forebears—and found that here, in the synagogue, on the Day of Atonement in 1913, he had met the living God.[33] So Rosenzweig returned to Judaism and did not become a Christian.

The letters subsequently written between Rosenzweig and Rosenstock-Huessy in 1916 represent a stage in the encounter between Judaism and Christianity "at the end of modernity" that has already moved beyond the exchanges of Harnack, Geiger and Baeck. Both writers accepted "the law under which all our thinking has stood, *post Hegel mortuum*," after Hegel's death.[34] This law is explained in terms of the shift from the presumption of an impersonal, neutral standpoint as the basis for all-embracing theory to the practice of a kind of thinking that consciously begins from the fragmentary location of the individual person. The law "after Hegel's death" therefore implied rejection of the systematic comprehension of historical existence to which the liberal culture of the nineteenth century—including Harnack—aspired. For both writers, it was the war of 1914 that had finally buried that culture with its ideals. The Foreword and Concluding Remark to Rosenzweig's study *Hegel and the State*, which was written for the most part before the war but only published afterwards, reflect on the decade between 1909 and 1919 as one in which a whole civilization came to an end: "When the edifice of a world collapses, then both the thoughts that imagined it and the dreams that were woven through it are buried under the debris."[35] Both authors wished to postulate instead a different approach that gave a cardinal place to revelation—named by Rosenzweig as "The New Thinking."[36] Yet while Rosenstock-Huessy advocated a Christianity that had left Judaism entirely behind, Rosenzweig's response was a sustained reflection on the complex and ambivalent intertwining of Christianity with Judaism in the dawning post-Christendom era.

Rosenstock-Huessy on Christ and the End of Judaism

In the opening letters of the correspondence, both men rather skirt around the difficult issue of their contrasting religious responses to the shared concern for an appeal to revelation. When this finally moves to the centre, Rosenstock-Huessy attempts at first to be irenic, but his passionate rejection of Judaism as a viable form of contemporary existence quickly becomes apparent. In a sequence of three letters, he sets out his view that Judaism after Christ can only combine a self-inflicted bondage and isolation from the creative historical process with an entirely reprehensible national pride that is no different in kind from that of the "pagan tribes" who claimed to have been descended from their gods. He wholly endorses the liberal Christian view that Judaism ceased to have any part to play in history since the destruction of the temple: "Since A. D. 70 there have only been peoples, and the chosen people has sunk into being a mere coloring reagent in all nations."[37]

For Rosenstock-Huessy as for Harnack, the redundancy of the Jewish people for the realization of God's purposes today is connected with the redundancy of their book, its Old Testament, from the perspective of the Church. Thus in a later letter, he explains to Rosenzweig that the Western world "will forget its Old Testament. 'The old things are passed away, and all things are become new.'"[38] At one point in the letter he suggests that Church history and the liturgical calendar have taken the place of the Old Testament in terms of the Church's self-understanding; later on he seems more concerned with how the Church treats whatever happens to be a society's dominant cultural inheritance as the "Old Testament" whose fulfilment in Christ it proceeds to preach.[39] At certain points in their correspondence, he insists on trying to persuade Rosenzweig to read various texts by standard antisemitic writers of the period on the grounds that there is genuine historical insight in the stereotypes and myths they contain.[40] In this letter, however, he explicitly relinquishes the legend of the "eternal Jew" and declares that Judaism is on the verge of disappearing entirely, its vestigial sense of identity about to be dissipated in the adventure of Zionism which he anticipates will be merely ephemeral.[41]

It is most important to register the connection, here as with Harnack, between the abandonment of the Old Testament as scripture and the abandonment of any conception of continuing Israel as the people of God with a stake in God's purpose for history. The transposition of the scripture judgment, Jewish interpretive blindness, again goes hand in hand with a radicalization of the people judgment, in that the division of history is now read as the dismissal of Judaism from history itself. Rosenstock-Huessy's conscious search for what we might already call an "after-modern" Christian theology, which included a deep aversion to the thought of Harnack himself,[42] certainly does not lead him away from theological modernity's tendency to consign both the Jewish people and the Jewish book to the ever receding past. That "after-modern" approach is indeed reflected in the way he re-describes the newness of Christ not by beginning from historical foundations and constructing a defence of Jesus' uniqueness in terms of his teachings and personality in the Locke-Harnack manner, nor by returning to the pre-modern pattern of prophecy and fulfilment, but by asserting the axiomatic reality of the incarnation:

> "The Word became flesh"—on that proposition *everything* indeed depends. While the word of man must always become a concept and thereby stagnant and degenerate, God speaks to us with the "word become flesh," through the Son.[43]

For Rosenstock-Huessy, the event of the incarnation is the divine revelation that provides the point in relation to which human life can become liberated from its own regressive self-referentiality.

In many ways this is indeed a sharp break with Harnack and the liberal tradition, but it remains an account of Christianity whose "content" appears to be exhausted by the figure of Christ; it is not clear that anything besides him constitutes divine revelation or that we need anything in particular to comprehend him besides faith. It is not surprising, therefore, that this newness with its potential to transform history renders everything that preceded it obsolete with its arrival. History after the incarnation is the story of how this revelation has been appropriated; Judaism, as indifference and resistance to it, only functions as a kind of "anti-history" which will soon pass into the void it might as well have entered 1900 years ago. This newness has so comprehensively displaced the particular law of Israel that veneration for the Old Testament itself must be recognized as a passing phase only in the life of the Church, while the Jewish people that still clings to it has no place in the present time. Rosenstock-Huessy's theology "beyond" the modernity of Harnack nonetheless leads him like Harnack to posit radical transpositions of the judgments from the classic framework, such that we seem to be moving toward a point where we approach, once again, the kind of radically Pauline option that Catholic Christianity rejected over the course of the second century. The endurance of Israel on this view is nothing other than the long dying echo of something that actually ended nearly two millennia previously.

Rosenzweig on Christianity's Enduring Need for Judaism

Already in this intimate correspondence with a friend, and much more fully in his major work, the *Star of Redemption*, published in 1921, Rosenzweig sought to develop an articulation of Judaism in relation to (still dominant) Christianity that would be neither polemical, nor apologetic.[44] Early on in the exchange with Rosenstock-Huessy, he identifies the Church's struggle with Marcion and with Gnosticism in the second century as definitive for Christianity's self-identity. By making Paul's conception of the relation between gospel and Law into "dogma," and thereby claiming the identity of the Creator with the Father of Jesus Christ and binding the Jewish Bible and the recognized apostolic writings into a single volume of its scriptures, "the Church established herself as a power in human history."[45] Unlike many modern Jewish critics of Christianity, Rosenzweig does not depict Christianity as an unstable amalgam of Jewish and pagan elements, but as achieving through its formative struggles a genuine *historical* originality. Thus far he is in agreement with Christian theology: the Church represents a new thing in history and makes a difference to history that contributes to the fulfilment of the divine purpose for the whole creation. This remains his position in the *Star of Redemption*.[46] Unlike the liberal tradition in European theology, however, in either its Christian or Jewish form, he avoids making any judgment on the uniqueness or otherwise of the so-called historical Jesus, and his comments elsewhere make it clear that he viewed the quest for that figure as fundamentally futile from the point of view of theology.[47]

Rosenzweig was also clear, however, that the positive historic "achievement" of orthodox Christianity carried with it a certain shadow side, precisely in its ambivalence towards the continuing presence outside it of those Jews whose God and whose scripture it claimed wholly for itself. For Rosenzweig, it is the third judgment, the division of history, that constitutes a locus of enduring tension in Christianity. As Rosenzweig sums matters up in the letter we are discussing, in characteristically dense and elliptical style:

Thus, in the firm establishment of the Old Testament in the Canon, and in the building of the Church on this double scripture (Old Testament and New Testament) the stubbornness of the Jews is in fact brought out as the other half of the Christian dogma (its formal consciousness of itself—the dogma of the Church—if we may point to the creed as the dogma of Christianity).[48]

For Rosenzweig therefore as for Harnack and Rosenstock-Huessy there is a vital connection within the self-understanding of Christianity between the place of the Old Testament and the place of the continuing existence of the Jewish people. But his evaluation of this connection and its implications for the Church is very different from theirs. He recognizes that a deeply engrained—and ultimately theologically driven—ambivalence towards Jews and Judaism, both contained and expressed by the political and social disenfranchisement of Jews in "Christian" Europe during the Middle Ages and earlier modernity, has become far more exposed since widespread Jewish emancipation in the later eighteenth and nineteenth centuries. As he would express a parallel point somewhat later,

When one seeks to reject the Jewish people's uniqueness through the frontdoor of reason, it forces a re-entry through the backdoor of faith in paroxysms of hatred of the Jews (which has never taken on greater forms than it has in the last hundred and twenty years, when one seeks to explain the Jews as totally ordinary).[49]

In this context of modernity's political emancipation and self-conscious rationalism, the Christian "dogma" of Jewish stubbornness becomes ever more nakedly expressed as "*hatred of the Jews*" for perpetuating the division of history and resisting the Church's grasp at global comprehension, and Rosenzweig does not hesitate to link contemporary antisemitism to these theological roots.[50]

The emerging Church of post-Hegelian modernity is defined by Rosenzweig, here following the German philosopher Schelling, as "Johannine", that is, as spiritual rather than institutional. The beginning of its epoch is dated 1789, not only the year of the French revolution and declarations of rights both there and across the Atlantic, but also when Jews were given full equality in the Constitution of the newly established United States of America.[51] Rosenzweig discerns a profound causal relationship between the political emancipation of the Jews that dates from 1789 and the spiritualizing Church of post-Enlightenment modernity. As the Jews begin to live in growing freedom from the political authority of the Church, Christianity experiences its ambivalence towards Jewish scripture and Jewish people more acutely. One way to resolve that growing tension is at once to dismiss continuing Jewish communities from its conception of theological history and the Old Testament from its scriptural canon—to place what is awkwardly at once "own" and "other" wholly outside itself.

According to Rosenzweig, this is the great dilemma for Christianity in the contemporary world. Jewish emancipation has left the Jews a more disturbing puzzle than ever for the Church that would still seek to comprehend them, and the drift towards Johannine Christianity brings with it the revival of a spiritualizing Gnosticism inclined to part company with actual Jews and remote Jewish scriptures altogether. Yet the Church in fact still needs the Synagogue, and Christianity still needs Judaism, if its original *novum* is not to be altogether dissipated in cultures always susceptible to regression into pagan forms of existence.[52] The only way it can resolve the increasingly uncomfortable ambivalence it has always carried towards Jews and Judaism is indeed to detach itself from the Old Testament, but that would leave it wholly exposed to absorption into that world of relativistic, ultimately monistic modernity which Rosenzweig and Rosenstock-Huessy had both agreed in 1913 must be resisted in the name of truth. The enduring tension within history *between* Church and Synagogue therefore needs to be reaffirmed by the Church for the sake of its own mission and indeed survival, beyond the political imposition of collective Jewish degradation under Christendom. A post-Christendom Church dreaming with Harnack and Rosenstock-Huessy of existence *beyond* enduring Judaism, with the division of history left only as a periodization of the past, is a Church that has become blind to the non-occurrence of redemption and to its own inadequacy as the sole agent of making present those "last things" that lie with God alone.

In this context, Rosenzweig regards the Church's enduring retention of the Old Testament as scripture as an important sign of its willingness to continue to grapple with Judaism as the needed "other" on its path through history, beyond the loss of the prophecy-fulfilment exegesis that underwrote the dual canon in pre-modernity.[53] Like modern Christian and Jewish liberalism, Rosenzweig did not see how the newness of Christ could be explicated in terms of prophetic fulfilment. Like modern Christians from Locke to Harnack, however, and unlike the Jewish writers reviewed in the next chapter, he did not therefore accept that Christian newness was either illusory or ultimately negative in its theological and practical implications. He accepted, in effect, versions of the covenant and people claims from the classic Christian framework—that there is an authentic newness expressed in the life of the Church and in its participation in the fulfilment of God's purposes in history—without accepting the corresponding judgments that Jewish Torah and Jewish existence based on Torah are thereby rendered "old" and overcome. Indeed, living Christianity is itself only comprehensible for him in relation to living Judaism, not as a self-sufficient entity, a closed system. It needs for its own life the people whom Rosenzweig in a letter to Rosenstock-Huessy called "the louse in your fur," and compared to the servant of ancient Rome whispering in the triumphal lord's ear, "Master, remember the last things."[54] He identified the urgency, after the perceived collapse of Enlightenment modernity, of theological reflection on Christianity *with* Judaism and on anti-Judaism *within* Christianity well before the important Christian writers to whom we now turn, and before the events in Germany of the 1930s that focused their attention on these matters.

Karl Barth: A New Framework?

Karl Barth, the subject of the third section of this chapter, belonged to the same generation of intellectuals as Rosenstock-Huessy and Rosenzweig. He became perhaps the single most important figure in Christian theology between the wars for the articulation of Christian newness in terms that were profoundly opposed to the liberal paradigm represented by Harnack. His work therefore represents a moment of opportunity for revisiting the classic framework described in chapters one and two, from the other side of modernity's dilemmas as set out in the third chapter and the first section of the present one. Moreover, the advent of Nazism in the 1930s and its overt advocacy of repressive antisemitism became the catalyst in Barth's case for critical awareness of anti-Judaism in modern theology and thereby for the attempt to outline a theology of Israel that could encompass the reality of continuing Jewish presence. In consciously attending to the judgments as well as the claims we have identified as the classic framework of Christian theology, Barth picks up the challenge of Rosenzweig that Christianity should understand itself in relation to continuing Judaism and face the internalized anti-Judaism somehow bound up with this. Yet as with the transition from pre-modern to modern approaches, the radical restatement of Christian claims about newness in Barth's "after-modern" theology refocused rather than removed the force of historic anti-Jewish judgments, not least because the covenant judgment of displacement of Torah (however differently conceived before, during and after modernity) remained a cardinal point of orientation.

Karl Barth was born in 1886, the same year as Franz Rosenzweig. In retrospect, we can view both his *Romans*, published first in 1918 with a second edition in 1922, and Rosenzweig's *Star of Redemption*, published in 1921, as examples of revolutionary modernism breaking out in the domain of theology.[55] Both works polemicize explicitly against the legacy of modernity generally and the nineteenth century in particular; both refuse to be bound by the norms of academic, university-oriented, encyclopaedic rationality; both celebrate revelation as a word coming from God to humanity from outside the closed circle of intra-historical immanence; both are receptive to elements of tradition regarded by modern liberalism as obsolete—original sin, for example, in Barth's case, and miracle in Rosenzweig's.[56] Is it possible that either was directly influenced by or even aware of the other during the critical years of gestation before and during World War I? A lecture Barth gave at Tambach in 1919 led Rosenstock-Huessy to initiate a correspondence with him. This made Barth aware of the Patmos group convened by Rosenstock-Huessy in 1915, which had a number of connections to Rosenzweig.[57] Still, the only evidence for any awareness of Rosenzweig from Barth's side indicates nothing other than complete incomprehension of his writings, despite the many parallels between them.[58] By contrast, Rosenzweig was an attentive reader and critic of Barth's publications during his too short life time.[59]

Indeed, it is difficult to speak of any direct theological dialogue between Barth and contemporary Jewish writers, in the way that we could in the case of Harnack and Jewish scholars such as Geiger and Baeck, and, still more strikingly, between Rosenstock-Huessy and Rosenzweig. Rather, the relationship between Barth's theological development, awareness of Judaism and expression of anti-Judaism needs to be understood against two primary horizons. The first is his emphatic rejection of the way in which Harnack and others had sought to re-describe the newness of Christ, in which there is an indirect relation to the Jewish-Christian exchanges of modernity. Barth thus cleared the space for radically different understanding of the claims and judgments of the classic framework—different from both modernity and pre-modernity. The second horizon is Barth's opposition to Nazism in the 1930s and his identification of antisemitism as a defining feature of it that required specifically theological resistance. This provides the context within which he began to work out systematically in the 1940s the new possibilities for the doctrine of Israel disclosed by his much earlier break with liberalism.

"The Word . . . Ever New"

Barth's *Romans* abounds with the language of newness; indeed, what we have treated as a mostly implicit theme in theological writing prior to World War I becomes an overt focus with this text. Yet it is a focus with a complexity of a different order from Harnack's response to "Jewish scholars" and their question about historical originality. This is indicated already by the opening pages of Barth's commentary, on the first verse of Paul's letter. In a dense paragraph shot through with paradox, Barth writes:

> The Gospel is not one thing in the midst of other things, to be directly apprehended and comprehended. The Gospel is the Word of the Primal Origin of all things, the Word which, since it is ever new, must ever be received with renewed fear and trembling.[60]

While it is true that "The point on the line of intersection at which the relation becomes observable and observed is Jesus, Jesus of Nazareth, the historical Jesus,"[61] Barth lays down an early marker that he will resist any attempt to read off the ever new word of the gospel from the historical study of even the unique "era of revelation and disclosure" marked by the calendar dating "A. D. 1-30."

> The effulgence, or rather, the crater made at the percussion point of an exploding shell, the void by which the point on the line of intersection makes itself known in the concrete world of human history, is not—even though it be named the Life of Jesus—that other world which touches our world in Him. In so far as our world is touched in Jesus by the other world, it ceases to be capable of direct observation as history, time, or thing.[62]

What is new about the gospel, then, is defined by Barth at the outset of *Romans* as something that cannot be directly observed or apprehended "as history, time, or thing"—and therefore this is not a newness that could either be defended by the historical apologetics of Harnack or attacked by the historical critique of Geiger. Indeed, Barth seems quite prepared to concede the historical arguments about Christian origins developed by Geiger, Baeck and other Jewish critics. He agrees that the "religion of Jesus" has no claim to superiority over that of the psalms and prophets, and he sees no need to ascribe some kind of special religious "genius" to him.[63] He concedes that early Christianity borrowed freely from the Greco-Roman religious environment, including the mystery cults in its rites of initiation.[64] At one point, he appears happy to abandon the entire case for Christian originality in relation to Judaism that Harnack and others had so carefully developed as an integral part of the defence of Christianity in modernity via historical superiority:

> Nothing that MEN can say or know of the Gospel is "new"; for everything which they possess is identical with what Israel possessed of old. Historically, and when it is treated as the negation of divine revelation, the NEW Testament appears to be no more than a clearly drawn, carefully distilled epitome of the OLD Testament. What is there in Primitive Christianity which has not its clear parallel in later Judaism? What does Paul know which the Baptist does not? And what did the Baptist know which Isaiah did not?[65]

The absence of religious, and therefore, human originality, whether on the part of Jesus or Paul or even the emerging Church of the second century, is of no consequence to Barth; such originality could only be, at best, "one thing in the midst of other things, to be directly apprehended and comprehended"—and therefore not the Gospel as Barth understands it. But "The action of God Himself is not a thing which has been DONE BEFORE. The action of God is *new*."[66] This action finds particular expression not in religious and ethical teaching, or historical progress, but in its concrete occurrence; and "this occurrence IS—Jesus Christ."[67]

Rather than seeking to make a case about the progress of human history and then propose a theological thesis on its basis, Barth re-describes the newness of Christ by speaking directly of Jesus as the breaking into human time of God's eternal—and always new—Word. In its deployment of such eschatological discourse, *Romans* stands in a particular relationship to the work of various scholars of Christian origins at the beginning of the twentieth century, including Weiss, Schweitzer and Overbeck. Their researches suggested that the religion of Jesus, Paul and the first Christians had as an intrinsic dimension the imminent expectation of divine disruption of the present order. Theologians such as Harnack claimed to have been recovering the religion of Jesus as the pattern for religion in the modern world, and yet this eschatological intensity appeared (not least to themselves) wholly incompatible with their own religious outlook.[68] That incompatibility led Schweitzer to seek a way of faithfulness to Christ that could bypass the eschatological element and drew Overbeck away from Christianity altogether.

Barth's response to this internal problem for Christian theology was quite different. By the time he wrote *Romans*, he was clear that, if integrating the new eschatological perspective meant dynamiting the inherited forms of liberal Protestantism, then that was exactly what should be done: "If Christianity be not thoroughgoing eschatology, there remains

in it no relationship whatever with Christ."[69] Yet while Barth affirms as
integral to Christian theology the eschatological tension that careful
scholars from the turn of the century had discerned within the New
Testament texts, he also radicalizes it in such a way that, at least in his
early works, the "last things" lose all apparent connection with any
historical future and are reconceived via the irruption into time of an
eternal "Moment" which never becomes a moment within time:

> With reference to before and after, the "Moment" is and remains strange
> and different; it neither has its roots in the past, nor can it be transmitted to
> the future. The "Moment" does not belong in any causal or temporal or
> logical sequence: it is always and everywhere wholly new: it is what
> God—who only is immortal—is and has and does.[70]

Newness and Narration: Re-Describing the Scripture Claim

The rigorous disjunction between the newness of Christ as this
"Moment" and the continuity of historical narration resulted in a virtual
denial at one point in *Romans* of any future orientation for eschatological
language, a point regarding which Barth would later seek to correct
himself.[71] Yet it also raises the question of what sort of relationship might
obtain between the re-description of the newness of Christ in *Romans*
through the discourse of eschatology and the first claim of the traditional
framework, the claim of prophetic fulfilment. After all, in the New
Testament itself, the claim of fulfilment seems to act at least as an impulse
to various kinds of narration, in which the story of Israel before Christ and
the story of Christ himself are "told" as two sequences that illuminate one
another, however differently this task might be approached by the authors
of Matthew, Acts, Romans and Hebrews, for example. Is Barth bound to
deny his "Moment" any kind of narrative shape? If so, it is hard to see how
anything like the traditional fulfilment claim could be sustained.

At the outset of *Romans* Barth speaks of the gospel as "the word
spoken by the prophets from time immemorial," and the idea of the Old
Testament as prophetic witness remains fundamental for him.[72] When he
comes to comment in a somewhat later work on Paul's summary of the
gospel at 1 Cor. 15:3-4, with its repeated refrain that Christ died and was
raised "according to the scriptures," he begins by explaining this in terms
of "the harmony of revelation . . . the consensus of voices." Yet it is hard
to escape the impression that for Barth as much as for Locke, however far
apart their theologies in other respects, such "harmony" forms
corroborative evidence only for something that is arrived at on other
grounds. In a striking image, Barth writes of this passage that Paul

> sees the fathers of the Old Testament all stranding around this one point in a wide circle, around this turning-point from death to life, from the end to the beginning, from an old to a new world, all gazing and pointing, knowing and participating, all expecting, believing and promising in many different tongues nothing else than this *one*.[73]

For Barth, no less than for Locke, Schleiermacher and Rosenstock-Huessy, indeed for any strongly Christocentric account of revelation, the question remains of what we have to gain, beyond corroboration, from attending to those standing around and pointing when we have direct access to the one at the centre—when we live this side of the incarnation, crucifixion and resurrection. Barth undoubtedly had a high doctrine of the authority of the whole of scripture, and his mature work in the *Church Dogmatics* is profoundly shaped by his immersion in what he himself once called "the strange new world within the Bible."[74] There are passages within it where he deploys a Christological exegesis of the Old Testament that has striking parallels with—as well as differences from—the sustained figural exegesis of pre-modernity.[75] It is at least worth noting, however, that during the two decades after *Romans*, when Barth's teaching activity reflected an intense engagement with the task of biblical commentary only lightly reflected in his publications, it was New Testament books alone that he seems to have considered for his courses.[76]

Not surprisingly, Barth's attempt to write Christian theology in a revolutionary new form that would practise a disjunction between revelation (as the newness of the eternal "Moment") and history (as continuity and repetition of the same) attracted the hostile attention of Harnack as well as other representatives of pre-war theological liberalism.[77] The hostility ran if anything even more strongly the other way: Barth had once studied under Harnack, but was horrified to see the name of his erstwhile teacher heading a list (which included other luminaries of liberal theology) presented to the Kaiser in 1914 that pledged support for the military action on which Germany had embarked; *dies ater*, as Barth referred to it.[78] From Harnack's side, the title of his opening salvo of 1923 against what he saw as the new trend in Christian theology indicated what he believed to be at stake: "Fifteen Questions to the Despisers of Scientific Theology."[79]

Barth, however, was not prepared to concede that Harnack's approach was "scientific" and his own in contrast arbitrary and subjective. The objectivity of theology for Barth was bestowed not by its compliance with accepted norms of academic practice in modernity (such as the methods of historical criticism), but by its rigorous attention to the word of divine revelation.[80] Such attention meant that theology could not turn to revelation only as a second or subsequent move; must it not begin with

> the *really* scandalous testimony that God himself has said and done something, something *new* in fact, outside of the correlation of all human words and things, but which *as* this new thing he has injected *into* that correlation, a word and a thing next to others but *this* word and *this* thing?[81]

If this new thing cannot be fitted into the flow of human history, then it cannot be expressed within a narrative of progress or growth such as that which had become intrinsic to Harnack's theology. Indeed, Barth's theology of revelation becomes a critique of all such narratives, whether or not they are overtly religious: "The way from the old world to the new world is *not* a stairway, *not* a development in any sense whatsoever; it is a being born anew."[82]

Harnack, on the other hand, argued that a great deal of evidence, including the conversion narratives of Christians such as Augustine, showed that this process of development was precisely how people move "from the old world to the new world"; moreover, Barth's bald statements seemed "to condemn all Christian pedagogy and sever, like Marcion, every link between faith and the human."[83] It might appear somewhat paradoxical that Harnack, who actually defended a kind of neo-Marcionism with regard to the Christian canon, should make such an accusation. Yet Harnack was surely right to press Barth on the question of how divine revelation as he understands it finds a point of "purchase" on human reality. How does eschatological newness actually make things new in human time?

In response, Barth develops the concept of the parabolic, which he had also used in *Romans*. Narratives such as Augustine's conversion story witness as parables to the non-sequential event of "being born anew."[84] While the question at stake here is how to understand the relation between the new thing God has done in Christ and everything that takes place in human time, there is a danger that Israel "after the flesh" before as since the incarnation is simply bundled up indiscriminately with all other manifestations of the "old world" from which we are delivered in Christ. Indeed, at several points in *Romans* Barth appears to intensify that problematic trajectory in Pauline thinking by quite deliberately "levelling down" Israel before Christ to the same status as every other culture and religion.[85] The charge of an affinity with Marcion is not really a just one in the sense that Harnack intended it, but if we use Marcion's name instead to denote an abstract, anthropological Paulinism which hinges on Christ alone against the world, and in which Israel and the Law are ultimately ranged with the world against Christ, then it becomes a more revealing objection.

The Law as the Form of the Gospel: Re-Describing the Covenant Judgment

Having outlined Barth's radically different understanding of the newness of Christ in *Romans* and other early works, we now turn our attention to the implications of this understanding for his account of the covenant judgment from the traditional framework, the displacement of Torah—a subject inseparable from the complex and contested topic of his theological ethics. Already in the first edition of his commentary on *Romans*, Barth had written: "From the last standpoint, which we have to take in Christ, there are no ethics."[86] Over 20 years later, in *Church Dogmatics* II/2, Barth could pepper the opening section of his programmatic chapter on theological ethics with comparably confrontational statements.[87] Yet Barth wrote extensively about theological ethics throughout his life and, although his death cut short his full development of it in the *Church Dogmatics*, the architecture of that unfinished work reflects his conviction that doctrine and ethics are in fact inseparable within the task of Christian theology.[88] In *Romans* itself, Barth explicitly rejects the idea that with the start of chapter 12, Paul "is turning his attention to practical religion, as though it were a second thing side by side with the theory of religion."[89] Moreover, far from suggesting that the concern with ethics in nineteenth-century theology was mistaken, Barth claims its problem lay in not being rigorous enough in this regard, as he makes clear in an address he gave in 1922, on "The Problem of Ethics Today."[90]

In that address and in *Romans* itself, Barth begins to sketch out his own response to the utter collapse—as he sees it—following World War I of the plausibility of modernity's solution to the dilemmas of ethical thought. We gain a clearer indication of the shape of his mature thinking, however, in the course of lectures he gave in the later 1920s on theological ethics.[91] Here we encounter "command" as the cardinal concept that mediates between "Law" as an exegetical and theological category and "ethics" as a field of human endeavour and reflection. The title for chapter VIII of the later *Church Dogmatics*, introducing Barth's account of theological ethics in volume II/2, is "The Command of God." The starting point of theological ethics, according to Barth, is that "all ethical truth is enclosed in the command of God."[92] What God wants, on Barth's account, from the human partner in the covenant is "this office of witness," "his obedience," "the action of a hearer."[93]

Command, then, will be the hinge both for Barth's critique of Law and ethics and for his carefully qualified recovery of them both, his "no" and his "yes" as a dialectical theologian. The command of God requires complete obedience to the will of God as something that cannot be deduced by human beings from anything within the world, including the instructions or examples of (human) others, the writings contained in scripture or even the description of Christ himself. One might compare Barth's reference in his commentary on Philippians to

> that *ethic* that can never become morals, that moves like a spinning top only on its point, nowhere impinges, nowhere calls a halt, and yet remains truly ethic, law, inexorable demand.[94]

Barth defines command from the outset in terms of the event of encounter with the Word of God.[95] He was quite prepared to criticize the "biblicism" of those Christians who sought to equate the divine command with scriptural texts, whether the Ten Commandments or the Sermon on the Mount; such texts cannot as such constitute God's command, which is "always a *concrete individual command*."[96] This does not mean, however, that for Barth there is nothing we can say about it.[97] There is a consistency, a pattern, which Barth describes primarily in terms of the single command having a threefold form, as it arises from the divine Word of creation, reconciliation and redemption. While, as in the projected structure of the *Church Dogmatics*, this description in the earlier lectures underpins an explicitly trinitarian account of theological ethics, it also serves to emphasize the non-systematic character of Barth's account of the divine command: "And what we hear is threefold. This is why we cannot make of it a system." Instead, Christian moral understanding has to exist as a movement, "in the act of traversing these standpoints."[98]

The relationship between the account of theological ethics developed by Barth in the 1920s and 1930s and the judgment of the displacement of Torah can be approached through his address on "Gospel and Law," from 1935. Barth was, in fact, prevented from delivering the lecture in person by the Gestapo; while someone else read it out on his behalf, Barth was being taken across the border to his native Switzerland.[99] In treating Law as an integral element within Christian theology, Barth was not oblivious to the seriousness with which a Christianity wholly stripped of all relation with Judaism was being urged around him in Germany. By contrast, the essay articulates (rather than arguing for) the interrelatedness of its two cardinal terms. The word of God is one, and while the gospel has priority as the proclamation of that word, the Law also is God's word, both as that which follows from the gospel and as that from which the gospel itself follows.[100] The two are distinguishable but not separable, nor can the relationship between them be fixed in some kind of abstract and schematic way: seen from one point of view, the Law is "*hidden* and *enclosed* in it [sc. the gospel] as in the ark of the covenant"; from another, "the *Gospel* is always *in the Law* as that which is manifest, proclaimed."[101]

In developing this second perspective, the gospel in the Law, Barth perhaps comes closest to a formulation that might appear to put into question the inevitability of the displacement of the Law in Christian theology:

> the Law is nothing else than the necessary *form of the Gospel*, whose content is grace. Precisely this content demands this form, the form which calls for its like, the Law's form. If grace is manifested, if it is attested and proclaimed, it means demand and claim upon man.[102]

For Barth, however, there can be no simple movement from Law to grace, from human response to the knowledge of God, but only a dynamic that begins from God and proceeds by the broken way of the cross. The passage from Law to grace can only be understood Christologically. Therefore he shares the traditional judgment about the displacement of Law as something through which there could be a relation to God aside from Christ.[103] Jesus Christ provides for us an authoritative "interpretation" of God's Law as the demand for faith, glossed as "saying 'yes' to God's glory and thus to man's misery."[104] Not only does Barth virtually reduce the commandments of the Law to the demand for faith; he also rules out the idea that our faith can actually resemble the Law-fulfilling faith of Christ, for it is not open to us to imitate his obedience. Rather, for us, keeping the first commandment and every commandment can only mean

> that we believe *in* Jesus Christ, that we . . . acknowledge his representative faith, which we will never realize, and allow it to count as our life, which we do not have here in our hand and at our disposal but have above, hidden with him in God (Colossians 3:1 f.).[105]

Law, then, is affirmed—but only as witness to the command which eludes all identification with text, and only in relation to Christ as the one who both fulfils it directly and then mediates our own relationship to it through faith in him. Any attempt to treat the Law—written, oral, traditional—as revelatory apart from this relatedness to Christ must be deemed inadequate in the light of the gospel. Such an effort could only show that we stand under the wrathful judgment of God, in the "negative relation" of divine condemnation. The covenant judgment has been radically re-described, but its anti-Jewish force is hardly touched.

Two Forms of One Community of God:
Re-Describing the People Judgment

A similar conclusion could be reached about Barth's recasting of the people judgment, the division of history. From the 1930s onwards we find Barth giving serious consideration to the theological significance of the survival of Judaism; towards the end of his life, he even suggested that "the great remaining ecumenical question is our relations towards Judaism."[106] His most sustained investigation of the doctrine of Israel is the chapter on "The Election of God" in *Church Dogmatics* II/2, which was published in 1942. Here Barth refutes, clearly and emphatically, the "modern" theology of supersession according to which God has finished with Israel and therefore the Jewish people no longer hold any place in his unfolding plan for human history. In a fierce exchange with Brunner in the late 1930s he had already insisted that we must say salvation *comes* from the Jews, and not just *came*.[107] The thesis at the start of section 34, "On the Election of the Community," sets out Barth's dialectical conception of Israel and Church as two forms of the one community of God, both existing "according to God's eternal decree."[108] His initial articulation of this point draws him closer to Rosenzweig's thinking in the *Star of Redemption* than it does to the "Christian" approach of the modern Harnack, the "after-modern" Rosenstock-Huessy or even the pre-modern tradition. Indeed, Barth makes the continuing uniqueness of the Jewish people a matter of Christian doctrine.[109] Following on from these points, he explicitly rejects "Christian anti-semitism right up to our own time" and its rationalization that "The Church is the historical successor of Israel."[110] Here he contradicts directly not just the liberal account of progress beyond Judaism but also a fundamental element of the pre-modern Christian understanding of the Jewish other.

Still, we need to attend carefully to precisely what Barth says in this text as well as what he does not. His public engagement in the struggles with Nazism in the 1930s was focused on the freedom of the Church rather than on antisemitism as such, something about which he later expressed regret.[111] Within these passages of the *Church Dogmatics*, his "yes" to Israel is always bound up with a "no," and a "no" which appears to involve the contemporary retrieval of motifs from pre-modern anti-Jewish polemic.[112] Judas Iscariot's presence among the twelve emerges as a key "figure" for the inclusion of disbelieving Israel as a community alongside the believing community within the one divine election.[113] Barth writes of the Israel that has resisted Christ:

> This is the disobedient, idolatrous Israel of every age: its false prophets and godless kings; the scribes and Pharisees; the high-priest Caiaphas at the time of Jesus; Judas Iscariot among the apostles. This is the whole of Israel on the left hand, sanctified only by God's wrath.[114]

In more sober language, the opening thesis of the chapter already makes clear Barth's view of continuing Judaism as a negative witness to God's grace:

> This one community of God in its form as Israel has to serve the representation of the divine judgment, in its form as the Church the representation of the divine mercy. . . . To the one elected community of God is given in the one case its passing, and in the other its coming form.[115]

The separate existence of enduring Israel can only be affirmed in terms of a revived division of history between the community representing judgment and the community representing mercy (i.e. the Church). The only "hope" for Israel is that this separate existence as witness to God's wrath is a passing form of the one community, and that it will ultimately be brought within the coming form of the Church.

Two shorter pieces from the immediate post-war period show Barth expressing the same fundamental ideas in more succinct form. The first is the second of the lectures on the Apostles' Creed that Barth gave amidst the rubble in Bonn in 1946. While articulating very clearly his own interpretation of the first claim of the traditional paradigm, Christ as the fulfilment of Israel and its scripture, Barth is most careful to emphasize that this in no way implies that Israel's election has been terminated. That election is God's choice, not "an historic fact," and God shows himself in Christ to be faithful to his promise; hence we are in no position to regard the continuing existence of the Jewish people

> as something that has ceased to affect us, so that the Christendom of to-day might turn out to be, as it were, a balloon trip, separated from the history of Israel. If as Christians we thought that Church and Synagogue had ceased to affect each other, everything would be lost.[116]

Because the endurance of Israel is the most concrete witness to God's grace and faithfulness in history, Barth tells his audience it should be no surprise that the radical godlessness of National Socialism found its characteristic expression in antisemitism.[117]

Here again, with the "yes" to Israel's election there is also a "no." Israel remains elect despite the fact that its story is one of repeated disobedience to God's command, resistance to God's call and rejection of God's chosen, culminating in its treatment of Jesus Christ. Hence while remaining elect, Israel is also sentenced by God to continual "wandering," and to a history in which we see

> the strangeness and absurdity of the Jew, his obnoxiousness which repeatedly made him odious among the nations—and now you may give the anti-Semitic register full play.[118]

Although Barth continues his lecture to affirm the witness to grace as well as judgment in the history of Israel, his qualification of the point is instructive: "And of this the Old Testament also speaks, not as a continuity of Israelite man, but as of a 'nevertheless' of God."[119] The endurance of Israel, as the people of God refusing faith in Christ, testifies to the "nevertheless" of God's grace, but the actual life of the Jewish people can only show this as its dark shadow. Thus while the modern, liberal, historicizing version of the people judgment is firmly repudiated, and certain features of the pre-modern version decisively qualified, the judgment of the division of history as such is certainly not taken away or rescinded, and the rhetoric traditionally associated with it is invoked as entirely legitimate.

Ultimately, Barth's rigorously Christocentric account of revelation and redemption makes it difficult to comprehend the history of Judaism since the first century as anything other than testimony to God's judgment.[120] The second short piece we will consider from the post-war years, a radio address Barth gave in 1949 entitled "The Jewish Problem and the Christian Answer," is both another direct rejection of theological supersessionism and also another clear restatement of the view that God's "yes" to Israel is always bound up with Jesus Christ and therefore with the response of God's faithfulness to human faithlessness. The continuing existence of the Jewish people is, as in the Bonn lectures, the clearest sign of God's covenant faithfulness, and hence "a sign of what the one true God has done for us all, once and for all, in this one Jewish person [i.e. Jesus]."[121] God meets the failure of the Jewish people to recognize and acknowledge their Messiah, the divine Son, with unrestrained grace, but while they continue as a nation, their existence is diminished, even as this diminution of existence also belongs to the truth which they signify:

> Yet they are no more than the shadow of a nation, the reluctant witnesses of the Son of God and the Son of Man. . . . He it is, from whose sake they were once a nation and under whose sovereignty they are once more to be united.[122]

The division of history—understood, as in pre-modern theology, as temporary, something to be overcome in the ultimate fulfilment of God's purposes in history—persists beyond its re-description. It is also qualified by a clear affirmation that the Church cannot expect any kind of privileged place in history, any political and material blessing that will demonstrate by contrast with the fortunes of Israel the bestowal of divine favour. It is in this context that Barth is able to makes one of his most powerful statements of Jewish-Christian solidarity, toward the end of his address:

> The Christian community exists in the same way as the Jews; miraculously sustained throughout the years, it too is a people of strangers; and just as the anti-semites are offended by the Jews, so the Christian community will necessarily arouses the same feelings.

Yet he immediately proceeds to identify the "barrier" between Christian and Jews as

> the same as what unites us, namely the one Jew, on the cross of Golgotha, whom we acknowledge as the fulfilment of the promise to Israel and as the Saviour of the whole world.[123]

The road from World War I and *Romans* to this address from 1949 is a long one. Barth's early refusal to equate the Gospel with "one thing in the midst of other things" required a break with the liberal adaptation of the classic framework and opened up new possibilities for its re-description. The challenges of Nazism and of the explicit intertwining of racist antisemitism with religious anti-Judaism that accompanied its rise prompted Barth to reflect carefully on the covenant and people judgments of that framework and to assert against "enlightened" modern theology the dialectical relationship between law and grace in revelation and between Judaism and Christianity in history. One can see his teaching about Israel as a powerful counterpoint to Rosenzweig's thinking about the Church: for both of them, identity is constituted through relation to what is other, and understanding ourselves involves a reckoning with that which faces us. Barth's articulation of Christian theology at the end of modernity, then, is marked by attention to both Judaism and anti-Judaism in unprecedented ways. Yet it also re-inscribes anti-Judaism at the heart of the Christian theological enterprise through its re-description of the covenant and people judgments and renders participation in deliberate exchange with living Judaism at best a distraction from its urgent priorities.

New Perspectives from Roman Catholicism

In the final section of this chapter, three Roman Catholic thinkers active in the first half of the twentieth century are reviewed. In each case, there are recurring themes from the analysis presented so far. Here too, the three-dimensional process of interchange between formulations of Christian teaching, Jewish-Christian exchanges and the replication of anti-Judaism can be seen at work. None of these thinkers was seeking to change traditional Christian doctrine, only to rearticulate it for the contemporary world; indeed as Roman Catholics, they had a very different sense of the value of tradition (and in particular pre-modern tradition) than the modern and after-modern Protestant thinkers whom we have been considering up to this point. Yet in their responses to the events of the 1930s and 1940s in Western Europe, each registers certain tensions with what we have been calling the classic framework and introduces elements which at least retrospectively have the potential to disrupt the continuity of its anti-Jewish judgments. Together they shed further light on the dilemmas beginning to confront Christian theology at the end of modernity as it became intermittently aware of the relationships between its own practice, the representation of Judaism and the treatment of actual Jewish people within its immediate social context.

Jacques Maritain: Earthly Activisation

The connections between Jacques Maritain, who became a highly influential Roman Catholic philosopher in the mid-twentieth century, and Christian reflection on Judaism reach deep into his life story. Maritain attributed great importance in his conversion from atheism to the Catholic writer León Bloy, and in particular to a text Bloy wrote in 1892 called *Salut par les Juifs*. Maritain converted to Catholicism together with his wife, Raïssa, who came from a Russian Jewish family; Bloy acted as godfather to both, while in gratitude the couple paid for the printing in 1906 of a new edition of *Salut par les Juifs*, which Bloy dedicated to Raïssa. Maritain and Bloy continued to meet regularly until Bloy's death in 1925.[124] Maritain eventually became a notable opponent of antisemitism in the 1930s and an advocate after the war of the need for clarification of the Church's teaching on Israel and the Jews. He is seen by some as a pioneer along the way leading to the paragraphs on Judaism in the decree *Nostra aetate* from the Second Vatican Council affirming the permanence of Israel's election.[125]

In retrospect, the alliance between Bloy and Maritain arising from Bloy's text of 1892 seems somewhat curious, given its use of highly emotive if not indeed violent language in writing about contemporary Jews.[126] Bloy, a novelist, pamphleteer and diarist rather than a theologian, had originally published *Salut par les Juifs* as a riposte to one of the seminal works of French antisemitism, Drumont's *La France juive*. Bloy castigated Drumont for his failure to recognize the unique place of the Jewish people within the continuing drama of redemption, a drama suspended since the crucifixion by their very persistence in unbelief. It was the conscious adoption of an anti-modern discourse of eschatology that for Bloy as for Barth cleared the space for articulating an overt *theology* of enduring Israel to set against racist antisemitism diagnosed at its roots as anti-Christian, however popular it might have been with modern Christians feeling threatened by the eclipse of Christendom. Nicolas Berdyaev, another after-modern retriever of pre-modern traditions, cited Bloy enthusiastically in his writings on Jews and Judaism as a vital force within world history.[127] For all the stark differences between Bloy and Barth, the recovery of the sources of Christian theology beyond Enlightenment modernity had to include for both of them an attentive reading of Romans 9-11 which, as for the pre-modern traditions analysed in chapter two, placed continuing Israel inescapably within the horizons of Christian eschatology and therefore bound the Church to speak of actual, contemporary Judaism with some reference to divine providence and salvific purpose. Indeed, Bloy himself rather immodestly described *Salut par les Juifs* as

> without any doubt, the most energetic and the most urgent Christian testimony in favor of the Elder Race, since the eleventh chapter of Saint Paul to the Romans.[128]

Although Maritain had written some pieces on Judaism during the 1920s, this was not a major focus of his work until the rise of Hitler in the 1930s and the strengthening of antisemitic rhetoric in France brought it again to the forefront of his attention. In a number of publications in the later 1930s and early 1940s,[129] Maritain restated in his consciously rational and philosophical style the enduring insights he had gained from Bloy: the centrality of Romans 9-11 for Christian understanding of contemporary

Jews as remaining chosen by God; the unique place of the Jewish people within world history as well as God's purpose of salvation; and the incompatibility of Christian belief with participation in any kind of antisemitic violence. In *Antisemitism*, for instance, a short text published in English in 1939 and based on lectures he gave in both Paris and New York the previous year, Maritain is careful to begin by surveying the social and political condition of contemporary Jews in different countries and noting some of the factors working both for and against the spread of antisemitic attitudes. Then in the second section, he turns to a theological perspective on the situation:

> whatever may be the economic, political or cultural forms, which are superficially covered by the problem of the dispersion of Israel among the nations, this problem is and remains in truth a sacred mystery, of which St. Paul, in the Epistle to the Romans, gives us in sublime summary the principal elements.[130]

Such a perspective establishes for Maritain as for Bloy the impossibility of conscious Christian participation in antisemitic action. It also discloses the reality of antisemitic ideology as a refusal of revelation, a desire to erase by human violence the difficult testimony to God's faithfulness which the endurance of Israel represents—and hence it also shows the close relation between hostility to Jews and hostility to Christians as witnesses to the same rejected revelation, the same unwanted God. "Thus hatred of Jews and hatred of Christians springs from a common source," Maritain concludes.[131]

Maritain's consistent defence of post-biblical Judaism in its continuing history as a mystery in biblical terms, and therefore an expression of God's revelatory and redemptive will, places him firmly among those opposed to the "total" supersessionism that emerged in the theology of Western modernity. Like Barth, Maritain reached back to pre-modern sources—above all to Paul in Romans—to affirm that God's covenant with Abraham remains unbroken for Jews, even as it now also embraces Gentiles who believe in Christ and belong to the life of the Church. Yet as for Barth, it is also clear that this is in spite of the collective failure of the Jewish people to recognize Jesus as Messiah and Lord; it is a matter of divine faithfulness in the face of human faithlessness. Jewish adherence to Torah without belief in Christ cannot therefore represent God's purposes, and it is in the light of the covenant judgment of the traditional framework, the displacement of Torah, that we need to read Maritain's assertion that Christianity is "the over-flowing expansion and the supernatural fulfilment of Judaism," i.e. Jewish life based around Torah observance.[132]

Up to this point, we have been able to observe Maritain reaching parallel positions to Barth by somewhat different routes. It is the relation between his long-standing theological perspective on Judaism, his developing political philosophy and the rise of extreme antisemitism in Europe in the 1930s that makes Maritain also worth considering in his own right, however. In a text from 1921, Maritain had spoken of the Jews being sentenced to remain both permanent outsiders in any human society and permanent seekers of missed messianic fullness—and therefore they "must play in the world a fatal role of subversion."[133] He argued from this that societies were right to seek to defend themselves against such a continual threat through appropriate action. Such views were fully allied with the standard right-wing tendencies of French Catholic thought in the 1920s, and from here it was but a small step to the kind of overt advocacy of antisemitic measures that was found among anti-Dreyfusard Catholic writers at the time, including the refusal of all rights of citizenship to Jews. Such a combination of theological anti-supersessionism on the one hand with defence of antisemitic policies on the other would continue in French Catholicism through the 1930s and into the Vichy regime, with a plausible appeal to Thomas Aquinas and medieval Christendom.[134] We can identify the same combination of views among critics of Nazism in Germany, both Protestant and Catholic; even Bonhoeffer seemed prepared to accommodate it.[135] Yet by the later 1930s we no longer find Maritain in such company—indeed, he is distinguished as one of the few Christian intellectuals to oppose restrictive legislation against Jews as a matter of principle. Moreover, whereas Bloy took it for granted that suffering was inevitable for Jews given their dual condition of being both uniquely chosen by God and also uniquely disobedient to God's will in rejecting their Christ, Maritain was now seeking to act in defence of the Jewish people whom he rightly perceived to be in great danger.

These developments in Maritain's approach to Judaism are inseparable from related changes in his wider political outlook, crystallizing in his overt support for the anti-Franco side in the Spanish Civil War (to the consternation of many French Catholics). His advocacy of "a pluralism based on the human person" in politics meant that he no longer conceived of the ideal society as culturally homogenous, and therefore the co-existence of diverse cultural, religious and ethnic groups could be accepted as a positive feature.[136] Hence the persistence of Jewish distinctiveness ceases to be a political "problem" justifying discriminatory legislation or negative cultural attitudes. Furthermore, Maritain now openly supported the need for reform of institutions and societies as well as individuals as a theological imperative, a position that horrified conservative Catholics such as Claudel. In this context, the restlessness that in 1921 had seemed to mark out Jews as a uniquely subversive element now helped them to be a uniquely progressive element. In 1939, Maritain was still deducing from his theology of the mystery of Israel a particular role for Judaism within the grand narrative of world history—but this is now a valued one,

> a task of *earthly activisation* of the mass of the world. . . . Like an alien body, like an activating element injected into the mass, it gives the world no peace, it bars slumber, it teaches the world to be disoriented and restless as long as the world has not God; it stimulates the movement of history.[137]

We might well hear echoes of Rosenzweig in this context—paradoxically perhaps of his account of Christianity as a driving force in world history and the overcoming of paganism, though also of his comment about Judaism being "the louse in your fur" that goads Christianity into activity. Like Barth, Maritain goes beyond the dominant Christian tradition in describing Church and Israel as parallel realities within the purpose of God; like Rosenzweig, though to a much lesser extent, he seeks to discern positive and complementary characteristics on each side, rather than leaving Israel after Christ as the negative impress only of divine faithfulness in the face of human failure. Maritain even ventures more directly into the realms of theological speculation on this point, writing that from the understanding of Israel's being as mystery follows the understanding of the people Israel as a mystical body analogous to the Church. His comments about its role of "earthly activisation" follow on from a question about what could be the proper vocation of this mystical body; he briefly mentions testimony to the scriptures, the conventional Augustinian answer, but then sketches out the additional dimension of stimulating "the movement of history."

It is as Maritain takes the theological risk of suggesting that Israel after Christ has a distinct vocation which contributes alongside the Church towards God's one purpose of redemption that the creativity of his reflection on Christianity and Judaism comes into focus. Moreover, it is evident that what enabled the clearing of the space into which he thereby ventures is a conversion to political pluralism and the abandonment of the ideal of the unified society as one that legitimates discrimination against those who do not conform. In relation to the people claim and judgment, once strong cultural differences are seen as compatible with and indeed conducive to full human flourishing within a particular society, it becomes possible to begin to think about the "other" people as a source of blessing, not the object of a necessary curse.

Henri de Lubac: Unpredictable Grace

Maritain worked primarily as a philosopher seeking to relate the Thomist tradition within Roman Catholicism to the challenges of the contemporary world. Henri de Lubac, on the other hand, is a major figure for Roman Catholic theology in the mid-twentieth century; indeed, it has recently been argued that he is one of the most important theological voices from the twentieth century as a whole.[138] There are parallels with both Maritain and Barth in relation to the attempt to move beyond the impasse of modernity and its liberal / conservative dilemmas by the creative recovery of discourses from pre-modernity.[139] Yet de Lubac's major works are much more oriented towards the sustained exposition of such discourses, with correspondingly fewer attempts at synthesis. Barth is a systematic theologian in a way that de Lubac never really attempted to be, not least perhaps because of the opposition he encountered within the Roman Catholic Church during the 1950s in particular, when he might have been expected to be at the height of his powers. [140]

From the point of view of this study, however, the most important reason for dwelling on de Lubac is that he as a Roman Catholic, like the Reformed Barth, was developing his "after-modern" theology with self-consciously pre-modern roots in the 1930s and 1940s, the period of the emergence of Nazism, the Second World War and the Holocaust. Like Barth, de Lubac was a passionate theological critic of contemporary antisemitism and sought to deploy his new mode of doing theology to oppose what he saw as widespread Christian indifference to this; in subjugated France while Barth was in neutral Switzerland during the war, de Lubac worked clandestinely with ecclesial opposition to Hitler and the Vichy regime to disseminate theological attacks on the prevailing antisemitism, alongside some who would lose their lives for their involvement in such circles.[141] One important question, then, is the extent to which de Lubac's writings from the time parallel Barth's in their partial critique and partial reaffirmation of the judgments we have associated with the classic framework.

A particular difficulty in determining de Lubac's thinking is the nature of much of his work as scholarly commentary on the writings of others, generally from much earlier periods. One occasion where he does speak clearly in his own voice on Judaism and antisemitism is in his contribution to a short collection of essays, titled *Israël et la foi chrétienne*, which a group of French Catholic writers managed to have printed in Switzerland in 1942.[142] It is a powerful and, as one would expect from de Lubac, meticulously researched critique of modern attacks on the Jewish God and the Jewish Bible as covert attacks on Christianity. De Lubac is warning that no Christian can nod sympathetically at such antisemitic propaganda without also undermining the orthodox faith of the Church. He notes that from the beginning of Christianity there have been voices calling for the repudiation of Israel's scriptures, with contemporary antisemitic writers taking over the ancient Gnostic position. He also observes that the rise of historical criticism caused something of a crisis for the Church in how to handle the Old Testament, with the consequent unease sometimes leading to its relegation to a secondary place in Christian teaching and practice. Rather than the legitimation of such a development offered by the neo-Marcionism of Harnack and Rosenstock-Huessy, however, de Lubac offers a brief but forceful restatement of Patristic teaching on the fundamental unity of both Testaments in their witness to Christ. Because they point always to Christ, the stories and prophecies of Israel belong to the Church in perpetuity; de Lubac closes by quoting Pius XI— "Spiritually, we are semites."[143]

The retrieval of pre-modern theological hermeneutics, rooted in the scripture claim from the classic framework of fulfilment in Christ, became one of de Lubac's major scholarly tasks in the post-war period.[144] While it already shows his conviction that such retrieval holds the clue to overcoming the impasse of modern Christian theology regarding the Old Testament brought about by historical criticism, his contribution to *Israël et la foi chrétienne* does not however indicate very much about his approach to theological anti-Judaism, rather than its contemporary secular counterpart whose genealogy he traces back to Nietzsche. The collective editorial foreword makes passing reference to the Catholic Church as "true Israel" and to old Israel's lack of faith in rejecting the Messiah.[145] Elsewhere in the book, something of the same ambivalence that was found in Barth's treatment of Judaism is discernible. Scripture, above all chapters 9-11 of Romans, is repeatedly invoked to defend the permanence of God's election of Israel and therefore the continuing place of Judaism within the purpose of divine providence. The four editors had worked together on the so-called Chaine declaration from 1941, whose final main paragraph stressed that contemporary Jews were the descendants of God's chosen people, shared with Christians their holy scriptures and remained like Christians children of Abraham; hence "the blessing promised to his descendants is still upon them."[146]

That affirmation might appear to represent at the very least a sharp qualification of the people judgment in particular—the division of history. Yet it is not clear just how far such qualification extended in the minds of these writers. The conclusion of the final chapter of *Israël et la foi chrétienne* by Joseph Bonsirven, on "the mystery of Israel", is particularly striking. Paul established a fundamental solidarity between Jews and (Gentile) Christians in Romans, Bonsirven asserts, but he then notes, following the same line of thought as that set out in de Lubac's opening chapter, that modern secular antisemitism has created a new dimension to such solidarity in that Christians and Jews find themselves together as its hated targets.[147] One could hardly ask, it might appear, for a clearer rejection of the polemic historically associated with the judgment of the division of history. Yet even at this point Bonsirven insists, like Barth until much later, that the divine will that keeps Judaism alive also blocks its political fulfilment, preventing any kind of national restoration.[148] Judaism still exists, it would seem, to confirm Christianity by its eternal frustration with regard to its own conscious goals; and although Bonsirven has ruled out Christian complicity in anti-Jewish action, he has still preserved the people judgment, the division of history between the Church that can flourish in time and Israel which, since Christ's coming, cannot, but only survive with a necessary measure of suffering. In an earlier chapter by Louis Richard, which also closes with a reaffirmation of Romans 9-11 and the enduring significance of Israel for the Church, the verdicts of liberal Protestant scholarship on the legalism and particularism of Judaism in Jesus' time are nonetheless reproduced without qualification, together with the assertion that it was necessary for Israel "to die as a people-nation, closed in upon itself, to become people-Church, open to all."[149] We do not actually seem to have come very far at all from Harnack's *Das Wesen des Christentums* on Jesus and Judaism.

This review of the rather mixed thinking encountered in *Israël et la foi chrétienne* is not intended to detract from the courage and wisdom of those who took great risks to combat what seemed to many at that time to be an invincible force that would crush all who sought to resist it. It is only intended to convey the fact that clarity about the nature of the enemy to be resisted did not necessarily result instantly in clarity about the consequences of that resistance for the positive articulation of Christian convictions. Racist and secular forms of anti-Judaism focused—at least for after-modern thinkers like Barth and de Lubac—the shortcomings of "modern" Christian theologies that considered Judaism and, increasingly, that part of the Christian Bible shared with Judaism to be a thing of the past, not least because such theologies agreed with secular anti-Judaism on the disposability of continuing Judaism. Yet beyond the rehearsal of Paul's thinking in Romans 9-11, the reassertion of God's will to keep his chosen people in existence until the consummation of history and the suggestion of a new solidarity between Jews and Christians in the face of the godless threat of Nazi ideology, it is hard to find any conscious evaluation of historic Christian anti-Judaism in the essays of these four authors. They clearly did not want the three judgments of the classic framework— Judaism's interpretive blindness, the displacement of Torah and the division of history—to be considered as pretexts for complicity with antisemitism in any way, and they strove to emphasize other aspects of the Christian tradition that would strengthen good will towards contemporary Jews. On the other hand, there is no evidence of a questioning engagement with the judgments themselves to set alongside the wrestling with Israel's election that is evident in Barth's work from the 1940s.

There is a vital strand in de Lubac's other work that is, however, at least suggestive of a question mark against standard articulations of the judgments from the classic framework. De Lubac, like Barth, made newness a central theme of his writing, although he approached it from a very different tradition and standpoint. He often quoted a phrase from St Irenaeus of Lyons, that Christ "brought all newness in bringing himself"[150]—a phrase which also indicates that for de Lubac, as for Rosenstock-Huessy, Barth and the entire pre-modern tradition, the newness of Christ is not primarily a historical truth, based on the (relative) originality of Jesus and the Christianity he founded as historical developments, but a theological truth, deriving from the incarnation as the decisive, transformative, self-communicating act of the triune God for creation. Yet while Barth began to articulate what such "newness" might mean in terms of contemporary theological discourse in the context of his recovery of the concept of revelation, de Lubac's formative theological struggles revolved around the theme of nature and grace and the related set of questions that stretched back through Western theology, via the complex refractions of the Protestant Reformation, to the early fifth-century controversy between Augustine and the Pelagians: what is the new thing that grace brings to created (human) nature, and to what extent is its work continuous with what that nature already possesses in itself?

For de Lubac, the real "newness" of grace as something other than an extension or development of what is already given in human nature was a distinguishing feature of the Christian faith, setting it apart, for instance, from the great religious traditions of Asia which he studied with great seriousness.[151] On the other hand, like the Catholic tradition in general he was wary of the antithetical thinking about (fallen) nature and grace that Protestant thinkers—including, at times, Barth himself—appeared eager to promote;[152] the newness brought by Christ could not be something that had as it were no connection at all with the existing condition of the creation he came to redeem. Critical of the treatments of this set of issues in the scholastic thought of Roman Catholic modernity down to his own time, de Lubac saw the answer required for the twentieth century clearly present in the pre-modern mainstream: human beings are created with a desire—we could even say *as* a desire—for the God who utterly transcends them, and whom they have no *natural* path or right to knowing. "You have made us for yourself, and our hearts are restless until they find their rest in you," as Augustine had so memorably written.[153] Because the desire for God is an ineluctable dimension of the nature of humanity, then, the newness of Christ does not come as something unrelated to our existing condition as human creatures; hence the antithetical thinking of Protestantism is inadequate. Because our nature does not give us the means to achieve or even truly conceive what we desire, however, the newness of Christ in offering to us the knowledge and love of God communicates a free, gracious and unimaginable gift;[154] hence the Protestant accusation that the Catholic tradition collapses grace back into nature as merely nature's immanent development is misplaced.

If an echo were heard at this point of the teaching of Aquinas on the self-transcending dynamic of the human person, noted in relation to his arguments for the necessity of divine as well as natural law in chapter two above, then de Lubac would be only too pleased. He regarded his teaching on nature and grace, the natural and the supernatural, as nothing more than the contemporary restatement of the great Catholic tradition, of which Aquinas was one of the most important exponents. Yet while Aquinas used the dynamic relation of nature and grace in this context primarily to set out the place of divine law by contrast with natural law, de Lubac suggests that this relation can also be illuminated in turn by the movement from old to new in God's economy, from the covenant with Israel to the covenant of Christ. In a short but intriguing passage in *The Mystery of the Supernatural*, he notes that the characterization of Israel's history as preparation for the coming of Christ does not mean that this coming was anything other than "totally new and gratuitous." He then continues,

> But further, just as the coming of Christ, though fulfilling the history of Israel and giving it meaning, marks the passing into a new order, which wholly transcends the order that preceded it—"omnem novitatem attulit" ["He brought all newness"]—so it is with our supernatural finality. Between nature as it exists and the supernatural for which God destines it, the distance is as great, the difference as radical, as that between being and non-being: for to pass from one to the other is not merely to pass into "more being", but to pass to a different type of being.[155]

Now, de Lubac stresses that he is using the relation between old and new covenants as an analogy in this context: he is not equating Israel with un-graced nature, as for instance Barth appears to do at certain moments of the dialectic in *Romans*. The force of the comparison for the theological understanding of Israel is rather to emphasize both the ineradicable orientation of Israel at every point in its history towards Jesus Christ, and also the truly surprising character of Christ's newness as not simply predictable from nor indeed simply continuous with the history of Israel.

There is therefore an unmistakeable distancing in de Lubac of the concept of fulfilment, which he sought to recover in his work on biblical interpretation, from the rhetoric of "demonstrating" Jesus as Christ from the Old Testament—a rhetoric, as we noted in chapter one, that goes right back to the New Testament itself and to the conflict between the emerging Christian assemblies and other Jewish groups that marks it throughout. Here too there is an affinity with Barth, whose dialectical theology arrived at a similar point.[156] The connection made by de Lubac, however, with a central theme of his theology is particularly powerful in undermining both the "old" anti-Judaism of pre-modernity which asserted wilful perversity in Jewish refusal after Christ to acknowledge the plain meaning of the texts they continued to read, and the "new" anti-Judaism of modernity which asserted Israel's irrelevance after Christ, as historic scripture and contemporary social presence, to the work of God in creation, revelation and redemption. Just as nature is not abolished by grace, so Israel remains at the heart of God's purposes for the world. While there are plenty of passages in de Lubac's writings that express conventional theological anti-Judaism,[157] his restatement of the newness of grace—which proved so troubling to the guardians of Roman Catholic orthodoxy in the mid-twentieth century—invites an articulation of radical newness in Christ that does not involve either the condemnation or the erasure of continuing Israel.

Edith Stein: Communion in Suffering

Joseph Roth, the secular Jewish novelist and journalist, wrote in 1937:

Only a very small, select minority of devout Christians have understood that—for the first time in the long and shameful history of Jewish persecutions—the plight of the Jews is identical to that of the Christians. They beat up Moritz Finkelstein from Wroclaw, but the intended victim is Jesus of Nazareth.[158]

It is an insight that, as we have seen, Maritain and de Lubac both to some extent shared. Yet Roth's remark stretches beyond solidarity between Jews and Christians in the face of Nazi persecution. It suggests that there is actually a solidarity between Jews and Jesus—that when historically "Christian" nations inflict suffering on Jews, their Christ now stands against them, with their victims, with the others. The same possibility appears in the famous *White Crucifixion* of Marc Chagall from 1938. Chagall sets alongside one another the image of Christ crucified, the suffering of the Jewish people and the practice of Torah: through the conjunction of faithfulness to Torah and the experience of persecution, Jews are sharing in the reality of Jesus.[159] There is no representation of the Church in this picture, but we might say that we can only imagine the Church in this context as turning away from the Jew on the cross at its centre, as broken in its soul and in its power by its collusion with what is happening—in other words as the counterpart of Synagoga in the medieval iconographic tradition that put Church and Synagogue on the right and left hand side respectively of the cross of Christ. Indeed, for Chagall as a Jewish artist, there was also an element of personal identification with the figure of Christ; poetry he wrote around the outbreak of World War II, when he left France, his first home in exile, for America, includes the lines,

> Day and night I carry a cross
> I am shoved, dragged by the hand
> Already night surrounds me. And you
> Abandon me, O God. Why?[160]

The theme of an implicit and unacknowledged solidarity between Jesus, faithful in suffering, and the Jewish people in the present becomes perhaps more problematic when it is used by Christians who in other ways appeared to legitimate Jewish suffering as an expression of the will of God. Paul Claudel, for instance, remarked in 1939, "All the sacred writers call Israel a witness; but the Greek word for witness is martyr."[161] There are traces of the same motif in Protestant writers as well. In the aftermath of Kristallnacht, Barth is reported to have said that "Whoever rejects and persecutes the Jew, rejects and persecutes the one who died for the sins of the Jews and only *thereby* for our sins."[162] Bonhoeffer wrote in the text of what was posthumously published as his *Ethics* that "An expulsion of the Jews from the west must necessarily bring with it the expulsion of Christ. For Jesus Christ was a Jew."[163] While the interpretation of Jewish suffering through Christian categories must be regarded with caution in a post-Holocaust context, the historical significance of these remarks—

however isolated and elliptical—needs to be appreciated. One simply cannot imagine influential Christians in any earlier period suggesting an identification between Jesus and contemporary Jews, let alone a profound communion in suffering and witness. Such comments therefore mark an important if also difficult moment in the history of the relationship between Judaism, anti-Judaism and Christian theology.

This same motif receives expression also in Edith Stein, the phenomenological philosopher who converted to Roman Catholicism from a Jewish background, eventually becoming a Carmelite nun, and died at Auschwitz with her sister in 1942.[164] Stein had a clear sense of the dangers facing the Jewish people as soon as Hitler came to power in 1933 and wrote a confidential letter to the Pope that year urging him to take action or risk complicity in evil. Commenting on the number of Jewish people who had already committed suicide in the face of state-sponsored persecution, Stein told Pius XI that responsibility for their deaths "must fall, after all, on those who brought them to this point and it also falls on those who keep silent in the face of such happenings"—and she makes it clear that she regards the Roman Catholic Church up to this point as having done precisely that.[165] Stein cannot easily be accused, therefore, of legitimating acquiescence in Jewish suffering through linking it theologically to the suffering of Jesus Christ.

Nor did Stein share the difficult ambivalence about Jewish identity that characterized many Jews attracted to Christian belief, an ambivalence clearly present for Rosenstock-Huessy and perhaps most notable in Simone Weil.[166] While many of her Jewish philosophical contemporaries who turned towards Christianity made much of their admiration for the New Testament as a separate text from the Jewish Bible, Stein loved both together and delighted in finding overlaps between Jewish and Christian forms of prayer by taking her Breviary with her when accompanying her mother to synagogue services, as she continued to do after her conversion to Christianity.[167] It is noteworthy that one of Stein's responses to the political success of Nazism in 1933 was to start writing memoirs about the family life she knew in childhood and adolescence—in order to present a simple, positive and sympathetic account of what Jewish existence was actually like.[168] Remarkably, although she shared in broad terms the theological perspectives on continuing Judaism that we found in Maritain and other Roman Catholic writers who persisted in assuming the cessation of the covenant with Moses, though not that with Abraham, she admired the devotion of family and friends who practised Judaism and after the death of her mother, a deeply religious Jewish woman, expressed her confidence that "she found a very merciful judge and is now my most faithful helper on my way, so that I, too, may reach my goal."[169]

One of the key passages in Stein's writing on the relation between Jewish suffering and the way of the cross comes from a letter she wrote to Petra Brüning in 1938, concerning her name in religion, Teresa Benedicta of the Cross, and her arrival at the Carmel in Cologne in the fateful year 1933:

> I must tell you that I already brought my religious name with me into the house as a postulant. I received it exactly as I had requested it. By the cross I understood the destiny of God's people which, even at that time, began to announce itself. I thought that those who recognized it as the cross of Christ had to take it upon themselves in the name of all. Certainly, today I know more or what it means to be wedded to the Lord in the sign of the Cross. Of course, one can never comprehend it, for it is a mystery.[170]

For Stein, suffering with Christ was integral to Christian faith; the drama of the cross is something each of us has to re-enact in the story of our life, something that may include the voluntary sharing in his (continuing) expiatory suffering.[171] Yet the passage from this letter makes it clear she also regarded the Jewish people, "God's people" without qualification, as somehow participating in this defining activity of Christian faith in a unique although hidden way. As a Jewish convert to Christianity who never ceased to consider herself Jewish, and who valued the religious practice of Torah observing contemporaries, she could consciously embrace Judaism's unacknowledged solidarity with Jesus in his sufferings—a solidarity not accessible to Gentile Christians—as cardinal for her vocation. The words of her last will and testament that speak of her life and death as an offering "for the Jewish people" indicate that this motif remained at the heart of her sense of identity as the prospect of sharing in the mass executions of that people drew closer. Stein never harboured the illusion shared by such culturally prominent Jewish figures as the philosopher Henri Bergson that the waves of antisemitism would pass by those who converted to Christianity;[172] she knew that for the Nazi regime her religious faith made no difference at all to her Jewishness, and indeed she never flinched from regarding herself as Jewish in her Christianity, not because she shared the mystique of race and blood but because of theological belief in the mystery of Israel's election.

Once again, it is a matter of identifying tensions arising from the thinking of these figures in relation to Christian theology, Judaism and anti-Judaism; tensions that remained undeveloped by them, perhaps in part because they could ultimately generate significant conflict with much that they took for granted. Finding Christ with and among the Jewish people in the death camps could be seen as the ultimate gesture of Christian theology desperate to make even this Jewish tragedy a passage within its wholly Christian drama, rather than actually attending to the realities of both alterity and responsibility, and Stein's legacy undoubtedly raises troubling questions around precisely such issues.[173] Yet her discernment of vocation can also be considered an affirmation of the presence of Christ as exceeding the comprehension of the Church, and therefore as interrupting the procession from claim to judgment via the hermeneutics of history that defines the classic framework and its subsequent variations, both modern and after-modern. For Stein, the mystery of Israel, as a theological mystery, is bound to the mystery of Christ: somehow there exists a communion between living Judaism and Jesus of Nazareth that Judaism does not understand—but neither does the Gentile Church, which is therefore not in a position to "tell" Judaism the meaning it does not own. Stein did not let her Catholic loyalty and indeed her profound Christian faith displace her barely formulated confidence, unparalleled in any of the other Christian writers considered in this chapter or indeed in previous ones, that the Word, the beloved Son of God, also dwells in and with Israel as the ever elect people of God, whom she always called her people. It is Christianity believing it comprehends God's redemption that presumes to pass judgment on "Judaism" as outside and against it, to interpret the history in which it participates as if it could stand over it as its judge. Stein's dissent from the dominant position of nearly two thousand years is none the less powerful for being so undemonstrative, so close to silence.

Tensions in Relation to the Judgments

Rosenzweig and Barth can both be described as dialectical thinkers. It would hardly be helpful to use the same term of the three Roman Catholic figures whose work we have just very briefly reviewed. Yet in each of them there are traces of theological tension in relation to the judgments from the classic framework which, it has been argued, carried the tradition of anti-Judaism across the epochal shifts in Christian theology we have been reviewing, from pre-modernity to modernity and its end. Maritain's treatment of the distinctive vocation of Judaism in unfolding history renders the endurance of Judaism a potential sign of God's blessing rather than God's curse and thus begins to subvert the force of the people judgment. De Lubac's analysis of the relation between nature and grace and the suggestive analogy with old and new covenants suggests that

Jewish non-recognition of Christological readings of the Hebrew scriptures does not in fact disclose interpretive blindness of a culpable kind, undermining the condemnation of Jewish people and their religious life implied in the scripture judgment. Finally, while she uncritically rehearsed the language of the covenant judgment, displacement of Torah, Stein disturbs its fixity in her acceptance both that those who continue to observe Torah without Christ stand in relation to Christ and the grace of God given through him, and that this relation is not something that the Gentile Church can comprehend or judge. Together with Barth, they raise from within Christian theology the question that, in the next chapter, we consider from the perspective of some Jewish commentators contemporary with them: how has anti-Judaism misshaped the development of Christian theology? Yet they also suggest that anti-Judaism as Christian judgment on Judaism comes in many forms, some of them evil and requiring resistance, but others to be accepted (with appropriate vigilance) as intrinsic to the shaping of Christian theology by its internal foe. That is an issue to which we will need to return in the final, concluding chapter.

Notes

[1] Cf. John M. Oesterreicher, *Walls Are Crumbling: Seven Jewish Philosophers Discover Christ* (London: Hollis and Carter, 1953); Alasdair MacIntyre, *Edith Stein: A Philosophical Prologue* (London: Continuum, 2006).

[2] The term "after-modern" is being used both to invoke and avoid the highly contested terminology of "postmodernity". For the relevance of the category of the postmodern, coined in the 1970s, to understanding the earlier history of twentieth-century theology, and in particular Karl Barth, see Graham Ward, "Barth, Modernity, and Postmodernity," in *The Cambridge Companion to Karl Barth*, ed. John Webster (Cambridge: Cambridge University Press, 2000), 274-95.

[3] See the editor's introduction to Adolf von Harnack, *Liberal Theology at Its Height*, ed. Martin Rumscheidt (London: Collins, 1989), 9-41.

[4] Cf. Mark D. Chapman, *Ernst Troeltsch and Liberal Theology: Religion and Cultural Synthesis in Wilhelmine Germany* (Oxford: Oxford University Press, 2001), 3-8.

[5] Adolf Harnack, *What is Christianity?* trans. Thomas Bailey Saunders, 5th ed. (London: Ernest Benn, 1958).

[6] Quoted in Hans Martin Rumscheidt, *Revelation and Theology: An Analysis of the Barth-Harnack Correspondence of 1923* (Cambridge: Cambridge University Press, 1972), 72.

[7] Adolf von Harnack, *History of Dogma*, trans. Neil Buchanan, 7 vols in 4 (New York: Dover, 1961).

[8] Harnack, *Liberal Theology*, 16.

[9] Harnack, *What is Christianity?* 28-29.

[10] Harnack, *What is Christianity?* 23. Wright places Harnack within a line of scholars from F. C. Bauer in the nineteenth century to Mack and Crossan in the present for whom early Christianity was, in its core, "only marginally or tangentially Jewish" (*New Testament*, 343).

[11] Harnack, *What is Christianity?* 43

[12] Harnack, *What is Christianity?* 44

[13] Quoted in Stanley Hauerwas, "Walter Rauschenbusch and the Saving of America," in *A Better Hope: Resources for a Church Confronting Capitalism, Democracy, and Postmodernity* (Grand Rapids: Brazos, 2000), 84. On the place of the historical Jesus in Jewish-Christian dialogue in the nineteenth and twentieth centuries, see David Novak, *Jewish-Christian Dialogue: A Jewish Justification* (Oxford: Oxford University Press, 1989), 73-92.

[14] Walter Jacob, *Christianity through Jewish Eyes: The Quest for Common Ground* (Cincinnati: Hebrew Union College Press, 1974), 40-50; Susannah Heschel, "1857," in *Yale Companion*, ed. Gilman and Zipes, 193-198.

[15] Quoted in Jacob, *Christianity through Jewish Eyes*, 71.

[16] Barbara Ellen Galli, *Franz Rosenzweig and Jehuda Halevi: Translating, Translations, and Translators* (Montreal: McGill-Queen's University Press, 1995), 259-60.

[17] Harnack, *What is Christianity?* 44-45. Walter Homolka stresses Harnack's indebtedness to Wellhausen's disjunction of (prophetic) Hebraism and (post-exilic, legalistic) Judaism in *Jewish Identity in Modern Times: Leo Baeck and German Protestantism* (Providence: Berghahn, 1995), 22-24.

[18] Harnack, *What is Christianity?* 45-46

[19] Harnack has already developed the theme of the exceptional qualities of Jesus' personality at the end of the previous lecture (*What is Christianity?* 36-37); he "translates" the title "Son of God" into the historical Jesus' "consciousness of the unique character of his relation to God as Son" at 97-99.

[20] On the universality of Christianity, see for instance Harnack, *What is Christianity?* 24, 55, and 99; on its interiority and focus on the individual, 49, 86, 90, 110 and 130.

[21] Harnack, *What is Christianity?* 130-132.

[22] "The last and highest stage of humanity had been reached" (Harnack, *What is Christianity?* 138).

[23] Harnack, *What is Christianity?* 46.

[24] Harnack's sublimation of biblical eschatology in ethical idealism in commented on by Rumscheidt, *Revelation and Theology*, 77-78.

[25] Cited in Robert Davidson and A. R. C. Leaney, *Biblical Criticism*, vol. 3 of *The Pelican Guide to Modern Theology*, ed. R. P. C. Hanson (Harmondsworth: Penguin, 1970), 157. Cf. Rumscheidt, *Revelation and Theology*, 86-100.

[26] Homolka, *Jewish Identity*, 18-38. Leo Baeck's response originally appeared as "Harnack's Vorlesungen über das Wesen des Christentums," *Montasschrift für Geschichte und Wissenschaft des Judentums* 45 [N. F. 9] (1901): 97-120. It is partly translated in "Harnack's Lectures on the Essence of Christianity," in *Jewish*

Perspectives on Christianity: Leo Baeck, Martin Buber, Franz Rosenzweig, Will Herberg, Abraham J. Heschel, ed. Fritz A. Rothschild (New York: Continuum, 2000), 42-45.

[27] Baeck, "Harnack's Lectures," 44; "Harnack's Vorlesungen," 118.

[28] Baeck, "Harnack's Lectures," 44; "Harnack's Vorlesungen," 118. Baeck set out what he believed could be recovered by critical historical study about the historical and thoroughly Jewish Jesus in a later essay, "The Gospel as a Document of the Jewish Faith," translated in *Judaism and Christianity: Essays by Leo Baeck*, trans. Walter Kaufmann (Cleveland: Meridian, 1961), 41-136.

[29] For a recent attempt by a conservative Protestant theologian to redress that balance, with interesting echoes of Harnack's presentation, see Paul F. M. Zahl, *The First Christian: Universal Truth in the Teachings of Jesus* (Grand Rapids: Eerdmans, 2003).

[30] On Rosenzweig's life, see Nahum N. Glatzer, *Franz Rosenzweig: His Life and Thought*, 3rd ed. (Indianapolis: Hackett, 1998). I have previously written about his analysis of Christianity in "Beginning without End: Christianity in Franz Rosenzweig's *Star of Redemption*," *Journal of Ecumenical Studies* 39:3-4 (Summer-Fall 2002): 340-362.

[31] See the letter cited by Paul Mendes-Flohr in his article "1914," in *Yale Companion*, ed. Gilman and Zipes, 323.

[32] Alexander Altmann, "Franz Rosenzweig and Eugen Rosenstock-Huessy: An Introduction to their 'Letters on Judaism and Christianity,'" in *Judaism despite Christianity*, ed. Rosenstock-Huessy, 26-48, especially 27-33. Cf. also Harold Stahmer, *"Speak That I May See Thee!" The Religious Significance of Language* (New York: Macmillan, 1968).

[33] Glatzer, *Franz Rosenzweig*, 23-29. See also his much later letter to Meinecke (translated in full 94-98).

[34] Rosenstock-Huessy, ed., *Judaism despite Christianity*, 91.

[35] Franz Rosenzweig, *Philosophical and Theological Writings*, trans. and ed. Paul W. Franks and Michael L. Morgan (Indianapolis: Hackett, 2000), 73-83; the quotation is from 82. Cf. also the opening remarks of his essay from 1918, "Science and Life," in Franz Rosenzweig, *God, Man, and the World: Lectures and Essays*, ed. and trans. Barbara E. Galli (Syracuse: Syracuse University Press, 1998), 123-133. Later on, in the notes to his translations of the poems of Jehuda Halevi, he would even compare World War I to Sinai as "a comparable revealing experience for mankind" (Galli, *Rosenzweig and Halevi*, 188). For Rosenstock-Huessy's views, see *Judaism despite Christianity*, 79 and 143.

[36] Franz Rosenzweig, "The New Thinking," in *Franz Rosenzweig's "The New Thinking"*, ed. and trans. Alan Udoff and Barbara E. Galli (Syracuse: Syracuse University Press, 1999), 67-102.

[37] Rosenstock-Huessy, ed., *Judaism despite Christianity*, 124; see letters 12-14, 118-129.

[38] Rosenstock-Huessy, ed., *Judaism despite Christianity*, 140.

[39] Rosenstock-Huessy, ed., *Judaism despite Christianity*, 140-41, 144.

[40] Rosenstock-Huessy, ed., *Judaism despite Christianity*, 84-88, 107.

[41] Rosenstock-Huessy, ed., *Judaism despite Christianity*, 140-42; cf. 88.

[42] Rosenstock-Huessy, ed., *Judaism despite Christianity*, 121, 141.

[43] Rosenstock-Huessy, ed., *Judaism despite Christianity*, 122.

[44] Rosenzweig, "Apologetic Thinking," in *Philosophical and Theological Writings*, 95-108. Commenting on his own work in the *Star of Redemption*, Rosenzweig suggested that its treatment of Judaism and Christianity "goes beyond the usual apologetics and polemics in this area—indeed for the first time" (*Rosenzweig's "New Thinking"*, 94).

[45] Rosenstock-Huessy, ed., *Judaism despite Christianity*, 110.

[46] Franz Rosenzweig, *The Star of Redemption*, trans. Barbara E. Galli (Wisconsin: University of Wisconsin Press, 2005); see also Worthen, "Beginning without End."

[47] Cf. Franz Rosenzweig, "Atheistic Theology," in *Philosophical and Theological Writings*, 10-24.

[48] Rosenstock-Huessy, ed., *Judaism despite Christianity*, 110.

[49] Galli, *Rosenzweig and Halevi*, 241.

[50] Rosenstock-Huessy, ed., *Judaism despite Christianity*, 112-13.

[51] Rosenstock-Huessy, ed., *Judaism despite Christianity*, 157-59. Cf. Rosenzweig, *Star of Redemption*, 296-306. On Rosenzweig's use of Schelling here, see Robert Gibbs, *Correlations in Rosenzweig and Levinas* (Princeton: Princeton University Press, 1992), 124-128; for the wider background to Rosenzweig's thinking, Alexander Altmann, "Franz Rosenzweig on History," in *Studies in Religious Philosophy and Mysticism* (London: Routledge and Kegan Paul, 1969), 275-291.

[52] Rosenstock-Huessy, ed., *Judaism despite Christianity*, 160; see also the final major section of Rosenzweig, *Star of Redemption*, Part III, Book III, "The Star or Eternal Truth," 403-440.

[53] On Rosenzweig's own efforts, in collaboration with Martin Buber, to recover the Hebrew Bible for the German culture of his time, see Martin Buber and Franz Rosenzweig, *Scripture and Translation*, trans. Lawrence Rosenwald with Everett Fox (Bloomington: Indiana University Press, 1994).

[54] Rosenstock-Huessy, ed., *Judaism despite Christianity*, 130, 135.

[55] On the political, social and cultural context for Barth's commentaries on Romans, see Timothy J. Gorringe, *Karl Barth: Against Hegemony* (Oxford: Oxford University Press, 1999), 24-72.

[56] For Barth on original sin, see Karl Barth, *The Epistle to the Romans*, trans. Edwyn C. Hoskyns (Oxford: Oxford University Press, 1933), 85-86; for Rosenzweig on miracle, *Star of Redemption*, 103-121. On the encyclopaedia as a paradigm of rationality in the nineteenth century, see Alasdair MacIntyre, *Three Rival Versions of Moral Enquiry: Encyclopaedia, Genealogy, and Tradition* (London: Duckworth, 1990).

[57] Eberhard Busch, *Karl Barth: His Life from Letters and Autobiographical Texts* (London: SCM, 1976), 112. Cf. Stahmer, *"Speak!"* 121-23, and Maurice Friedman, *Martin Buber's Life and Work: The Middle Years, 1923-45* (Detroit: Wayne State University Press, 1988), 106-7.

[58] Gorringe, *Karl Barth*, 78; Randi Rashkover, *Revelation and Theopolitics: Barth, Rosenzweig and the Politics of Praise* (London: T & T Clark, 2005).

[59] Galli, *Rosenzweig and Halevi*, 194-95, 204-06, and Buber and Rosenzweig, *Scripture and Translation*, 25-26, 108.

[60] Barth, *Romans*, 28.

[61] Barth, *Romans*, 29; cf. 96.

[62] Barth, *Romans*, 29.

[63] Barth, *Romans*, 97-98; cf. 366.

[64] Barth, *Romans*, 192-93.

[65] Barth, *Romans*, 338.

[66] Barth, *Romans*, 339.

[67] Barth, *Romans*, 76.

[68] Cf. Jürgen Moltmann, *Theology of Hope: On the Ground and Implications of a Christian Eschatology*, trans. James W. Leitch (London: SCM, 1967), 37-42, and *Coming of God*, 1-22.

[69] Barth, *Romans*, 314. Cf. Ingolf U. Dahlferth "Karl Barth's Eschatological Realism," in *Karl Barth: Centenary Essays*, ed. S. W. Sykes (Cambridge: Cambridge University Press, 1989), 20.

[70] Barth, *Romans*, 112.

[71] Barth, *Romans*, 499-500, and *Church Dogmatics* II/1, 635; references to the *Church Dogmatics* (hereafter *CD*) are to the English translation in *Church Dogmatics*, ed. G. W. Bromiley and T. F. Torrance, 14 vols (Edinburgh: T & T Clark, 1956-1977). Already in his 1928-29 lectures on theological ethics, Barth was carefully distinguishing two aspects of eschatological truth, that it is both "final" and present "*as* the future, coming to us" (Karl Barth, *Ethics*, ed. Dietrich Braun and trans. Geoffrey W. Bromiley [Edinburgh: T & T Clark, 1981], 464-66). Cf. also Moltmann, *Coming of God*, 17-18; Gorringe, *Karl Barth*, 288.

[72] Barth, *Romans*, 28. Cf. Francis Watson, "The Bible," in *Cambridge Companion to Barth*, ed. Webster, 57-71.

[73] Karl Barth, *The Resurrection of the Dead*, trans. H. J. Stenning (London: Hodder and Stoughton, 1933), 148.

[74] Karl Barth, "The Strange New World within the Bible," in *The Word of God and the Word of Man*, trans. Douglas Horton (Boston: Pilgrim Press, 1928), 28-50. Cf. the comments from a Jewish perspective on this aspect of Barth's writing by Michael Wyschogrod, "Why Was and Is the Theology of Karl Barth of Interest to a Jewish Theologian?" in *Footnotes to a Theology: The Karl Barth Colloquium of 1972*, ed. Martin Rumscheidt (Toronto: Corporation for the Publication of Academic Studies of Religion in Canada, 1974), 95-111, especially 100-102.

[75] E.g. Barth, *CD* II/2, 355-409; cf. the comments of Frei in the preface to *Eclipse of Biblical Narrative*, vii-viii.

[76] See Bruce L. McCormack, "The Significance of Karl Barth's Theological Exegesis of Philippians," in *Epistle to the Philippians: 40th Anniversary Edition*, by Karl Barth, trans. James W. Leitch (Louisville: Westminster John Knox, 2002), v-xxv.

[77] Cf. McCormack, "Significance of Barth's Exegesis," vi-ix.

[78] Gorringe, *Karl Barth*, 35; cf. Katherine Sonderegger, *That Jesus Christ Was Born a Jew: Karl Barth's "Doctrine of Israel"* (University Park, PA: Pennsylvania State University Press, 1992), 34-35.

[79] The whole correspondence is reproduced with extensive analysis in Rumscheidt, *Revelation and Theology*.

[80] Cf. his reply to Harnack's fifteenth question (Rumscheidt, *Revelation and Theology*, 35).

[81] Barth, "Barth to Harnack," in Rumscheidt, *Revelation and Theology*, 44.

[82] Rumscheidt, *Revelation and Theology*, 34.

[83] Rumscheidt, *Revelation and Theology*, 37-38.

[84] Rumscheidt, *Revelation and Theology*, 47-51; cf. e.g. Barth, *Romans*, 107-09, 495-96.

[85] Barth, *Romans*, 79 (on "the oracles of God"), 132 ("The Jewish religion forms but a part of the wider world to which the revelation of God is promised and in which it is encountered. The world is not broken up into fragments").

[86] Quoted in Gorringe, *Karl Barth*, 43.

[87] Barth, *CD* II/2, 517-18.

[88] This has been emphasized in recent studies, such as Nigel Biggar, *The Hastening That Waits: Karl Barth's Ethics* (Oxford: Clarendon, 1993), and John Webster, *Barth's Moral Theology: Human Action in Barth's Thought* (Edinburgh: T & T Clark, 1998). Cf. also Barth, *Ethics*, 15-18.

[89] Barth, *Romans*, 426-27.

[90] The address can be found in Barth, *Word of God*, 136-82; cf. Barth, *Romans*, 424-438, a sub-section itself titled "The Problem of Ethics."

[91] Barth, *Ethics*.

[92] Barth, *CD* II/2, 527.

[93] Barth, *CD* II/2, 510-511, 546.

[94] Barth, *Epistle to the Philippians*, 50.

[95] Barth, *Ethics*, 49-50.

[96] Barth, *Ethics*, 76.

[97] This is stressed in particular in Biggar, *Hastening that Waits*.

[98] Barth, *Ethics*, 53-54.

[99] Karl Barth, "Gospel and Law," in *Community, State, and Church: Three Essays* (Gloucester: Peter Smith, 1968), 71-100.

[100] Barth, "Gospel and Law," 96.

[101] Barth, "Gospel and Law," 71-72, 80.

[102] Barth, "Gospel and Law,"80.

[103] On the implications of law without gospel, see "Gospel and Law," 84-94.

[104] Barth, "Gospel and Law," 81.

[105] Barth, "Gospel and Law," 83.

[106] Quoted by David Burrell, "Introduction: How Christians Share in the Destiny of Israel," in *Voices from Jerusalem: Jews and Christians Reflect on the Holy Land*, ed. David Burrell and Yehezkel Landau (New York: Paulist Press, 1992), 14.

[107] Gorringe, *Karl Barth*, 157.

[108] Barth, *CD* II/2, 195, 198.

[109] Barth, *CD* II/2, 287.

[110] Barth, *CD* II/2, 290.

[111] Franklin H. Littell and Hubert G. Locke, eds., *The German Church Struggle and the Holocaust* (Detroit: Wayne State University Press, 1974); see the short note Barth wrote in 1967 calling for "'Jewish-Christian Solidarity' today!" and recognizing his own earlier failures, cited for instance in Sonderegger, *Jesus Christ*, 136-37.

[112] See the catena of passages cited by Wyschogrod, "Theology of Karl Barth," 106-07.

[113] Cf. Sonderegger, *Jesus Christ*, 112-133.

[114] Barth, *CD* II/2, 287.

[115] Barth, *CD* II/2, 195.

[116] Karl Barth, *Dogmatics in Outline*, trans. G. T. Thomson (London: SCM, 1949), 74-75. Barth returns to this theme at the end of the lecture (81).

[117] Barth, *Dogmatics in Outline*, 74-77.

[118] Barth, *Dogmatics in Outline*, 79.

[119] Barth, *Dogmatics in Outline*, 80.

[120] On reversion to the "witness people" tradition of Christian understanding of Judaism among both supporters and opponents of the Nazi regime in Germany in the 1930s, see Haynes, *Bonhoeffer Legacy*, 50-53; cf. also Saperstein, *Moments of Crisis*, 41-42.

[121] Karl Barth, "The Jewish Problem and the Christian Answer," in *Against the Stream: Shorter Post-war Writings, 1946-52*, trans. E. M. Delacour and Stanley Godman (SCM: London, 1954), 197.

[122] Barth, "Jewish Problem," 198.

[123] Barth, "Jewish Problem," 200-01. The talk led to Barth's meeting with a group of Jews in Basle to discuss his views in 1950, an occasion that does not seem to have been particularly comfortable and was not repeated (Busch, *Karl Barth*, 368-69).

[124] Bernard Doering, "The Origin and Development of Maritain's Idea of the Chosen People," in *Jacques Maritain and the Jews*, ed. Robert Royal (Mishawaka: American Maritain Association, 1994), 17-35.

[125] See for instance the essay by Vittorio Possenti, "Maritain and the Jewish Question," in *Maritain and the Jews*, ed. Royal, 104-122.

[126] Cf. John Hellman, "The Jews in the 'New Middle Ages': Jacques Maritain's Anti-semitism in Its Times," in *Maritain and the Jews*, ed. Royal, 89-103.

[127] Nicolas Berdyaev, *The Meaning of History*, trans. George Reavey (London: Geoffrey Bles, 1936). Berdyaev's short essay from 1940, *Christianity and Anti-semitism*, trans. Alan A. Spears and Victor B. Kanter (Aldington: Hand and Flower, 1952), opens with a quotation from Bloy.

[128] Cited from Doering, "Origin and Development," 23.

[129] For a list of these, see Charles P. O'Donnell, "A Select Bibliography on Jacques Maritain's Writings on Jews, Christians, and Anti-semitism," in *Maritain and the Jews*, ed. Royal, 273-75.

[130] Jacques Maritain, *Antisemitism* (London: Geoffey Bles, 1939), 16.

[131] Maritain, *Antisemitism*, 20.

[132] Maritain, *Antisemitism*, 16.

[133] Cited in Doering, "Origin and Development," 27.

[134] Doering, "Origin and Development," 28-34; Hellman, "'New Middle Ages.'"

[135] Dietrich Bonhoeffer, "The Church and the Jewish Question," in *No Rusty Swords: Letters, Lectures and Notes from the Collected Works*, ed. Edwin H. Robertson (London: Collins, 1970), 217-25; Haynes, *Bonhoeffer Legacy*, 57-67.

[136] Maritain, *Antisemitism*, 23-24.

[137] Maritain, *Antisemitism*, 19-21.

[138] John Milbank, *The Suspended Middle: Henri de Lubac and the Debate concerning the Supernatural* (London: SCM, 2005).

[139] Cf. George A. Lindbeck, *The Church in a Postliberal Age*, ed. James J. Buckley (Grand Rapids: Eerdmans, 2003), 6.

[140] Hans Urs von Balthasar, *The Theology of Henri de Lubac: An Overview*, trans. Joseph Fessio, Michael M. Waldstein and Susan Clements (San Francisco: Ignatius, 1991); Henri de Lubac, *At the Service of the Church: Henri de Lubac Reflects on the Circumstances That Occasioned his Writings*, trans. Anne Elizabeth Englund (San Francisco: Ignatius, 1993).

[141] See de Lubac's own account of this period, *Christian Resistance to Anti-semitism: Memories from 1940-44*, trans. Elizabeth Englund (San Francisco: Ignatius, 1990).

[142] Henri de Lubac, "Un nouveau 'front' religieux," in *Israël et la foi chrétienne*, by Bonsirven et al. (Fribourg: Éditions de la Librairie de l'Université, 1942), 9-39; on the origins of the article, see de Lubac, *Resistance to Anti-semitism*, 108-09, and *Service of the Church*, 57-58.

[143] De Lubac, "Un nouveau 'front' religieux," 39.

[144] Henri de Lubac, *Histoire et esprit: L'intelligence de l'Écriture d'après Origène* (Paris: Aubier, 1950); *Exégèse médiévale*, 4 vols. (Paris: Éditions Montaigne, 1959-64).

[145] Bonsirven et al., *Israël et la foi*, 7-8.

[146] De Lubac, *Resistance to Anti-semitism*, 66-68; for the origins of the declaration, see 50-62.

[147] Bonsirven, "Le mystère d'Israël," in *Israël et la foi*, by Bonsirven et al., 151-53. Klein cites Bonsirven's pre-war writings at a number of points as clear evidence of anti-Judaism in Roman Catholic theology in the twentieth century, e.g. *Anti-Judaism*, 37-38, 65-66 and 121.

[148] Bosirven, "Le mystère d'Israël," 150.

[149] Louis Richard, "Israël et la Christ," in *Israël et la foi*, by Bonsirven et al., 92; my translation.

[150] Von Balthasar, *Henri de Lubac*, 61.

[151] See e.g. Henri de Lubac, *The Mystery of the Supernatural*, trans. Rosemary Sheed (New York: Herder and Herder, 1967), 157.

[152] Cf. Henri de Lubac, *The Christian Faith: An Essay on the Structure of the Apostles' Creed*, trans. Richard Arnandez (San Francisco: Ignatius, 1986), 158-59.

[153] The first part of this sentence from the *Confessions* is quoted at the very end of the Preface to *Mystery of the Supernatural* (xiv); de Lubac returns to it again at 84.

[154] So e.g. de Lubac, *Mystery of the Supernatural*, 35-42, 64-65, 308-10.

[155] De Lubac, *Mystery of the Supernatural*, 107-08.

[156] "That the promises of the faithfulness of God have been fulfilled in Jesus the Christ is not, and never will be, a self-evident truth, since in Him it appears in its final hiddenness and its most profound secrecy" (Barth, *Romans*, 98).

[157] E.g. Henri de Lubac, *Catholicism: A Study of Dogma in Relation to the Corporate Destiny of Mankind*, trans. Lancelot C. Sheppard (London: Burns, Oates and Washbourne, 1950), 89-90 and 197.

[158] Joseph Roth, *The Wandering Jews*, trans. Michael Hofmann (London: Granta, 2001), 133.

[159] For a brief discussion of the picture, see Harries, *After the Evil*, ix-x.

[160] Quoted in Monica Bohm-Duchen, *Chagall* (London: Phaidon, 1998), 245. Bohm-Duchen comments on Chagall's various representations of the suffering Christ, beginning as early as 1912, at 227-34 and 242-49.

[161] Quoted in Sylvie Courtine-Denamy, *Three Women in Dark Times Edith Stein, Hannah Arendt, Simone Weil; or Amor fati, amor mundi*, trans. G. M. Goshgarian (Ithaca: Cornell University Press, 2000), 109.

[162] Quoted in Haynes, *Bonhoeffer Legacy*, 52.

[163] Dietrich Bonhoeffer, *Ethics*, ed. Eberhard Bethge and trans. Neville Horton Smith (London: SCM, 1955), 90.

[164] For overviews of Stein's life and work, see Sarah Borden, *Edith Stein* (London: Continuum, 2003), and Josephine Koeppel, *Edith Stein: Philosopher and Mystic* (Scranton: University of Scranton Press, 2007).

[165] Edith Stein, "Text of Letter to the Pope from Edith Stein," http://geocities.com/baltimorecarmel/stein/1933let.html (accessed 17th October, 2008).

[166] George Steiner, "Sainte Simone—Simone Weil," in *No Passion Spent: Essays, 1978-1996* (London: Faber, 1996), 171-79.

[167] Oesterreicher, *Walls Are Crumbling*, 305-6 and 323; on Husserl's privileging of the New Testament, see e.g. 43, 79-80 and 84.

[168] Edith Stein, *Life in a Jewish Family: Her Unfinished Autobiographical Account*, trans. Josephine Koeppel (Washington, DC: ICS Publications, 1986); see Stein's Foreword written in September 1933, 23-25. Koeppel suggests that the Jesuit theologian Erich Przywara played an important role in encouraging her to write this (*Edith Stein*, 17).

[169] Edith Stein, letter 227, in *Self-Portrait in Letters, 1916-1942*, trans. Josephine Koeppel (Washington, DC: ICS Publications, 1993), 238. Cf. also letters 280 and 281 (290-92).

[170] Stein, letter 287, in *Self-Portrait in Letters*, 295.

[171] Borden, *Edith Stein*, 129-30. Cf. Stein, "Love of the Cross: Some Thoughts for the Feast of St. John of the Cross," in *The Hidden Life: Hagiographic Essays, Meditations, Spiritual Texts*, trans. Waltraut Stein (Washington, DC: ICS Publications, 1992), 91-93.

---

[172] This is the implication of Bergson's last will and testament, noted in Courtine-Demay, *Three Women*, 196. The husband of the novelist Irène Némirovsky wrote to the German ambassador in 1942 requesting that she be released on the grounds that, amongst other things, although she was of Jewish descent, "we are Catholic and so are our children who were born in Paris and are French"; see the correspondence in Appendix II of Irène Némirovsky, *Suite Française*, trans. Sandra Smith (London: Chatto and Windus, 2006), the passage quoted being from 379.
[173] David Novak, "What Does Edith Stein Mean for Jews?" in *Talking with Christians: Musings of a Jewish Theologian* (Grand Rapids: Eerdmans, 2005), 146-166.

CHAPTER FIVE

THE MISSHAPING OF CHRISTIAN THEOLOGY?

The previous chapters of this book have sought to sketch some of the ways in which Judaism and anti-Judaism have contributed together to the shaping of Christian theological traditions in the West, through a dynamic process in which awareness—however limited and distorted—of the continuing reality of Jewish existence has been an important agent of creative disturbance. Those chapters have developed the idea of a classic framework for Christian self-understanding in relation to Judaism that emerges by the later second century. The framework carries within it religious anti-Judaism by the judgments it requires on "old" Israel that correspond to the claims it makes about newness in Christ. Chapter two showed how that framework survived and adapted in the face of the manifold challenges of the millennium we call the Middle Ages; in chapter three, we analysed the much more radical changes to it made by some thinkers in response to modernity and the Enlightenment. Finally, in the preceding chapter, it was argued that the intersection between the critique of liberal theology and the rise of antisemitism in the first half of the twentieth century precipitated creative re-description of major features of that framework in both its pre-modern and characteristically modern forms. Nonetheless, the linkages between claims about newness and judgments about Judaism tended to become re-forged with new materials. Even as anti-Judaism emerged as a conscious object for Christian theological thought in the first five decades of the twentieth century, the judgments of the classic framework remained a horizon of that thought beyond which there were only a few very tentative excursions. Examples of such hesitant, ambivalent exploration included Maritain on Judaism's calling to "earthly activisation", de Lubac on the unpredictability of grace and Stein on the hidden communion between Jesus and the Jewish people.

The case this book has sought to establish, that there is a problematic intertwining between the constructive development of Christian theology and a deeply embedded hostility towards a Jewish "other" that this theology is thereby sentenced to keep confronting, is not a wholly new one. At just the point where Christian thinkers such as Barth and Maritain were first struggling to articulate Christianity's understanding of Judaism in a way that would not give cover to antisemitism, contemporary Jewish writers were making the case that anti-Judaism was much more profoundly and much more insidiously part of the Christian theological "system" than those Christian thinkers might have been comfortable to contemplate. The hypothesis of this book, that one can narrate the story of Christian theology as one of both response to Judaism and legitimation of anti-Judaism, has some important precedents in Jewish texts on Christianity from the first half of the twentieth century. The present chapter reflects on two of the substantial analyses from that period of the "misshaping" of Christian theology through its problematic location in relation to Judaism and anti-Judaism. For these voices, the formation of Christian theology by its oppositional stance towards integral elements of continuing Judaism left deep flaws that rendered Christian practice liable to fracture when put to the test in the crises of human history—above all the crisis that was unfolding around them in the 1930s and 1940s.

The first writer to be considered is Leo Baeck, whose criticism of Harnack was mentioned in the previous chapter. For Baeck, the points where anti-Judaism had most effectively shaped Christian theology—the covenant and people judgments which we have found continually resurfacing across profound internal shifts in that theology's history— were precisely its points of greatest weakness. Then we turn our attention to Martin Buber, a contemporary of Baeck's with a very different relationship to Jewish tradition. Buber makes a strong case for viewing the collapse of the dream of European civilization through the events of the first half of the twentieth century as also the point where some of the deepest fault lines in the Christian theological tradition became apparent. Yet for all the power in the critiques of Christianity presented by Baeck and Buber, on the basis of the preceding chapters it is not clear that they adequately reckon with either the complexity or the creativity of the relationship between Christian theology, Judaism and anti-Judaism that we have been tracing through the shifting pattern of claims and judgments.

Leo Baeck: Christian Newness as Romantic Survival

Leo Baeck is one of the great figures in twentieth-century Judaism.[1] He is particularly important from our point of view because of his sustained engagement with Christianity and in particular the liberal Christianity of modernity associated with Harnack in the previous chapter. While his treatment of the New Testament has been criticized by both Christian and Jewish scholars,[2] it is important to remember that he studied the Christian Bible not simply as a historical scholar but as a teacher and leader concerned, as Isaac Troki and Joseph Kimhi had been in their time, to defend the Jewish community from the intellectual power of a politically dominant Christian culture. Whereas they had seen the cardinal weakness of Christianity, however, in its Christological exegesis of the Hebrew scriptures, Baeck faced a liberal Christianity which had long since given up on such exegesis as outmoded. Instead, it sought to vindicate itself by arguing for Christianity's historical originality and superiority on the enlightened, "liberal" grounds of historical scholarship and the necessary correlation of religion with ethics.

Baeck's task was to show how these supposedly enlightened grounds could not, in fact, sustain the negative judgments about Judaism that liberal Christianity continued to make, thereby undermining the case of people like Harnack for Christian truth as authoritative within modernity. As a historian, Baeck affirmed liberal theology's assumption that the covenant and people judgments of the classic framework were constitutive of the origins of Christianity. Christianity was indeed defined—in its "newness"—by a rejection of Law and a division of history. The price of that rejection of Law was, however, according to Baeck a withdrawal from the public sphere of history which left the Church characterized by a vitiating irresponsibility. In questioning the newness of Christ, the displacement of Law and the division of history with the tools of historical scholarship and ethical reason, Baeck was, as much as Harnack, the heir of his nineteenth-century predecessors. Yet his awareness of the distinctive challenges and tragedies of the twentieth century, even before his experience of persecution, the ghetto and the Theresienstadt concentration camp under Nazism, gives his writing on Christianity a resonance that extends beyond his particular context.

Which Religion is Ethical?

In his review of Harnack's *Das Wesen des Christentums*, briefly discussed in the previous chapter, Baeck admired with Harnack the expression of the prophetic tradition of ethical religion in Jesus' ministry; but he flatly denied that a responsible reading of the relevant sources permits the judgment that this expression is in any way unique, new or unparalleled.

> What Harnack attributes to the Gospel as a "distinctive sphere of ethical thought," that the fundamental attitude is given priority over moral action, that all morality is brought back to love, that humility is the point at which morality becomes religion—all that is nothing other than the Jewish ethic

as it meets us in the Talmud, it is the spirit [*Geist*] of Judaism, which speaks to us from all of it.[3]

What is actually distinctive about the ethics of Christianity, as opposed to the ethics of Jesus, according to Baeck, is its tendency to blur the ethical demand for justice with the theological affirmation that God is just, as if the latter could do duty for the former; as if doctrines could stand in place of moral imperatives; as if having the right view about the divine attributes was not relatively easy, but tackling the reality of human evil far more costly and demanding.[4] And this kind of Christian distinctiveness is not so appealing, Baeck implies, to the humanity of post-Enlightenment modernity with its concern for ethical religion. Even in 1901, he reflected a keen sense of the tragic dimensions of human history, rounding off his attack on Christianity's historic confusion between dogma and duty by commenting, "The agonies of a millennium are illustrations for this history of theoretical and practical ethics."[5]

To understand the sharpness of Baeck's criticism on this point, we need to recall the cardinal relationship between religion and ethics for thinking shaped by the liberal theological project of the nineteenth century, a project whose proper direction had been indicated, for Harnack as for many others, by Albrecht Ritschl.[6] Christian theologians associated with the Ritschlian school were suspicious of metaphysics and philosophical idealism and confident that in the historical Jesus they encountered God's definitive revelation. They looked to Kant rather than Hegel as their guiding philosophical star, both for his anti-metaphysical approach and his vindication of religion via ethics. Kant had rejected the traditional philosophical arguments for theism, but without accepting atheism. Instead, Kant developed new arguments for the key postulates of "religion" from morality, claiming that moral behaviour committed its practitioners to belief both in the freedom of the human will and in a providential deity who would guarantee the ultimate achievement of justice.[7] He also sketched out, in his *Religion within the Bounds of Reason Alone*, a programmatic approach to religion which would deploy its moral functioning as a criterion for theological truth.[8] Ritschl, and Harnack as his follower, certainly had no intention of reducing the content of religion to ethics, a goal to which Kant might be thought to be leading, but they did conceive of the two as inextricably linked. Ritschl compared religion and ethics to two foci of an ellipse; in *Das Wesen des Christentums* Harnack describes Jesus' gospel as "an ethical message" and in a pivotal passage sets out the distinctive ways in which that message correlates religion with morality.[9]

Baeck's intellectual roots also included a concern for ethical religion among certain modern Jewish thinkers that both paralleled and countered the work of Kant, Ritschl and Harnack on Christianity. Moses Mendelssohn, Lessing's friend and Kant's contemporary, had argued in the eighteenth century that for Judaism, revelation was fundamentally constituted by law rather than doctrine.[10] That appeared to leave Mendelssohn's Judaism uniquely well-placed to meet the ethical and political challenges represented by modernity, while still respecting Spinoza's ban on any claim that revelation can introduce some new truth inaccessible to human reason. In the nineteenth century, the Orthodox writer Elijah Benamozegh argued for the ethical superiority of Judaism to Christianity along lines that anticipate Baeck's approach in many ways, including the perceived overemphasis in Christianity on individual over community and love over justice, resulting in an impaired engagement with the social and political.[11] In a book first published in 1921, Max Brod deployed the same line of attack, claiming that the "terrible guilt of Christianity for World War I" was irrefutable. According to him, this guilt derived from its effective denial of politics, arising in turn from the denial of this world implicit in its fundamental affirmations of original sin on the one hand and of grace through Christ's death alone on the other.[12]

Much the most comprehensive and subtle articulation of Judaism as the distinctive religion of ethical reason is found in the work of Baeck's older contemporary, the neo-Kantian philosopher Hermann Cohen. Cohen epitomized the confidence of liberal Jews in the nineteenth century that Judaism and modernity were, fundamentally, partners:

> As modern and civilized men, we could not cherish our own religion were we not unshakeably and utterly convinced that it is fully consonant with the ideals of modern culture. We know that our fundamental religious principles constitute the deepest roots of contemporary ethics.[13]

So, for instance, he argues that Kant's conception of ethics as foundation and criterion for theology is not something new but is already evident in Moses Maimonides in the twelfth century, for whom

> it is legitimate to make statements about God's moral attributes alone, that is, those attributes that bear upon man's actions. . . . God's essence is morality, and morality only; nothing else is divine nature.[14]

Moreover, for Cohen this is not simply an interesting feature of intellectual history but reflects the distinctive character of Jewish consciousness in which there is no division between religion and morality.[15]

Given such an approach, it is only natural that Kant should appear to
Cohen as a vital ally, despite Kant's own evaluation of Judaism by which
it barely counted as a religion at all, precisely because of the perceived
absence of grounding in morality.[16] Indeed, Cohen develops a kind of
messianic appropriation of Kant: God is not simply the guarantor of
morality and of its ultimate correspondence to reality in life beyond death,
as Kant suggested, but is also the pledge that goodness may become
complete here on earth, within history and time, as we approach the
horizon of the messianic future.[17] The concrete, historical and universal
messianic vision of Judaism is thereby brought into relation with Kant's
ethical religion—and contrasted with the other-worldly and individualistic
understanding of redemption in Christianity, floating free from any moral
or political accountability.[18] Such messianic realization as ethical task and
future horizon renders Christian talk of a Messiah from the past saving
individuals in the present in spiritual isolation from history and one
another at once misguided and irrelevant. We can hear an echo here of the
emphatic rejection by medieval Jewish thinkers of the rationalizing
Anselmian accounts of redemption presented to them by Christian
polemicists. For Cohen, it was a profound mistake to consider that the
prophetic, scriptural hope for reconciliation and redemption is anything to
do with releasing humanity from "this-worldly, finite existence. Rather
than create illusions and phantasmagoria, these concepts set up ideals for
the moral work of mortal beings."[19]

Polarity as the Essence of Judaism

Cohen's influence on Baeck is particularly evident in the book Baeck
published in 1905, in implicit comparison with Harnack's: *Das Wesen des
Judentums* ("the essence of Judaism").[20] After the First World War, in
which he served as a chaplain to the German army, Baeck produced a
much revised second edition of what had already become a widely read
work within the Jewish world, and it is here that we encounter more
distinctly Baeck's creative recasting of nineteenth-century Jewish thought
on Christianity, with its critique of liberal claims. In particular, his
distinctive presentation of Judaism as a religion of polarity moves more
into the foreground.[21]

This approach is signalled in the title of an essay that originally
appeared just before the second edition of *The Essence of Judaism*:
"Mystery and Commandment."[22] Baeck opens the essay by characterizing
human experience as having a twofold character. It contains "the
knowledge of what is real and the knowledge of what is to be realized";

the mystery which is "from God," and the commandment which is "to be achieved by man"; "humility and reverence"; "the consciousness that we have been created versus the consciousness that we are expected to create."[23] It is on the basis of this presentation of human experience as intrinsically bi-polar that Baeck proceeds to develop his theme of Judaism as the religion of polarity:

> What is peculiar to Judaism is that these two experiences have here become one. . . . From the one God comes both mystery and commandment, as one from the One, and the soul experiences both as one. Every mystery means and suggests also a commandment; and every commandment means and suggests also a mystery.[24]

Baeck is thereby able to give a more positive account of the place of the non-rational than Cohen, yet without surrendering Cohen's sense that religion can never float free from ethics and the command.[25] Judaism is no longer presented as an austere and rigorous ethical monotheism, but it remains distinguished in always holding the mystical *with* the ethical, the non-rational *with* the rational, faith with works and God's gift with human endeavour.[26] Judaism is still, as for Mendelssohn and Cohen, the religion that accords the ethical a unique and distinctive place; but this is not because it cannot comprehend a place for anything else. Rather, it is because it is constituted by a polarity in which the ethical is always one "pole" in creative tension and interrelationship with the non-ethical. As he expressed it in the book that he started writing in the ghetto and then continued in Theresienstadt, what is characteristic of Israel is that "everything which emanates out of the mystery enters into the sphere of the moral."[27]

In all of this there is, implicitly and on occasions explicitly, a continuing polemic against Christianity and its judgment about the displacement of Torah. In "Mystery and Commandment" itself, Baeck recognizes that within the history of Judaism, the creative tension between moral act and religious awe has been reflected in a diversity of expressions, some emphasizing one pole more than the other; but he still wants to argue that Judaism is defined by the preservation of the tension.

> Only where one or the other was supposed to constitute the whole of religion, only where the whole of piety was exclusively identified with one or the other, did the religion cease to be Judaism.[28]

If Judaism is the religion of polarity, then a religion that ceases to be Judaism moves, by definition, out of that creative polarity in one direction

or another. Christianity emerges both here and in *The Essence of Judaism*
as the cardinal case study of this process, with a diagnosis of collapsing
the polar tension of Judaism into the pole of mystery.

At the beginning of part II of *The Essence of Judaism*, Baeck
introduces the polarity of secret and commandment as the central theme
for his chapter on "Faith in God," and almost immediately contrasts
Judaism that holds the two together with other religions that allow the
secret, the knowledge of the mystery, to begin and end aside from
commandment and law. While Buddhism is the first example he mentions,
it is clear that certain forms of Christianity at least are in his sights when
he writes:

> For Judaism, salvation is not a ready-made possession, a miraculous
> treasure presented to man by divine grace, but rather a task imposed by
> God which man has to fulfil "in order that he may live" (Lev. 18:5).[29]

The separation of the secret from the commandment leads to the secret's
fixation in the sub-ethical shapes of myth, fate and dogma.[30] That Baeck
sees Christianity as opening the door to all three of these becomes clear in
the following chapter, "Faith in Man: In Ourselves." Here he develops the
creative polarity of mysticism and ethics in Judaism, by way of contrast
with Christian doctrines about original sin as a "fate" that we ineluctably
experience and redemption as something that is achieved aside from our
ethically responsible endeavour. In scripture's account of the human being
before God, Baeck writes, "In his deed is the beginning of his atonement";
and for this deed there can be no substitute, "no mediator and no past
event, no redeemer and no sacrament."[31]

So how does Christianity lose the polarity of Judaism? Baeck follows
both Christian and Jewish scholarship in fingering Paul as the critical
individual who pushed the early Christian movement outside the limits of
Judaism; "the creator of the Christian church," as Baeck calls him.[32] In
"Mystery and Commandment," he relates this evaluation of Paul to his
own understanding of Judaism as the religion of polarity in order to trace
the fateful origin of historical Christianity:

> The world of Judaism is to be found only where faith has its
> commandment, and the commandment its faith. That is why Paul left
> Judaism when he preached *sola fide* (by faith alone) and thereby wound up
> with sacrament and dogma.[33]

Faith relates to the "mystery" pole of the polarity of mystery and
commandment, and by isolating faith as the fundamental principle of

knowing God and attaining salvation, Paul loses the polar rhythm of Judaism and so inevitably tries to stabilize the new religion of mystery that has emerged in other ways:

> Hence mystery finally had to become for him something tangible, namely sacraments, and something that can be molded, namely dogma. For it is always thus: sacraments are a mystery into which man enters, a mystery of which man can take hold; and dogma, like myth, is a mystery which man can build up and shape.[34]

Baeck is aware of the complexity of Paul's thought and identifies in his letters a commendable refusal to follow his destabilization of Judaism's polarity through to its natural end. With redemption and sacraments replacing commandment and Law, there was really no defence left against the dilemma of asceticism or libertinism, according to Baeck—yet Paul, unlike his more consistent second-century followers, persisted in resisting it.[35] It is as if, for Baeck, the Jew in Paul sensed that something was missing once he found himself outside the dialectic of mystery and commandment that he had known in Judaism, and so he responded by seeking to supplement the loss by the reassertion of the ethical that can be found periodically in his letters. Baeck has been accused, with some justice, of minimizing the strong ethical element within Paul's writings,[36] but if pressed on this point he could respond that Paul's attempts to integrate the ethical and the non-ethical within the Christianity he had helped to create only serve to demonstrate the extent to which they had been originally disintegrated by his version of Christianity's message. Hence the ethical could only be reintegrated as a second moment, a second thought, a supplement to the first truth of faith and grace alone. Outside Judaism's polar field, on Baeck's analysis, the Christian movement was bound to mutate into a very different kind of religion, and its development needs to be understood as a series of reactions, of what we might by analogy with psychology call coping mechanisms, precipitated by this fundamental break.

Christianity as the Victory of Romanticism

Baeck's understanding of the displacement of Law instigated by Paul as a tragic flaw that runs across the history of Christianity and into the present day receives its most vivid and forceful presentation in the essay "Romantic Religion," first published in 1922 and then appearing again in revised form in 1938.[37] Here it is the dichotomy of classical and romantic that provides the interpretive key to understanding the history of religion and the contrast between Judaism and Christianity.[38] Initially, Baeck's description of romantic religion seems to relate rather to the romantic movement in modern culture than to Christianity as a historical phenomenon:

> Tense feelings supply its content, and it seeks its goals in the now mythical, now mystical visions of the imagination. Its world is the realm in which all rules are suspended; it is the world of the irregular, the extraordinary and the miraculous, that world which lies beyond all reality, the remote which transcends all things.[39]

Baeck cites Schlegel, Novalis and Lessing in his opening exposition, hardly reputable spokesmen for the Christian tradition; even the invocation of Schleiermacher could be counted as scarcely representative.[40] Baeck, however, is quite serious about the specific relevance of romanticism to Christianity: the romanticism which, in the late eighteenth and nineteenth centuries, grows outside the Church grows from the Church which had carried it for nearly two millennia—and cannot shed it now. He looks to modern, cultural romanticism to distil the "essence" of romantic religion as that which remains once the classical—i.e. Jewish—residue has been wholly siphoned off from Christianity. Although Christianity functions historically as the paradigm of a romantic religion, because of the admixture of Judaism it is easiest to begin with the more transparent examples. "To be sure," Baeck acknowledges, "historical types, just like human types, never appear quite pure."[41] Hence Baeck need not try to prove that Christianity, as a historical phenomenon, is romantic religion without remainder; only that this is the "type" of religion that has always dominated it and will always necessarily dominate it, as its primary place is always already implied in the separation and distinction from Judaism, no matter how strong the internal counter-reactions against it may be at various places and times.

If romantic religion can surface beyond the church, in "secular" romanticism, it also existed before the church, within the pagan cultures of antiquity. The "traditional national religion in the Hellenic lands" had some kind of affiliation to classical religion, however inferior to Judaism, but it was disrupted at an early stage by a "victorious intruder... the Dionysian or Orphic cult." Furthermore, this cult

> had all the traits of romanticism: the exuberance of emotion, the enthusiastic flight from reality, the longing for an experience. Holy consecrations and atonements were taught and ecstatically tasted with reeling senses. They aimed to relate man to the beyond; they aimed to

make him one with the god and thus grant him redemption from primordial sin and original guilt.[42]

In this and the passage that follows, Baeck seeks to show that the ancient, pre-Christian form of romantic religion exhibited the same fundamental trait of escaping reality in emotion, fantasy and interior experience that he had identified in modern, secular romanticism, but that it expressed this trait in specific religious forms, including cultic practices and theological themes. From the Greek to the Egyptian mystery cults, from Mithras to Attis, the same basic pattern is discernible, and the same basic message too: "the faith in a heavenly being that had become man, died, and been resurrected, and whose divine life a mortal could share through mysterious rites."[43] Without having—so far—discussed Christianity at all, Baeck has already set up the premises for his central claim in the essay: "What is called the victory of Christianity was in reality this victory of romanticism."[44]

According to Baeck, the architect of the victory of romanticism in Christianity is Paul, although Paul is "not so much a creator as connector of ideas":[45] he takes the pieces that have already been forged in the romantic religion within Hellenism and arranges them in a new way around the figure of Jesus Christ, while still holding on to some residual Jewish elements. Paul adopts the already existing template of the divine redeemer mystically unified with his devotees and finds in Jesus Christ "the savior, who became man and had been god. . . . he was the resurrected, miracle-working, redeeming God, he that had been from eternity."[46] From this beginning come on the one hand Christology and the whole panoply of Christian doctrine, and on the other sacramental activity and the distinctive ritual practices of the Christian church. Against Harnack, for whom the struggle against "Hellenization" is something that happens *after* Paul, Baeck finds the essential victory of one vital strand within Hellenism—the romantic—already achieved in Paul himself. There is then no "essence" to Christianity other than its distinctive variations on the abiding themes of romantic religion.

Classical religion, represented by Judaism, is still defined here by the polarity of mystery and commandment; so it is no surprise that romantic religion is defined by the rupture of that polarity and a weighting towards the mystery that exceeds all attempts at correction. Everything in romantic religion is oriented towards a relatedness to God that abstracts from ethics, from human responsibility, from historical activity and from shared life. Salvation is achieved apart from all these by the divine mediator and then accessed by the believer also before and aside from them, through faith in the myth, mystical experience and sacramental practice. "For the believer

there is no command to do anything. 'Christ is the end of the law': the new
justice annuls the old: thus Paul formulated it."[47]

As has already been noted, Baeck was aware that Paul sometimes tried
to "rein in" those who apparently took such talk at face value by
developing a new law and a new framework for moral duties. According
to Baeck, however, this remains unstable and unsustainable because the
ground for moral activity has in fact been liquidated by Paul's most basic
teaching. So Baeck writes:

> The Pauline dogma removes the very ground from under man's rights as a
> moral subject, as an ethical individual. . . . The Pauline faith deprives
> ethics itself of its basis. . . . Where the will that decides for itself is
> considered the path of destruction, no place is left for ethics; indeed it is
> expressly repudiated.

For him, Paul and Luther present us with a choice: "Either faith or ethics!"
It follows for them that "Man becomes good only through the miracle that
has been accomplished. . . . Law and the miracle cannot be reconciled."[48]
If the miracle saves, then law is irrelevant; only faith is required and
passive union with the mystery. Finally, Baeck is able to present as the
logical outcome of Pauline religion the self-absorption of modern
romanticism, the religion of Schlegel and Novalis with which he began.
What motivates romantic religion is the desire to be saved, for something
to happen to me that will bind me forever to the eternal; and therefore its
end is in surrender, ecstasy and self-absorption.

> Everything revolves around the yearning to be saved; the self is central in
> the meaning of religion. The hope of becoming eternal dominates and
> decides everything.[49]

No ethical impulse, no concern for the neighbour, can ultimately hope to
compete with this primary motivation within romantic religion; it will
always win out, before, within and after the age of the church. We cannot
forget that the definitive version of this essay was published in 1938—and
immediately confiscated and destroyed by the Nazi authorities.[50]

We are also bound to read Baeck's "inversion" of the people judgment
in this historical context. In the same essay, he affirms the link between
the displacement of the Law and the division of history—but as a way of
accounting for the historic failures of the Church in the realm of social and
political ethics. The real division of history is between classical religion,
which strives for justice in the historical world, and romantic religion,
which gives up on it. As Baeck recounts church history, wherever the

Pauline discourse of the displacement of Law has led to the dominance of romantic religion, there has been a natural alliance with political authoritarianism and an apparently limitless capacity for indifference to human suffering.[51] Baeck links the passivity of humanity in the redemption of Christian theology—"redemption is something that happens to man; man is only the object"[52]—with the political passivity of actual Christians. Where feeling is valued above acting, the freedom to act is devalued and not likely to find religious defenders;[53] where the ordinary world of sense and action is discounted, submission to the powers that be makes more sense than striving for the realization of the good here on earth.[54]

Baeck sees the problem going still deeper than this, however. Romantic religion not only tolerates but actually encourages political submission. Romantics aching for the beyond are liable to disorientation in the here and now; consequently,

> the more romantic the faith and the more passive it therefore feels, the more it must feel the need to lean against something established and firm in order to find a tangible certainty in it, this being the only source of security for those who find nothing of the sort in themselves.[55]

Baeck is even able to quote Harnack to support his thesis here. Church history is full of swift action against those who challenged established authority, and of inaction where suffering and injustice were deemed not to impinge upon the specialized sphere of religious experience. Hence church history is properly as much about what Christians did not do as about what they did:

> A good deal of Church history is the history of all the things which neither hurt nor encroached upon this piety, all the outrages and all the baseness which this piety was able to tolerate with an assured and undisturbed soul and an untroubled spirit.[56]

Romantic religion, inseparable on Baeck's account from the "newness" of Christianity relative to first-century Judaism, is far more than a theological mistake or an intriguing historical specimen. It is a tragic collusion with evil, because it enervates human power to resist the activity of evil and to struggle for the good in the here and now. It does indeed divide history— between those who give in to its spell and those who, inside or outside the Church, fight against it. Those who resist it, however, will always be fighting, whether consciously or not, on the side of enduring Judaism.

Judaism as the Refusal of Finality

In another essay, "Two World Views Compared," the contrast underpinning the differences between Judaism and Christianity is restated by Baeck as one between a Hellenic preoccupation with perfection as stasis and a biblical-Jewish hope for the realization of the good through the endeavour of humanity and the unpredictable contingencies of its history before God. Baeck knows that the future orientation he attributes to Judaism would be considered positively by many Christians. But he nonetheless argues that if they adopt this orientation it is not, so to speak, by right. Christianity begins with Paul, and it begins when Paul proclaims that the Messiah has come; and if the Messiah has come, the kingdom of God is no longer a future goal for our striving but an achieved reality to which we now need to connect ourselves.[57] Vestiges of a future orientation may remain in Paul, but that is in spite of, not because of, the logic of his position.

Harnack would have agreed with Baeck thus far; he saw the overcoming of a future-directed messianism in early Christianity as one of its most praiseworthy achievements.[58] Baeck, by contrast, regards it as the point where Christianity turns its back on ethical engagement with humanity's history to demand instead assent to a specific narrative of revelatory events. He is aware, of course, that Judaism, like Christianity, has its identity shaping narratives; both of them claim, against Lessing, that revelation arises from the singular, the unique, the historically contingent. "Yet," he continues, "it makes a difference whether, as in this case, a *beginning* is posited or, as in the Pauline religion, the absolute goal and the ultimate fulfilment." Where the revelatory singular is a beginning, an opening—as with the story of the gift of Torah—the polarity of creation and the future discussed in *The Essence of Judaism* takes concrete form. Where the revelatory singular is presented as accomplishment and closure—as in the story of divine incarnation in Christ—then stasis and repose become preferred modes of response to it:

> Movement and becoming appear as an alienation from religion, an alienation from faith which is everything. What is good here is characterized by repose; and what has a history, is the ungodly and anti-godly.[59]

For Baeck, Christianity must always struggle against the grain of its inherent romantic religiosity in order to engage positively with history as the arena of change, chance and choice. Therefore it must always struggle too against the grain of the positive insights of modernity, including the conscious shaping of history as an ethical endeavour and the study of history as a cultural activity that cannot retrieve in an isolated figure from the past a definitive summation of history's meaning. The "turn" to history and the historical Jesus in modern theology cannot save Christianity:

> After it has given up most dogmas, a completed story remains almost its only axiom of faith. The question of the "unique" personality of Jesus becomes for it the question of the very existence of religion.[60]

It is a claim that historical study, of necessity, can never make good. Yet neither can Christianity let go of the claim. For it, humanity is already "finished" in the God-man, Jesus Christ: human fulfilment lies in the past, and participation in human fulfilment comes by looking backwards. The sacrament of baptism binds the believer to the achievement of perfection, and nothing further, nothing new, can unfold beyond this.[61] Belief and ritual celebrate a "finished perfected justice"; why struggle for greater justice for the present and future?[62] Christianity after Paul cannot articulate a positive vision of present ethical engagement aimed at a still-to-be-realized ethical goal, at a coming kingdom and its justice, because it "narrates" salvation in the past tense as the work of the divine redeemer.

Writing in the shadow of Nazism, Baeck could recognize the strengths of the "world view" that contemplated achieved perfection; but he also prophesied its demise.

> Century after century can turn to it to contemplate what is permanent and rejoice in what is complete and final. But when the world of finality and perfection once totters, when it once collapses, it is forever broken. . . . When finality dies, its death is final.[63]

Contrast the world view that looks forward to the infinite future out of the tension that comes from seeking to obey the commandment, to realize the good:

> Every day on this path man struggles with the commandment, is often wearied but then triumphs nevertheless, and in this struggle he is reconciled, renewed and reborn again and again. . . . In it there is no permanent rest, but no death, either. The religion of tension, the culture that lives in it, cannot die.[64]

Judaism, the religion of polarity, is a religion of (messianic) tension; as such, it is indestructible. Baeck never claimed that with the attempted and ultimately thwarted implementation of the Final Solution in the lands of "Christian" Europe, his prophecy had come to pass: "When finality dies, its death is final"—though others have located in the history of the Holocaust the ultimate death of Christendom, if not of Christianity itself. Nor did he claim that the terrible history of the 1930s and 1940s vindicated the critique of Christianity and its descendent cultures in secular modernity that he had developed between the wars, a critique which discerned an agent of ethical corrosion in the inmost heart of that religion from the very beginning, carried within its historically distinctive "newness". His silence on these matters, however, is surely eloquent. On Baeck's reading, the historical ambivalence of Christian tradition to the Jewish elements bound up with its origins and their continuing trajectory outside the Church was not simply a matter of scholarly interest for learned investigation but an abiding reality with repeatedly tragic implications.

Martin Buber: Christian Faith as Mistaking Redemption

In the previous section, we have seen how what we have been calling the covenant judgment of the classic framework, the displacement of Torah, decisively weakens Christianity's ability to grasp the priority of ethical action in the world according to Baeck's analysis. Furthermore, the people judgment, the division of history, following from the assertion of the essential completion of messianic achievement, ultimately encourages a tendency of indifference to continuing history, both to its tragedies and sufferings and to the continuing openness of human time to the God who makes all things new. In this reading of Christianity, Baeck was not being radically innovative but rather creatively synthesizing a tradition of Jewish critique of Christianity stretching back to its early centuries. Martin Buber can be seen as a parallel figure in this respect, although one with different priorities. For Baeck, it was the displacement of Torah in Paul's Christianity that collapsed the polarity of Judaism and resulted in a false understanding of the messianic, and hence the disabling of Christianity for the real moral work that faces flesh and blood humanity. For Buber, on the other hand, a mistaken construal of the relationship between messianic hope and continuing history is at the root of the misshaping of Christian theology, with the issue of attitudes to Torah and to the ethical more generally taking a secondary role.

Martin Buber was undoubtedly one of the most important figures in Jewish-Christian theological dialogue in the twentieth century, but also perhaps one of the most complex. Born in 1878, he gave up Jewish observance as a teenager but found his way back into Judaism through the study of Hasidism in the first decade of the twentieth century. Although there were important changes in his thinking between his early publications on Hasidism and his writings in the 1950s and 1960s, his understanding of Judaism was not rooted in the collective life of Torah study and synagogue worship in the same way as that of Baeck or Rosenzweig. Buber had already established himself as an important thinker within and beyond the German Jewish community prior to World War I, about which he, like many others in that community, displayed an initial enthusiasm.[65] It was during the war, however, that he began to shift from a "mystical" to a "dialogical" perspective,[66] leading to the publication of his lectures at Rosenzweig's *Lehrhaus* in Frankfurt as the hugely influential book *I and Thou* in 1923 and then to the collaboration with Rosenzweig on a new translation of the Hebrew Bible, a task he only completed in 1961, long after the death of his collaborator.[67]

Dialogue across the Divide

Buber's accent on dialogue in his work between the wars found one expression in a range of conversations with Christian thinkers, though his engrained anti-institutionalism made him wary of anything like "official" dialogue between the two religions. The Protestant minister and writer Florens Christian Rang became a particular friend and later Buber's colleague on the editorial board of the journal *Die Kreatur*, which published work by a range of creative figures, both Christian and Jewish, in the later 1920s. Rang also provided a bridge into the milieu of Christian Socialism, which gave Buber particular hope for inter-religious collaboration.[68] In the 1930s, Buber continued his engagement with Christianity, but the tone necessarily changed with the context. His writings from the period include a sequence of exchanges with Christian scholars, some of whom were overtly sympathetic to Nazism, prior to his settling in Israel in 1938.[69] It was there that he wrote, in the aftermath of World War II, both the text that sums up much of his thinking about Christianity, *Two Types of Faith*, and the novel that reprises some of its themes in fictional form, *For the Sake of Heaven*.[70]

Although Buber was an early advocate and indeed practitioner of dialogue between Judaism and Christianity, his view of Christianity remained at root a deeply critical one. The final sentence of *Two Types of Faith* suggests that the present moment is not a propitious one for dialogue between Israel and Church, and Buber himself is reported to have said that the book was "really about the failure of Christianity."[71] It was certainly interpreted as a significant attack on the credibility of Christianity by both the Protestant theologian Emil Brunner and the Roman Catholic Hans Urs von Balthasar.[72] The very title of *Two Types of Faith* places his thinking about Christianity in a Jewish tradition stretching back at least to Joseph Kimhi, which identifies what Christians mean by "faith" as something different from and ultimately alien to what "faith" means within Judaism. Pauline faith is seen as "belief that" certain things are true rather than "trust in" God as the one who addresses and is addressed by us. For Buber, this represents a declension into the I-It dimension, away from the affirmation of the I-Thou as primary which he discerns in the paradigmatic forms of Judaism. Buber had already argued in earlier writings that Judaism involves a response to God with the whole of life, including action;[73] Pauline faith in Christ, defined as merely mental assent, was bound to seem a drastic attenuation of that. Moreover, the relegation according to Buber's analysis of the sphere of ongoing historical action to a secondary level in Pauline faith left supposedly Christian societies dangerously vulnerable to quiescent acceptance of the morally unacceptable, a point Baeck was simultaneously making from a parallel perspective, as we have seen.[74]

In retrospect, Buber can be seen as more directly in the succession of nineteenth-century liberal Jewish thinking about Christianity than might have appeared to be the case in the 1920s and 1930s, and therefore as someone who never in fact wholly relinquished the tradition of polemic in the name of dialogue. Rather, like Hermann Cohen and many others, he entered dialogue hoping that Christians would come to put to one side many of their normative doctrines from earlier centuries. It was Buber's explicit relegation of Torah to a secondary position within Judaism and his evident respect for Jesus himself that made him seem such a sympathetic figure to Christians, but in both respects he was only intensifying certain strands within the "progressive" Judaism of the previous century.[75] From his *Lectures on Judaism* before and during World War I to *Two Types of Faith*, Buber continued earlier traditions of critique of Christianity but also brought his particular intelligence and interests to bear upon it. This is evident in his treatment of two themes in Jewish writing on Christianity that we have met repeatedly before: Christianity's (mis)understanding of Jesus as the incarnate Son of God, and its interpretation of history AD as a series of footnotes to already-achieved redemption. In each case, Buber will locate a fatal distortion at the heart of historic Christianity in its handling of the theme of the messianic.

Jesus' Innocent Messianic Mistake

Like Baeck and indeed Gilbert Crispin's Jewish interlocutor from the eleventh century, Buber draws a sharp line between Jesus who belongs within Judaism and Paul who moves Christianity decisively outside it and is to be regarded as "the real originator of the Christian conception of faith."[76] Yet unlike them, he presents Jesus as an exceptional and decisive figure *within* Judaism, while still resisting the theological narratives that the Church has accumulated around him. In a frequently quoted phrase, he wrote in the Foreword to *Two Types of Faith* that "From my youth onwards I have found in Jesus my great brother," adding that

> I am more than ever certain that a great place belongs to him in Israel's history of faith and that this place cannot be described by any of the usual categories.[77]

Jesus was always central to Buber's dialogue with Christianity; in a brief account of his initial encounter with Rang in 1914, he recalls how his own words about the Jewishness of Jesus were the catalyst for the beginning of their relationship.[78] He gave a lengthy defence of Jesus as belonging within Judaism in an address given in 1918 and made significant references to him as an example of someone who lived the I-Thou reality in relation to God in *I and Thou*.[79] In 1917 he wrote that he was fighting for Jesus and against Christianity.[80] Pauline Christianity, according to Buber, profoundly misreads Jesus' story—not because it makes something of nothing, as if Jesus was "just" an ordinary Galilean Jew, but because it misconstrues the relationship between history and the messianic that indeed comes to the fore in Jesus' life in a wholly original yet also deeply problematic way.

Buber begins chapter VII of *Two Types of Faith* by asserting that for Judaism generally, "fulfilment of the divine command is valid when it takes place in conformity with the full capacity of the person and from the whole intention of faith," while in Jesus' case specifically "the conception of the intention of faith receives an eschatological character" related to a conviction that the kingdom of God draws near.[81] Buber regards the dynamic movement towards wholeness as characteristic of Judaism, but for Jesus "the breaking-in of God's rule" was an imminent reality, whereas for his contemporaries such as the Pharisees it was to be waited for in patience, requiring a suitable survival strategy in the meantime.[82] Buber does not see Jesus' distinctive sense of an eschatological "charge" in the unfolding present as an unfortunate error or weakness. Indeed, it is responsible in part for the parallels between him and the early Hasidism

Buber so much admired, which also nurtured a sense of the proximity of
the messianic future to life here and now in all its mundane diversity and
called for active love of the enemy as an extreme sign that this future is
coming to us, indeed is overtaking us.[83] Yet in chapter X Buber will
present the case, already sketched out in his earlier work on Hasidism, that
Jesus nonetheless breaks with all previous manifestations of the messianic-
prophetic strand in Judaism, in a way that contrasts too with Hasidism's
later "messianism of continuity".[84]

   Buber believes that Jesus recognized the messianic power of God at
work through his ministry and interpreted it in the light of the suffering
servant figure of deutero-Isaiah. Being chosen to be the prophet through
whom the kingdom draws near would bring with it experience of suffering
and rejection, a view shared by other notable movements in Jewish
history, including Hasidism. By way of contrast with traditional Christian
exegesis of the Servant Songs in Isaiah, for Buber Isa. 49:2 is critical: "He
made my mouth like a sharp sword, in the shadow of his hand he hid me;
he made me a polished arrow, in his quiver he hid me away." According to
Buber, those within Judaism who—like Jesus—understand the messianic
in terms of deutero-Isaiah expect the Messiah to come initially not as a
figure of public recognition but as someone hidden and neglected. Yet if
the Messiah begins in hiddenness, he does not remain there: at a certain
moment, God calls him out of the quiver and draws the bow. The trick,
however, is to know when that moment has come; "the man who believes
acts in God's tempo," but the changes in time signature, so to speak, may
not be unambiguously marked.[85] According to Buber, Jesus "understood
himself . . . to be a bearer of the Messianic hiddenness," and found that
understanding confirmed in his disciples.[86] Yet still he remained hidden—
hence his injunctions to them to tell no one. Only at the very end, at his
trial, does Jesus step out of the shadow to declare his messianic identity—
and in doing so invokes a rather different strand of the messianic tradition
in Judaism, Daniel's Son of Man who descends from above, the figure of
the conquering king rather than Isaiah's suffering prophet. From this
elliptical remark and the consequent constellation of two quite different
messianic themes around this one man and his tragic death, there will
emerge, according to Buber, from a Hellenistic milieu the assertion of
Jesus' deification and ultimately the Gentile Church's doctrinal apparatus
of incarnation and Trinity.[87]

   Christianity as such therefore begins, for Buber, with a mistake, which
can be traced back to the mistake of Jesus himself in stepping out of the
shadow, out of the quiver, under the hostile interrogation of the Jerusalem
authorities. Buber emphatically rejects the charge that this mistake

attributes any sort of "guilt" to Jesus: to know oneself to be the bearer of Messianic hiddenness is to live with the constant question of when—if ever—God may call you out, may draw the bow, and there is no wholly reliable way to answer it; indeed, Jesus acts "in highest innocence."[88] Still, Buber will elsewhere contrast the declining series of those who follow his example of stepping out from the shadow—ending with the wholly impure figure of Sabbatai Zvi—with the model of Hasidism, which struggled profoundly with the same question and yet, in some cases at least, accepted a vocation to preserve the messianic power within hiddenness, a struggle that Buber presents in the form of historical fiction in *For the Sake of Heaven*.[89]

Upon Jesus' wholly innocent misreading of the unfolding narrative of his own life, his followers built the framework of historic Christianity in Buber's account. Rather than accepting, the other side of his death, that it was such an innocent and even tragic misreading, they tried to "save" it by translating his final glimpse of the coming Son of Man into an alternative ending to his story, in which he is rendered as the present and future heavenly, then divine saviour. This is not a narrative, Buber is clear, that Jesus himself could have comprehended or countenanced; Christianity renders him as the image for the imageless God and in doing so breaks with "the Old Testament proclamation of the non-humanity of God and the non-divinity of man" that Jesus himself explicitly affirmed and that ultimately underpins the possibility of I-Thou relatedness between humanity and God.[90] And yet it is this narrative that would be rendered by Paul and the Pauline churches as the one necessary and sufficient object for faith, replacing trust in the God of Israel. Jesus' momentary and innocent mistake becomes the trigger for a denial of the continuing opacity of history, in its intimate but remote connection to the messianic, for the sake of an assertion of messianic clarity in the midst of history which points unambiguously here and now to its end. Failure to acknowledge that such clarity obtains then becomes interpreted as wilful faithlessness, an unbelief deserving divine punishment, in the eyes of Paul's successors in the Christian Church.

The Case for Holy Insecurity

The misreading of the historical narrative of Jesus of Nazareth as one of deification also, according to Buber, gives rise to dangerous possibilities for the misreading of subsequent history. At their root is the determination to assert a fixed point for the possession of redemption in the midst of an unredeemed world. This is another theme that we can trace back to medieval Jewish writing on Christianity but which finds a particular articulation in Buber, for whom the renunciation of the stable presence of messianic redemption is a characteristic feature of Judaism. Thus he can write that:

> the Jew, as part of the world, experiences, perhaps more intensely than any other part, the world's lack of redemption. He feels this lack of redemption against his skin, he tastes it on his tongue, the burden of the unredeemed world lies on him.[91]

On the other hand, Christianity's failure to sustain this Jewish renunciation of messianic presence leads it to persistent misreading of ongoing history that is not only theologically flawed but also catastrophic in its potential— and actual—political implications. Such misreading results, Buber's work suggests, in oscillation between two contrary but ultimately connected positions: one which gives up on actual history as the locus of redemption, and another which wants to attach messianic power to particular figures and events within it. In chapter two of this book, it was suggested there was a related oscillation in medieval Christian thought between a simple equation of the Church and its public history with the reign of God and an identification of salvation with an act wholly removed from this world, untouched by it and therefore—as in Nahmanides' sardonic aside— unfalsifiable by historical realities. Either redemption achieved is a reality that continues to have identifiable manifestations, or it is not; to put it crudely, either Christianity must repeat the Eusebian vision of redemptive fulfilment in Church history, or the Anselmian account of redemption as an intradivine transaction which secures us entry beyond death into the heavenly city. Buber's writings suggest that the Christian theology of his own time has to face its own variants of this abiding dilemma.

On the one hand, then, there is according to Buber the view found already in Paul's writings of an utter divorce between human time and messianic possibility, such that concrete history is regarded as the domain of darkness, under the power of the Evil One, and salvation in the present can be considered only as proleptic deliverance from it. Buber aligns himself fully with the likes of Cohen and Baeck in seeing rigorously Pauline Christianity as virtual Gnosticism, which requires belief in the devil alongside God to guarantee its dualistic universe; he can write without even Baeck's caveats about "Paul's Gnostic view of the world."[92] It is important to remember that he had argued in the 1930s against the use of original sin as a theological legitimation for totalitarian politics in the hands of "Christian" writers such as Schmitt and Gogarten. He even corresponded with Karl Barth on this point; the dualism of Pauline Christianity was not for him an intellectual problem only.[93]

On the other hand, however, there is also a strong implication in Buber's writing that Christianity's willingness to identify the presence of the messianic in history straightforwardly with one person, one sequence of events, stands as a precedent for other, much more destructive historical messianisms, both within Judaism—such as that triggered by Sabbatai Zvi—and in Western history more generally. *For the Sake of Heaven* is, on the face of it, a historical novel about Hasidism; but Buber did not write in the final days of the Second World War a book about the Napoleonic upheavals at the start of the nineteenth century out of some kind of literary escapism. The central theme of the novel is the conflicting interpretation of violent political change: is Napoleon, who at one point claimed he would restore the Jews to the land of Israel, saviour or destroyer? Is he a false saviour who will turn out to be an enslaver? Is he the destroyer who, despite himself and his own wickedness, will clear the way for salvation to come? Or—and this is the perspective with which Buber himself acknowledges he identifies—is the compulsion to read the grand dramas of history as fraught with messianic meaning ultimately a temptation to be resisted, in the name not just of Judaism but also of humanity? Yet this is more than the recommendation of a meagre pragmatism; Buber does not want us to abandon the prospect of redemption. Instead, his concern is that our preoccupation with the sensational story of a Napoleon's career invariably blinds us to the real presence of the messianic power amongst us—represented in the novel in the hidden, humble form of the Holy Yehudi. *For the Sake of Heaven* can be read both as a critique of the hopes and fears invested in the great political and military adventures of the modern age and their complex entanglements with vestigial and actual religion, and as a plea not to respond in despair by cutting human history adrift from the horizon of redemption. Instead, Buber invites us to seek that redemption in hiddenness, outside the grand narratives, in the ordinary extraordinariness of encounter.

In the remarkable penultimate chapter of *Two Types of Faith*, Buber announces his preference for the "Paulinism of the unredeemed"— represented by the Jewish Kafka—as against the Paulinism of those who regard redemption as an identifiable achievement, represented by the Protestant Christian theologian Emil Brunner.[94] He accepts that the temper of the times is attuned to a Pauline vision of existence as hemmed in by powers that exceed our comprehension and control, marked by a terrible contradiction between the persisting hope of fulfilment and a world of mocking emptiness. Yet rather than "stabilizing" that contradiction as a dualism, from the secure standpoint of the (already) redeemed, Kafka embraces it outside any achievement of redemption—which paradoxically permits the possibility of signs of redemption arising in the midst of the contradiction, for its instability is also a space for hope. Kafka's is simply an extreme version of the Jewish vision, shared by Jesus, of the necessary hiddenness of God's messianic presence. Hence Buber's conclusion to the chapter:

> That He hides Himself does not diminish the immediacy; in the immediacy
> He remains the Saviour and the contradiction of existence becomes for us a
> theophany.[95]

Buber's reading of Kafka here coincides with his analysis of the "Jewish soul" generally, whose second great focus is "the basic consciousness that God's redeeming power is at work everywhere and at all times, but that a state of redemption exists nowhere and never." [96]

By implicit contrast, Christianity's insistence on regarding the narrative of Christ and his followers as leading to an actually existing "state of redemption" blinds it to the redeeming power of the messianic surprise within the still unfolding present. This is certainly a theme in Buber's writing on Hasidism, whose "holy insecurity" derives from sustaining a messianic horizon for the whole of life without allowing that horizon to become fixed in any particular individual or sequence of events and thereby closed.[97] As the Maggid advises Prince Czartoryski in *For the Sake of Heaven*, who cannot see where to begin because he cannot see where things should end, "The beginning and the beginning alone is placed into the hands of men. But it *is* placed in them."[98] There is a direct parallel here with Baeck's essay "Two World Views Compared," even if Buber's appropriation of Hasidism colours his articulation of the point rather differently. For Buber, we are only called to make a beginning of "turning" towards the coming rule of God;[99] we should not expect to comprehend how it will arrive in its fullness, and should practise resistance towards all the siren voices—Christian, Nationalist, Fascist, Communist—that persist in claiming they can.

The corollary of this is made explicit in the conclusion to the first section of an earlier essay, "Dialogue," which covers the same ground from the viewpoint of a more general religious anthropology: "Revelation will tolerate no perfect tense, but man with the arts of his craze for security props it up to perfectedness."[100] How can Christianity, with its demand for faith-assent to a perfect tense narrative of revelation and redemption, avoid being the paradigm case of this understandable but unfortunate failure? For Buber, all its other theoretical, social and political failings stem from this original mistake in identifying the messianic event with a specific, past and ever receding narrative—that is, in making the scripture claim of fulfilment in Christ. In terms of the framework by which Christian theology has made sense of Christian identity in relation to Judaism and whose history we have been describing in previous chapters, all the other dilemmas follow from that, according to Buber's analysis.

Critical History

Baeck and Buber provide critical histories of Christianity that have significant parallels as well as contrasting emphases. Their Christian contemporaries such as Barth, Maritain and de Lubac were beginning to raise anti-Judaism as an issue requiring urgent attention, as we saw in the previous chapter, yet did not conceive of its elimination as requiring radical surgery for historic Christianity. Baeck and Buber interpreted the Christian story as far more profoundly implicated in a distorting alienation from the Judaism within which it originated.

At one level, they can be read as confirming the hypothesis of the preceding chapters that the judgments about scripture, covenant and people, directed against the "other" of continuing Judaism, functioned as powerful parameters for Christian thought and practice over two millennia that have also proved enduringly problematic. Sustaining them, and the legitimating anti-Judaism conveyed by them, has shaped the development of Christian theology at the deepest level. It has implicated that theology in difficult dilemmas about the priority of ethics and the openness of history in particular. The question of anti-Judaism cannot therefore be treated simply as a minor issue when seeking to understand Christian thought and practice. Where Baeck and Buber go beyond this study is in arguing that this shaping has also been a profound misshaping, by implication one that tragically distorted Christianity's capacity to be attentive and responsible in arguably its greatest hour of historical judgment. While it is not my intention to refute or affirm that verdict, it does seem to me that it still needs to be heard and pondered with great care.

On the other hand, their approach shows no real awareness of the three-dimensional process of exchange that we have also repeatedly traced, and therefore no awareness of the importance of continuing exchanges between Christians and Jews, as well as the Christian image of Judaism, for the development of Christian theology. It is not perhaps accidental that what is true for their analysis of history also holds true to some extent for their sense of the present. While they were both important

participants in the exchange between Christian thinking and continuing
Judaism, it is hard to see the past reality or present potential of that
exchange acknowledged in their work. Their version of critical history,
therefore, while providing both precedent and inspiration for attempts to
take seriously the relationship between anti-Judaism and the shaping of
Christian theology, also has its limitations. Above all, we have found
reason to question their presumption, shared with most Christians of the
time, of a clear boundary between the two religions fixed since the time of
Paul, one across which hostility, or occasionally a more friendly attitude,
could be expressed from the security of independent territories. One of the
reasons for highlighting in the Foreword and Introduction the rather
different perspective of Franz Rosenzweig, their contemporary, is the
affinity between his insights and the hypothesis this book has sought to
establish, according to which Judaism *and* anti-Judaism together
profoundly shape Christian theology over two millennia. The extent of that
affinity is a subject to which we need to return in the last chapter, together
with its potential implications for Christian theology today.

Notes

[1] For a brief biography of Baeck, see Albert H. Friedlander, *Leo Baeck: Teacher of Theresienstadt* (London: Routledge and Kegan Paul, 1973), 11-50.
[2] See, for instance, Samuel Sandmel, *Leo Baeck on Christianity: The Leo Baeck Memorial Lecture 19* (New York: Leo Baeck Institute, 1975), and J. Louis Martyn, "Leo Baeck (1873-1956): Introduction," in *Jewish Perspectives on Christianity*, ed. Rothschild, 21-41.
[3] Baeck, "Harnack's Vorlesungen," 114-115. Translations from parts of the article that do not appear in Baeck, "Harnack's Lectures" are my own.
[4] Baeck, "Harnack's Vorlesungen," 105.
[5] Baeck, "Harnack's Vorlesungen," 105.
[6] Harnack, *Liberal Theology*, 12; Chapman, *Troeltsch*, 14-22.
[7] Allen Wood, *Kant's Moral Religion* (Ithaca: Cornell University Press, 1970).
[8] Immanuel Kant, *Religion within the Limits of Reason Alone*, trans. Theodore M. Greene and Hoyt H. Hudson (New York: Harper, 1960).
[9] Chapman, *Troeltsch*, 16; Harnack, *What is Christianity?* 59-62. Cf. Rumscheidt, *Revelation and Theology*, 80.
[10] Moses Mendelssohn, *Jerusalem and Other Jewish Writings*, trans. and ed. Alfred Jospe (New York: Schocken, 1969), 61-73. Cf. also Schoeps, *Jewish-Christian Argument*, 95-107; David Sorkin, "1783," in *Yale Companion*, ed. Gilman and Zipes, 93-100.
[11] See the review of Benamozegh's treatment of Christianity in Jacob, *Christianity through Jewish Eyes*, 34-39.

[12] Max Brod, *Paganism–Christianity–Judaism: A Confession of Faith*, trans. William Wolf (Alabama: University of Alabama Press, 1970); the quotation is from page 10.

[13] *Reason and Hope: Selections from the Jewish Writings of Hermann Cohen*, trans. Eva Jospe (New York: W. W. Norton, 1971), 53. Cohen was not uncritical of Mendelssohn's presentation of Judaism; see Hermann Cohen, *Religion of Reason out of the Sources of Judaism*, trans. Simon Kaplan, 2nd ed. (Atlanta: Scholars Press, 1995), 357.

[14] Cohen, *Reason and Hope*, 83; see also 45-46, and *Religion of Reason*, 108-09.

[15] Cohen, *Religion of Reason*, 33.

[16] Cohen, *Reason and Hope*, 88. Kant's negative evaluation of Judaism is attributed to his dependence on Spinoza for his understanding of it (*Religion of Reason*, 331). For a brief survey of Kant's understanding of Judaism, see Yirmiyahu Yovel, *Dark Riddle: Hegel, Nietzsche, and the Jews* (Oxford: Polity, 1998), 7-20.

[17] Cf. Kenneth Seeskin, "How to Read *Religion of Reason*," introductory essay to Cohen, *Religion of Reason*, 24-26.

[18] Cohen, *Reason and Hope*, 121-122.

[19] Cohen, *Reason and Hope*, 212; cf. *Religion of Reason*, 204-05, 309-10.

[20] Leo Baeck, *The Essence of Judaism*, rev. ed. (New York: Schocken, 1948). On the two editions of the book, see Friedlander, *Leo Baeck*, 61-102.

[21] In making the term "polarity" central to the interpretation of Baeck's thought, I am following the lead of Friedlander, *Leo Baeck*. Baeck himself contrasts Judaism with "mere" mysticism and rationalism, "both of which lack that distinctive unity composed of polar opposites" which is found in Judaism (*Essence of Judaism*, 141).

[22] Baeck, "Mystery and Commandment," in *Judaism and Christianity*, 171-185.

[23] Baeck, "Mystery and Commandment," 171-173.

[24] Baeck, "Mystery and Commandment," 173.

[25] On the broader context for the changes introduced in the second edition, see Mark H. Gelber, "1916," in *Yale Companion*, ed. Gilman and Zipes, 343-47. Baeck articulated the understanding of Jewish mysticism that is introduced in "Mystery and Commandment" in his essay "The Origin of Jewish Mysticism," in *The Pharisees and Other Essays* (New York: Schocken, 1966), 93-105. Contrast Cohen on "the difference that exists between monotheism and all mysticism" (*Religion of Reason*, 90).

[26] Baeck comments on the shortcomings of ethical monotheism as a characterization of Judaism in his final book, *This People Israel: The Meaning of Jewish Existence*, trans. Albert H. Friedlander (Philadelphia: Jewish Publication Society, 1964), 23-24.

[27] Baeck, *This People Israel*, 35.

[28] Baeck, "Mystery and Commandment," 177.

[29] Baeck, *Essence of Judaism*, 88.

[30] Baeck, *Essence of Judaism*, 88-94.

---

[31] Baeck, *Essence of Judaism*, 166-167. Baeck argues at greater length that Christianity is bound to myth (the myth of the heavenly redeemer) in a way that is wholly unacceptable for Judaism in "Romantic Religion," in *Judaism and Christianity*, 202-203.

[32] Baeck, "Judaism in the Church," in *Pharisees*, 72.

[33] Baeck, "Mystery and Commandment," 177.

[34] Baeck, "Mystery and Commandment," 177.

[35] Baeck, "Judaism in the Church," 74-78; cf. "Romantic Religion," 203.

[36] Cf. Martyn, "Introduction," in *Jewish Perspectives on Christianity*, ed. Rothschild, 34-35.

[37] Baeck, "Romantic Religion," 189-292. On the history of this essay, see Friedlander, *Leo Baeck*, 120-121.

[38] The idea that the relationship of Christianity to Judaism might be compared to that between romanticism and classicism can be traced in Geiger (cf. Jacob, *Christianity through Jewish Eyes*, 47) and Cohen (e.g. *Reason and Hope*, 83, 89), although for Cohen the fundamental concern with Christianity is its failure to resist pantheism completely and uphold with Judaism the uniqueness of God (so for instance the first two chapters of *Religion of Reason*, 35-58).

[39] Baeck, "Romantic Religion," 189-190.

[40] Baeck, "Romantic Religion," 189-192.

[41] Baeck, "Romantic Religion," 195.

[42] Baeck, "Romantic Religion," 196.

[43] Baeck, "Romantic Religion," 197.

[44] Baeck, "Romantic Religion," 198.

[45] Baeck, "Romantic Religion," 199.

[46] Baeck, "Romantic Religion," 201. In the later essay "The Faith of Paul," Baeck acknowledges that the tendency of early twentieth-century scholarship to explain every aspect of Paul's development through the ancient mystery cults has been corrected in subsequent scholarship, but he is concerned that it should not be over-corrected (in *Judaism and Christianity*, 155-156). For a more recent attempt to reinvigorate the "Hellenistic" reading of Paul against the prevailing preference to locate him within the context of first-century Judaism's diversity, see Hyam Maccoby, *Paul and Hellenism* (London: SCM, 1991).

[47] Baeck, "Romantic Religion," 240.

[48] Baeck, "Romantic Religion," 248-249.

[49] Baeck, "Romantic Religion," 278.

[50] The German political theorist Carl Schmitt glorified Nazism as a romantic politics; see Friedlander, *Leo Baeck*, 122-123.

[51] On Baeck's analysis, this dominance has not been without resistance; thus for instance he affirms precisely what Harnack decries, the renewed attention to the Old Testament in Calvinist thinking. See Baeck, "Judaism in the Church," in *Pharisees*, 86-88, and *This People Israel*, 313-314.

[52] Baeck, "Romantic Religion," 276.

[53] Baeck, "Romantic Religion," 232.

[54] Baeck, "Romantic Religion," 212-214.

[55] Baeck, "Romantic Religion," 232-233.
[56] Baeck, "Romantic Religion," 275.
[57] Cf. Baeck, "The Faith of Paul," especially 160-163.
[58] Cf. Harnack, *What is Christianity?* 47-49 and 53.
[59] Baeck, "Romantic Religion," 219.
[60] Baeck, "Romantic Religion," 218-219.
[61] Baeck, "Romantic Religion," 270.
[62] Baeck, "Romantic Religion," 275.
[63] Baeck, "Two World Views Compared," in *Pharisees*, 144.
[64] Baeck, "Two World Views Compared," 145.
[65] Maurice Friedman, *Martin Buber's Life and Work: The Early Years, 1878-1923* (London: Search Press, 1982), 178-202.
[66] I am borrowing this terminology from Dan Avnon, *Martin Buber: The Hidden Dialogue* (Lanham: Rowman & Littlefield, 1998), which describes three major phases in Buber's thought, mysticism, dialogue and attentive silence.
[67] Martin Buber, *I and Thou*, trans. Ronald Gregor Smith, 2nd ed. (T & T Clark, 1958); Buber and Rosenzweig, *Scripture and Translation*. For a brief survey of how Buber influenced contemporary Protestant theology, through *I and Thou* in particular, see Helmut Gollwitzer, "The Significance of Martin Buber for Protestant Theology," in *Martin Buber: A Centenary Volume*, ed. Haim Gordon and Jochanan Bloch (New York: Ktav, 1984), 385-402.
[68] For an account of his initial meeting with Rang, see Martin Buber, "Dialogue," in *Between Man and Man*, trans. Ronald Gregor-Smith (London: Routledge, 2002), 6-7. Cf. Friedman, *Buber's Life: Middle Years*, 95-119.
[69] Martin Buber, "Church, State, Nation, Jewry," in *Jewish Perspectives on Christianity*, ed. Rothschild, 132-142; "An Open Letter to Gerhard Kittel," in *Disputation and Dialogue*, ed. Talmage, 51-54; "The Question to the Single One," *Between Man and Man*, 47-97.
[70] Martin Buber, *Two Types of Faith*, trans. Norman P. Goldhawk (New York: Macmillan, 1951); *For the Sake of Heaven: A Chronicle*, trans. Ludwig Lewisohn (New York: Meridian Books, 1958).
[71] Buber, *Two Types of Faith*, 174; Lorenz Wachinger, "Buber's Concept of Faith as a Criticism of Christianity," in *Martin Buber*, ed. Gordon and Bloch, 437.
[72] Maurice Friedman, *Martin Buber's Life and Work: The Later Years, 1945-1965* (New York: E, P. Dutton, 1983), 94-97.
[73] So e.g. Martin Buber, "The Two Foci of the Jewish Soul," in *Jewish Perspectives on Christianity*, ed. Rothschild, 126-27; cf. also "The Faith of Judaism," in *Mamre: Essays in Religion*, trans. Greta Hort (Melbourne: Melbourne University, 1946), 1-17.
[74] Cf. e.g. Buber, "Two Foci," 125-30; "Church, State, Nation, Jewry," 138-41; and from an earlier period Martin Buber, *On Judaism*, ed. Nahum N. Glatzer (New York: Schocken, 1967), 126-28.
[75] Novak, *Jewish-Christian Dialogue*, 80-86.
[76] Buber, *Two Types of Faith*, 44; cf. also 55 and 79-81. Buber also contrasts John's Gospel with the Synoptics in a complementary way (32-34).

[77] Buber, *Two Types of Faith*, 12-13.

[78] Buber, "Dialogue," in *Between Man and Man*, 6-7.

[79] Buber, "The Holy Way," in *On Judaism*, 122-25; *I and Thou*, 90, 110-11.

[80] Friedman, *Buber's Life: Early Years*, 363-34.

[81] Buber, *Two Types of Faith*, 56.

[82] Buber, *Two Types of Faith*, 68.

[83] Buber, *Two Types of Faith*, 75-78.

[84] Buber, *Two Types of Faith*, 78; Martin Buber, *The Origin and Meaning of Hasidism*, ed. and trans. Maurice Friedman (New York: Harper & Row, 1966), 107-11, 249-51.

[85] Buber, *Two Types of Faith*, 22.

[86] Buber, *Two Types of Faith*, 107-08.

[87] Buber, *Two Types of Faith*, 108-13.

[88] Buber, *Origin of Hasidism*, 249-51.

[89] Buber, *Origin of Hasidism*, 109-11; cf. the Foreword to the second edition of *The Sake of Heaven*, xii-xiii.

[90] Buber, *Two Types of Faith*, 114-16, 129-34; cf. "Two Foci" and *Origin of Hasidism*, 91-92.

[91] Buber, "Two Foci," 127; compare also comments in two letters Buber wrote during successive world wars on the same theme, in Friedman, *Buber's Life: Early Years*, 363-65, and *Buber's Life: Later Years*, 47.

[92] Buber, *Two Types of Faith*, 148; cf. also 81-83, 89-90, 135-42, 161.

[93] Buber, "The Single One," 46-97, especially 89-91. On the correspondence with Barth, see Busch, *Karl Barth*, 272; Sonderegger, *Jesus Christ*, 106-08; Gollwitzer, "Significance of Martin Buber," 396-98.

[94] Buber, *Two Types of Faith*, 162-69.

[95] Buber, *Two Types of Faith*, 169.

[96] Buber, "Two Foci," 127.

[97] Buber, *Origin of Hasidism*, 86-88, 105-07, 111-12.

[98] Buber, *The Sake of Heaven*, 202.

[99] Cf. the comments of the narrator in Buber, *The Sake of Heaven*, 246.

[100] Buber, "Dialogue," in *Between Man and Man*, 21.

CHAPTER SIX

CONCLUSION:
THE INTERNAL FOE

The purpose of this final chapter is to reflect on the extent to which the detailed studies in theological tradition presented in previous chapters confirm the insights about the relationship between Christianity, Judaism and anti-Judaism that Franz Rosenzweig initially articulated in his correspondence with Rosenstock-Huessy during the First World War. While Rosenzweig subsequently developed those insights at much greater length in the *Star of Redemption* and then also in other writings in the 1920s, his early letters already sketched in bold outline a dynamic interchange between Christian theology, Christian anti-Judaism and continuing Christian encounter with Judaism that is at once fraught with tension and rich in creativity. It is this outline, reviewed briefly in chapter four and summed up in the metaphor of Judaism as Christianity's "internal foe", which serves as our point of departure here.

We might begin by noting that Rosenzweig's analysis of Christianity in relation to Judaism more or less leaves to one side the detailed narrative of their historical development prior to modernity and treats them as abiding and contrasting "historical forms of revelation."[1] Unlike Baeck and Buber, whom we discussed in the previous chapter, Rosenzweig makes no attempt to engage with the scholarly debate about Christian origins and its associated questions, such as how much Christianity owes to Judaism and at what point it broke away from it. Nor does he show much interest in analysing specific examples from subsequent history of how the relationship he so powerfully asserts between Christian theology, Christian anti-Judaism and Christian encounter with Judaism has actually worked. His concern to identify the unchanging structure of that relationship in the *Star of Redemption*, via a methodology that sits somewhere between philosophy, theology and sociology, leads him to write at a level of abstraction from historical contingency that has incurred significant criticism.[2] Yet it is also perhaps inseparable from the way his work has sustained a sense of actuality that the more conventionally "scholarly" writings of Baeck and Buber have not.

This book, then, while it may ultimately substantiate a Rosenzweigian thesis does not follow a Rosenzweigian method. The first question that the final chapter will therefore seek to answer is: to what extent do the exercises in the excavation of Christian theological history it contains tend to affirm Rosenzweig's model of Judaism as Christianity's "internal foe" as the key for interpreting that history? In order to answer that question, the first section compares this model with two others that have been much more influential over the last forty years and are evident in the literature reviewed in the Introduction. These two models are identified as "exterior other" (most obvious in Neusner and Haynes) and "estranged sibling" (implicit in e.g. Yoder and Bader-Saye). Both are shown to have significant shortcomings for making sense of the material presented in the book so far.

The following two sections seek to show how Rosenzweig's alternative model can help to synthesize the various parts of this study with regard to two important themes: the hermeneutics of history; and the relationship between reason, ethics and Law. Yet if the understanding of Judaism as Christianity's "internal foe" indeed fits best with the realities of historical exchange, does this mean that anti-Judaism is in fact inseparable from the enterprise of Christian theology insofar as it seeks to work in continuity with its historic traditions? That is not a question that Rosenzweig, as a Jewish thinker, answered directly, but it is surely unavoidable for Christian theologians in the contemporary context. The final section offers a tentative response to this question by returning to the issue of how claim implies judgment in Christian teaching, the pivot for the classic framework we have been tracing since chapter one. If it is accepted that claim about gospel must imply some judgment on those who consciously ignore that gospel, then a "minimal" and carefully circumscribed form of anti-Judaism would indeed appear to be intrinsic to Christian theology. If on the other hand we follow the lead of MacKinnon in questioning the inevitability of judgments about history flowing from claims about the resurrection of the crucified, then Christianity's difficult non-comprehension of the stranger crossing its borders can be sustained without being resolved into anti-Jewish judgment.

Models of Relationship

It is integral to Rosenzweig's model of relationship for Christianity and Judaism that Judaism somehow falls inside Christianity's self-understanding as well as existing outside it, *and* that its existence across the boundary of Christian self-definition is inevitably an occasion for tension and conflict.

It is a model repeatedly corroborated in the detailed work of the previous chapters. This is hardly accidental, of course: the hypothesis set out in the Introduction, of a significant relationship between Christian theology's primary subject of newness in Christ, its secondary subject of Judaism as (apparently) enduring Israel without Christ and Christians' experience of and response to Jews, owes much to Rosenzweig's profoundly suggestive work. The Introduction also noted that if this hypothesis was correct, it would show the importance of tracing the "three-dimensional" historical process of intersection between changes within Christian theology, the theological exchange between Judaism and Christianity and the (more or less hostile) Christian understanding of Judaism. We have seen numerous examples in the preceding chapters of how changes in the experience of Jews and Judaism had effects on Christian theology. We have seen cases too where the direction of influence has also flowed in the opposite direction. In chapter two, it was argued that new levels of exposure to Jewish culture, including anti-Christian polemic, in the twelfth century helped to precipitate shifts in Christian theology that then fed back into altered evaluations of Judaism and ultimately allowed new mentalities to emerge regarding the treatment of Jews as a minority community in Western societies in the centuries that followed. Chapter three argued a closely parallel thesis about the seventeenth century, with results that were then touched on in chapter four. Jewish voices (mixing with others) challenge Christian discourse about newness; Christian thinkers creatively restate what newness means; altered understandings of good news remain bound up with judgments on the old Israel that resists it, judgments that may or may not then themselves shift and change Jewish-Christian relations.

Nonetheless, other models of relation besides that of the "internal foe" have been persistently encountered in the book, particularly in the post-war Christian works discussed in the Introduction and to some extent also in the Christian and Jewish writings from between the wars considered in the previous two chapters. Indeed, it needs to be acknowledged that these other models have in fact been far more influential than Rosenzweig's for both academic studies and more popular communication. The two most significant might be summed up as "exterior other" and "estranged sibling", and they therefore need to be reviewed before proceeding.

Exterior Other

The model of Judaism as "exterior other" to Christianity is arguably the distinctive contribution of modernity. Thinkers in the line that we traced from Locke to Harnack assumed that Judaism after Jesus is simply nothing to do with the Christian Church. Judaism and Christianity are related merely via overlapping origins. In terms of their continuing reality, they are wholly separate from one another.

Of course, almost all Christians who thought in this way until the 1960s believed that the historical exteriority of Judaism to Christianity was bound up with Judaism's theological exteriority to the redeeming work of God in the world. It is possible to see the perspective of Jews such as Baeck as an inverted image of this Christian view: according to them, Judaism is exterior to Christianity because Christianity has become exterior to sustaining witness to the God of Sinai. Baeck and Harnack would have agreed on the utter distinction of Judaism from Christianity; they disagreed fiercely, of course, as to the side of the distinction on which God, truth and goodness were ultimately anchored.

Influential recent commentators from both religions have sought to adapt this model in order to make it fit for a post-polemical era. One approach here from the Christian side would be the kind of "two-covenant" thinking that proposes God, truth and goodness to be as it were anchored on both sides of the distinction between Judaism and Christianity.[3] The two religions can then remain exterior to each other without passing any judgment upon each other. The powerful attraction of this approach in certain quarters is reflected in the way that Rosenzweig has been appropriated as its first protagonist, despite the fact that his actual writings, as we have seen, clearly point in a very different direction.[4] To some extent, such thinking could look for historical substantiation in the work of Neusner. Neusner tried to provide an account of Jewish and Christian origins which would show that there never was any such thing as a "common tradition", only two always and essentially independent traditions.[5] An alternative to arguing that Christians should accord independent theological value, rather than judgment, to Judaism is to urge that they abandon the task of making theological sense of Judaism altogether. Haynes, for instance, proposes that Christians renounce the theological interpretation of Judaism, on the grounds that any attempt to make sense of Judaism on Christian terms has to become an act of intellectual violence that leaves space for the repetition of actual violence against Jews.[6] His is perhaps the most extreme version of this model: Judaism is so wholly "exterior" to Christianity that Christians cannot say anything *about* Judaism at all but only listen passively to what Jews might say about themselves.

In the light of the previous chapters, there are perhaps two major criticisms that might be directed against the various ways in which the model of the exterior other has been developed. First, historically, Christianity has in fact lived with and been shaped by constant interaction with Judaism, as a persisting neighbour and as a cultural adversary, real and imagined. Every chapter has produced significant examples of this process, while it should also be evident that the book as a whole is not in the remotest sense a comprehensive account. Furthermore, it would need a historian of Judaism to begin to assemble the evidence for the complementary thesis of the shaping of Jewish thought through interaction with Christianity, a thesis which has already received considerable attention in Jewish studies. It is simply not the case that in terms of their history, Christianity and Judaism have been "separate" religions, entirely exterior to one another.

The second criticism would be more theological. If continuing Judaism is wholly exterior to Christianity, then Christian thought can either deny it all value (as Harnack did) or recognize its value on the basis of a discourse that transcends and thereby effectively relativizes Christianity itself. The characteristic dilemma of "modern" theology traced in chapter three, between the path of historical superiority and the path of religious relativism, is bound to recur in modified form for all variants of this fundamentally modern model. Denying Judaism all value tends to proceed via a historicizing mode of rationality that ultimately struggles to make sense of the pre-modern sources and traditions of Christian theology, as reflected in Harnack's affinity with Marcion. On the other hand, well-intentioned attempts to accord Judaism value without assimilating it to Christianity must ultimately appeal to criteria of truth and goodness that do not "belong" to Christianity but validate both it and its exterior other, Judaism. The exteriority of Judaism to Christianity thereby invokes the exteriority of truth to both religions and beckons us down the way to religious relativism.

Estranged Sibling

One of the reasons why the writings of Baeck and Buber discussed in the previous chapter might sound somewhat dated today is the narrative they presume about Christian origins. Like contemporary Christian scholars, Baeck and Buber presupposed that "Christianity" became distinct from "Judaism" with Paul. The issues that were thought to separate the two religions from that point onwards were then taken to represent fixed and abiding contrasts which could reliably guide the understanding of contemporary theological difference.

Chapter one reflected the very different narrative of Christian origins that has been current for some time in contemporary scholarship. This locates New Testament texts, including those written by and attributed to Paul, within the diversity of first-century Judaism and the multiple debates and divisions it both generated and (at some level) embraced. The emergence of Christianity to become a separate form of religious life from simultaneously developing Judaism is understood as a complex and contested process that took centuries to reach a relatively stable terminus. Experiencing the resistance of many fellow Jews to their message about Jesus Christ undoubtedly generated for the first believers in that message fierce exchanges both with the unconvinced and between themselves regarding the implications of the newness they celebrated for changes to existing traditions. One crucial issue here, as we can see from Paul's letters, was how to treat Gentiles, perhaps from the fringes of Diaspora synagogues but not full proselytes, who came to believe in Jesus as Lord and Christ. While this rendered problematic the location of Christian groups within the broad comprehension of first-century Judaism, no New Testament text consistently proposes Judaism as a separated "other" which Christianity then mirrors and opposes. Even when we do find precisely this presentation of Christianity and Judaism in Justin Martyr's writings from the second half of the second century, it should not be taken uncritically to reflect historical reality when it might also be plausibly read as an attempt to shape that reality in the face of those who continued to be happy within Boyarin's spectrum of "Judaeo-Christianity". In terms of the history of Christian origins, therefore, the division between Christianity and Judaism cannot be taken to be as early or as straightforward as Baeck and Buber on the one hand, and Harnack and Barth on the other, all presumed.

This new narrative of Christian origins raises the possibility of a quite different model of relation between Christianity and Judaism from either the "exterior other" or Rosenzweig's internal foe: the estranged sibling. The model is suggested in the title of a seminal work by Segal, which argued that both normative Christianity and normative (i.e. Rabbinic) Judaism should be seen as successors to the pluriformity of first-century Judaism prior to the destruction of the temple in 70 CE.[7] While this model allows for continuing competition and thereby some mutual influence as dimensions of estrangement, it also raises questions about the necessity, and hence possible reversibility, of the estrangement itself. If Christianity and Judaism were conceived in a common womb, and if there was no single overwhelming *theological* reason why they could not continue to coexist within loose but shared structures of authority and identity, can two millennia of estrangement be overcome in a post-Holocaust world?

The possibility that thereby arises from the new narrative of Christian origins for "repair of the tradition"[8] could be seen as the animating force for the some of the most important recent work by Christian thinkers on understanding Judaism. Writers such as Soulen, Yoder and Bader-Saye seek to discern the factors that led to the estrangement of Christianity from Judaism in the first four centuries, and while they offer somewhat different diagnoses they agree that the primary causes of the estrangement are both non-essential to the Christian tradition and theologically undesirable.[9] Therefore the effects deriving from those causes, including the continued teaching of supersessionism, can and should be reversed, with hope thereby invoked of ultimately overcoming Christianity's estrangement from its historic sibling, Judaism.

Again, we can register both more historical and more theological objections to this model. Historically, while it is undeniably important to register that "the partings of the ways" between Christianity and Judaism need to be understood as an extended and complex process, it can nonetheless be asked whether at least some versions of the new narrative still perpetuate a distinction between "before" and "after" that is too absolute to do justice to the evidence. Rosenzweig's refusal to allow developments within the histories of Christianity and Judaism final significance should not be interpreted too hastily as mere critical naivety. To begin with, we have seen repeatedly that the interaction between these purported "siblings" does not stop with their communal and institutional separation, even if we date this, with Yoder, as late as the fourth century. Estrangement did not in fact lead to total alienation; the border crossings keep happening. Perhaps still more importantly, the hope for "repair of tradition" tends to make implicit appeal to a "before" when there was once peace between Christians and (other) Jews, as the precedent for the peace we are striving for today. Yet there is simply no evidence that the siblings ever did live together all that peaceably, though undoubtedly they coexisted without violence in many different contexts, before and after the asserted point of final estrangement. The claim that God had raised the crucified prophet of Nazareth from the dead in fulfilment of Israel's scriptures was an inherently divisive claim: either it was true, and everything potentially had to change, or it was not, in which case it was wrong to give it any credibility. This was the case in 33 CE as it was in 433, or 1933.

Theologically, the danger with this model might be that it stakes too much on enduring commonality. It may be the case that Christian theologians need to face the possibility that Judaism as it has developed historically is not, at its deepest roots, *like* Christianity, as the sibling metaphor implies. Of course there are many points of similarity, but that does not necessarily mean that Judaism and Christianity are actuslly two things of the same kind. Moreover, why suppose that the estrangement was somehow accidental, and therefore must derive from factors that are ultimately external to the Christian tradition? This book has made central to its understanding of Christianity claims about newness, beginning with Jesus, which are simply irreconcilable with any version of Judaism that does not accept that its belief and practice need to be reinterpreted in the light of that newness. The best way for Christianity to live peaceably with such versions of Judaism, in the first century or the twenty first, might be to see them as something actually profoundly *unlike* it, but in that very unlikeness nonetheless sharing—however differently—in the life of the one God.

While the models of exterior other and estranged sibling have been far more influential than Rosenzweig's for thinking about the relation between Christianity and Judaism over the past hundred years, they are both open to serious question as interpretations of history and as proposals for theological understanding. In the two sections that follow, two themes that have recurred at various points in the preceding chapters are reviewed in order to provide examples of how the model of the "internal foe" might be put to work. Rosenzweig's approach is shown to express in schematic form a much more productive explanatory framework for synthesizing the conclusions of different parts of this study.

The Model at Work (1): Hermeneutics of History

In the preceding chapters, it has been argued that the preservation of anti-Judaism through the repetition in varying forms of the cardinal judgments of interpretive blindness, displacement of Torah and division of history has been profoundly formative for the development of the Western Christian theological tradition. Moreover, it has been suggested that such repetition faced more attentive Christian thinkers in particular, from Augustine to Aquinas and from Limborch to Barth, with difficult questions for which they struggled to find resolution. The theological hermeneutics of history—past, present and future—has emerged time and again as the site where these questions tend to converge: how to interpret God's action in the past, in establishing the covenant at Sinai; in the present, in allowing the persistence of disobedient Judaism; and in the future, in achieving the fulfilment of all the divine promises to which the scriptures bear witness, including those that speak of the salvation of Israel. Buber, Baeck and Rosenzweig might also have agreed from their distinctive perspectives that the interpretation of history is finally the critical issue for Christian theology, and moreover the one with which Judaism in its persistence keeps confronting it.

The decisiveness of this issue is apparent in the account of Christian separation from Judaism given in chapter one. The separation, as it was presented there, was not primarily "about" faith or Law, sacrifice or its cessation, God alone or God working through a supreme agent, the Messiah arrived or the Messiah awaited. Tensions and debates about such things could—and did—exist within Jewish contexts, and not only prior to the mid-second century. What we can discern in Justin's text, however, is the transposition of New Testament interpretations of history's resistance to the good news such that "Judaism" becomes objectified as the externalized site of such resistance, and therefore an enduring symbol of disobedience to the will of God. The earliest and foundational Christian claims about fulfilment relate directly to the life of Jesus, and most specifically to his suffering and death. Scripture is reread in the light of the resurrection to disclose the possibility that God was at work even and supremely in these apparently terrible events—acting to bring about the fullness of all that had been promised in the history of Israel. Yet the proclamation of Jesus' death and resurrection did not compel assent from other Jews in most cases, in Judea, Galilee or the Diaspora, while it also started to attract Gentiles from the penumbra of Jewish life in the cities of the Hellenized Roman empire. Now the pattern from the interpretation of Jesus' life and death was extended forwards: these developments— opposition from God's own people and the gathering in of the nations— were recognized in turn as the fulfilment of scripture. For Paul and many others who may have only dimly known or grasped his writings, such a revised understanding then required the re-evaluation of Torah observance within the life of the people of God now existing in the new assemblies of Jews and Gentiles.

This incipient theological hermeneutics of continuing history in the New Testament documents intersected with the social reality of increasingly entrenched estrangement between groups of Jewish and Gentile Christians and groups of non-Jesus Jews in at least some of the cities of the empire during the second century. At this point, it becomes possible for a Christian teacher to conceive of such non-Jesus Jews as representatives of an entity named Judaism that mirrors and opposes his Christianity, the two appearing as parallel elements within a fully fledged interpretation of God's work in human history. Given the persistence of resistance to the gospel among most Jews for the foreseeable future, the narration of Christianity as the unfolding fulfilment of God's promises of blessing elicited as its counterpoint the narration of Judaism—now defined by the "literal" observance of Torah—as the successive confirmation of divine judgment, for which the events of 70 and 135 CE provided decisive points of reference.

Such an analysis implicates not only anti-Judaism but also continuing Judaism itself within the subsequent trajectory of Christian theology, as the "internal foe". The theological hermeneutic that becomes integral to Christianity's self-understanding and the articulation of its gospel of divine newness must provide a space for Israel in terms of scriptural past, historical present and eschatological future, a space which cannot be entirely purged of the perceived reality of actual Judaism, regardless of the hostility directed towards it. The particular interpretations that such a hermeneutics must generate of Mosaic Torah, Judaism's persistence and Israel's final salvation are liable to questioning whenever Christianity's understanding of itself within theological history changes and also when those interpretations encounter resistance from the shifting experience of the Jewish "other"—and therefore fresh interpretations are called for that must be adjusted with Christianity's understanding of its own movement through historical time.

This is something that we have encountered repeatedly in the preceding chapters. In chapter two we had to consider the impact of awareness of the Islamic world, including its rich Jewish culture, on Christianity's inherited framework for understanding itself in relation to Judaism. In chapter three the irrevocable rupturing of Western Christendom's unity and the attack on the argument from prophecy, associated with Jewish voices, were presented as factors contributing to profound alterations in the replication of that framework. Finally, the background to the creative re-description of Christian newness discussed in chapter four was constituted in part by the disintegration of confidence in progress after World War I and in part also by both Jewish cultural influence and the politicization of antisemitism.

The story of Christian theology therefore needs to be told as one marked by restless engagement with living Judaism in tandem with the shifting restatement of anti-Judaism. Baeck and Buber were right to identify Christianity's theological hermeneutic of history as the critical issue in relation to Jewish concerns but did not recognize—unlike Rosenzweig—the extent to which that hermeneutic drew Christianity into a continuing exposure to the living presence of actual Judaism, because of its correspondence to a certain necessary space in Christianity's interpretive scheme. As a result of that correspondence, changing perceptions of Judaism may have consequences for the interpretive scheme as a whole while, conversely, changes elsewhere in the scheme may entail revisiting the theological understanding of Judaism / Israel. It is precisely because Judaism can neither be wholly externalized nor wholly domesticated and comprehended that it acts as such a powerful agent for change in Christian theology.

The Model at Work (2): Reason, Ethics and Law

In a contrasting but complementary way, the value of Rosenzweig's model of the "internal foe" can be seen and perhaps extended in relation to another theme that has recurred throughout the preceding chapters: reason, ethics and Law. Here Christianity and Judaism have very clearly borrowed from, been influenced by and developed in parallel with each other; yet they have also at the same time continually sought to demonstrate that they represent opposing and incompatible positions. Such a conclusion not only confirms the Rosenzweigian thesis of this book but also suggests that the "non-exteriority" of Judaism to Christianity might be reflected in a parallel, though doubtless different, "non-exteriority" of Christianity to Judaism.

At various points in the preceding chapters, the common challenge of shifting forms of reasoning has been the catalyst for interchange and shared responses between Jewish and Christian thinkers.[10] Changing conceptions of rationality trigger disorientation in the theological hermeneutics of the twinned realities of Christianity and Judaism that Christian theological discourse then seeks to stabilize, sometimes in relatively conscious engagement with Jewish thinking. Christian theology therefore participates in a dynamic process of exchange with Judaism not in isolation but as one dimension of its openness to changing presentations of reason that are also interacting with contemporary Judaism. Re-descriptions are thereby generated (on both sides) of their own identity and that of the "other", to which the other may then in turn respond. This pattern can be seen in the re-appropriations of the reasoning of ancient philosophy by Saadia and Abelard, Maimonides and Aquinas, touched on in chapter two; in the interplay of Jewish heretics and Christian radicals in the early history of the Enlightenment and the consequent scramble for reinterpretation among the more orthodox, in chapter three; in the struggle over the bodies of Kant and Hegel amongst leading figures within both Judaism and Christianity in the nineteenth century and their abandonment for the sake of new thinking following World War I, in chapter four.

Such interchange, however, was not always acknowledged and affirmed. Indeed, around the issue of reason, ethics and Law it seemed particularly important to writers on both sides to present the image of a chasm that could not be crossed. We encountered examples in the first four chapters from over two millennia of how Judaism served Christian teachers as the symbol of what they were *not* saying about the relationship between scriptural text, community practice and ethical reason. Jewish hermeneutics was castigated as "carnal" in pre-modern Christianity, on the basis that it rejected the mediation of the Spirit between ancient text and God's people in the present in favour of a misconceived literalism. Growing recognition from the twelfth century onwards that Judaism in fact had extensive and highly developed traditions for the interpretation of Torah put a puzzling question mark against this older discourse. It also opened the space for Aquinas to argue that such traditions were inherently incapable of spanning the divide from ancient Israel, by contrast with a Christian architecture of law in its manifold forms. Modern theology, epitomized by Harnack, depicted continuing Judaism with its adherence to Torah as a refusal of the universality and interiority of the ethics of Jesus that define Christianity and make it alone a viable religion for modernity.

In the last chapter, we showed Christianity serving Jewish writers in much the same way. Yet while Baeck celebrated Judaism as the religion of polarity in which mystery and commandment belong to one another and flow into each other, Barth was devoting his mature years to the task of integrating doctrine and ethics, gospel and command, into a single whole, both within his own theological thought and in the very architecture of the *Church Dogmatics*.[11] For him, the "what" of Christian belief certainly does not stand alone as a complete object for assent, proclaiming achieved perfection and therefore affirming the supremacy of stasis (Baeck and Buber's portrayal of Christianity). Rather, to receive this message *is* to be overturned from one's deepest roots of moral complacency and reborn into God's righteousness and thereby obedience to God's command here and now. Nor did Barth regard this as anything other than utter fidelity to the Pauline thinking of the New Testament. Chapter 11 of his *Ethics* sets out the relationship between indicative and imperative, Christ's sacrifice and our love, and arrives at the startling conclusion that "We cannot forget that we do not ever stand in a direct relationship to Jesus Christ if we take his humanity seriously," for that relationship must always also include our relationship to the neighbour.[12] For Barth, it is in Christian theology alone that the ethical lacuna generated by modernity—and beneath that indeed by human existence—is overcome. We might also note that this insistence on the inseparability of doctrine and ethics has continued to occupy the attention of Christian theologians from a wide range of confessional and theological standpoints up to the present day.[13]

It would seem, then, that in fact Christianity and Judaism both face a common task around the relationship between the indicative and the imperative, doctrine and ethics, sacred texts and contemporary practices, and aspire to broadly parallel frameworks for articulating their responses. Indeed, this point is explicitly accepted by David Novak, an influential Jewish voice in contemporary theological dialogue between Jews and Christians.[14] Yet Baeck and Buber did not acknowledge that the greatest contemporary Christian theologian was engaged in working out a profound account of the unity between faith and action whose rupture they located at and as the origin of Christianity itself. Moreover, neither did they attend in this context at least to how the task of articulating that unity had also emerged as profoundly problematic within modern Judaism, which had been characterized since the mid-nineteenth century by intellectual and institutional divisions over the relationship between Torah, history and ethical reason. The failing attributed to Christianity—that it did not know how to relate the command of God to the demands of moral life in the present—was hardly an area of unanimity and harmonious resolution within contemporary Judaism.

Buber is a particularly interesting case in this respect. Because he did not regard Torah observance and the Talmudic traditions of its interpretation as constitutive of Judaism, the fact that early Christianity did not preserve these things is not actually the critical point for him in its break with Judaism; rather, the ways parted when it rendered faith as *pistis* through its demand for belief in the resurrection rather than as *emunah*, trust in God in I-Thou relation. There is something slightly anomalous, then, in Buber's desire to preserve the charge of traditional Jewish polemic that Christianity displaces the command, the ethical, while leaving to one side the specific issue of its displacement of Torah to which that charge had been characteristically related. Buber's own understanding of Judaism is actually open to something very close to the Jewish critique of Christianity on just this point. Rosenzweig, for instance, tried to persuade him that his disregard of Torah left a serious gap in his treatment of Judaism. Arguing from their shared understanding of revelation, he suggested that one could value Judaism as Law in a way that ran parallel to Buber's recovery of Judaism as teaching, i.e. beyond the liberal-conservative dichotomies of the nineteenth century, which both agreed could lead only to dead ends. Buber, however, politely but curtly reiterated his rejection of these attempts on the grounds that "God is not a law-giver" and each human being has a unique responsibility to decide what is to be done in a given situation.[15]

Rosenzweig's original, lengthy letter on this subject was written in the summer of 1923; between then and the exchange of shorter letters around its publication in 1924 there had been a major breach between Buber and Ernst Simon, one of their colleagues at the Frankfurt Lehrhaus, again involving Buber's refusal to accept Law as integral to revelation or even as compatible with it. Simon, like Rosenzweig, disagreed with Buber's "meta-nomianism", which he interpreted specifically as the result of a failure to reckon with the tragic; the fallenness of humanity, according to Simon, meant humanity was sentenced to the tragedy of work, within which it could only draw near to God through a voluntary acceptance of the tragedy of law.[16] While Rosenzweig attempted to highlight the inconsistencies within Buber's thinking, his own account of the relationship between divine command and the category of Law has in turn been analysed by Gillian Rose as a turning away from the difficult realities of seeking justice in the modern world. In effect, Rose argues that the displacement of Law / displacement of the ethical which Jewish writers saw in Christianity and some other Jews saw in Buber is actually replicated within the thought of Rosenzweig, considered by many Jews as the outstanding thinker of twentieth-century Judaism.[17]

Of course, Barth himself showed no interest at all in what Jewish writers might be saying about ethics and Law, despite the close cultural proximity of their reflections to his own in the 1920s and 1930s. The terminology and the fundamental issues at stake in Rosenzweig's correspondence with Buber are not at all far removed from Barth's explorations of similar territory in his lectures on ethics in the later 1920s. Was there some kind of unacknowledged, even subliminal border crossing happening between the two sides? And what might have been gained by acknowledging it?

At this point I would like to touch on a more contemporary example of how questions about reason, ethics and Law demonstrate in a particularly powerful way the "interiority" of Judaism to Christianity and the residual hostility that inhibits insightful exchange. Enrique Dussel, one of the leading thinkers associated with South American Liberation Theology, is an especially interesting figure for our purposes. His encounter with the writings of the Jewish philosopher Emmanel Levinas in 1971, from which he proceeded to engage also with Rosenzweig, marked something of a watershed in his own intellectual development.[18] Yet the terms in which he praises Levinas along with Rosenzweig are revealing: "I have studied the Jewish theologians in considerable depth because they give a good account of the way things were before the Incarnation."[19] Moreover, Dussel shows no signs of engagement with Levinas' powerful reformulation of the critique of Christianity we reviewed in relation to Leo Baeck: that the covenant judgment, displacement of Torah, leads directly to the displacement of ethics and a weakening of moral resolve in Christianity.[20] Instead, the good news for Dussel is all about the loss of law. He wishes to propose Christian newness as recovery of Israel's authentic heritage: Jesus wanted to inaugurate the restoration of the original constitution of Israel in the wilderness to be a "utopian community" and not a state, and of the law given at Sinai as an ethic of liberation rather than a moral code. It is not clear whether the actual Torah as written down in Genesis to Deuteronomy with its orientation towards settled life in the land should therefore be seen as recording the corruptions of the original purity of community and ethic for the sake of the state and morality, Jerusalem already degenerated into Babylon.[21] What is clear is that the "old law" that was "destroyed" by Jesus and "opposed" by Paul is most certainly to be associated with Babylon as the sign of domination legitimating itself as morality.[22] Dussel thus overtly rehearses what Rose diagnosed as the covert dualism between law and love implicit in Levinas and Rosenzweig and symptomatic of the unresolved dilemmas at the heart of European modernity.[23] Indeed, Dussel proudly makes it axiomatic for his account of Christianity.

Dussel, like Harnack, wants to identify the newness of Christ *as* a new ethics, but that seems in his case as in Harnack's to require a profoundly negative evaluation of the prevailing forms of Judaism at the time of Christ—i.e. forms believed to focus on observance of Torah—to a point that veers close to the edge of Marcionism. The tendency of Liberation Theologians to resort to unscholarly caricatures of first-century Judaism in order to present Jesus' ministry as good news for the oppressed might be paralleled in the work of Christian feminists.[24] Furthermore, unlike Harnack's reformist ethics, Dussel's revolutionary ethics cannot rely on existing institutions to provide the matrix for their purchase. With no institutions, and no law, Dussel can only posit a "holy community" in the midst of history, something that Rose identified as the delusive mirage haunting Rosenzweig and Levinas on the one hand and contemporary Christian theologians seeking images of liberation on the other.[25]

The case of Dussel's approach to ethics and Law shows us how the dynamics of Rosenzweig's model of the "internal foe" continue to replicate themselves. Judaism provides a powerful spur for Christian thinking, yet it is a thinking that is constantly wanting to legitimate anti-Judaism and place itself beyond the Judaism with which it in fact remains bound up. The question that arises from these reflections is whether the

Rosenzweigian analysis which has been defended here thereby sentences Christian theology to perpetual anti-Judaism—to casting Judaism as its "foe", despite the determination repeatedly expressed since the 1960s to avoid this. That is the issue to which we turn in the final section.

Is Anti-Judaism Intrinsic to Christian Theology?

Part of the attraction of the two other models for understanding the relationship of Christianity to Judaism reviewed in the first section of the chapter is that they can provide a plausible basis for giving a negative answer to this crucial question. If Judaism is ultimately exterior to Christianity, then Christianity is not *bound* to say or think anything about Judaism at all, as Haynes urges. Alternatively, it may, to follow the line pursued by Boys and many others, come to regard Judaism as a different but parallel path for the sharing of God's covenantal blessing. Either way, anti-Judaism is a mistake from which Christian theology can and should recover. This same fundamental conclusion follows from the representation of Judaism as Christianity's estranged sibling. Soulen, Yoder and Bader-Saye all seem to be clear enough that the estrangement is the Church's fault in terms of history and that in terms of the present it can be corrected by good theology that overcomes the distorting legacy of anti-Judaism.

Conversely, perhaps one reason why Rosenzweig's model of the "internal foe" has found few advocates in the post-Holocaust world is that it provides far less reassurance that Christian belief and practice can be neatly severed from anti-Judaism. It has, however, been repeatedly borne out in this study of Christian theological history. If anything, texts from the decades after his death provide the clearest confirmation of it. Even as Christian thinkers, from Barth to Dussel, recognized that anti-Judaism constitutes a problem for Christian doctrine, they have nonetheless continued to replicate it across very different theological paradigms in moves inseparable from their fractured encounters with contemporary Judaism. On the other hand, neither does Rosenzweig's model make easy the dismissal of Christianity with its embedded anti-Judaism as simply alien to Judaism, which would perhaps be the ultimate conclusion for Baeck and Levinas at least. Anti-Judaism via its rationalization also becomes the site in Christian theology of exchange with Judaism in the present, and of the creative struggle inseparable from it to interpret God's work in history in a way that makes sense of the original call and final redemption of the people of Israel.

If one accepts in the contemporary context the interpretive power of the Rosenzweigian model for understanding the relationship between Christianity and Judaism, then it is inevitable both that Christian theology deals *with* the Jewish reality within its own frame of reference (against the "exterior other" model) and that it cannot fully comprehend or reconcile the Jewish reality *within* that frame of reference (against the "estranged sibling" model). Is it therefore bound to perpetuate anti-Judaism? In this final section, two possible responses are outlined. The first accepts that the move from claim to judgment that constitutes the classic framework is inescapable: Judaism that sets aside the good news of Jesus Christ has to be an object of judgment for those who believe in this good news. Yet it argues that this "minimal" anti-Judaism needs to be and indeed can be very clearly demarcated from the outgrowths of the classic framework in Christian history that have given rise to prejudice, interpersonal hostility, discrimination and violence. The second response by contrast questions the original need for judgment in the classic framework and sees Judaism rather as the locus for an enduring aporia in Christian theology. The perplexity it thus generates must create tension, but the tension is not inevitably discharged in an act of judgment on Judaism. It can set up instead an energizing balance of struggle, within which the one who appears as an internal foe can be recognized with less assurance as a stranger continually encountered on "Christian" territory.

First Response: The Inevitability of Judgment

It could be argued with some plausibility that any form of Christianity which resists the religious relativism pioneered by Spinoza and others in the seventeenth century is bound to make the judgment that there is something wrong with Jewish life that takes no account of the new thing that Israel's God has done in Jesus Christ. If that judgment constitutes anti-Judaism, then such "minimal" anti-Judaism may well be intellectually inevitable for non-relativistic forms of Christian belief. We might compare the view of Novak, who asserts that some form of supersessionism is simply intrinsic to Christian belief, despite the well-meaning efforts of so many Christians to argue the contrary.[26] This is likely to be the conscious view of many conservative or traditional Christians, while we have also found it present in different but equally powerful forms in traditions of theological liberalism.

Is the necessary persistence of such minimal anti-Judaism in Christian theology cause for concern, or even for the rejection of Christian claims on the grounds of their implication in evil? While we have sought to follow the interplay between theology of newness, theology of Israel and Jewish-Christian relations in many different settings, we have also found reason time and again to refrain from oversimplifying the link between cause and effect. Aquinas helped to provide the intellectual foundations for the gradual unravelling of the Augustinian policy of protecting Jewish communities within Christendom in the later Middle Ages, yet he consistently defended it in his own writings. Those who followed the lead of pioneers of modern liberal theology such as John Locke abandoned the traditional rationale for considering contemporary Jews as theologically or politically "special", and thereby paved the way both for their political emancipation in Western Europe and for Christian indifference to collective Jewish survival. Both developments were unthinkable in pre-modernity, yet they are liable to be valued rather differently from each other in a post-Holocaust context.

If we turn to the twentieth century, Harnack might have the greatest claim of all the theologians we have considered to be free from the witness people myth that Haynes alleges was so dangerous for the Jews, yet it was not his intellectual heirs who were prominent in the public resistance to Hitler. Nor is it really plausible that Barth could have provided more effective theological opposition if he had never broken with Harnack's theology.[27] On the other hand, Haynes is right to stress that, as we saw in chapter four, Christians sharing an anti-supersessionist understanding and insisting against the successors of Locke that Jews remained God's (disobedient) people could nonetheless occupy a wide variety of positions on the spectrum of responses to Nazi antisemitism, from courageous opposition to broad support.[28] How Jews as a vulnerable minority in a particular Christian society were treated was in fact likely to be determined by the interaction between a variety of factors, including theologies of Israel / Judaism but also at least as importantly general views on the legitimacy of coercion and discrimination and on the political imperative for cultural and religious uniformity. This is a point that became particularly clear in the discussion of Jacques Maritain in the final section of chapter four: Maritain's change of heart about discrimination against Jews was not caused by a shift in his doctrine of Israel so much as a shift in his understanding of the state precipitated by the emergence of European fascism.

The previous chapters suggest that the practical implications of "minimal" anti-Judaism in non-relativistic forms of Christianity will also depend on the extent to which this becomes interwoven with other strands of Christian anti-Jewish tradition. We might list three theological theses in

particular that we have found associated with the anti-Jewish judgments of
the classic framework:

1. Jewish resistance to Christian claims implies the culpable failing
   of the Jewish people, individually and collectively, to be e.g.
   obedient to the manifest will of God, spiritual rather than carnal
   in their faith, or willing to heed reason and conscience;
2. The coming of Christ means that the calling of Abraham's
   biological children to be a distinct people, Israel in contrast to the
   nations, has come to an end, and with it any observance of the
   Torah given to Moses that contributes to the enduring distinction
   of Jews from Gentiles;
3. Judaism since the second Christian century has needed to be
   instructed by the Gentile Church as to what it means for Jews to
   be part of the faithful people of God, while the Church has
   nothing at all to learn from continuing Judaism.

The first thesis can be related to the scripture judgment of interpretive
blindness, the second to the covenant judgment of displacement of Torah
and the third to the people judgment of the division of history. Each thesis
expresses a high degree of confidence in the Church's ability to interpret
God's purposes in history generally, and specifically with regard to the
Jewish people.

These additional theses from the history of Christian anti-Judaism,
unlike the minimal judgment that Judaism without Christ is missing
something, do indeed lend themselves relatively directly to the
legitimation of anti-Jewish practices, though even here we need to be
careful of oversimplification. To make only some preliminary points, the
first thesis implies that Jews deserve punishment, which might encourage
the promotion of or at least acquiescence in repressive measures taken
against them. The second thesis indicates that Jews who seek to join the
Christian Church must abandon everything that makes them distinctive as
Jews, including all observance of Torah as mediated through Talmudic
traditions.[29] The third sets up the ideal relationship between Christians and
Jews as one in which Christians speak with authority and Jews listen with
deference; in the absence of such a situation, it would be hard to see what
point there could be for Christians in deliberately relating to Jews at all.

Yet is also needs to be said, on the basis of the preceding study, that
these additional theses do not necessarily appear to be intrinsic to
Christian doctrine in the same way as the first, minimal judgment,
although they have repeatedly been proposed across two millennia. From
the writings of the New Testament on the one hand to the life of Edith
Stein on the other, it is clear that being critical of Judaism for its resistance

to Christ is not the same thing as being prejudiced against Jews or as being committed to the erasure of all distinctions between Jews and Gentiles. A minimal theological anti-Judaism only leads Christians to treat Jews as anything other than neighbours to be loved as themselves when other, truly toxic ingredients are added to foster the illusion that somehow the commandment is suspended in their case or that it is properly expressed through the infliction of suffering. Criticism of Judaism only becomes an objection to the existence of Torah observant Jews in abiding distinction from Gentiles via a hermeneutics of history that believes it is entitled to relegate the mystery of Israel's election to the past, a view which we have seen continually resurfacing in Christianity from the second century to the twentieth but which has never been established as any kind of formal doctrinal consensus.

Second Response: Suspending Judgment, Sustaining Perplexity

Is it actually inevitable that Christian claims lead to Christian judgment on Judaism, as has certainly happened throughout Christian history despite important shifts within the classic framework? Rosenzweig's own analysis identifies Christian hostility to Judaism as stemming from the way that continuing Judaism by its mere existence refutes Christian claims to total comprehension, political and theological. He suggests that Christianity inevitably seeks and dreams of such comprehension and therefore needs Judaism to guard it from the illusion of actually attaining it. If that is right, then the tension between Christianity and Judaism has to be expressed in some kind of Christian hostility towards Judaism, however carefully sublimated, as that which contradicts its deepest ambition. Such hostility will be expressed in judgment on Judaism, whether minimal or maximal in the terms set out above. What, though, if this analysis is not right, and it is possible for Christian theology to accept the reality of non-comprehension, both politically and intellectually? The tension would remain, in that (against Haynes) Judaism would be a necessary object *for* Christian theology yet at the same time one it cannot fathom. And because it cannot fathom it, neither can it confidently attribute failure to it even in the minimal sense described above, of asserting that there is something wrong with Judaism that does not here and now accept the claims about Jesus made by the Church. The cardinal claim of Christianity that the God of Israel has done a new and decisive thing in Jesus binds Christianity to thinking about continuing Judaism, the children of Abraham who do not receive this new thing, as a theological question at once demanding and resisting resolution.

Would such an abstention from judgment not in fact lead back to religious relativism and thus prove once again that non-relativistic Christian faith cannot be sustained without some minimal level of anti-Judaism? There is clearly a fine line here, but a line can nonetheless perhaps still be drawn. It would be possible to conceive of the caesura between Christianity and Judaism in history as a sign that something is wrong and something is missing in humanity's participation in the work of God in Christ, without placing oneself in a position to say *who* is wrong and what is wrong with them. Judaism would be a figure with which Christian theology must wrestle, but as with a stranger whose identity remains always elusive, not as an adversary one intends to overcome. Indeed, one might believe that ultimately its identity cannot be separated from the Word made flesh amongst us: the stranger who makes you limp may be the messenger of God.

Such a proposal also brings us back, once again, to the hermeneutics of history. Does the good news of Christ crucified and risen place those who receive it in a position to interpret authoritatively the work of God through the whole scope of human history? One theologian who strongly urged a negative answer to that question was Donald MacKinnon. According to him,

> The events of the present century and in particular what happened in Germany between 1933 and 1945 rob any serious theologian of the remotest excuse for ignoring the tragic element in Christianity.[30]

For MacKinnon, including the tragic within Christian theology was not primarily a matter of making space for lament but of renouncing the dream of comprehending human experience and its long history from a secure vantage point for making judgments about divine providence and human decisions. He identified the resistance to tragedy in Christianity as constituting only part of a deeper and more long term problem for Western culture, one that could be traced back all the way to Plato and his hostility to the tragedians in the name of philosophy.[31] Attempts to produce from Christian faith in the crucified and risen one an "answer" to the problem of evil or an all-encompassing interpretation of history tell us less about what is distinctive of such faith than about our fundamental aversion to contemplating what MacKinnon calls the "intractable surd element" of suffering and evil in human experience.[32] The *theological* value of tragic literature for him is precisely its relentless invitation to contemplation of this surd element.

MacKinnon's writings on theology and tragedy are potentially relevant for developing this second response to the question about anti-Judaism in two ways. First, if their plea that Christian theology should renounce the project of a total hermeneutics of history is accepted, then the drive for it to reach a verdict on the nature and purpose of the continuing Judaism so strangely bound up with its own identity would also be broken. It could instead accept that Judaism as another, different kind of surd; a mystery not just to the world but to itself, to be explored with care and rigour, yet without the expectation of comprehending it within its work of interpretation and being able to arrive at settled judgment.

Second, MacKinnon's writings indicate that the separation of Judaism and Christianity itself participates in tragedy. The profoundly tragic choice faced by Jesus of Nazareth, according to MacKinnon, concerned whether to allow his confrontation with the authorities in Jerusalem to develop and unravel into the abyss of his own death, trusting somehow that this was the will of God, or whether to stop that unravelling, convince his people of his own authority and use his power and influence instead to avoid the catastrophe that he could prophetically foresee and that would in fact finally overtake the city itself in 70 CE. The price of Jesus refusing the prudential reasoning of a Caiaphas whose highest good is collective political survival was a high one: not just the tragedy of 70, and then of 135, but the unfolding history of Christian antipathy to the continuing existence of the Jewish people that paves the way towards the Nazis' Final Solution.[33] Hence MacKinnon's description of Auschwitz itself as "surely among the most terrible *sequelae* of Calvary, as its mystery has been distorted and perverted in the Christian ages."[34] On this account, there can be no reassurance in reversion to the model of the estranged sibling with its hopes for repairing the rent fabric of the past: the tragic is precisely not that which, with hindsight and better intention or information, could have been avoided. It is a limit for the human ability to translate goodness into act and reality, a limit that needs to be faced without the illusion that somehow we can see or exist beyond it—and a limit which the truly incarnate God must also share.

To give a full evaluation of the two responses to the final question of this book would be a very substantial undertaking. Nonetheless, my own view would be that the second response opens up paths that deserve to be followed, with appropriate caution and critical engagement. The danger of the first answer is not, as I have tried to show, that it inevitably implicates theology in the acting out of violence, as so many writers on Christian anti-Judaism have feared, but rather that it keeps it locked in the Rosenzweigian cycle of always seeking to render what is partly interior to it as a separate object of external judgment. As we saw in the previous section in relation to ethics and Law, the cycle continually generates

Christian attempts—not always acknowledged—to identify the failings of Judaism that at once say little about actual Judaism and hide much about the internal dilemmas of Christianity. Not only is the perpetuation of that cycle hard to reconcile with the nurturing of non-polemical, non-apologetic dialogue in the contemporary world; it also suggests that in hiding from ourselves our own dilemmas by projection onto the nearest perceived outsider, our theological reasoning itself will not satisfy our hopes for the growth of understanding. For Christians to accept Judaism not as exterior other, estranged sibling or even perpetual foe but as a perplexing stranger who paradoxically makes claims upon their "own" territory might prompt them to attend more carefully not only to actual Jews but also to their actual selves, in order to understand more truthfully the fractured and multilayered ground on which we all have to stand.

Notes

[1] *Rosenzweig's "New Thinking"*, 90.

[2] Cf. Emil L. Fackenheim, *To Mend The World: Foundations of Post-Holocaust Jewish Thought* (New York: Schocken, 1982), 58-101.

[3] E.g. Boys, *Only One Blessing?* See also the brief discussion in the Introduction, at 2-6 above.

[4] Cf. Worthen, "Beginning without End," 341-43.

[5] Neusner, *Jews and Christians*.

[6] Haynes, *Reluctant Witnesses*.

[7] Alan F. Segal, *Rebecca's Children: Judaism and Christianity in the Roman World* (Cambridge: Harvard University Press, 1986).

[8] I owe this phrase to Susannah Ticciati, via personal correspondence.

[9] See 2-6 above.

[10] Cf. Burrell, *Faith and Freedom*.

[11] See 181-84 above. The ethical dimension of Barth's understanding of revelation is also stressed in Rashkover, *Revelation and Theopolitics*.

[12] Barth, *Ethics*, 345.

[13] E.g. Stanley Hauerwas, *The Peaceable Kingdom: A Primer in Christian Ethics* (Notre Dame: University of Notre Dame Press, 1983); Michael Banner, *Christian Ethics and Contemporary Moral Problems* (Cambridge: Cambridge University Press, 1999); Gustavo Gutierréz, *Theology of Liberation: History, Politics and Salvation*, trans. Caridad Inda and John Eagleson, rev. ed. (London: SCM, 1988); Mahoney, *Making of Moral Theology*.

[14] David Novak, "Avoiding Charges of Legalism and Antinomianism in Jewish-Christian Dialogue," in *Talking with Christians*, 26-45; cf. also "Karl Barth on Divine Command: A Jewish Response," in the same volume, 127-145.

[15] See Rosenzweig's open letter to Buber, "The Builders," and the subsequent exchange of correspondence in Franz Rosenzweig, *On Jewish Learning*, ed. N. N. Glatzer (New York: Schocken, 1965), 72-92 and 109-18

[16] Friedman, *Buber's Life: Middle Years*, 32-33.

[17] Gillian Rose, *The Broken Middle: Out of Our Ancient Society* (Oxford: Blackwell, 1992), 267-72; *Judaism and Modernity: Philosophical Essays* (Oxford: Blackwell, 1993), 43 and 156; *Mourning Becomes the Law: Philosophy and Representation* (Cambridge: Cambridge University Press, 1996), 85-86. Rose provides an extended analysis of Rosenzweig's *Star of Redemption* in chapter 10 of *Judaism and Modernity*, "Franz Rosenzweig: From Hegel to Yom Kippur," 127-54.

[18] On the development of Dussel's thought, see Linda Martín Alcoff and Eduardo Mendieta, eds., *Thinking from the Underside of History: Enrique Dussel's Philosophy of Liberation* (Lanham: Rowman & Littlefield, 2000), 13-25. Cf. the references to Levinas in Dussel's outline essay on liberation ethics in Enrique Dussel, *Ethics and Community*, trans. Robert R. Barr (Maryknoll: Orbis, 1988), 238-39.

[19] Enrique Dussel, *Ethics and the Theology of Liberation*, trans. Bernard F. McWilliams (Maryknoll: Orbis, 1978), 28-29.

[20] Some of the essays reflecting this are collected in Emmanuel Levinas, *Difficult Freedom: Essays on Judaism*, trans. Seán Hand (Baltimore: John Hopkins, 1990).

[21] Dussel, *Ethics and Community*, 42-70.

[22] Dussel, *Ethics and Community*, 76-77.

[23] Rose, *Broken Middle*, 247-67; *Judaism and Modernity*, especially chapters 5, "Shadow of Spirit" (37-51), and 13, "Angry Angels—Simone Weil and Emmanuel Levinas" (211-223); also, more succinctly, *Mourning Becomes the Law*, 35-39.

[24] Cf. Rachel Montagu, "Anti-Judaism in Christian Feminist Theology," in *Renewing the Vision: Rabbis Speak out on Modern Jewish Issue*, ed. Jonathan A. Romain (London: SCM, 1996), 26-37; Boys, *Only One Blessing?*, 12-14.

[25] Cf. Rose, *Broken Middle*, 289-294, commenting specifically on Emil Fackenheim and Johann Baptist Metz.

[26] E.g. Novak, *Talking with Christians*, 41 and 164.

[27] As would appear to be implied by Haynes, *Reluctant Witnesses*, 80-81.

[28] Haynes, *Reluctant Witnesses*, 87-89.

[29] Cf. Michael Wyschogrod, "A Letter to Cardinal Lustiger," in *Abraham's Promise: Judaism and Jewish-Christian Relations*, ed. R. Kendall Soulen (London: SCM, 2006), 202-210.

[30] Donald M. MacKinnon, *The Problem of Metaphysics* (Cambridge: Cambridge University Press, 1974), 130.

[31] Donald M. MacKinnon, "Theology and Tragedy," in *The Stripping of the Altars* (London: Collins, 1969), 41-51; this is also woven into the argument of *Problem of Metaphysics*.

[32] See e.g. Donald M. MacKinnon, "Order and Evil in the Gospel" and "Atonement and Tragedy," in *Borderlands of Theology and Other Essays* (London: Lutterworth, 1968), 90-104.

[33] MacKinnon's thoughts on this theme are scattered across various articles and essays; perhaps the most compact and comprehensive treatment is that in chapter 11 of *Problem of Metaphysics*, 122-35. On Caiaphas and the reasoning of institutional leaders, see "Kenosis and Establishment," in *Stripping of the Altars*, 26-29.

[34] Donald M. MacKinnon, *Themes in Theology: The Three-fold Cord* (Edinburgh: T & T Clark, 1987), 235-36.

BIBLIOGRAPHY

Abelard, Peter. *Dialogue of a Philosopher with a Jew, and a Christian.* Translated by Pierre J. Payer. Toronto: Pontifical Institute for Mediaeval Studies, 1979.

—. *Peter Abelard's Ethics: An Edition with Introduction, English Translation and Notes.* Edited by D. E. Luscombe. Oxford: Clarendon, 1971.

Abulafia, Anna Sapir. *Christians and Jews in the Twelfth-century Renaissance.* London: Routledge, 1995.

—. "From Northern Europe to Southern Europe and from the General to the Particular: Recent Research on Jewish-Christian Coexistence in Medieval Europe." *Journal of Medieval History* 23:2 (1997): 179-90.

Aelred of Rievaulx. *Aelred of Rievaulx: Treatises and Pastoral Prayer.* Kalamazoo: Cistercian Publications, 1971.

Alcoff, Linda Martín and Eduardo Mendieta, eds. *Thinking from the Underside of History: Enrique Dussel's Philosophy of Liberation.* Lanham: Rowman & Littlefield, 2000.

Altmann, Alexander. "Franz Rosenzweig on History." In *Studies in Religious Philosophy and Mysticism*, 275-291. London: Routledge and Kegan Paul, 1969.

Anselm of Canterbury. *Cur deus homo.* Edited by F. S. Schmitt. Bonn: Hanstein, 1929.

Aquinas, Thomas. *Summa theologiae.* Edited by Petrus Caramellus. 3 vols. Turin: Marietti, 1948-50.

Asiedu, F. B. A. "Anselm and the Unbelievers: Pagans, Jews, and Christians in the *Cur deus homo.*" *Theological Studies* 62.3 (September 2001): 530-548.

Augustine of Hippo. *The City of God against the Pagans.* Edited and translated by R. W. Dyson. Cambridge: Cambridge University Press, 1998.

Avnon, Dan. *Martin Buber: The Hidden Dialogue.* Lanham: Rowman & Littlefield, 1998.

Bader-Saye, Scott. *Church and Israel after Christendom: The Politics of Election.* Boulder: Westview, 1999.

Baeck, Leo. *The Essence of Judaism.* Rev. ed. New York: Schocken, 1948.

—. "Harnack's Vorlesungen über das Wesen des Christentums." *Montasschrift für Geschichte und Wissenschaft des Judentums* 45 [N. F. 9] (1901): 97-120.

—. *Judaism and Christianity: Essays by Leo Baeck.* Translated by Walter Kaufmann. Cleveland: Meridian, 1961.

—. *The Pharisees and Other Essays.* New York: Schocken, 1966.

—. *This People Israel: The Meaning of Jewish Existence.* Translated by Albert H. Friedlander. Philadelphia: Jewish Publication Society, 1964.

Balthasar, Hans Urs von. *The Theology of Henri de Lubac: An Overview.* Translated by Joseph Fessio, Michael M. Waldstein and Susan Clements. San Francisco: Ignatius, 1991.

Banki, Judith H. and John T. Pawlikowski, eds. *Ethics in the Shadow of the Holocaust: Christian and Jewish Perspectives.* Franklin: Sheed & Ward, 2001.

Banner, Michael. *Christian Ethics and Contemporary Moral Problems.* Cambridge: Cambridge University Press, 1999.

Barnes, Timothy D. *Constantine and Eusebius.* Cambridge: Harvard University Press, 1981.

Baron, Salo Wittmeyer. *A Social and Religious History of the Jews.* 2nd ed. Vol. 5. New York: Columbia University Press, 1957.

Barth, Karl. *Against the Stream: Shorter Post-war Writings, 1946-52.* Translated by E. M. Delacour and Stanley Godman. SCM: London, 1954.

—. *Church Dogmatics.* Edited by G. W. Bromiley and T. F. Torrance. 14 vols. Edinburgh: T & T Clark, 1956-1977.

—. *Community, State, and Church: Three Essays.* Gloucester: Peter Smith, 1968.

—. *Dogmatics in Outline.* Translated by G. T. Thomson. London: SCM, 1949.

—. *Epistle to the Philippians: 40th Anniversary Edition.* Translated by James W. Leitch. Louisville: Westminster John Knox, 2002.

—. *The Epistle to the Romans.* Translated by Edwyn C. Hoskyns. Oxford: Oxford University Press, 1933.

—. *Ethics.* Edited by Dietrich Braun and translated by Geoffrey W. Bromiley. Edinburgh: T & T Clark, 1981.

—. *Protestant Theology in the Nineteenth Century: Its Background and History.* London: SCM, 1972.

—. *The Resurrection of the Dead.* Translated by H. J. Stenning. London: Hodder and Stoughton, 1933.

—. *The Word of God and the Word of Man.* Translated by Douglas Horton. Boston: Pilgrim Press, 1928.

Benson, Robert L., and Giles Constable, eds. *Renaissance and Renewal in the Twelfth Century.* Cambridge: Harvard University Press, 1982.

Berdyaev, Nicolas. *Christianity and Anti-semitism.* Translated by Alan A. Spears and Victor B. Kanter. Aldington: Hand and Flower, 1952.

—. *The Meaning of History.* Translated by George Reavey. London: Geoffrey Bles, 1936.

Biggar, Nigel. *The Hastening That Waits: Karl Barth's Ethics.* Oxford: Clarendon, 1993.

Blumenkranz, Bernhard. *Les auteurs chrétiens latins du moyen âge sur les Juifs et le judaïsme.* Paris: Mouton, 1963.

Bohm-Duchen, Monica. *Chagall.* London: Phaidon, 1998.

Bonhoeffer, Dietrich. *No Rusty Swords: Letters, Lectures and Notes from the Collected Works.* Edited by Edwin H. Robertson. London: Collins, 1970.

—. *Ethics.* Edited by Eberhard Bethge and translated by Neville Horton Smith. London: SCM, 1955.

Bonsirven, Joseph, Joseph Chaine, Henri de Lubac and Louis Richard. *Israël et la foi chrétienne.* Fribourg: Éditions de la Librairie de l'Université, 1942.

Borden, Sarah. *Edith Stein.* London: Continuum, 2003.

Boyarin, Daniel. *Border Lines: The Partition of Judaeo-Christianity.* Philadelphia: University of Pennsylvania Press, 2004.

Boys, Mary C. *Has God Only One Blessing? Judaism as a Source of Christian Self-Understanding.* New York: Paulist Press, 2000.

Braaten, Carl E., and Robert W. Jenson, eds. *Jews and Christians: People of God.* Grand Rapids: Eerdmans, 2003.

Bradshaw, Paul F. *Eucharistic Origins.* London: SPCK, 2004.

Bradstock, Andrew. *Faith in the Revolution: The Political Theologies of Müntzer and Winstanley.* London: SPCK, 1997.

Brod, Max. *Paganism—Christianity—Judaism: A Confession of Faith.* Translated by William Wolf. Alabama: University of Alabama Press, 1970.

Brown, Peter. *The Body and Society: Men, Women and Sexual Renunciation in Early Christianity.* London: Faber, 1989.

Buber, Martin. *Between Man and Man.* Translated by Ronald Gregor-Smith. London: Routledge, 2002.

—. *For the Sake of Heaven: A Chronicle.* Translated by Ludwig Lewisohn. New York: Meridian Books, 1958.

—. *I and Thou.* Translated by Ronald Gregor Smith. 2nd ed. Edinburgh: T & T Clark, 1958.

—. *Mamre: Essays in Religion*. Translated by Greta Hort. Melbourne: Melbourne University, 1946.

—. *On Judaism*. Edited by Nahum N. Glatzer. New York: Schocken, 1967.

—. *The Origin and Meaning of Hasidism*. Edited and translated by Maurice Friedman. New York: Harper & Row, 1966.

—. *Two Types of Faith*. Translated by Norman P. Goldhawk. New York: Macmillan, 1951.

Buber, Martin, and Franz Rosenzweig. *Scripture and Translation*. Translated by Lawrence Rosenwald with Everett Fox. Bloomington: Indiana University Press, 1994.

Burrell, David. *Faith and Freedom: An Interfaith Perspective*. Oxford: Blackwell, 2004.

— and Yehezkel Landau, eds. *Voices from Jerusalem: Jews and Christians Reflect on the Holy Land*. New York: Paulist Press, 1992.

Busch, Eberhard. *Karl Barth: His Life from Letters and Autobiographical Texts*. London: SCM, 1976.

Byrne, Brendan. "Interpreting Romans Theologically in a Post-'New Perspective' Perspective." *Harvard Theological Review* 94:3 (2001): 227-41.

Cassiodorus. *Historia tripartita*. Patrologia Latina, vol. 69. Paris: J. P. Migne, 1848.

Chadwick, Owen. *The Victorian Church*. Vol. 1. London: A. and C. Black, 1966.

Chapman, Mark D. *Ernst Troeltsch and Liberal Theology: Religion and Cultural Synthesis in Wilhelmine Germany*. Oxford: Oxford University Press, 2001.

Chauvet, Louis-Marie. *The Sacraments: The Word of God at the Mercy of the Body*. Translated by Madeleine Beaumont. Collegeville: Liturgical Press, 2001.

Chazan, Robert. *Daggers of Faith: Thirteenth-century Christian Missionizing and Jewish Response*. Berkeley: University of California Press, 1989.

—. *European Jewry and the First Crusade*. Berkeley: University of California Press, 1987.

Chenu, Marie-Dominique. *La théologie au douzième siècle*. Paris: J. Vrin, 1957.

Chilton, Bruce and Jacob Neusner. *Jewish and Christian Doctrines: The Classics Compared*. London: Routledge, 2000.

—. *Judaism in the New Testament: Practices and Beliefs*. London: Routledge, 1995.

Cohen, Hermann. *Reason and Hope: Selections from the Jewish Writings of Hermann Cohen*. Translated by Eva Jospe. New York: W. W. Norton, 1971.

—. *Religion of Reason out of the Sources of Judaism*. Translated by Simon Kaplan. 2nd ed. Atlanta: Scholars Press, 1995.

Cohen, Jeremy. *The Friars and the Jews: The Evolution of Medieval Anti-Judaism*. Ithaca: Cornell University Press, 1982.

—. *Living Letters of the Law: Ideas of the Jew in Medieval Christianity*. Berkeley: University of California Press, 1999.

—. *"Synagoga conversa*: Honorius Augustodunensis, the Song of Songs, and Christianity's 'Eschatological Jew'." *Speculum* 79 (2004): 309-40.

—, ed. *Essential Papers on Judaism and Christianity in Conflict: From Late Antiquity to the Reformation*. New York: New York University Press, 1991.

Cohn, Norman. *The Pursuit of the Millennium: Revolutionary Millenarians and Mystical Anarchists of the Middle Ages*. London: Pimlico, 1993.

Court, John M., ed. *New Testament Writers and the Old Testament: An Introduction*. London: SPCK, 2002.

Courtine-Denamy, Sylvie. *Three Women in Dark Times: Edith Stein, Hannah Arendt, Simone Weil; or Amor fati, amor mundi*. Translated by G. M. Goshgarian. Ithaca: Cornell University Press, 2000.

Croner, Helga, ed. *Stepping Stones to Further Jewish-Christian Relations: An Unabridged Collection of Christian Documents*. New York: Paulist Press, 1977.

Cyprian of Carthage, *Three Books of Testimonies against the Jews*. Ante-Nicene Christian Library, vol. 12, part 2. Edinburgh: T & T Clark, 1869.

Dahan, Gilbert. *The Christian Polemic against the Jews in the Middle Ages*. Translated by Jody Gladding. Notre Dame: University of Notre Dame, 1998.

Dahlferth, Ingolf U. "Karl Barth's Eschatological Realism." In *Karl Barth: Centenary Essays*, edited by S. W. Sykes, 14-45. Cambridge: Cambridge University Press, 1989.

Davidson, Robert and A. R. C. Leaney. *Biblical Criticism*. Vol. 3 of *The Pelican Guide to Modern Theology*, edited by R. P. C. Hanson. Harmondsworth: Penguin, 1970.

Dawson, John David. *Christian Figural Reading and the Fashioning of Identity*. Berkeley: University of California Press, 2002.

Dronke, Peter, ed. *A History of Twelfth-century Western Philosophy*. Cambridge: Cambridge University Press, 1988.

Drury, John, ed. *Critics of the Bible, 1724-1873*. Cambridge: Cambridge University Press, 1989.

Dunn, James D. G. *The Partings of the Ways between Christianity and Judaism and Their Significance for the Character of Christianity*. London: SCM, 1991.

Dussel, Enrique. *Ethics and Community*. Translated by Robert R. Barr. Maryknoll: Orbis, 1988.

—. *Ethics and the Theology of Liberation*. Translated by Bernard F. McWilliams. Maryknoll: Orbis, 1978.

Eckhardt, A. Roy. "Salient Christian-Jewish Issues of Today: A Christian Exploration." In *Jews and Christians: Exploring the Past, Present and Future*, edited by James H. Charlesworth, 151-184. New York: Crossroad, 1990.

Edwards, John. *The Jews in Christian Europe, 1400-1700*. London: Routledge, 1991.

Elon, Amos. *The Pity of It All: A Portrait of Jews in Germany, 1743-1933*. London: Penguin, 2004.

Epistle of Barnabas. In *The Apostolic Fathers in English*, translated and edited by Michael W. Holmes, 177-98. 3rd ed. Grand Rapids: Baker Academic, 2006.

Evagrius. *Altercatio inter Theophilum Christianum et Simonem Judaeum*. Patrologia Latina, vol. 20. Paris: J. P. Migne, 1845.

Evans, Craig A., and Donald A. Hagner, eds. *Anti-semitism and Early Christianity: Issues of Polemic and Faith*. Minneapolis: Fortress, 1993.

Fackenheim, Emil L. *To Mend The World: Foundations of Post-Holocaust Jewish Thought*. New York: Schocken, 1982.

Fishbane, Michael. *Biblical Interpretation in Ancient Israel*. Oxford: Clarendon, 1985.

Fisher, Eugene J. Introduction to *Catholic Jewish Relations: Documents from the Holy See*. London: Catholic Truth Society, 1999.

Ford, David F. and C. C. Pecknold, eds. *The Promise of Scriptural Reasoning*. Oxford: Blackwell, 2006.

Frank, Daniel H., Oliver Leaman and Charles H. Manekin, eds. *The Jewish Philosophy Reader*. London: Routledge, 2000.

Franks, Robert S. *The Work of Christ: A Historical Study of Christian Doctrine*. London: Nelson, 1962.

Frei, Hans W. *The Eclipse of Biblical Narrative: A Study in Eighteenth and Nineteenth Century Hermeneutics*. New Haven: Yale University Press, 1974.

Friedlander, Albert H. *Leo Baeck: Teacher of Theresienstadt*. London: Routledge and Kegan Paul, 1973.

Friedman, Maurice. *Martin Buber's Life and Work: The Early Years, 1878-1923.* London: Search Press, 1982

—. *Martin Buber's Life and Work: The Later Years, 1945-1965.* New York: E. P. Dutton, 1983.

—. *Martin Buber's Life and Work: The Middle Years, 1923-1945.* Detroit: Wayne State University Press, 1988.

Fry, Helen P., ed. *Christian-Jewish Dialogue: A Reader.* Exeter: University of Exeter Press, 1996.

Fulbert of Chartres. *Tractatus contra Iudaeos.* Patrologia Latina, vol. 141. Paris: J. P. Migne, 1853.

Galli, Barbara Ellen. *Franz Rosenzweig and Jehuda Halevi: Translating, Translations, and Translators.* Montreal: McGill-Queen's University Press, 1995.

Gibbs, Robert. *Correlations in Rosenzweig and Levinas.* Princeton: Princeton University Press, 1992.

Gilbert Crispin. *The Works of Gilbert Crispin, Abbot of Westminster.* Edited by Anna Sapir Abulafia and G. R. Evans. London: British Academy, 1986.

Gilman, Sander L., and Jack Zipes, eds. *Yale Companion to Jewish Writing and Thought in German Culture, 1096-1996.* New Haven: Yale University Press, 1997.

Glatzer, Nahum N. *Franz Rosenzweig: His Life and Thought.* 3rd ed. Indianapolis: Hackett, 1998.

Gordon, Haim, and Jochanan Bloch, eds. *Martin Buber: A Centenary Volume.* New York: Ktav, 1984.

Gorringe, Timothy J. *Karl Barth: Against Hegemony.* Oxford: Oxford University Press, 1999.

Grant, Robert M. *Greek Apologists of the Second Century.* London: SCM, 1988.

Grosseteste, Robert. *De cessatione legalium.* Edited by Richard C. Dales and Edward B. King. London: British Academy, 1986.

Guibert of Nogent. *Tractatus de incarnatione contra Judaeos.* Patrologia Latina, vol. 156. Paris: J. P. Migne, 1853.

Gutierréz, Gustavo. *Theology of Liberation: History, Politics and Salvation.* Translated by Caridad Inda and John Eagleson. Rev. ed. London: SCM, 1988.

Harnack, Adolf von. *History of Dogma.* Translated by Neil Buchanan. 7 vols in 4. New York: Dover, 1961.

—. *Liberal Theology at Its Height.* Edited by Martin Rumscheidt. London: Collins, 1989.

—. *What is Christianity?* Translated by Thomas Bailey Saunders. 5th ed. London: Ernest Benn, 1958.

Harries, Richard. *After the Evil: Christianity and Judaism in the Shadow of the Holocaust.* Oxford: Oxford University Press, 2003.

Harries, Richard, Norman Solomon and Tim Winter, eds. *Abraham's Children: Jews, Christians and Muslims in Conversation.* London: T & T Clark, 2005.

Haskins, Charles Homer. *The Renaissance of the Twelfth Century.* Cambridge: Harvard University Press, 1927.

Hauerwas, Stanley. *A Better Hope: Resources for a Church Confronting Capitalism, Democracy, and Postmodernity.* Grand Rapids: Brazos, 2000.

—. *The Peaceable Kingdom: A Primer in Christian Ethics.* Notre Dame: University of Notre Dame Press, 1983.

Haynes, Stephen R. "Beware Good News: Faith and Fallacy in Post-Holocaust Christianity." In *Good News after Auschwitz? Christian Faith within a Post-Holocaust World*, edited by Carol Rittner and John K. Roth, 3-20. Macon: Mercer University Press, 2001.

—. *The Bonhoeffer Legacy: Post-Holocaust Perspectives.* Minneapolis: Fortress, 2006.

—. *Reluctant Witnesses: Jews and the Christian Imagination.* Louisville: Westminster John Knox Press, 1995.

Hays, Richard B. *Echoes of Scripture in the Letters of Paul.* New Haven: Yale University Press, 1989.

Hazard, Paul. *The European Mind, 1680-1715.* Translated by J. Lewis May. Harmondsworth: Penguin, 1973.

Herbert of Bosham. *Vita sancti Thomae, archiepiscopi et martyris.* In *Materials for the History of Thomas Becket, Archbishop of Canterbury*, vol. 3, edited by James Craigie Robertson. London: Longman, 1877.

Herbert, George. *A Priest to the Temple or The Country Parson with Selected Poems.* Edited by Ronald Blythe. Norwich: Canterbury Press, 2003.

Herman-Judah. "A Translation of Herman-Judah's *Short Account of His Own Conversion*." In *Conversion and Text: The Cases of Augustine of Hippo, Herman-Judah, and Constantine Tsatsos*, by Karl F. Morrison, 76-113. Charlottesville: University Press of Virginia, 1992.

Hobbes, Thomas. *Leviathan.* Edited by J. C. A. Gaskin. Oxford: Oxford University Press, 1998.

Homolka, Walter. *Jewish Identity in Modern Times: Leo Baeck and German Protestantism.* Providence: Berghahn, 1995.

Horbury, William. *Jews and Christians in Contact and Controversy.* Edinburgh: T & T Clark, 1998.

Irenaeus of Lyons, *Adversus haereses.* Ante-Nicene Fathers, vol. 1. Grand Rapids: Eerdmans, 1985.

Israel, Jonathan I. *The Dutch Republic: Its Rise, Greatness and Fall, 1477-1806.* Oxford: Clarendon, 1995.

—. *Radical Enlightenment: Philosophy and the Making of Modernity, 1650-1750.* Oxford: Oxford University Press, 2001.

Jacob, Walter. *Christianity through Jewish Eyes: The Quest for Common Ground.* Cincinnati: Hebrew Union College Press, 1974.

Jerome. *Commentariorum in Isaiam libri octo et decem.* Patrologia Latina, vol. 24. Paris: J. P. Migne, 1845.

Joachim of Fiore. *Adversus Iudeos.* Edited by Arsenio Frugoni. Rome: Istituto Storico Italiano per il Medio Evo, 1957.

John Chrysostom. *Discourses against Judaizing Christians.* Translated by Paul W. Harkins. Fathers of the Church, vol. 68. Washington DC: Catholic University of America, 1979.

Johnson, Luke Timothy. *The Gospel of Luke.* Collegeville: Liturgical Press, 1991.

Josephus, Flavius. *Against Apion.* Translated by H. St. J. Thackery. Loeb Classical Library, vol. 186. Cambridge: Harvard University Press, 1926.

Judah Halevi. *The Kuzari: An Argument for the Faith of Israel.* Translated by Hartwig Hirschfeld. New York: Schocken, 1964.

Julian of Toledo. *De comprobatione aetatis sextae.* Patrologia Latina, vol. 96. Paris: J. P. Migne, 1851.

Justin Martyr. *Dialogue with Trypho, a Jew.* Ante-Nicene Fathers, vol. 1. Grand Rapids: Eerdmans, 1985.

—. *The First Apology of Justin.* Ante-Nicene Fathers, vol. 1. Grand Rapids: Eerdmans, 1985.

Kant, Immanuel. *Religion within the Limits of Reason Alone.* Translated by Theodore M. Greene and Hoyt H. Hudson. New York: Harper, 1960.

Kaplan, Yosef. *From Christianity to Judaism: The Story of Isaac Orobio de Castro.* Translated by Raphael Loewe. Oxford: Littman Library of Jewish Civilization, 2004.

Kermode, Frank. *The Genesis of Secrecy: On the Interpretation of Narrative.* Cambridge: Harvard University Press, 1979.

Kerr, Fergus. *After Aquinas: Versions of Thomism.* Oxford: Blackwell, 2002.

Kimhi, Joseph. *The Book of the Covenant.* Translated by Frank Talmage. Toronto: Pontifical Institute of Mediaeval Studies, 1972.

Klein, Charlotte. *Anti-Judaism in Christian Theology.* Translated by Edward Quinn. London: SPCK, 1978.

Koeppel, Josephine. *Edith Stein: Philosopher and Mystic.* Scranton: University of Scranton Press, 2007.

Lambert, Malcolm. *Medieval Heresy: Popular Movements from the Gregorian Reform to the Reformation.* 2nd ed. Oxford: Blackwell, 1992.

Lancel, Serge. *St Augustine.* Translated by Antonia Nevill. London: SCM, 2002.

Lane, William L. *Hebrews 1-8.* Dallas: Word, 1991.

Langmuir, Gavin I. *History, Religion, and Antisemitism.* Berkeley: University of California Press, 1990.

Lasker, Daniel J. *Jewish Philosophical Polemics against Christianity in the Middle Ages.* New York: Ktav, 1977.

Le Grys, Alan. *Preaching to the Nations: The Origins of Mission in the Early Church.* London: SPCK, 1998.

Lerner, Robert E. *The Feast of St Abraham: Medieval Millenarians and the Jews.* Philadelphia: University of Pennsylvania Press, 2001.

Lessing, Gotthold Ephraim. *Nathan the Wise: A Dramatic Poem in Five Acts.* Translated by Bayard Quincy Morgan. New York: Frederick Ungar, 1955.

Levenson, Jon D. *The Death and Resurrection of the Beloved Son: The Transformation of Child Sacrifice in Judaism and Christianity.* New Haven: Yale University Press, 1993.

Levinas, Emmanuel. *Difficult Freedom: Essays on Judaism.* Translated by Seán Hand. Baltimore: John Hopkins, 1990.

Lieu, Judith. *Image and Reality: The Jews in the World of the Christians in the Second Century.* Edinburgh: T & T Clark, 1996.

Limborch, Philippus van. *De veritate religionis Christianae amica collatio cum erudito Judaeo.* Gouda, 1687.

Lindbeck, George A. *The Church in a Postliberal Age.* Edited by James J. Buckley. Grand Rapids: Eerdmans, 2003.

Littell, Franklin H., and Hubert G. Locke, eds. *The German Church Struggle and the Holocaust.* Detroit: Wayne State University Press, 1974.

Locke, John. *The Correspondence of John Locke.* Edited by E. S. de Beer. 8 vols. Oxford: Clarendon, 1976-89.

—. *An Essay concerning Human Understanding.* Edited by Peter H. Nidditch. Oxford: Clarendon, 1975.

—. *The Reasonableness of Christianity as Delivered in the Scriptures*. Edited by John C. Higgins-Biddle. Oxford: Clarendon, 1999.

—. *A Second Vindication of the Reasonableness of Christianity etc.* In vol. 7 of *The Works of John Locke: A New Edition, Corrected*. London: Thomas Tegg, 1823.

Löwith, Karl. *Meaning in History: The Theological Implications of the Philosophy of History*. Chicago: University of Chicago Press, 1949.

Lubac, Henri de. *At the Service of the Church: Henri de Lubac Reflects on the Circumstances That Occasioned his Writings*. Translated by Anne Elizabeth Englund. San Francisco: Ignatius, 1993.

—. *Catholicism: A Study of Dogma in Relation to the Corporate Destiny of Mankind*. Translated by Lancelot C. Sheppard. London: Burns, Oates and Washbourne, 1950.

—. *The Christian Faith: An Essay on the Structure of the Apostles' Creed*. Translated by Richard Arnandez. San Francisco: Ignatius, 1986.

—. *Christian Resistance to Anti-semitism: Memories from 1940-44*. Translated by Elizabeth Englund. San Francisco: Ignatius, 1990.

—. *Exégèse médiévale*. 4 vols. Paris: Éditions Montaigne, 1959-64.

—. *Histoire et esprit: L'intelligence de l'Écriture d'après Origène*. Paris: Aubier, 1950.

—. *Medieval Exegesis: The Four Senses of Scripture*. Translated by Mark Sebanc. 2 vols. Edinburgh: T & T Clark, 1998-2000.

—. *The Mystery of the Supernatural*. Translated by Rosemary Sheed. New York: Herder and Herder, 1967.

Maccoby, Hyam. *Paul and Hellenism*. London: SCM, 1991.

—, ed. *Judaism on Trial: Jewish-Christian Disputations in the Middle Ages*. London: Littman Library Of Jewish Civilization, 1993.

MacIntyre, Alasdair. *Edith Stein: A Philosophical Prologue*. London: Continuum, 2006.

—. *Three Rival Versions of Moral Enquiry: Encyclopaedia, Genealogy, and Tradition*. London: Duckworth, 1990.

MacKinnon, Donald M. *Borderlands of Theology and Other Essays*. London: Lutterworth, 1968.

—. *The Problem of Metaphysics*. Cambridge: Cambridge University Press, 1974.

—. *The Stripping of the Altars*. London: Collins, 1969.

—. *Themes in Theology: The Three-fold Cord*. Edinburgh: T & T Clark, 1987.

Mahir, Nabil I. "John Locke and the Jews." *Journal of Ecclesiastical History* 44:1 (1993): 45-62.

Mahoney, John. *The Making of Moral Theology: A Study of the Roman Catholic Tradition.* Oxford: Oxford University Press, 1987.

Maimonides, Moses. *Epistles of Maimonides: Crisis and Leadership.* Translated by Abraham Halkin. Philadelphia: Jewish Publication Society, 1993.

—. *Ethical Writings of Maimonides.* Edited by Raymond L. Weiss and Charles Butterworth. New York: Dover, 1983.

—. *The Guide for the Perplexed.* Translated by M. Friedländer. 2nd ed. New York: Dover, 1956.

Manuel, Frank E. *The Broken Staff: Judaism through Christian Eyes.* Cambridge: Harvard University Press, 1992.

Maritain, Jacques. *Antisemitism.* London: Geoffey Bles, 1939.

Markus, R. A. *The End of Ancient Christianity.* Cambridge: Cambridge University Press, 1990.

—. *Saeculum: History and Society in the Theology of St Augustine.* Cambridge: Cambridge University Press, 1970.

Meeks, Wayne A. *The Origins of Early Christian Morality: The First Two Centuries.* New Haven: Yale University Press, 1993.

Mendelssohn, Moses. *Jerusalem and Other Jewish Writings.* Translated and edited by Alfred Jospe. New York: Schocken, 1969.

Milbank, John. *The Suspended Middle: Henri de Lubac and the Debate concerning the Supernatural.* London: SCM, 2005.

Moltmann, Jürgen. *The Coming of God: Christian Eschatology.* Translated by Margaret Kohl. London: SCM, 1996.

—. *History and the Triune God: Contributions to Trinitarian Theology.* Translated by John Bowden. London: SCM, 1991.

—. *Theology of Hope: On the Ground and Implications of a Christian Eschatology.* Translated by James W. Leitch. London: SCM, 1967.

Montagu, Rachel. "Anti-Judaism in Christian Feminist Theology." In *Renewing the Vision: Rabbis Speak out on Modern Jewish Issues*, edited by Jonathan A. Romain, 26-37. London: SCM, 1996.

Moore, R. I. *The Formation of a Persecuting Society: Power and Deviance in Western Europe, 950-1250.* Oxford: Blackwell, 1987.

Moyise, Steve. *The Old Testament in the New.* London: T & T Clark, 2001.

Myers, David N. *Resisting History: Historicism and Its Discontents in German-Jewish Thought.* Princeton: Princeton University Press, 2003.

Nanos, Mark D. *The Irony of Galatians: Paul's Letter in First-Century Context.* Minneapolis: Fortress, 2002.

—. *The Mystery of Romans: The Jewish Context of Paul's Letter.* Minneapolis: Fortress, 1996.

Némirovsky, Irène. *Suite Française*. Translated by Sandra Smith. London: Chatto and Windus, 2006.

Neusner, Jacob. *Jews and Christians: The Myth of a Common Tradition*. London: SCM, 1991.

Novak, David. *Jewish-Christian Dialogue: A Jewish Justification*. Oxford: Oxford University Press, 1989.

—. *Talking with Christians: Musings of a Jewish Theologian*. Grand Rapids: Eerdmans, 2005.

Odo of Tournai. *On Original Sin and A Disputation with the Jew, Leo, concerning the Advent of the Son of God: Two Theological Treatises*. Translated by Irven M. Resnick. Philadelphia: University of Philadelphia Press, 1994.

O'Donovan, Oliver. *Resurrection and Moral Order: An Outline for Evangelical Ethics*. 2nd ed. Leicester: Apollos, 1994.

Oesterreicher, John M. *Walls Are Crumbling: Seven Jewish Philosophers Discover Christ*. London: Hollis and Carter, 1953.

Origen. *Homilies on Leviticus 1-16*. Translated by Gary Wayne Barkley. Fathers of the Church, vol. 83. Washington, DC: Catholic University of America Press, 1990.

Pascal, Blaise. *Pensées*. Translated by A. J. Krailsheimer. Harmondsworth: Penguin, 1966.

Pelikan, Jaroslav. *Christian Doctrine and Modern Culture (since 1700)*. Vol. 5 of *The Christian Tradition: A History of the Development of Doctrine*. Chicago: University of Chicago Press, 1989.

Peter Damian, *Dialogus inter Judaeum requirentem, et Christianum e contrario repsondentem*. Patrologia Latina, vol. 145. Paris: J. P. Migne, 1853.

Petrus Alfonsi. *Dialogi*. Patrologia Latina, vol. 157. Paris: J. P. Migne, 1854.

Popkin, Richard H. *The History of Scepticism from Erasmus to Spinoza*. 2nd ed. Berkeley: University of California Press, 1979.

Porter, Jean. *Natural and Divine Law: Reclaiming the Tradition for Christian Ethics*. Grand Rapids: Eerdmans, 1999.

Radner, Ephraim. *The End of the Church: A Pneumatology of Christian Division in the West*. Grand Rapids: Eerdmans, 1998.

Rashkover, Randi. *Revelation and Theopolitics: Barth, Rosenzweig and the Politics of Praise*. London: T & T Clark, 2005.

Reeves, Marjorie. *The Influence of Prophecy in the Later Middle Ages: A Study in Joachimism*. Oxford: Clarendon, 1969.

Reeves, Marjorie, and Beatrice Hirsh-Reich. *The "Figurae" of Joachim of Fiore*. Oxford: Clarendon, 1972.

Richmond, Colin. *Campaigner against Antisemitism: The Reverend James Parkes, 1896-1981*. London: Vallentine Mitchell, 2005.

Rooden, Peter van. "The Amsterdam Translation of the Mishnah." In *Hebrew Study from Ezra to Ben-Yehuda*, edited by William Horbury, 257-67. Edinburgh: T & T Clark, 1999.

Rooden, Peter van, and Jan Wim Wesselius. "The Early Enlightenment and Judaism: The 'Civil Dispute' between Philippus van Limborch and Isaac Orobio de Castro (1687)." *Studia Rosenthaliana* 21 (1987): 140-153.

Rose, Gillian. *The Broken Middle: Out of Our Ancient Society*. Oxford: Blackwell, 1992.

—. *Judaism and Modernity: Philosophical Essays*. Oxford: Blackwell, 1993.

—. *Mourning Becomes the Law: Philosophy and Representation*. Cambridge: Cambridge University Press, 1996.

Rosenstock-Huessy, Eugen, ed. *Judaism despite Christianity: The "Letters on Christianity and Judaism" between Eugen Rosenstock-Huessy and Franz Rosenzweig*. Alabama: University of Alabama Press, 1969.

Rosenzweig, Franz. *Franz Rosenzweig's "The New Thinking."* Edited and translated by Alan Udoff and Barbara E. Galli. Syracuse: Syracuse University Press, 1999.

—. *God, Man, and the World: Lectures and Essays*. Edited and translated by Barbara E. Galli. Syracuse: Syracuse University Press, 1998.

—. *On Jewish Learning*. Edited by N. N. Glatzer. New York: Schocken, 1965.

—. *Philosophical and Theological Writings*. Edited and translated by Paul W. Franks and Michael L. Morgan. Indianapolis: Hackett, 2000.

—. *The Star of Redemption*. Translated by Barbara E. Galli. Wisconsin: University of Wisconsin Press, 2005.

Roth, Joseph. *The Wandering Jews*. Translated by Michael Hofmann. London: Granta, 2001.

Rothschild, Fritz A., ed. *Jewish Perspectives on Christianity: Leo Baeck, Martin Buber, Franz Rosenzweig, Will Herberg, Abraham J. Heschel*. New York: Continuum, 2000.

Royal, Robert, ed. *Jacques Maritain and the Jews*. Mishawaka: American Maritain Association, 1994.

Ruether, Rosemary Radford. *Faith and Fratricide: The Theological Roots of Anti-semitism*. New York: Seabury Press, 1974.

Rumscheidt, Hans Martin. *Revelation and Theology: An Analysis of the Barth-Harnack Correspondence of 1923*. Cambridge: Cambridge University Press, 1972.

Saadia Gaon. *The Book of Beliefs and Opinions*. Translated by Samuel Rosenblatt. New Haven: Yale University Press, 1948.

Sanders, E. P. *Paul and Palestinian Judaism: A Comparison of Patterns of Religion*. London: SCM, 1977.

Sandmel, Samuel. *Leo Baeck on Christianity: The Leo Baeck Memorial Lecture 19*. New York: Leo Baeck Institute, 1975.

Saperstein, Marc. *Moments of Crisis in Jewish-Christian Relations*. London: SCM, 1989.

Schoeps, Hans Joachim. *The Jewish-Christian Argument: A History of Theologies in Conflict*. Translated by David E. Green. London: Faber, 1965.

Scholem, Gershom. *Major Trends in Jewish Mysticism*. 3rd ed. New York: Schocken, 1995.

—. *The Messianic Idea in Judaism and Other Essays on Jewish Spirituality*. New York: Schocken, 1995.

Schreckenberg, Heinz. *The Jews in Christian Art: An Illustrated History*. Translated by J. Bowden. New York: Continuum, 1996.

Segal, Alan F. *Rebecca's Children: Judaism and Christianity in the Roman World*. Cambridge: Harvard University Press, 1986.

Shagrir, Iris. "The Parable of the Three Rings: A Revision of Its History." *Journal of Medieval History* 23:2 (1997): 163-77.

Simon, Marcel. *Verus Israel: A Study of the Relations between Christians and Jews in the Roman Empire (AD 135-425)*. Translated by H. McKeating. London: Littman Library of Jewish Civilization, 1996.

Sirat, Colette. *A History of Jewish Philosophy in the Middle Ages*. Cambridge: Cambridge University Press, 1985.

Smalley, Beryl. *Studies in Medieval Thought and Learning: From Abelard to Wyclif*. London: Hambledon, 1981.

—. *The Study of the Bible in the Middle Ages*. 3rd ed. Oxford: Blackwell, 1983.

Sonderegger, Katherine. *That Jesus Christ Was Born a Jew: Karl Barth's "Doctrine of Israel"*. University Park, PA: Pennsylvania State University Press, 1992.

Soulen, R. Kendall. *The God of Israel and Christian Theology*. Minneapolis: Fortress, 1996.

Southern, R. W. *Saint Anselm: A Portrait in a Landscape*. Cambridge: Cambridge University Press, 1990.

Spinoza, Baruch. *Tractatus theologico-politicus*. Translated by Samuel Shirley. Leiden: Brill, 1989.

Stahmer, Harold. *"Speak That I May See Thee!" The Religious Significance of Language*. New York: Macmillan, 1968.

Stein, Edith. *The Hidden Life: Hagiographic Essays, Meditations, Spiritual Texts.* Translated by Waltraut Stein. Washington, DC: ICS Publications, 1992.

—. *Life in a Jewish Family: Her Unfinished Autobiographical Account.* Translated by Josephine Koeppel. Washington, DC: ICS Publications, 1986.

—. *Self-Portrait in Letters, 1916-1942.* Translated by Josephine Koeppel. Washington, DC: ICS Publications, 1993.

—. "Text of Letter to the Pope from Edith Stein." http://geocities.com/baltimorecarmel/stein/1933let.html (accessed 17th October, 2008).

Steiner, George. *No Passion Spent: Essays, 1978-1996.* London: Faber, 1996.

Sutcliffe, Adam. *Judaism and Enlightenment.* Cambridge: Cambridge University Press, 2003.

Talmage, Frank Ephraim. *David Kimhi: The Man and the Commentaries.* Cambridge: Harvard University Press, 1975.

—, ed. *Disputation and Dialogue: Readings in the Jewish-Christian Encounter.* New York: Ktav, 1975.

Tertullian. *Apology.* Translated by T. R. Glover. Loeb Classical Library, vol. 250. Cambridge: Harvard University Press, 1931.

Theissen, Gerd. *The Shadow of the Galilean: The Quest of the Historical Jesus in Narrative Form.* Translated by John Bowden. London: SCM, 1987.

Tindal, Matthew. *Christianity as Old as the Creation, 1730.* New York: Garland, 1978.

Tolan, John. *Petrus Alfonsi and His Medieval Readers.* Gainesville: University Press of Florida, 1993.

Trapnell, William H. *The Treatment of Christian Doctrine by Philosophers of the Natural Light from Descartes to Berkeley.* Oxford: Voltaire Foundation, 1988.

Troki, Isaac. *Faith Strengthened.* Translated by Moses Mocatta. New York: Ktav, 1970.

VanderKam, James C. *The Dead Sea Scrolls Today.* Grand Rapids: Eerdmans, 1994.

Webster, John. *Barth's Moral Theology: Human Action in Barth's Thought.* Edinburgh: T & T Clark, 1998.

—, ed. *The Cambridge Companion to Karl Barth.* Cambridge: Cambridge University Press, 2000.

Wilken, Robert L. *The Land Called Holy: Palestine in Christian History and Thought.* New Haven: Yale University Press, 1992.

Williams, Rowan. "Bulgakov and Anti-semitism." Appendix to *Towards a Russian Political Theology*, by Sergii Bulgakov, edited by Rowan Williams, 293-303. Edinburgh: T & T Clark, 1999.

—. *Teresa of Avila.* London: Continuum, 2003.

Wood, Allen. *Kant's Moral Religion.* Ithaca: Cornell University Press, 1970.

Worthen, Jeremy. "Beginning without End: Christianity in Franz Rosenzweig's *Star of Redemption.*" *Journal of Ecumenical Studies* 39:3-4 (Summer-Fall 2002): 340-362.

Wright, N. T. *Jesus and the Victory of God.* London: SPCK, 1996.

—. *The New Testament and the People of God.* London: SPCK, 1992.

Wyschogrod, Michael. "A Letter to Cardinal Lustiger." In *Abraham's Promise: Judaism and Jewish-Christian Relations*, edited by R. Kendall Soulen, 202-210. London: SCM, 2006.

—. "Why Was and Is the Theology of Karl Barth of Interest to a Jewish Theologian?" In *Footnotes to a Theology: The Karl Barth Colloquium of 1972*, edited by Martin Rumscheidt, 95-111. Toronto: Corporation for the Publication of Academic Studies of Religion in Canada, 1974.

Yoder, John Howard. *The Jewish-Christian Schism Revisited.* Edited by Michael G. Cartwright and Peter Ochs. London: SCM, 2003.

Yovel, Yirmiyahu. *Dark Riddle: Hegel, Nietzsche, and the Jews.* Oxford: Polity, 1998.

Yuval, Israel Jacob. *Two Nations in Your Womb: Perceptions of Jews and Christians in Late Antiquity and the Middle Ages.* Translated by Barbara Harshav and Jonathan Chipman. Berkeley: University of California Press, 2006.

Zahl, Paul F. M. *The First Christian: Universal Truth in the Teachings of Jesus.* Grand Rapids: Eerdmans, 2003.

INDEX